Poland, the United States, and the Stabilization of Europe, 1919–1933

Poland, the United States, and the Stabilization of Europe, 1919–1933

NEAL PEASE

New York   Oxford
OXFORD UNIVERSITY PRESS
1986

Oxford University Press

Oxford New York Toronto
Delhi Bombay Calcutta Madras Karachi
Petaling Jaya Singapore Hong Kong Tokyo
Nairobi Dar es Salaam Cape Town
Melbourne Auckland
and associated companies in
Beirut Berlin Ibadan Nicosia

Copyright © 1986 by Oxford University Press, Inc.

Published by Oxford University Press, Inc.,
200 Madison Avenue, New York, New York 10016

Oxford is a registered trademark of Oxford University Press

Library of Congress Cataloging-in-Publication Data
Pease, Neal.
Poland, the United States, and the stabilization of
Europe, 1919-1933.
Bibliography: p. Includes index.
1. United States—Foreign relations—Poland.
2. Poland—Foreign relations—United States.
3. United States—Foreign relations—1921-1923.
4. United States—Foreign relations—1923-1929.
5. United States—Foreign relations—1929-1933.
6. Poland—Politics and government—1918-1945.
7. Europe, Eastern—Politics and government. I. Title.
E183.8.P7P43 1986 327.438073 85-31062
ISBN 0-19-504050-3

2 4 6 8 10 9 7 5 3 1
Printed in the United States of America
on acid free paper

Preface

Only during the years spanning the world wars has a Poland independent both in name and fact coexisted with the United States. Even so, when I first resolved to write a study of relations between the two countries during that era, the initial question was whether such an exercise was at all necessary. If anything, the burden of proof appeared to rest with the affirmative. The conventional view held that the United States had paid meaningful attention to Polish matters only while they formed a conspicuous part of the diplomatic agenda of the global wars of this century but had ignored them almost entirely during the intervening peace. Citing Washington's presumed desire for isolation and Warsaw's preoccupation with the threats posed by its continental neighbors, scholarly opinion agreed that American-Polish contacts in the interwar epoch were strictly limited and scarcely worth mention. While over the years some valuable studies, both Polish and American, have plainly indicated the inadequacy and oversimplification of this verdict, to date no comprehensive treatment of U.S.-Polish interwar ties based on the archival resources of both countries has appeared in any language.

This volume represents the result of my conclusion that such a book would serve a useful purpose, but during its preparation the conception and approach of the work changed in a fashion that bears explanation. In recent years a general reexamination of American relations with Europe in the period 1919–1933 has taken place. The central contention of the newer scholarship has been that the primary goal of U.S. policy concerning Europe during the presidencies of Coolidge and Hoover was not seclusion from the continent but rather "stabilizing" it as a peaceful and reliable element of a world in which American influence, wealth, and overseas investment now played a crucial role, one no less important for its reliance on dollar diplomacy rather than the more visible instruments of alliances or the League of Nations. Acceptance of this insight transforms understanding of interwar American dealings with Europe, redefining a seemingly passive epoch as one of cautious, painstaking transition from traditional isolation to the formal and fixed Atlanticism of the past four decades.

Gradually this idea became the backbone of my own project. Research convinced me not only of the validity of the "stabilization" theory as an interpretation of U.S. diplomacy in Europe, but also of its particular relevance to the case of Poland. My arguments, in short, are these: that the Polish authorities of the mid-1920s recognized the American yearning for stability in Europe and sought to derive political and economic benefit from it, that this theme and its consequences dominated the relationship between the two countries in the fifteen years following World War I and enmeshed it in many of the foremost diplomatic and financial issues of the day, and that the Polish courtship of the United States ultimately failed for reasons largely inherent in the structure of the interwar world.

The decision to organize the work about the device of European stabilization has, I think, both narrowed and broadened it in certain ways. For one, it inclined me to excise lengthy discussion of the period 1933–1939, when the United States temporarily retreated into a condition very like isolation after the policy of stabilization had played itself out. The omission is not significant. These were years of genuinely minimal intercourse between Poland and the United States, and I am content to forgo them in return for the sharper focus provided by the stress on stabilization and its utility in linking my subject to a series of other interesting and significant issues of interwar history, such as Polish domestic politics, international financial questions, and European boundary disputes.

The book deals with all these matters, but upon reflection I am persuaded that its core is accurately described in the answer I habitually gave to acquaintances who asked about the subject of my labors: that it was a detailed account of something that did not happen. While meant as jocular, the reply is apt. The "something" in this case is the creation of a solid economic and diplomatic partnership between the United States and Poland in the mid-to-later 1920s. In a sense, the topic of the following pages is not so much the interwar American-Polish relationship that was as the one that might have been but for the prohibitive realities of the times. Explanation of how and why this vision failed to materialize may help to illuminate both the nature of that epoch and the reasons for the historical detachment of the United States from the fate of Poland despite the customary bonds of sympathy between these nations.

Help has come to me from numerous quarters. The International Research and Exchanges Board, the American Council of Learned Societies, the Hoover Presidential Library Association, and the Kościuszko Foundation donated generous and indispensable financial support. I am beholden as well to many individuals, far more than I can acknowledge by name, who deserve much credit for the book's merits and bear no responsibility for its shortcomings. Prof. Piotr S. Wandycz of Yale University first suggested to me the need for such a study and then patiently supervised its incubation in its original form as a doctoral dissertation. I count myself fortunate to have spent seven years under the tutelage of this erudite and dedicated scholar. With gratitude I also recall the assistance of Profs. Ivo Banac, Hans W. Gatzke, and Gaddis Smith of Yale; Prof. Anna M. Cienciała and the late Prof. Oswald P. Backus III of the University of Kansas; Profs. Teresa Małecka and Zbigniew Landau of the Szkoła Główna Planowania i Statystyki, Warsaw; Prof. Mieczysław B. Biskupski of St. John Fisher College; Prof. Peter Hayes of Northwestern University; and Mrs. Florence Thomas, registrar of the Department of History, Yale University. My editors at Oxford University Press, Nancy Lane, Joan Bossert, and Catherine Clements, have done their work with skill, precision, and courtesy. I have benefited as well from the expertise and aid of the curators and librarians of various archives and research centers, notably Carl Backlund of the Federal Reserve Bank of New York, Dr. Ronald E. Swerczek of the National Archives, and, in particular, Robert Balay and the reference staff of Yale's Sterling Library.

Special mention must be accorded a few dear people whose contributions to this volume cannot be measured merely in scholarly or professional terms. My friend and sometime colleague Dr. Thomas S. Dyman, an accomplished specialist in matters of interwar Poland, participated in the evolution of this enterprise from its beginnings, and its virtues, such as they are, would be far fewer and lesser without his judicious suggestions and sympathetic criticism. Thanks, Tom, for these and countless other services and kindnesses I will never forget. Of my wife and children—last in this roster but first always in my thoughts—there is nothing to say except that they make everything worthwhile.

July 1986   N. P.
Milwaukee Wisconsin

For Ewa, Andrzej, and Krystyna

Contents

Stabilization is a blesseder word than Mesopotamia, and when I am President I'm going to ask you to stabilize something and the whole country will applaud. I confess to an absolute ignorance of what stabilization is or how it is done but I share with all other statesmen the conviction that it ought to be done.

William Hard to Edwin W. Kemmerer, April 20, 1926

Poland, the United States, and the Stabilization of Europe, 1919–1933

CHAPTER I

Introduction: Poland and the American Retreat from Europe, 1919–1924

Is the existence of a free, socially-sound Poland as a great Central European Republic . . . an essential condition of restoring the normal health of Europe, consequently of the world, or is it not? Does Poland constitute a danger for the peace of the world, or does she constitute a security against two or three grave possibilities of danger for the future of the world?

Władysław Wróblewski, February 16, 1924

Interwar Poland began her existence amid inauspicious circumstances. Although Allied victory in World War I had assured the recovery of Polish independence after more than a century of political dismemberment, the new state faced a host of internal and foreign difficulties which threatened to extinguish it in infancy. Confronted by massive tasks of reconstruction, flanked by her traditional enemies, menaced by revolutionary chaos in the East, Poland scarcely possessed the resources necessary to overcome these challenges to her future. Accordingly, Poland's directors counted on aid and support from abroad. During the summer of 1919, barely a week after the conclusion of the Paris Peace Conference, the deputy minister for foreign affairs, Erazm Piltz, observed that Warsaw should seek "the closest relations and an eventual alliance with the great powers to which Poland owes the recovery of her sovereignty, and above all with France and America. It must be remembered that Poland will need the assistance of these countries for a long time to come."[1]

Only a few months later Piltz's coupling of the United States with the country that was Poland's natural ally would have seemed fanciful, but in midyear of 1919 Washington had not yet defined its future role in postwar Europe, and the custodians of the Polish Foreign Ministry (MSZ) could still reasonably hope to win the patronage of the transatlantic giant, which had emerged abruptly during the war as the foremost power in the world. Despite a perceptible shift of American sentiment toward the traditional policy of aloofness from Europe, the prevailing view held that the wartime Allied coalition would endure as a device for the regulation of the peace through the League of Nations and that the participation of the United States in this process was indispensable.

Among the proponents of an active American presence in the Old World was Benjamin Strong, the governor of the Federal Reserve Bank of New York, who argued that upon entering the war "we assumed not only military but financial, political and moral obligations to Europe which cannot be terminated . . . without prolonged disorder and suffering."[2] Those Americans who shared Strong's position agreed that the efforts of their country were essential to the maintenance of the European political balance and to the economic revival of Europe from the ravages of war, and they were convinced that a peaceful and prosperous Europe was necessary to the well-being of the United States.

Strong contended that America bore a particular responsibility for the fate of the new states that had arisen from the shambles of Central and Eastern Europe,[3] and none of these countries welcomed the prospect of American support more than Poland. The fundamental challenge facing the fledgling government in Warsaw was simply to preserve Polish statehood in defiance of Germany and Russia, the defeated great powers whose temporary eclipse accounted for the reappearance of Poland on the map. The Poles recognized France as their principal foreign backer, and at the peace conference the French had reinforced this judgment by their consistent advocacy of a robust Polish state that would stand as a bastion of French influence on Germany's eastern frontier. The Americans had not promoted Poland at Paris as wholeheartedly; according to the enigmatic definition of the American delegation's adviser for Polish questions, Washington's policy had been to see "that Poland should get neither too much nor too little, but just what belonged to her."[4] Put into practice, this hazy formula meant that the United States tended to examine Polish territorial claims through the prism of national self-determination and adopted a stance midway between British conceptions of a minimal Poland and French plans to create a Poland that would be "big and strong—very, very strong."[5] The powers settled their differences by compromise, and Poland emerged from Paris with her territorial ambitions only partially fulfilled.

The ambivalent American performance at Paris did not shake Warsaw's conviction that Washington remained committed to the defense of basic Polish interests. Memories of the decisive intervention of the United States in the war and of Woodrow Wilson's conspicuous assertion of Poland's right to independence remained fresh, and the experiences of the war had strengthened the traditional bonds of sympathy between the two peoples.[6] In the flush of liberation, Polish opinion expected the United States to continue her association with her wartime partners and loudly proclaimed Poland's solidarity with the countries of the Allied coalition. While the MSZ recognized the tenacity of the noninterventionist viewpoint in the United States, it nonetheless anticipated that the American republic would take an important part in European political affairs and would exert her influence on behalf of republican Poland and against Germany and Bolshevik Russia.[7] America appeared all the more valuable to Warsaw as London sought increasingly to redress what it considered a serious imbalance of power favoring Paris over Berlin, meaning that Poland could not count upon British partnership.

Desirable though the United States appeared to the Poles as a potential guarantor of Polish security against their most likely foreign rivals, many shared the view of Socialist leader Ignacy Daszyński that what the country needed most from the Americans was not good will but "a loan at low interest."[8] For if the war had enriched the United States, vaulting her into dominance of world finance and permitting her to capture the markets of European combatants, it had ruined the Polish lands. Much of the country had been leveled by battle and stripped by occupation forces. Agricultural production had dropped to half the output of 1913, and industry was so devastated that in 1918 the factories of former Russian Poland employed only 15 percent of the number of workers engaged in 1914. Altogether, the official Polish estimate of war-related damages amounted to 10 billion American dollars.[9]

At the same time, the problem of the economic recovery of Poland transcended mere restoration of losses. The forcible separation of Polish territories in the preceding century had sundered the economic unity of the region and caused the gradual absorption of the three zones of partition into the economies of the conquerors. The parts of the reconstituted Poland did not fit together in an economic sense, just as the character and civic traditions of the different sections of the country bore the visible marks of German, Russian, or Austrian custody. The magnitude of the job of integration was best illustrated by the Polish railway system, which was, in fact, not a system at all but rather a hodgepodge of incompatible lines inherited from the vanished empires. In addition to the task of stitching together these dissimilar areas into a thriving economic organism, Poland required thoroughgoing modernization. The predominantly agrarian economy could not support the population of twenty-seven million, and a majority of the peasantry of southern and eastern Poland lived in squalor. Only a great expansion of industry and the exploitation of untapped natural resources could raise Polish living standards and relieve the chronic pressure of rural overpopulation.

In the long run, the attainment of these economic goals would be no less crucial to the survival of Poland than her ability to withstand foreign armies. This massive chore of reconstruction and development demanded an enormous amount of investment capital, but Poland, like all of postwar Eastern Europe, suffered a critical shortage of this asset. The war had destroyed $1.8 billion of physical capital in the Polish territories, and the collapse of the imperial currencies had obliterated Polish savings.[10] The paucity of domestic capital made apparent that the rebuilding of

Poland would have to be financed largely from abroad, and accordingly the Poles adopted a course of wooing foreign lenders and investors. Warsaw pursued this strategy so ardently that a deputy to the Sejm (parliament) complained to his colleagues that the government's financial policy consisted of little more than the slogan "borrow, borrow and borrow again."[11]

Not surprisingly, the United States became a special target of the Polish courtship of foreign finance. In the first place, America had replaced the war-ravaged countries of Western Europe as the world's principal pool of disposable capital. At the same time, many Poles hoped that the introduction of American money, enterprise, and economic expertise would invigorate their republic through the implantation of American methods of business and administration.[12]

Political reasons likewise took a hand in inclining Polish overtures toward Wall Street. A history of external interference in their affairs predisposed the Poles to an acute sensitivity toward the possible political dangers of the admission of foreign capital, and they particularly dreaded the implications of falling under the economic domination of a revived Germany. To reduce this risk, they sought to develop financial ties with countries that posed no political hazard, such as France and the United States. Furthermore, the MSZ argued that the engagement of large amounts of American money in the country represented the surest method of inspiring Washington's friendly interest in the safety and prosperity of the Polish commonwealth.[13] In short, Poland coveted American capital and energetically set about to attract it in the form of loans, investments, and trade. The newly appointed Polish minister to Washington, the unfortunately maladroit Prince Kazimierz Lubomirski, went so far as to offer his country to American businessmen as an "opportunity to start some kind of colony for [your] nation."[14]

The outstanding Polish exponent of close association with the United States was Ignacy Jan Paderewski, the famous musician-turned-politician who held the combined posts of premier and foreign minister for an eleven-month period beginning January 1919. During the war Paderewski had acted as the American agent for the Paris-based Polish National Committee, which eventually won recognition from the Allies as the legitimate political voice of the Polish nation. The Committee largely owed its success to Paderewski's labors in America, where he mobilized Polish-American groups and won the confidence of Wilson and his chief adviser, Colonel Edward M. House. In the process Paderewski acquired an exalted and perhaps exaggerated opinion of America's power and her importance to the fate of Poland.[15] In this he differed from Józef Piłsudski, the military hero of the Polish struggle for independence, who served as head of state in the uneasy mixture of opposing political forces that governed Poland. Piłsudski regarded the United States as a promising source of economic assistance, but Washington did not figure greatly in his diplomatic calculations.[16] However, it was Paderewski who operated as Poland's spokesman in the world, and he tirelessly commended his country to the United States as a deserving pillar of stability, democracy, and Allied loyalties in disordered Eastern Europe.[17]

At first this appeal found a favorable response in the United States. One of the original premises underlying American sponsorship of Polish statehood had been the conviction that a strong Poland was necessary to combat the revival of German imperialism and to contain the revolutionary ferment in Russia.[18] During the war American attention toward Poland had focused on her potential value as part of an East European *barrière de l'est* against Berlin, while after the armistice the emphasis shifted to consideration of Poland's role as the crucial link in the proposed *cordon sanitaire* against Bolshevism.

The problems posed by the tenacity of the Soviet government in Russia permeated the deliberations of the peace conference. The Allies had no clear idea of what to do about Russia. Wilson balked at the suggestions of Marshal Ferdinand Foch that Poland be designated the spearhead of an offensive strategy to root out the Bolsheviks, but during the course of 1919 the Americans cautiously endorsed tentative Allied decisions to support Poland as a defensive bulwark against the westward spread of revolution.[19] An influential segment of American opinion feared that if Poland succumbed either to Soviet armies or internal revolution, the red tide would sweep through weakened Germany and endanger Western Europe. Paderewski considered these apprehensions his trump card and attempted to play it by relentlessly broadcasting the theme that Poland needed strengthening and foreign assistance if she was to subdue revolutionary threats from without and within.[20]

While Poland trusted in Washington's benevolence as a natural development of the realities of international diplomacy, she also expected to benefit from the homelier logic of American domestic politics. Successive waves of migration to the New World had brought the number of immigrant Polish-born and their descendants to an estimated 2.4 million, or roughly 2.5 percent of the total population of the United States. Much of this Polish diaspora—collectively known as Polonia—had taken American citizenship, and it had clustered in the industrial cities of the northeastern and Great Lakes regions. For these reasons, it formed a significant electoral bloc whose votes comprised an important element of the Democratic Party's urban and ethnic constituency. During the war the Polish-Americans had distinguished themselves by their efforts on behalf of the Polish cause.[21] Now that independence had been attained, Warsaw banked heavily on the expectation that the one-tenth of the Polish nation resident in America would continue its service to the homeland by subscribing to Polish loans, sending dollars to Polish friends and relatives, and urging Washington toward directions advantageous to Poland.[22]

The Polish petition to the United States met a generally approving reception during the year that followed the armistice. Eager to reinforce Poland against the Bolshevik peril, American officials encouraged the extension of loans and war credits to that country, and the U.S. Liquidation Board provided quantities of military supplies to the Poles.[23] However, the principal agent of American aid to Poland was Herbert Hoover's American Relief Administration, which operated in various lands of eastern and central Europe. The activities of the ARA were jointly founded on humanitarian impulse, American commercial self-interest, and the assumption—shared by Hoover and Wilson—that Bolshevism was a political disease that fed on misery, a malady that "cannot be stopped by force, but . . . can be stopped by food."[24] Beginning in 1919, the ARA dispensed victuals, medicine, and advice to Poland for three years. Nor did the ARA confine its efforts to the alleviation of immediate distress. Upon Paderewski's request, Hoover submitted detailed suggestions for the reorganization of Polish economic life and sought unsuccessfully an American willing to serve as financial adviser to the new government, while his deputies hunted for ways to improve the crippled transportation system.[25]

Aside from material aid, Washington bestowed tokens of political favor upon the Poles. In the spring of 1919 Hugh Gibson assumed the post of American minister to Warsaw. A protégé of Hoover and a pronounced hater of Bolshevism, Gibson was respected as a capable and influential diplomat.[26] For his part, the appointee congratulated himself upon his assignment to "the most important legation we now have." He subscribed to a belief in Poland's mission to stand guard over Germany and Russia and consistently urged the State Department to encourage her in this role.[27] To protect Poland's international reputation against widespread, if exaggerated, accusations of mistreatment of her large Jewish minority, Washington dispatched an investigatory commission led by Henry Morgenthau, one of the most prominent American Jewish political figures. Morgenthau was selected for the job precisely because he was known to be sympathetic to Poland, and his report largely exculpated the Polish government, exactly as expected.[28]

The United States also entered discreetly into the Polish domestic scene to bolster the friendly but sagging cabinet of Paderewski. Despite his many shortcomings as an administrator, the Polish premier enjoyed the esteem of American officials. As an Allied loyalist and representative of the political center-right, he stood out in favorable contrast to Piłsudski, whose past affiliations with the Polish Socialist Party and the Central Powers compromised him in American eyes.[29]

The refusal of the Senate to accept Wilsonian conceptions of collective security subverted the assumptions upon which Paderewski had based his American policy. As the tide of American opinion began to turn against the peace treaties in the later months of 1919, so it swung against Poland as well. Already in June the journalist Walter Lippmann had advised his friend Gibson that "the American appetite for guaranteeing the frontiers of your domain is, I am afraid, rapidly diminishing." Liberal critics of the "Carthaginian peace" stigmatized Poland as a tool of French continental hegemony, and the persistence of military action on her unsettled eastern frontier left her open to charges that she was more a factor of disruption than of order in Europe.[30] Continuing internal disarray prompted predictions of an unavoidable Polish demise, and as animosity toward Germany abated, some American officials began to argue that German domination of Eastern Europe was inevitable or, alternatively, that the *Reich* and not Poland constituted the natural barrier to the extension of Bolshevism.[31] In December the Paderewski government fell, leaving Piłsudski the most visible political figure in the country. The Americans feared for the course of Polish policy in the hands of a man they considered an unreliable military adventurer—a "high-class pirate" in Morgenthau's estimate—and their interest in Poland as a diplomatic partner correspondingly waned.[32] In the wake of the senatorial rejection of the Treaty of Versailles in November, Vice-President Thomas Marshall assured Prince Lubomirski that "America stands by Poland." Marshall was more acute a student of cigars than of diplomacy; in fact, the brief phase of association between the two countries already had drawn to a close and given way to a gradual deterioration of relations that would continue for the next five years.[33]

The first significant divergence of American and Polish diplomatic interests surfaced in the question of Russia. From the first the Allies had followed an equivocal policy in the east, hesitant to spell out either Poland's frontiers or her rights and obligations in the region pending the outcome of the Russian civil war. Believing in the eventual victory of White elements, Wilson's government consistently upheld the principle of Russian territorial integrity lest a fragmented Russia become a source of international instability. On the other hand, Piłsudski had elected to seize the opportunity presented by Russian disorder to effect a historic alteration of European power relations by detaching Russia's western marches and molding them into a vast Polish-sponsored "confederation" reminiscent of the realm of the Jagiellon kings.[34]

Polish appeals for American diplomatic and material support against the Bolsheviks elicited a mixed reaction: despite Gibson's enthusiastic advocacy of such measures, Washington threatened to cut off the flow of war credits and economic aid to Poland if Warsaw did not take steps to suspend hostilities in the east.[35] The possibility of assistance was made conditional on Polish adherence to a strictly defensive posture toward Russia, and the State Department repeatedly counseled the Poles to moderate their eastward territorial ambitions.[36] When Piłsudski launched a full-scale offensive in the spring of 1920, Washington announced its neutrality in the contest, but American representatives privately expressed dismay and annoyance at the Polish gamble, which they feared would strengthen the Bolsheviks by making them appear the champions of Russian patriotism.[37]

Poland's push into the Ukraine met with initial success, but her position became critical in the summer when a Red Army counteroffensive arrested her advance and drove the Polish forces in full flight westward. When Warsaw turned to the Allies and America for help in what suddenly had turned into a struggle for survival, its distress evoked sympathy but little effective aid. Embittered and ill, Wilson could not rouse himself even to make a statement on behalf of the country whose independence he had sponsored. The State Department turned aside Polish entreaties for emergency war supplies and credits in spite of the supplications of Gibson and the Polish-American community.[38]

On August 10, as the Soviet troops neared Warsaw, Secretary of State Bainbridge Colby issued the definitive American pronouncement on the crisis in the form of an open letter to the Italian ambassador. The Colby Note, as it came to be known, asserted Washington's refusal to recognize the Bolshevik regime or approve the fragmentation of Russia. As a corollary, it proclaimed the intention to employ "all available means" in defense of a homogeneous Polish state whose eastern boundary would approximate the so-called Curzon Line, which the Allied Commission on Polish Affairs had put forward as a minimum frontier in December 1919.[39] The weakness of the Colby Note's assurance to Warsaw, as its author confessed to Wilson, was that it was "impossible to say what we will do, if anything." In an election year dominated by growing public and congressional opposition to an active European policy, the answer was: very little.[40] Aside from the contributions of Polonia, American assistance to Poland consisted largely of moral support.

The emergency passed in mid-August when the Polish armies rallied at Warsaw and regained the offensive. Once again the United States, among other countries, called on Poland to exercise restraint, sue for peace, and rein in at the Curzon Line, but the Poles disregarded this advice and pushed the military frontier eastward until an armistice was reached in October.[41] In the aftermath of the Polish-Soviet war, the MSZ appraised the importance of the Colby Note for the course of future relations with Washington, and its conclusions were surprisingly sanguine. While admitting the inconvenience of the American attitude toward Russian issues, Foreign Minister Eustachy Sapieha considered it an exception to a general posture of support of Polish interests.[42] This was the rosiest possible reading of American conduct during the Soviet campaign, and it represented a refuge in wishful thinking against an accumulating body of evidence that Poland was no longer a significant concern of the United States. The cardinal lesson of the episode was, in fact, that Washington could offer the Poles no protection at a time of extreme peril.

The American shift toward disengagement from Europe appeared to receive confirmation when the Republicans and Warren Harding swept to victory in the 1920 elections on a platform of resolute opposition to the League of Nations and interventionism abroad. The defeat of Wilson's party seemed to mark a turning point in the course of American foreign relations, and the event induced the MSZ to reassess its policy toward the United States.

The Poles did not take seriously the popular outcry in America for a complete withdrawal from European affairs: the question, as they saw it, was not whether the United States would participate in Europe, but rather in what way and in whose interests.[43] The MSZ accepted the view that the American colossus was ready to resume an active part in international politics after two years of hesitation and debate, and that the logic of its worldwide economic interests compelled it to seek the "stabilization of European relations and the restoration of the European economy." The consequent focal points of American concern, so the analysis continued, would be the rejuvenation of German industry and access to the natural resources of a Russia rid of Bolshevik rule. In the glum estimate of Prince Lubomirski, the concentration of American interest in Poland's neighbors and rivals was a dangerous sign that his government "should not expect any improvement, *but rather fear more pronounced indifference,* if not complete *désintéressement"* from Harding's administration.[44] However, this somber judgment did not represent the prevalent sentiment of Polish officials. The Foreign Ministry still believed it possible to fit Poland into an American anti-Bolshevik strategy and even to secure Washington's eventual political favor of France and her Polish ally.[45]

Polish aspirations to make a fresh start at cooperation with the new Republican government met a rebuff over the question of the disposition of Upper Silesia, the valuable industrial and mining district that straddled the Polish and German ethnographic borders. At first the Allies had intended to award the region to Poland, but British and German protests forced France and the United States to submit the matter of Silesian allegiance to a plebiscite. Poles comprised a majority of the local population, but the vote of March 20, 1921, went to Germany by a wide margin. Since the Allies had reserved the right to make the final decision on the fate of Silesia, Poland initiated a diplomatic campaign to win the province in spite of the vote. The MSZ regarded Washington as central to its hopes: America, it believed, might swing the balance between France and Britain and discredit England's benign policy toward Germany. In April Lubomirski began to lobby the State Department and its new head, Charles Evans Hughes, for a vote of confidence on Silesia. The Americans were not encouraging, but Lubomirski mistook politeness for agreement and persuaded himself that he was on the way to winning the American card.[46]

In fact, the new secretary of state vetoed U.S. involvement in the Silesian dispute, and as Hughes was the final authority for foreign policy in Harding's administration, that settled the issue. Hughes perceived an American interest in safeguarding the economic health and productivity of Silesia, but he insisted that the drawing of national boundaries in the area was "merely of European significance," and he had no intention of violating an unmistakable public and congressional consensus of opposition to trespassing in the European political arena. The outbreak of an armed uprising among the Polish populace of Silesia in early May dispelled the remaining traces of American sympathy for the Polish argument.[47] Ignoring the handwriting on the wall, Lubomirski badgered Hughes pointlessly throughout the next month and succeeded only in irritating his interlocutors through his tactlessness.[48] At the same time, Hughes fended off British pressure to endorse London's tilt toward the German claim. Above all he wished to avoid taking any stand in what he regarded as essentially a dispute between France and England.[49]

The Americans reacted with relief when in August the Allied Conference of Ambassadors—with the silent approval of the American observer—referred the Silesian question to the League of Nations and thus safely out of Washington's hands.[50] In the end, the League of Nations partitioned Silesia between the contestants. The American silence on the controversy at last convinced the Poles that Paderewski's view of the United States as a champion of the new Poland had lost its last shred of validity. Twice within a year successive American governments had declined Polish invitations to offer diplomatic reinforcement against Russia and Germany: the United States was no longer a partisan of Poland, but a neutral which no longer recognized Eastern Europe as a sphere of interest.

As the Harding government reduced Washington's political activity in Europe to the vanishing point, Poland devoted a greater share of her attention to the solicitation of Wall Street. Her earlier attempts to attract American capital had not proved fruitful. Pioneering American entrepreneurs, many of them Jewish, found themselves bewildered by the chaotic condition of the new state and occasionally became targets of harassment by imperious, suspicious, or anti-Semitic provincial authorities. The State Department accused Poland of discrimination against American business and, to demonstrate its displeasure, quietly recalled Gibson for four months during the perilous spring and summer of 1920.[51]

At the same time, the first major Polish loan obtained in the United States proved a disappointment. Desirous of tapping the pockets of Polonia, Warsaw in June 1919 awarded authorization to arrange a loan to John Smulski, a Polish-American banker from Chicago with close ties to Paderewski. Four months later, at the instance of Finance Minister Leon Biliński, the Poles dumped Smulski and granted the rights to the loan to another American firm, the People's Industrial Trading Corporation. The agreement with PITC angered Smulski and provoked dissension in the ranks of Polonia, and when Lubomirski moved to annul the offensive arrangement the State Department reluctantly intervened to confirm the PITC contract.[52] The embarrassing altercation alienated much of Polonia, and subscriptions were depressed further by the inopportune timing of its offer, which coincided with the nadir of Polish fortunes in the Soviet campaign of 1920. Despite the efforts of American and Polish notables on its behalf, the loan netted barely 40 percent of an anticipated $50 million at 6 percent interest, a sum that aided the Poles in their war with the Bolsheviks but donated little to the long-range task of national reconstruction.[53]

Poland's financial position at the end of 1920 had scarcely improved since the chaotic days of 1918. The country had failed to import meaningful amounts of foreign capital during this highly unstable interlude. The war against the Soviets had inflicted yet more damage on the Polish lands, and the extraordinary expenses of the campaign had overburdened the resources of the treasury and fed the fires of a serious inflation. So long as Poland's boundaries remained unsettled and the extent of her assets uncertain, she could not plan for future development, and the advent of restrictive immigration policies in the United States indirectly added to the list of economic woes by stemming the exodus of destitute peasants.

American finance did not regard the vulnerable and disorganized Poland of this period as a safe or promising location for its money,[54] but as Poland's condition steadily deteriorated the MSZ and Ministry of Finance redoubled exertions to attract American capital.[55] Aside from purely economic considerations, the hope lingered that Washington's cooled political enthusiasm for Poland could be rekindled if the United States acquired a significant financial stake in the country.[56] The Poles invited Americans to invest in Polish enterprise and, coincidentally, to establish Poland as an element of social and economic soundness on the flank of the Soviet Union. As a concession to what they now considered America's principal interest in Russia, they added a new twist to the anti-Bolshevik theme and began to tout Poland as a base from which to penetrate the vast Russian market once it was restored from socialism.[57]

One of the few Americans to respond to Poland's call was Samuel M. Vauclain, the president of the Baldwin Locomotive Works of Philadelphia. Upon the conclusion of the war, Baldwin sought to expand its European operations and focused its attention particularly on Poland and Romania. In 1919 the company sold 160 locomotives and 4,600 railroad cars to Poland, then desperately short of rolling stock, and Vauclain liked to boast that his engines "kept the Bolshevists from overrunning [Poland] and so preserved that western bulwark for sane Europe." Vauclain combined a repugnance for Bolshevism with a limitless faith in the commercial potential of Russia. He considered Warsaw the key to the containment and eventual "rehabilitation" of Russia and dreamed of making Poland a great crossroads of European trade, handling traffic from east to west and from the Baltic to the Black Sea.[58] In fact, Vauclain talked more about Poland than he spent on her, but he became the Poles' most devoted advocate within the American business community, assuring his colleagues that "when you go before God you will learn that your acts toward this new government have been recorded."[59]

During the Harding years, however, not even the promise of divine gratitude could persuade American finance to locate in Poland. In the first place, the immediate postwar period was not a time of great American commercial activity in Europe. The Washington authorities discouraged foreign loans for reasons related to the domestic economy. Furthermore, the instability and barely controlled animosities of the Old World frightened off the cautious American investor. Fears of a renewal of European warfare explained the principal cause of the reluctance of American capital to take an interest in Poland: a simple disbelief in the ability of the state to survive. The prevailing mood was expressed by William R. Castle of the State Department, who reported that Poland was:

> a country of fine ideals, a country which may well have a brilliant future if it has any future at all, but with a thoroughly disorganized and dangerous Russia on one side and with a still intriguing, revengeful and dangerous Germany on the other side, one cannot look forward to a future with much hope.[60]

Far from convincing Americans of Poland's ability to surmount her perilous geography, the successful repulsion of the Soviet thrust of 1920 fortified the conviction in the United States that the hostilities would unavoidably resume sooner or later. American businessmen regarded Poland's costly maintenance of a large army at great budgetary sacrifice as proof that the government expected foreign attack or intended to launch aggressive military adventures of its own, and they found neither alternative alluring.[61]

Many felt that Poland required no pressure from without to collapse but that she might break down under her own weight. To the outside observer, Poland appeared a cauldron of feuding parties and disaffected national minorities. American opinion appreciated the conservative cast of the Polish governments of the early 1920s,[62] but none of the contentious political factions seemed able to master the challenges that confronted them. Cabinets rose and fell quickly—five governments ruled in 1922 alone—and the first president of the republic, Gabriel Narutowicz, was assassinated in December of the same year. Unable to meet expenses and plagued by an inadequate tax base, the treasury resorted to the printing press until Poland's inflation rivaled that of Germany. Originally pegged at a rate of 9.8 to the American dollar, the Polish mark dwindled to 17,800 to a dollar by 1922.

American observers placed the blame for Poland's hyperinflation on an unwillingness to submit to fiscal self-discipline; her public finance, in the verdict of the *Wall Street Journal*, could "only be called the finest bid for bankruptcy ever made by any modern State in Europe with the sole exception of Russia."[63] Warsaw objected, with some justice, that the inflation was as much the result of six years of unbroken warfare as of faulty management, but the steady degeneration of politics and finances discouraged foreign capital and revived the stereotyped reproach that the Poles lacked a capacity for statecraft.

The Poles hurt their own cause by slipshod conduct of their first financial transactions in the United States. The 6 percent loan of 1920 had ended in a fiasco of litigation and ill-will, and its failure cast a pall over Polish credit in America.[64] Moreover, the State Department accused Lubomirski and various officials in Warsaw of resorting to untruth and obstruction to avoid settlement of grievances filed by PITC.[65] Because Poland was considered a bad credit risk in America, she could attract the attention only of speculative firms of low repute, and her association with these dubious partners further compromised her standing among the more substantial houses.[66] In this era of revolving-door cabinets, the lines of governmental responsibility for financial affairs were blurred, and a multitude of departments despatched missions in search of loans with little regard for coordination. To a considerable extent, the Poles were also handicapped by inexperience in foreign trade and unfamiliarity with the accepted practices of American finance. This combination of confusion and lack of know-how with the general mediocrity of Poland's financial emissaries to the New World made Polish business methods an object of derision in American commercial circles.[67]

Particular forms of economic intercourse between Poland and the United States suffered from special impediments. Potential investors in Poland typically demanded tax concessions, controlling interest and pledges that their operations would not be subjected to governmental intrusion. The Poles were reluctant to cede so broad an authority over the nascent national economy to outsiders, and Warsaw's steps to promote Polish ownership of pivotal enterprises prompted American charges that the Polish climate was inhospitable to foreign capital. Gibson complained that Poland's insistence on a "dog in the manger" policy could only end in the retardation of her development.[68] As it was, the opportunities presented by Poland—chiefly petroleum, timber, minerals, and construction—held little attraction for American business, which dismissed them as too small to warrant serious attention.

Trade between the two countries remained at low levels in spite of Polish eagerness to expand commercial ties and obtain freedom from economic dependence on Germany while making up for the loss of the Russian market. As an infant state, Poland found it difficult to make inroads into established American trading patterns with Europe and to combat the common impression that she had nothing to sell to the United States.[69] Hungry for quick profits, the inexperienced Polish exporters routinely quoted exorbitant prices and lost orders to foreign competitors. As a consequence Poland bought much more from America than she sold, and the American trade became entrenched as a small but persistently negative entry on the books of Poland's foreign exchange.[70]

The Poles wanted loans above all other forms of American economic assistance, but in the unfavorable conditions of the Harding years their efforts yielded only a handful of insignificant credits. Their inability to borrow in the United States stemmed in part from the determination of the State Department to avoid the pitfalls of actual or potential entanglement in the snarls of European affairs. In August 1921, Herbert Hoover, recently elevated to stewardship of the Department of Commerce, proposed that Governor Strong of the New York Federal Reserve Bank enlist the participation of European central banks in a plan for economic reconstruction of East and Central Europe. Hoover contended that differences among the great powers prevented the presentation of aid to the region through the concerted endeavors of governments and concluded that "if these states are to recover it must be . . . through the healing power of private finance and commerce." Hoover claimed to have the support of Harding, and the idea appealed as well to Strong and his British counterpart, Governor Montagu Norman of the Bank of England; but the project died when Hughes rejected it on the grounds that it would inevitably draw the United States into European politics.[71]

The Poles also discovered that their prospects for success in the American loan market would not brighten until they had squared their accounts from the World War. By the end of 1920 Poland's American debt amounted to roughly $170 million—65 percent of the total indebtedness of the Polish state—mostly stemming from the "Hoover relief," which fell into the category of war liabilities owed the U.S. government. In 1922 the State Department began to exert pressure on Poland, as on all debtor governments, to arrange for payment of these sums.[72] The beleaguered Ministry of Finance pleaded for postponement until it had weathered the economic crisis, quietly planning to use the extra time to bargain for better terms. American officials proved amenable to the Polish request for deferment, conceding the futility of forcing the issue until Warsaw had created some order in its finances. However, the very fact that Poland had not settled her war debts greatly diminished her attractiveness to lenders.[73] Taken by itself, the outstanding obligation would have closed the doors of most American banks to Poland; when added to her other difficulties, it reduced her credit in the United States to rock bottom.

Despite warnings from American sources and the Polish legation in Washington that Poland could not hope to obtain a major loan in the United States in such adverse circumstances, the unsteady Polish cabinets of 1922–1923 looked desperately for angels on Wall Street to cover their budget deficits and, not least, to win political points at home. In April 1922 the nonparty government of Antoni Ponikowski authorized Finance Minister Jerzy Michalski to seek an American credit of $50 million against the lease of the Polish tobacco monopoly and fed the newspapers wildly exaggerated reports of its imminent fruition.[74] Michalski's successor, Zygmunt Jastrzębski, abandoned the chase, admitting that "American financial interests would be entirely justified in refusing to consider any such proposal," but his subordinates in the ministry remained convinced of the need to win an American loan on any terms.[75]

In the summer of 1923, as inflation raced out of control, a right-center coalition took office under the leadership of Wincenty Witos, the head of the Piast (Peasant) party. Witos energetically resumed the hunt for loans, concentrating on the United States and England. In July an attempt to conclude an offer of $100 million through Hallgarten and Co. came to nothing.[76] A month later Władysław Kucharski, the minister of industry and commerce, approached J. P. Morgan and Co. to propose a small loan. The bid was leaked to the Warsaw press, which, eager to publicize even so slight an association with such a prominent house, indulged in speculation that the amount under consideration reached as high as $150 million. Although Kucharski reported to Witos that Morgan had shown interest in the project, the bank declined Poland's suit on the grounds of her financial instability. Meanwhile, the conspicuous journalistic accompaniment backfired by irritating Morgan and stimulating unwelcome slights on the creditworthiness of Poland. The financial commentator of the Hearst chain declared that only "boobs" would lend money to Poland in her present condition.[77]

In the view of Hipolit Gliwic, the counselor to the legation in Washington, Warsaw's undignified scramble for an American loan was as unwise as it was unseemly. A professional economist who later filled a number of high positions in the era of Piłsudski's later dominance, Gliwic served continuously in Washington from 1919 to 1925. Although he never attained top rank at the mission, his abilities outshone those of his lackluster superiors, and he displayed a keen understanding of the reasons for the American financier's misgivings about Poland. At the time of Kucharski's negotiations with Morgan, Gliwic protested that "a more inappropriate moment could not have been chosen." Realizing that American banks would not consent to lend money to Poland just so the Finance Ministry could temporarily make good its shortfall, he argued that Warsaw's helter-skelter pursuit of benefactors on Wall Street should be abandoned in favor of a patient policy of restoring Poland's financial reputation in the United States. At a minimum, such a program would require internal financial reorganization, the ending of inflation, the balancing of the budget and assurance that the proceeds of a loan would be applied to "constructive" purposes and not used to subsidize an avoidance of hard choices such as raising taxes. Gliwic contended that careful preparation might produce the ideal result: a large "breakthrough" loan from a solid American firm and the secure establishment of Polish credit in the world's greatest capital market. Until Poland gained the confidence of American banking circles by a demonstration of fidelity to the tenets of financial orthodoxy, her chances to borrow in the United States would remain chimerical.[78]

These observations corresponded with the findings of Paderewski, then in political semiretirement after his unsuccessful ministry. Aware of the admiration Paderewski commanded in America, the faltering Witos cabinet sent him to the United States in December 1923 to sound out the prospects for a loan of at least $400 million. On all sides Paderewski heard the same response: Poland could expect no loans until she had settled her war debts and overhauled her finances. At the same time, Hoover ruled that the Department of Commerce would frown on any Polish loan contracted for the purposes of covering deficits or maintaining the armed forces.[79] In short, American capital considered Poland a risky proposition in every respect and refused to commit any funds to her custody in the absence of guarantees that she could not or would not give during the first five years of her independence. The American economic stake in Poland remained minute, and in finance as in politics, Polish expectations of the United States had failed to materialize.

Far from producing an expansion of ties between Poland and the United States, the era of Harding's presidency witnessed a souring of relations through a series of petty but nettlesome disputes. In 1921 Washington registered its objections to a Franco-Polish trade agreement that, in the opinion of the State Department, violated the Open Door principle by granting preferential treatment to French commerce.[80] Much to the annoyance of Gibson and other American authorities, complaints of arbitrary discrimination against American business interests continued to accumulate.[81]

The State Department ascribed much of the blame for American-Polish discord to Prince Lubomirski, regarding him as incompetent and untrustworthy. Responding to repeated American requests, the MSZ sacked Lubomirski in the autumn of 1922; his successor, Władysław Wróblewski, admitted to Gibson that "Polish-American relations were in such an unsatisfactory state that his position would be difficult."[82] A brief improvement of the atmosphere between Washington and Warsaw followed Lubomirski's departure, only to be dispelled in 1923 by an acrimonious six-month quarrel over the rights of American shipping in Polish harbors.[83] Patience was not Gibson's long suit, and he and his subalterns bristled with barbed appraisals of the abilities of the Polish government, the sincerity of its friendship for the United States, and the viability of the new state.[84]

Disenchantment with Poland mounted as American opinion became exasperated with Polish foreign policies. Early misgivings that Poland was but a vassal of France hardened into conviction after Paris and Warsaw concluded an alliance in 1921. As the view spread that the French system of East European security pacts constituted a needless provocation of Germany and a permanent barrier to European harmony, so Poland's stock declined.[85] American disillusionment with the wisdom of the postwar order created by the peace treaties deepened, and the press began to question the propriety of the Polish frontiers with Germany—especially the so-called Polish Corridor[86]—with increasing frequency. The struggle to fix the Polish frontiers had repeatedly erupted in violence—the war with Soviet Russia, the seizure from Lithuania of the contested city of Vilna in 1920, the Silesian rebellions—and many Americans believed that Warsaw had grown intoxicated with imperial designs. In one intemperate dispatch, Gibson flailed "this lawless and unruly government . . . [which thinks] that Poland can do exactly as she likes and the world can go to the devil [because] . . . nobody is going to send an army here to hold them down." Although Poland's boundaries had become peaceful and relatively stable after 1922, the recollection of her disputatious youth lingered in the American memory and branded her a potential international troublemaker.[87]

Polish spokesmen attempted to remedy the situation by continuing to advertise their country as a bulwark against the twin threats of German imperialism and Russian communism,[88] but this appeal had grown threadbare. The time had long since passed when Americans perceived Germany as a menace, and American militancy toward the Bolshevik regime had cooled as well. The Republican administrations of 1921–1933 never decided quite what to make of Soviet Russia. The State Department refused to admit the legitimacy of the Red government, but neither did it believe that the Soviets possessed the strength to export their revolution. The Americans were content to follow a waiting game, and Hughes honored the principles of the Colby Note of 1920: disdain for the Bolsheviks, hope for the triumph of counterrevolution and insistence on the integrity of Russian territories. The Poles welcomed Washington's official snubbing of their socialist neighbor, but they lamented both American adherence to the idea of an undivided Russia—which appeared to contradict the eastern frontier accorded Poland by the Treaty of Riga of 1921—and the Colby Note's implicit recognition of Russia, not Poland, as the leading power in Eastern Europe and the natural focus of American attention in the area.[89] Although Warsaw achieved a small diplomatic victory when the United States agreed to acknowledge the Riga boundaries on April 5, 1923, Polish efforts to influence American policy toward Russia gained no more than this minor accomplishment.

By the middle of the postwar decade American sympathy for Poland had fallen off sharply from the heady levels of 1919. For the most part, the circle of her enthusiasts had dwindled to the ranks of resolute anti-Bolsheviks who regarded Poland as the shield of Western civilization against the latest manifestation of Eastern barbarism.[90] Largely the property of conservatives and Catholics, these opinions also retained the allegiance of a minority within the American diplomatic community. Despite his tendency to fulminate against the Poles in his letters and dispatches, Hugh Gibson never recanted the conviction that a powerful Poland would benefit the European balance, and he placed ultimate blame for the shortcomings of her foreign policies on the failure of the Allies to make her formidable.[91] However, these views remained uncommon within the State Department and atypical of public sentiment.

Even the American Polonia became an asset of dubious value to Poland. During the immediate postwar period Polish-Americans maintained their support of Poland through agitation and donations, but the passage of time eroded their effectiveness as a lobby for Polish interests. Already during the war the Polonia had split into factions supporting Piłsudski or his opponents on the right, but the rival elements had managed to keep their differences under control for the sake of the common goal of Polish independence. Once the wartime need for unity passed, the coalition of Polish-American political groups splintered into a rancorous heap of cliques roughly corresponding to the constellation of parties in Poland. The infighting within Polonia inhibited its ability to undertake useful work for Poland on American soil.[92]

Warsaw also discovered the limitations of Polonia's weight in the balance of American political forces. The customary preference of the Polish voter for Democrats restricted his leverage on a Republican government in Washington, and the ballot was virtually the only political weapon Polonia possessed.[93] Overwhelmingly a working-class population of peasant origin and minimal education, Polish-Americans kept to themselves, rarely made their way into city halls or corporate boardrooms, and played a decidedly subordinate role in American society. Even Polish diplomats in Washington regarded their American cousins with mild contempt, privately describing them as "benighted masses" and "white Negroes."[94] Nor was Polonia the only ethnic group that could marshal support for a European homeland. The German-American bloc had emerged from the limbo of the World War to reassert its political importance, and when the question of Upper Silesia arose in 1921 the Polish legation refrained from calling upon Polonia for fear of inciting counteraction from the better-organized and better-placed German-Americans.[95]

Polish-Americans gradually drifted away from preoccupation with Poland and turned inward. The natural processes of Americanization received the blessing and promotion of the American government and Polonia's ecclesiastical authorities in the Roman Catholic hierarchy, and the new curbs on immigration prevented fresh infusions of Polish blood. Warsaw regretted these tendencies but hesitated to combat them, unwilling to arouse American ire at intereference in domestic matters.[96] For much of Polonia, the troubled Poland of reality bore little resemblance to the idealized ancestral land of their earlier reveries, and many of them became embittered by financial losses incurred in dealings with the old country. The political eclipse of their favorite, Paderewski, also disappointed and disillusioned them. For the most part, Polish-Americans decided that they had discharged their obligation to their former homeland and that the time had come to improve their own lot. The American economic slump of 1920-1921 bit painfully into the pocketbooks of Polonia and directed its attention toward problems close to home. Polish-American organizations hurriedly adopted the standard of *Wychodźtwo dla Wychodźtwa*—"Polonia for Polonia"—and American politicians found that evocations of Poland elicited a weakened response in Polish neighborhoods.[97]

The five years that followed the end of the World War had not rewarded Polish hopes for close peacetime collaboration with the United States. One by one the links of interest between the two countries had snapped. Washington had chosen to remove itself from the theater of European diplomacy and felt no need of a Polish ally against Germany and the Soviet Union. American capital shunned Poland as a hazardous business. Warsaw had lost the favor of American opinion, which turned against France and her allies, as well as the sponsorship of Polonia. As Hipolit Gliwic noted, a small state like Poland could do little to gain the notice, much less the allegiance, of a global power like the United States. Their attention turned toward home, the Far East and Latin America, the Americans paid little heed to Poland. "It is a completely one-sided relationship," Gliwic wrote; "We have no chance to win over America directly to our policy." Already in the summer of 1922 he had arrived at the unwelcome conclusion that:

> it is hard to imagine that our efforts toward a broadening of relations with America, such as in finance and economics, can attain the desired results. . . . We must not delude ourselves that we can expect to find ourselves in greater political favor here within the near future.[98]

As Gliwic viewed the problem, Poland's only choice was to wait and hope that future developments would cause American and Polish interests to coincide. A few months later a bored Hugh Gibson reported to Hughes that the Warsaw legation found itself "not doing much that is of interest."[99] By the end of 1923, significant political and economic contact between Poland and the United States had lapsed.

CHAPTER II

The Resumption of Financial Contact, 1924–1925

What can America do for [the countries of Eastern Europe] now? So far as my observation goes, most of them have ceased to think of America as anything except the nation with money.

Elmer Davis, 1922

The obvious waning of American interest in Poland in the first years of Republican government produced disappointment and occasional dismay in Polish circles. "The U.S. has done too much to help in the reestablishment of independent Poland," insisted a disbelieving member of the Sejm in 1923, "for it not to participate in the final stages of that task."[1] Yet the combination of Poland's financial demoralization and America's profession of indifference to Europe persuaded the harried Polish authorities of the early 1920s that they would have to get by without the United States. Official declarations of reliance on the good will and material assistance of America, so hearty in 1919, gradually dwindled into ritualistic recitations of thanks for past favors expressing little hope of future collaboration. However, in the closing weeks of 1923 two simultaneous but seemingly unrelated developments laid the foundations for the revival of economic relations between the two countries. In Warsaw a new government entered into office with a mandate to repair the tattered Polish finances, while at the same time the State Department was choosing delegates to take part in the international conferences that would bring forth the Dawes Plan and inaugurate a fresh American approach to European affairs.

The Polish economic plunge persisted during the final months of 1923. In mid-November the Polish mark plummeted to a value of 2.3 million to the American dollar, having declined by a factor of ten in less than three months, and continued its free fall through December toward a low of 10.1 million to a dollar. A wave of strikes swept the country, raising the specter of revolution. Powerless to resolve the mounting crisis, the Witos government collapsed on December 15.

For a successor, the president of the republic turned to Władysław Grabski, an economist and veteran of five previous cabinets. Grabski belonged to no political party, and because no faction found his nomination for a second term as premier intolerable, the nod went to him almost by default. Determined to bring order into Polish finances and allay the threat of social unrest, Grabski demanded and received from the Sejm freedom to enact special decrees on fiscal and budgetary matters for a period of six months. Armed with more authority than any prior peacetime leader of the new Poland, Grabski formed a nonpartisan government of center-right complexion in which he doubled as minister of finance.

The man assigned the task of rescuing the country from economic chaos ranks as one of the more intriguing personalities of the era of parliamentary dominance in interwar Poland. Professorial in mien, Grabski was in fact a disciple of the Central European tradition of political *Kuhhandel*, a skillful though erratic operator who excelled in the delicate art of managing the notoriously balky Sejm. Lacking a parliamentary majority, he nonetheless managed to keep his government afloat for nearly two years by dexterously maneuvering among the parties of left and right through the judicious exercise of bribery and economic legerdemain. These traits did not endear the new prime minister to all observers; as early as 1920 Hugh Gibson dismissed him as "a man without strength of character, of poor judgement; and not above deliberate deception."[2] Yet despite his reputation as a shady dealer, Grabski rose and clung to power because he could offer what his rivals could not: a broad if unorthodox economic expertise and a comprehensive plan to extricate Poland from her financial distress.

Buoyed by the acquiescence of the Sejm and the Polish business community in his ambitious reform program, Grabski set to work with a will in the first months of his ministry. He slowed the pace of inflation and, with the aid of some budgetary sleight of hand, brought Polish expenditures into seeming equivalence with revenues. During the spring and summer of 1924 he withdrew the worthless mark and replaced it with a new unit, the złoty, based on gold and fixed at a rate of 5.18 to the dollar. A new central bank, the Bank Polski (Bank of Poland), was created as the sole agency of issue. Economic traditionalists gagged at Grabski's audacious attempt to introduce a new currency before the budget had been brought safely into equilibrium, but on balance his innovative improvisations produced visible if temporary benefits and helped to restore a modicum of international confidence in Poland.[3]

The enticement of foreign lenders occupied a position of high priority in Grabski's scheme to salvage Polish finances. On this subject, as in others, the premier's practice differed from his stated convictions. One of Grabski's foremost objectives was to accomplish Poland's internal renewal with a minimum of aid from outside, and he adopted the slogan *O własnych siłach*—"by our own efforts"—to describe his philosophy. As a logical consequence, he opposed loans from abroad on the grounds that

Poland, as a country with dangerous enemies, would do well to avoid mortgaging her interests to foreign influence.[4] He wished particularly to escape the predicament of Austria and Hungary—and, a few months later, of Germany—which received international stabilization loans at the price of foreign supervision over their finances.[5] The appeal for financial autonomy also struck responsive chords among certain sectors of the Polish population—peasants, entrepreneurs, nationalists, the left—which harbored misgivings about foreign capital.

But on inheriting responsibility for Poland's economic rescue, Grabski found the ideal of self-reliance impossible to realize. Bowing to necessity, he embarked on a course of seeking piecemeal loans to balance his budgets, betting that periodic small infusions of capital from various sources might reduce the political risk of dependence on a large foreign donor. Accepting foreign loans as "a necessary evil," he set out briskly to drum up business in the money markets of the world.[6] Because his reforms had broken down some of the instinctive resistance of foreign capital to Poland, his efforts yielded some initial successes. In February 1924 Poland obtained a loan of 400 million lire from the Banca Commerciale Italiana and a few months later a French consortium agreed to help stake the building of the new port of Gdynia.

Although Grabski had accomplished the removal of some of the impediments against Polish credit, he still lacked a suitable and willing source of steady foreign funding. Since 1921 the Poles had sought to forge economic ties with England, and several of Grabski's associates counseled him to concentrate his attention on the City of London.[7] The preceding Witos government had invited British advice, and in 1923–1924 Poland received an English exploratory expedition led by Hilton Young, a Liberal politician and financial expert. Young envisaged an influx of loans to Poland only after a thorough reorganization of the Polish financial apparatus carried out largely by British advisers. After some hesitation, Grabski snubbed the work of the Young commission as a gesture of independence, underlining both his freedom from the policies of earlier cabinets and his determination to prevent foreign dictation over the course of his program of reforms.[8] The failure of the Young mission discouraged British capital, but no competitor seemed eager to fill the void. In spite of the political alliance between Paris and Warsaw, French financial interest in Poland remained tepid, partially owing to France's own precarious state of financial health.[9] As for the United States, Grabski had concluded long before that American capital had written off Europe as a potential sphere of activity.[10]

These calculations altered abruptly when America returned to the European scene in the role of offstage arbiter and chief creditor. The origin of the American about-face can be traced back to December 1922, when Secretary Hughes publicly proposed an international conference to resolve the question of war reparations. This statement reflected Washington's tacit admission both that the far-flung economic interests of the

United States bound her inextricably to Europe and that the tangle of financial obligations stemming from the war could only be unsnarled with American help. The problem became critical in January 1923 when France and Belgium invaded the Ruhr in a bid to extract defaulted reparations payments from Germany. The adventure provoked the disapproval of London and Washington and proved unprofitable to the French, who in November abandoned the policy of coercion and bowed to the calls of the Anglo-American front for a reparations settlement along the lines of the Hughes suggestion.

Subsequent negotiations produced the blueprint for German recovery that bore the name of the American chairman of the proceedings, Charles G. Dawes. Adopted in the summer of 1924, the Dawes Plan revised the schedule of German reparations payments and placed German finances under the regulation of an international committee headed by S. Parker Gilbert, an American lawyer and former treasury official. The crux of the project was a loan of $200 million to Germany, mostly to be raised in the United States. When J. P. Morgan and Co. opened the American allotment of the Dawes loan to subscription in October 1924, the investing public responded with alacrity and fulfilled its quota ten times over.[11]

The construction of the Dawes Plan marked a decisive transformation of the international diplomatic balance and of the nature of the American presence in Europe. The event signaled the breaking of French resolve to enforce the postwar treaties by means of a strong hand. Admitting her ultimate dependence on Whitehall and Wall Street, France relaxed her truculent posture toward Berlin and edged nearer the more accommodating German policy espoused by Britain. The French renunciation of the goal of strict fulfillment of the Versailles accords initiated a five-year phase of diplomatic *détente* in Europe during which the great powers strove to compose their differences in a spirit of compromise. Convention has designated this interlude of relative calm and economic prosperity "the era of Locarno," after the famous European security pact of 1925. In truth, the surface tranquility of the Locarno period belied the continuation of intense diplomatic competition among the Europeans, but the milder tone of international discourse came as a relief to many contemporaries, particularly in Britain and the United States, whose apprehensions of renewed European war began to subside.

The wholehearted if unofficial support given the Dawes Plan by the governmental and financial authorities of the United States reflected an American decision, partly conscious and partly implicit, to reclaim a position of importance in Europe. The medium of American activity was to be the dollar; the goal, the promotion of European economic and political stability for the purposes of advancing peace and providing a secure outlet for American export and overseas investment. In essence, the United States, brimming with a surplus of capital, offered to open her pocketbook to nations that satisfied the American definition of a reliable client and inclined their policies along lines generally acceptable to

American investors. The advancement of stabilization became the hallmark of the American relationship with Europe during the tenure of Calvin Coolidge and Herbert Hoover, and the lure of American money provided Washington a large measure of leverage in Europe.

The notion of stability was nebulous, embracing many meanings, and it represented more a cumulative tendency of American actions than a fully articulated policy. Nevertheless, certain principles governed American behavior toward Europe. The first commandment of stabilization stipulated that a deserving European recipient of American largesse should honor the tenets of financial orthodoxy. By far the largest repository of precious metal, the United States also strongly encouraged adoption of the gold standard as a means of streamlining world trade and amplifying American commercial influence. These requirements carried with them a natural bias toward conservative government. By its very nature, a regime of radical stripe or a country menaced by social or political upheaval could not be accounted trustworthy and safe. The American investor preferred as well to deal with European partners that changed governments infrequently and afforded the continuity of policy and ministerial personality conducive to long-range planning.

In the realm of international relations, Washington upheld the polite fiction that economics was separable from politics and insisted upon retaining freedom from commitment to European political blocs and arrangements. In reality, the United States became a freelance participant in European diplomacy, occasionally intervening warily to advocate the amicable resolution of disputes. The American strategy of stabilization sought above all to serve the interests of the United States by fostering the peaceful and prosperous conditions in which commerce flourished. In design and intent, the policy was one of nonalignment and evenhandedness; put into practice, it often worked to the advantage of Germany, the European country that stood most to gain from political compromise and whose economic opportunities offered the greatest prizes to American investors.[12]

The success of the course of stabilization hinged on the willingness of the private sector to deliver large sums to Europe, and the reluctance of American capital toward Europe gave way before the stimulus of official encouragement and fortuitous political and economic developments. The relaxation of international tension in the mid-1920s made European investments thinkable, and the lure of high profits make them irresistible. When the thunderous reception of the Dawes loan demonstrated the extent of the demand for European securities, lenders rushed to join the bandwagon. The result was a five-year explosion of American capital outlay to Europe in the form of loans and investments, abetted by easy money and minimal governmental supervision over the boom in the export of dollars. Germany attracted by far the largest share of the American economic infatuation with Europe. Between 1924 and 1931 Americans committed nearly three billion dollars to Germany, and German securities amounted to 40 percent of the total volume of American lending to Europe.[13]

The new readiness of the United States to bankroll Europe necessarily led Grabski to look across the Atlantic for a source of foreign loans. Aside from the elementary fact that, as Grabski put it, "all the money was in the United States," recourse to America made sense in terms of the prime minister's aversion to foreign interference. Of all potential lenders, Grabski believed, the United States was least involved in the complex of European diplomacy and her money least tainted by political motivations. For that reason, American capital could be trusted not to intrude into Polish internal affairs or, worse yet, to demand political concessions as the price of aid.[14]

If the promulgation of the Dawes Plan presented the Poles with an opportunity to crack the money markets of New York, the awakening of American financial interest in their western neighbor also was profoundly unsettling. At the least, the concentration of American investment in Germany could dry up the pool of funds available to Poland. Many Poles perceived a political danger as well, seeing the Anglo-American effort to revitalize the German economy as evidence of an unwelcome intention of the great commercial nations to develop a special relationship with Berlin.[15] Alarmists foresaw the day when a revived Germany, fed by a steady stream of English and American capital, would extend a web of economic and political hegemony over Eastern Europe with the tacit approval of her western benefactors. This menacing vision gained plausibility from the unconcealed German desire to reclaim the lands lost to Poland by the peace settlement.[16] Grabski agreed that the sudden attractiveness of Germany to American finance constituted a threat that Poland could neutralize only by carving out her own foothold on Wall Street. In the wake of the adoption of the Dawes Plan, Grabski pondered aloud how it might "affect Poland politically and economically? American capital will flow into Germany; will it take an interest in Poland?"[17]

In fact, Polish stock in the United States had rebounded modestly from the depths of 1923. The virtual cessation of economic contact between the two countries meant at least that the injurious stream of accusations of Polish discrimination against U.S. enterprise trickled to a halt. At the same time, the swift enactment of the Grabski reform package prompted a recovery of confidence in Poland's future in some American quarters. Soundings within the American financial community now revealed faint stirrings of interest in the possibility of doing business with Poland.[18]

Grabski understood that to sustain the hopeful signs Poland needed to conclude an agreement on the funding of the American war debt.[19] The Americans had established fulfillment of these obligations as the acid test of European creditworthiness, and under the "Ruling of 1922" the State Department embargoed loans to delinquent countries, most notably France. Until the advent of the Grabski cabinet, Polish policy—pursued as well by Grabski in his occasional stints as minister of finance—had sought to stall the American bill collectors while assuring them that Warsaw intended to settle as quickly as its circumstances would permit.[20] American patience with Polish delay wore thin after the British came to terms midway through 1923,[21] and once he had installed his reforms Grabski could not easily justify avoidance of the debt question while simultaneously claiming to have stabilized Polish finances.

Mindful of the advantage to be gained in American opinion by appearing the conscientious debtor, Grabski instructed the Washington legation in February 1924 to set the train of debt negotiations into motion.[22] The Poles laid their proposition for a settlement before the U.S. War Debt Commission in June. Inviting praise for Poland's decision to discharge her liabilities at the earliest possible moment, Minister Wróblewski offered a preliminary figure and repayment over a span of 62 years.[23] The Americans accepted the main points of the proposal, leaving only a Polish request for minor deductions as an obstacle to an immediate agreement. Impatient to hasten an accord and convinced that haggling would not yield meaningful concessions, Grabski directed his representatives in Washington to avoid quibbling over details and to bring the proceedings to a speedy conclusion.[24]

Grabski's willingness to adopt the American conditions liquidated the issues separating the parties, and on November 14, 1924, Wróblewski and Secretary of the Treasury Andrew Mellon, meeting in Washington on behalf of their governments, signed a pact for payment of the Polish debt. The contract closely approximated the form of the English settlement of the preceding year. It called for Poland to satisfy a consolidated debt of $178.6 million in principal and accumulated interest by 1984. All in all, the Poles had not done badly for themselves. The schedule of amortization was calculated to ease the immediate burden on the young state by allowing payment in gradually increasing increments over the early years of the plan, and reductions in the original rates of interest to an average annual rate of 3.3 percent lessened the total anticipated debt by roughly a quarter.

Polish opinion received the settlement favorably as an acceptable if not optimal outcome,[25] and the measure obtained speedy parliamentary approval. For its part, the Grabski government from the beginning had considered the terms of the debt agreement secondary to the objective of eliminating the war obligations as an encumbrance on Polish credit. Wróblewski reported to Grabski that with the debt question safely laid to rest, the time had come to test the American waters for loans.[26]

In the late autumn of 1924 Poland's chances to make a favorable impression on lenders in America appeared better than at any time since 1919. Wróblewski noted that the debt compact had inspired "a deeper and friendlier echo in the United States" than any Polish action since the winning of independence, and Poland could point to her scrupulous discharge of her obligations to Baldwin Locomotive as proof of her trustworthiness.[27]

In the meantime, the arrival of a new American minister to Warsaw in June 1924 seemed an indication of revived American financial interest in the Polish market. Hugh Gibson's successor, Alfred J. Pearson, was an academic without a scrap of diplomatic expertise or acumen, but after five years of growing frustration Gibson clearly needed a change of scenery, and the Warsaw grapevine speculated that his replacement's mission was to quicken the flagging pace of American trade and investment.[28] The coincident timing of the American elections of 1924 also worked to Polish advantage. Despite the advice of the State Department not to inject domestic political factors into the equation of policy toward Warsaw, campaign strategists for President Coolidge saw merit in the idea of appealing to Polish-American voters by hinting approval of the participation of American capital in the reconstruction of Poland.[29]

In fact, the Poles already had managed to score a minor success on the American market before the conclusion of the debt settlement. In September an agent of Ulen and Co. of New York approached the state Bank Gospodarstwa Krajowego (National Economic Bank) with an offer to place a $9.7 million bond issue in the United States to finance a series of public works projects the company would undertake in a number of Polish cities. The Polish government responded with alacrity, and the Bank, bowing to official exhortations for acceptance, contracted with Ulen on September 27. The terms of the deal were hard for the Poles; the loan carried a steep price tag of 8 percent interest plus a 15 percent commission for the American firm. In its eagerness to land any sort of loan in the United States, Warsaw was not inclined to jeopardize the business by driving a hard bargain. Grabski accepted the severity of the Ulen loan as the cost of admission into the Wall Street market. The MSZ stressed to the Washington legation "the importance it ascribes to this first large transaction of American capital in Poland as well as its realization in a manner that will provide encouragement for other American investments."[30]

Despite the government's satisfaction at having broken the long string of Polish failures on Wall Street, the small Ulen loan could neither establish Polish credit firmly in America nor provide Grabski the coup he needed to justify his policy and cement his political position at home. The charge that Grabski's tinkering had given the Polish economy began to falter in the autumn of 1924. Imaginative bookkeeping had concealed an actual budget deficit of at least $33 million for 1924, and the złoty showed signs of weakening. Political pressure began to mount for the prime minister to produce a large loan from abroad.[31] For his part, Grabski believed such a credit was necessary to stave off economic disaster, but as no foreign takers appeared on the horizon his anxiety increased. Confessing his worries to a colleague in October, Grabski gave the impression of a man likely to "break down any day now."[32]

Poland began to cast for loans with a touch of the desperation of 1923, but inquiries in London and at the League of Nations proved barren.

Several American banks acknowledged interest in Warsaw's overtures but added the unwelcome proviso that the Poles would have to wait for six months until pending European business had been completed.[33] In early November, however, as the negotiations for the debt consolidation agreement drew toward completion, Grabski received word that Dillon, Read and Co. of New York was weighing the merits of a prompt loan to Poland and commanded Wróblewski to focus his efforts exclusively on that firm.[34]

At the close of 1924, Dillon, Read was one of the most dynamic investment houses in America, and its precocious president, Clarence Dillon, was approaching the pinnacle of a career that, in the contemporary evaluation of the *New York Times*, "has made even Wall Street wonder."[35] In 1916, at the age of thirty-four, Dillon had assumed the leadership of William A. Read and Co., and under his direction the renamed concern advanced rapidly toward the front ranks of American finance. Dillon's business method blended the customary prudence of the investment banker with a share of the exuberance of his native Texas; his characteristic procedure was to take carefully calculated risks on dubious propositions, and his burgeoning reputation rested on his knack for reaping spectacular dividends from these gambles. In 1921 he accomplished the rehabilitation of the troubled Goodyear Tire and Rubber Co., and four years later he outbid J. P. Morgan and Co. for the Dodge Brothers Automobile Co.—an acquisition that, at the time, stood as the largest industrial transaction in history. By no means merely a lucky hunch player, Dillon planned his moves cautiously and acted only upon the conviction that the odds of success lay in his favor. Dillon's speculative streak and rapid ascent bred resentment within the old guard of the financial fraternity, and his undisguised hunger for eminence on Wall Street led Dillon, Read into spirited and sometimes bitter competition with the older, established banks, and particularly with the House of Morgan.[36]

Dillon was one of the first American bankers to grasp the fact that the Dawes Plan had opened new vistas to United States enterprise, and he gladly would have replaced his rival Morgan as agent of the Dawes loan to Germany.[37] He moved Dillon, Read quickly into the field of European lending, joining other banks in an effort to enter the booming German market. Dillon did not limit his European horizons to Germany; by 1926 he had financed the governments of six continental states. Poland had attracted Dillon's notice even before the Dawes Plan riveted American attention on Europe. In 1922 Samuel Vauclain of Baldwin Locomotive had aroused his interest in floating a loan toward expansion of the Polish railways, but Dillon shelved the idea owing to illness and lack of confidence in European conditions.[38]

Dillon's thoughts returned to Poland late in 1924 at the instance of Trowbridge Callaway, a fellow banker and Harvard classmate. Receiving encouragement from the Polish legation in Washington, Dillon dispatched Callaway to Warsaw as head of a delegation empowered to negotiate on behalf of Dillon, Read. At the same time Morgan extended feelers for a Polish loan. Luxuriating in this unaccustomed abundance of suitors, Wróblewski advised Warsaw to seek a liaison with Morgan and use Dillon, Read as a fallback. Dillon's agents moved quickly, however, and a series of meetings in Warsaw with Polish treasury officials produced an understanding in principle that Poland would place a loan through his bank.[39]

The contracting parties agreed promptly that the proposed loan would yield a high interest of 8 percent and that Poland would apply the bulk of its proceeds toward railway development, but other points of the deal proved more difficult to resolve. The bank offered to float $25 million immediately and, in the event of its success, to follow with a second transfer of equal size; in rejoinder, the Poles insisted that Dillon, Read commit itself without reservation to an issue of $50 million. Negotiators for the bank warned that the American investing public would not absorb such an ambitious sum, but Grabski refused to allow the mood of the American market to dictate the size of the loan and held out for a full $50 million or $25 million on better terms. Against its judgment, Dillon, Read acquiesced in the larger figure while reserving the privilege to reduce the amount at a later date as a protection against unforeseen circumstances.[40] For their part, Dillon's representatives demanded the right to veto the placement of other Polish government loans in the United States during the term of the bank's option to prevent dilution of demand for the Dillon, Read offer. The Poles consented to this condition of priority but managed to procure an exception for subsequent dealings with Ulen and Co.[41] With these issues settled, Wróblewski arrived at an agreement with the Dillon bank in mid-January 1925.

No sooner had the bargain been struck than it began to buckle under the strain of adverse pressures. To a large degree these difficulties originated from Polish-German friction. Berlin hoped to render Warsaw more pliant through the perpetuation of Polish credit isolation, which would increase Poland's economic dependence on her western neighbor and reduce her ability to resist German political demands. Upon learning of the accord with Dillon, Read, the Auswärtiges Amt (Foreign Office) and its deputies in Warsaw and the United States initiated a campaign to denigrate Polish creditworthiness and undermine the loan.[42] During the opening weeks of 1925 the American press revived speculation on the likelihood of a Polish-German war, and the untimely resurrection of this topic gave the Dillon firm second thoughts about the security of its venture.[43] The spate of unfavorable publicity instantly chilled the American financial world's fragile confidence in Poland. When Dillon, Read approached other New York banks with invitations to form a syndicate in support of the loan, they unanimously declined to join the enterprise and counseled Dillon "to have nothing to do with Poland."[44]

Now apprehensive that it had overestimated the receptivity of the

American investor to Polish loans, Dillon, Read informed Wróblewski on February 4 that the failure to find allies on Wall Street left it no choice but to revise the terms of the agreement as provided in the bank's safety clause. Instead of $50 million, the firm proposed a first transfer of $35 million with an option to offer the remaining $15 million by August 1, when market conditions might prove more propitious. Grabski reluctantly gave assent to the new arrangement.[45] Its misgivings growing daily, Dillon, Read returned to Wróblewski on February 13, a mere two days before the loan was to go on sale, to impart its doubts that the weakened market would bear even $35 million. To protect themselves against undersubscription, the Americans requested a confidential Polish pledge to purchase unsold bonds up to a limit of $7.5 million. In other words, Dillon, Read was now prepared to guarantee a net loan of $27.5 million—roughly equivalent to the original offer of $25 million rejected by the Poles. The imposition of this requirement at the last minute annoyed Grabski, who had already claimed political credit at home for a $35 million windfall, but he gave in to avoid losing Dillon, Read altogether.[46] Acting on Grabski's instruction, Wróblewski on February 14 authorized the bank to issue the first transfer of the loan.

In its final form, the contract with Dillon, Read outlined a loan of up to $50 million with an initial transfer of $35 million, subject to the bank's eleventh-hour hedge, which remained secret so as not to alarm the market or embarrass Grabski. The bonds carried an interest of 8 percent and were to be repaid by 1950. The conditions of the agreement were not easy from the Polish perspective—a German diplomat scoffed that the Poles had been forced to swallow an interest rate "unheard of in any civilized country of the globe"[47]—but they reflected the risk of doing business with a state which lay in such a precarious geopolitical situation. On the positive side of the ledger, Grabski could point to the facts that the loan entailed fewer burdens at least than those of 1924 and that he had avoided the provisions of foreign financial supervision which had accompanied major loans to Germany and other Central European countries. The leading Polish economists of the day acknowledged that Dillon's terms, while relatively stringent, represented the best that Poland could expect in view of current market trends and practices.[48]

Poland and Dillon, Read finally sealed their bargain despite frictions and mutual reservations because both parties regarded the transaction as a means to larger ends. While Poland needed the money for immediate purposes, in Warsaw's eyes the crucial rationale for the Dillon loan lay in its utility in the long run. Grabski sought a large foreign loan not only to allay the distress of the moment, but also to cap and consolidate his series of reforms. Furthermore, he looked on the contract with Dillon as Poland's ticket of entry into the mammoth and safely apolitical American capital market, and as in the case of the Ulen loan he was willing to pay a price for this privilege.[49] German opposition to the project injected the additional element of Polish international prestige into the calculations.

Although irritated at the gradual shrinkage of the loan during the course of negotiations, Grabski believed that Poland could not afford to permit the appearance of success to Berlin's unconcealed endeavors to sabotage the deal.[50] Domestic political considerations came into play as well. The Polish press had whetted public anticipation of the loan to such a degree that the government preferred to accept difficult terms rather than face the consequences of standing its ground and possibly ending up empty-handed, and Grabski also found it convenient to shift the onus of fiscal austerity onto Dillon, Read by exaggerating the preconditions laid down by the bank.[51]

Clarence Dillon's primary motivation for concluding the Polish loan arose out of his desire to solidify the standing of his upstart house within the American banking community. The agreement embraced an understanding that the Polish government would regard Dillon as its permanent "banker" in the United States and grant his firm the right of first refusal in its future credit operations. This priority clause conformed to American banking convention in international lending. In theory, the arrangement conferred benefits on both lender and borrower: it allowed the bank, if it wished, to exercise a monopoly over a country's credit in the American market while providing the petitioner with a steady and presumably sympathetic source of funding and financial advice. The informal code of business ethics demanded respect for the tie between a bank and a foreign government, and any client who attempted to evade his commitment to his American banker ran the hazard of incurring a bad name as a faithless partner.[52] Dillon, Read wanted to forge just such a relationship with Warsaw, not only for the attractions of its business but also to advance the concern's broader strategic purposes. Attaining the status of banker for a foreign country lent prestige to a firm, and by establishing his primacy in Poland Dillon hoped to build a base from which to compete with the Morgan interests for a leading position in Europe.[53] The fact that the loan provided for railway expansion and owed its original inspiration to Samuel Vauclain suggests that Dillon accepted the rail magnate's argument that the development of the Polish transportation network would stimulate the pace of European commerce and consequently reward American investors in other continental ventures.

Aside from some disappointment within Polish business circles that the loan was no larger—rumored estimates had reached as high as $100 million[54]—Poland greeted the news of the Dillon, Read transaction with widespread approval. On February 23 Grabski commended the contract to the budget committee of the Sejm as an indispensable step toward the restoration of Poland's finances and international reputation. The deputies winced at the rigor of Dillon's conditions but admitted the overriding importance of cracking the American market and passed the measure without difficulty.[55] The normally raucous press endorsed the loan as a godsend that opened "a new era in the economic life of the country."[56] Poland's representatives in the United States congratulated themselves for achieving at last the long-sought principal aim of Polish policy toward America. Hipolit Gliwic, who had endured the long Polish credit drought, exulted that "finally we have managed to introduce Poland onto the world market and to interest one of the most prominent firms in the world in our affairs," while Wróblewski forecast a durable and mutually beneficial collaboration with Dillon, Read.[57] No less susceptible to the prevalent optimism, Polish banking circles looked forward to more American loans in the near future.[58]

The conclusion of the Dillon enterprise elicited a similar satisfaction on the American side. Clarence Dillon lavished praise on Poland—"that great country, that great nation"—and predicted coming eminence for her.[59] In keeping with its role as banker, the firm assumed responsibility for managing Polish public relations in the United States. The outcome of the negotiations also pleased the departments of Treasury and State. Desirous of encouraging the work of the Grabski reforms, American officialdom gave its tacit blessing to the Dillon project and maintained a benevolent attitude throughout the period of its incubation.[60]

By chance, the closure of the loan coincided with the successful resolution of a lengthy Polish effort to secure a provisional commercial accord with the United States. With an exchange of notes on February 10, Warsaw and Washington agreed to conduct trade relations according to the most-favored-nation formula. In removing the basis for long-standing American complaints of Polish discrimination in commercial matters, the Grabski government hoped to spur an influx of investment from the United States.[61] Prospects for the broadening of economic exchange between Poland and America had never looked brighter than in February 1925.

The celebrations of the Dillon loan proved premature. Soon after the bonds opened for public sale on February 15 the failure of the issue became evident. Subscriptions fell short even of the modest goal set by the bankers when they trimmed the loan drastically at the last minute. Many reasons contributed to the depression of sales. In the first place, the Polish offer made its debut during a temporary lull in the demand for foreign securities; the buying public was taking a breather in the wake of the initial burst of enthusiasm for European bonds.[62] Thrust hastily and without sufficient advance publicity into a soft and satiated market, the loan had no chance to overcome the ingrained wariness of the public toward Poland or induce it to choose the Polish bond over seemingly safer alternatives from Germany or Western Europe.[63] The Dillon loan's high interest rate, installed to attract buyers with the promise of lucrative yields, appeared instead to discourage investors by reminding them of the risks attached to Polish ventures. Subscriptions suffered as well from the inability of the loan to win favor from its natural client, the small Polish-American investor, who remembered the money he had lost in earlier dealings with postwar Poland, most notably the 6 percent loan of 1920.[64]

By far the most important cause of the unattractiveness of the Dillon loan to American buyers was its appearance at a time of great political uncertainty in Europe. In February 1925 Germany submitted a proposal for a European security pact that eventually found expression in the Locarno treaty of October. In essence Berlin, following the lead of Foreign Minister Gustav Stresemann, hoped to escape the most burdensome clauses of the peace treaties by voluntarily accepting those deemed tolerable. During the intervening months of negotiation and discussion, American investors held back to watch the evolution of the project and measure its impact on Europe and the safety of American investment.

The German proposition affected Warsaw in particularly intimate fashion: Berlin offered to recognize the inviolability of its western frontiers, but refused to rule out the possibility of peaceful modification of its boundaries with Poland and Czechoslovakia. This drawing of a distinction between the Rhine and the Vistula naturally led the American press to ponder the problematic longevity of the Polish Corridor and the disputed partition of Upper Silesia.[65] These speculations exerted a disastrous influence on the trade of Polish bonds. In April one of Dillon's lieutenants lamented the difficulties of selling the loan in the face of a barrage of newspaper reports "which would tend to indicate that Poland may lose a substantial amount of its territory eventually."[66] In spite of Polish assurances that "nothing endangers foreign investments in Poland,"[67] the timid reaction of American capital to the European political suspense of the spring and summer of 1925 demonstrated that Warsaw had not put to rest the killing doubt that the Polish state could survive.

The Dillon loan absorbed another blow when the influential Moody's Investors Service assigned the issue a mediocre rating for want of confidence in the European political condition.[68] The absence of any mechanism for foreign supervision over Polish finances also seemed to awaken the skepticism of the Moody analysts, who ranked the loan below other Central European offerings including such a provision. This disparaging evaluation from the most respected American guide to securities investments provoked futile Polish protests and brought the fitful sales of the Polish loan to a standstill. Buyers hurriedly moved to divest themselves of their holdings. By mid-April Dillon, Read had been forced to repurchase $5.5 million of bonds from frightened investors.[69]

In the meantime, the receipt of the first transfer of the Dillon loan had failed to arrest the erosion of the Polish economy. Even as Grabski extolled the beneficial effects of the loan toward reducing unemployment and stimulating railway and housing construction, Poland edged toward a new round of financial crisis. Tax revenues failed to cover governmental expenditures. Furthermore, a poor harvest in 1924 provoked an unfavorable balance of trade; the deficit compelled the Bank Polski gradually to liquidate much of its gold cover, imperiling in turn the position of the złoty, which had been fixed at an unrealistically high plateau. The infusion of dollars from Dillon, Read temporarily redressed the balance of foreign exchange, but by April the ominous economic winds threatened to overturn the premier's financial house of cards.[70] Confronted again by the likelihood of imminent fiscal disaster, Grabski looked abroad for rescue and turned to Dillon, Read with a request to release a second installment of the anticipated $50 million, of which $22.5 million remained.

On April 9 Wróblewski appealed to Dillon to forward the $7.5 million which the bank had chopped from the nominal amount of the first offer of $35 million. Dillon, Read refused, citing sagging sales and the long list of misfortunes the loan had encountered. While pledging their intention to furnish the remainder of the loan in good time, the bankers declined "to make any prediction as to when the remaining $7,500,000 of bonds can be taken up." Counselling patience and faith in their judgment of the market, they emphasized the need to outwait and reverse the tide of ruinous publicity before taking further action.[71] From the point of view of the bank, this advice was sound long-term strategy, but it provided cold comfort to the Polish officials preoccupied with pressing emergency.

If Poland had begun to grow impatient with her American bankers, Dillon, Read likewise developed second thoughts about its Polish partners. Clarence Dillon reaffirmed his desire to be "the banker of Poland in the fullest meaning of the term,"[72] but the miscarriage of the 8 percent loan bred in him the conviction that Polish issues required the utmost caution and preparation. Once burned, the firm determined not to carry out a second Polish operation until its chance of success was assured. Meanwhile, the anxious Poles angered Dillon, Read by looking elsewhere for loans in transgression of the bank's temporary monopoly over Polish credit in the United States. Dillon, Read protested the violation of its prerogatives, arguing for good measure that the placement of a rival Polish loan in a slow market inevitably would retard efforts to build public demand for its own issues.[73]

Warsaw reserved hope that Dillon would sanction the realization of all or part of the outstanding $22.5 million in the course of a forthcoming visit to Poland to survey the Polish condition at first hand. Feeling the heat from public and parliament, Grabski imprudently claimed that receipt of the second installment of $15 million was certain.[74] On June 10 Dillon arrived in the Polish capital. The financier maintained an outward satisfaction with the performance of the 8 percent loan for public consumption, but in his talks with Polish officials he proved reluctant to rush a further advance. He departed without comment on the question of the second transfer, leading American financial observers correctly to infer that he had resisted Polish entreaties and shelved the project for the immediate future.[75]

The outbreak of trade war between Poland and Germany in the summer of 1925 scarcely whetted Dillon, Read's appetite for the second installment of the Polish loan. The Upper Silesian convention of 1922 governing commercial relations between these Central European antagonists expired in June. Negotiations for a successive treaty proceeded poorly, complicated by mutual mistrust and Berlin's attempts to link an accord to Poland's treatment of her German minority. The standoff produced a customs war that dragged on until 1934. The contest appeared no even match, for the Poles depended heavily on the German market; the embargo affected 27 percent of the total Polish export trade, while Germany's stake in the economic struggle amounted to but 3 percent of her sales abroad. Poland weathered the test and even emerged from it stronger for having found new markets and reduced her reliance on the German trade, but in 1925 the consensus of financial opinion held that the customs war could only inflict further damage on an already weakened Poland.

The trade war with Germany completed the circle of renewed Polish credit isolation in the United States. Already discouraged by the European security pact discussions, Polish economic woes, and the obvious failure of the Dillon loan, American houses showed no interest in Poland.[76] The new complication provided Dillon, Read one more reason to put off the Poles until better times. Toward the end of July the bank confessed its inability to float the second transfer of $15 million until the market for Polish bonds recovered, and the firm asked for an extension of its option. While retaining the wish to keep Poland as a client, the bankers feared they "had a white elephant on their hands . . . and that it would be a long time before any further financing could be done."[77]

The extravagant Polish hopes that attended the winning of the first major loan from the United States since 1920 failed to materialize. The salutary economic effect of the initial transfer wore off quickly without perceptibly strengthening the złoty. Nor did the loan bring more foreign capital in its wake or improve Poland's standing in the world money markets. Far from furnishing Poland with her coveted "breakthrough loan," the Dillon transaction stigmatized the Polish state in the eyes of the financial community. The loan's checkered history and the postponement of its second transfer were taken as evidence of the financial sickness of Poland, and the exodus of foreign exchange persisted.[78] Business with Poland had proved risky in fact as well as in prospect.

The Polish government could not hide the failure of the American loan, and the Polish public soured in its estimate of the project. At the time of its announcement, criticism of the loan had been muted and uncommon. An undercurrent of press opinion had registered minor objections on technical grounds—that it was too small, or that its proceeds should have gone toward currency stabilization instead of investment.[79] However, as the Polish economy took a turn for the worse and months passed without a renewal of aid from the government's American banker, the conviction gained force in the newspapers and parliament that Grabski had given up too much for too little. In time the Dillon episode became a byword for the type of so-called "rotten loan" that did not pay. The failure of the venture turned into a standing reproach against Premier Grabski and contributed to the eventual fall of his cabinet in November 1925.[80]

Grabski encountered difficulty in defending himself against charges of mishandling the Dillon affair, owing partly and ironically to his own earlier success in overselling the significance of the loan for political effect. In his memoirs, Grabski insisted that the Dillon loan had been "almost essential" for Poland and attributed its disappointing outcome to the potency of German propaganda and mismanagement on the part of the bank. From time to time he hinted that the postponement of the second transfer stemmed from Dillon's use of the money as a club to compel Warsaw's submission to German conditions for a trade treaty, and a broad segment of Polish opinion developed the suspicion that Dillon actively sought to employ his position as creditor in promotion of inimical German political interests.[81]

The accusations of political motivation laid at Dillon's feet rested on the premise that Dillon, Read desired to protect its financial stake in Germany by fostering German economic dominion over Poland. As evidence of this tendency subscribers to this view pointed to the bank's refusal to provide successors to the first transfer of February while yet claiming a monopoly over Polish credit in the United States. The supposed design of Dillon's action was to frustrate Polish efforts to find foreign monetary assistance and render Poland vulnerable to the coercive pressure of the German trade embargo, facilitating the submission of Warsaw to Germany's demands.[82]

Business considerations, not intrigue, dictated the suspension of Dillon, Read's lending to Poland. The February issue had fallen through, and the bank could not expect a second operation to succeed in light of the diplomatic uncertainty of the moment and the weakness of the Polish economy. Furthermore, no bank in the world was prepared to lend significant sums to Poland in the summer of 1925, so Dillon's corner on Polish state credit in America—a normal feature of international banking relations—limited the Poles in name only. The conduct that triggered Polish doubts of Dillon's good intentions was fully explicable in apolitical terms as an attempt to make the best of a disappointing but potentially useful business relationship, and if the bank enforced its dictates with a minimum of tact, this demonstrated primarily that Polish credit was so weak that Warsaw lacked any leverage on the policies of its American associate.

In his eagerness to improve his firm's position in the scramble for European investment and gain the rank of banker to a European client government, Clarence Dillon failed to gauge the market with his customary acuity and underestimated the resistance of the buying public to Poland. Upon realizing his miscalculation, he placed Poland on the back burner. As Benjamin Strong later observed, by the summer of 1925, after a series of buffets to Polish credit, "the expectations in Poland of what

Mr. Dillon could do in the way of raising money and the terms on which it could be done were not justified by the circumstances, and Mr. Dillon was possibly expected to do the impossible."[83]

In the end, the interests of Poland and Dillon, Read were incompatible: Warsaw needed money and the bank wished to make money, and fulfillment of either of these aims negated the other. The Poles naturally cared less for Clarence Dillon's problems than for their own urgent need for foreign capital, and they believed Dillon, Read had not kept up its end of the bargain. With a year's hindsight, the vice-president of the Bank Polski, Feliks Młynarski, admitted that the indifferent performance of the first issue of the Dillon loan should have alerted Poland to the impossibility of receiving the second transfer at an early date.[84] However, in their extremity the Poles recognized only that their American banker had refused to provide for them—in the words of Grabski—"precisely at our moment of greatest need."[85] The brief revival of Polish fortunes over which Grabski presided had drawn to a close without satisfying the credit ambitions of the country. Through reform and assiduous courtship Poland had gained access in name to Wall Street, but a combination of diplomatic uncertainty, investor skepticism and her own financial relapse deprived her of the expected benefits. The American market had thrown open its doors to a boom in European investment, but the Poles still found themselves on the outside looking in.

CHAPTER III

The Poles in Search of the "Golden Fleece," 1925

There can be no doubt that the growing participation of the United States in European questions creates the need to take steps in our foreign policy that are calculated for long-range benefit.

Aleksander Skrzyński, June 22, 1925

In the spring of 1925 the tide of diplomatic and economic fortune appeared to have turned against Poland. The chief order of business on the European political agenda, the German security pact proposal, threatened to undermine the foundations of Polish foreign policy and further erode the already enfeebled international position of the Polish republic. In offering to acknowledge the inviolability of its boundaries with France and Belgium, Berlin sought the tacit recognition by the West European powers of the principle that renegotiation of its eastern frontier was a legitimate aim. At the same time, French adherence to the projected Rhine pact clearly would curtail the military and political significance of the Polish alliance with Paris, the bedrock upon which Poland had constructed her defensive policy of maintenance of the Versailles system and based her calculations of protection against German revenge. In Warsaw's eyes, the adoption of the security treaty might leave Poland dangerously isolated.

In the meantime, the sickening of Polish finance deepened, and in the aftermath of the disappointing Dillon, Read loan the state found itself unable to borrow its way out of trouble by recourse to foreign credit. So grave was the economic prognosis that even as the security pact talks quickened, a Polish diplomat returning from assignment abroad discovered that "the need for a foreign loan was so great that no one [in Warsaw] spoke of anything else."[1] In combatting the combined menaces of diplomatic vulnerability and financial disorder, the Polish authorities called on the United States to intervene on behalf of Poland in the name of a stable and sound Europe. As in 1919, the Poles attempted in 1925 to turn America's economic might and latent political influence to their own advantage.

The foremost proponent of this restored tendency in Polish policy was the foreign minister, Count Aleksander Skrzyński. Named by Grabski to his second term as head of the MSZ in July 1924, Skrzyński was a man of recognized abilities, a centrist of liberal instincts who commanded support across a broad range of the political spectrum. To his detriment, foreign statesmen found him oppressively vain and overbearing. According to French Premier Édouard Herriot, Skrzyński "plays the minister, he plays the count, he plays the diplomat and plays all ineptly." Many concurred in the verdict that Skrzyński was no more than a supercilious poseur—"all smiles and irony," in the phrase of British Foreign Secretary Austen Chamberlain.[2]

His personal quirks aside, Skrzyński was a logical choice to guide Polish foreign policies in a period of international flux. Clever and energetic, he understood that changing European conditions required Poland to meet the challenge of German revisionism by edging away from exclusive reliance on the French alliance and broadening her base of diplomatic support. He accepted the League of Nations and the doctrine of collective security as means to safeguard the status quo and, like his Czechoslovak counterpart Edvard Beneš, attempted to promote the interests of his country by identifying them with the overall European welfare. Upon his return to the helm of the MSZ the new foreign minister told an interviewer that he would found his policies "on the fact that Poland is the key to the problem of Eastern Europe and the problem of peace. Poland endangered is Europe endangered."[3]

The English-speaking powers occupied a rank of special importance in Skrzyński's worldview, and in bringing him into the government Grabski hinted an inclination to draw nearer to Britain and the United States. Known as an Anglophile, Skrzyński stressed the need to animate Warsaw's desultory ties with England and convince London to support the basic postulates of Polish policy.[4] He respected English and particularly American financial might, and his elevation to the foreign ministry fitted comfortably within the Grabski strategy of hunting loans in those markets. Skrzyński regarded the diplomatic backing of the United States as a possibility which, while momentarily unavailable, represented an asset of cardinal potential value. Addressing the Sejm in 1923, he allowed that the wartime mutuality of Polish and American objectives had dwindled to no more than an "alliance of the heart" but asserted that Poland awaited the day when the United States would enter the lists "to aid in winning the peace to the same degree that she aided in winning the war."[5]

Skrzyński believed that in time the United States, her interest in Europe already rekindled by the swelling flow of dollars across the Atlantic, would exert the decisive influence in European affairs. He held this view in common with a growing body of Polish official and public opinion. These circles considered American aloofness from European political questions an anomaly that would pass as Washington came to realize the extent to which its interests interlocked with those of the Old World.[6] As it was, some observers conceded the United States the dominant voice in Europe already by virtue of her financial preponderance, which could easily translate into political power. A Polish diplomat opined that the United States could, if she chose, force the retrocession of the Polish Corridor simply by denying credit to Poland and France: "Without taking direct part in European politics, America in fact decides if there is to be peace in Europe. Neither France, nor Poland, nor Germany as well can do without American money."[7]

From the Polish perspective, then, it proved all the more frustrating that the drift of American opinion and action in the spring of 1925 appeared to be moving in an unwelcome direction. American capital ignored Poland and, to the chagrin of many Poles, clamored instead for admission into Germany.[8] A significant segment of the American press demonstrated revisionist sentiments toward the Polish boundaries and many within the U.S. diplomatic establishment privately favored the return of Silesia, Danzig, and the Corridor to Berlin. Persistent allegations of Polish repression of Jewish and German minorities further corroded Poland's prestige in the United States.[9] In addition, Minister Wróblewski reported his suspicions that Hughes's recent replacement as secretary of state, Frank B. Kellogg, brought to his office an ingrained distaste for France and her allies.[10] Disenchantment with the unsatisfactory lot of Poland's relations with Washington at such an ominous time surfaced intermittently in the Polish press and parliament. A rightist deputy told the Sejm, "it is a disgrace to this government that our ties with [the United States] . . . are so weak. . . . This is one of the principal reasons for our economic and political debility, this neglect . . . which will require a long time to set right."[11]

To counter the growing threat of Polish isolation Skrzyński embarked on an extensive campaign of consultation with European powers, and he decided as well that the hour had arrived to cultivate better relations with the Americans. Skrzyński believed in the existence of a natural and traditional affinity linking the Polish nation with the distant republic, a fellowship strained by six years of American reclusiveness and mutual estrangement. He discerned in the expansion of American investment in Europe a sign that Washington had begun to emerge from its shell, and he reasoned that the Coolidge government, its political position secure after a resounding electoral victory in November 1924, was now free to assume a more confident stance in international affairs more in keeping with the strength of the United States. In short, as Skrzyński told the English minister to Warsaw in June:

> in view of the many indications that America was beginning afresh to play an important role in the settlement of the problems which still confronted Europe, he felt that he should do all in his power to assist in removing the misunderstanding that had arisen between the two countries.[12]

Skrzyński accordingly began in the early months of 1925 to impress upon Washington his desire that the United States should adopt his own conception of Warsaw's crucial importance to the international balance and cast a vaguely protective cloak of benevolence over the Polish state. In February Wróblewski suggested to the State Department an exchange of ambassadors in recognition of Poland's status as "a firstclass European power," contending that this symbolic gesture would reinforce the equilibrium of Europe by demonstrating American interest in a flourishing Poland.[13] Wróblewski explicitly disavowed any intention to draw Washington out of its settled course of neutrality in Europe, but in the diplomatically charged atmosphere of the day the Americans could not fail to grasp the nuances of Warsaw's effort to strengthen its American connection. Noting the growth of Polish anxiety over the security pact discussions, Minister Pearson reported in April that "it is to the United States that Poland is now preparing to turn for moral support" in her struggle to maintain her frontiers.[14]

Skrzyński decided to press his suit to America personally by undertaking a visit to the United States. In April he sent an MSZ functionary to Washington to join Wróblewski in soliciting an invitation from the State Department. The Americans reacted coolly to the idea, which placed them in a dilemma. Kellogg did not wish to offend Skrzyński, but he vetoed a state visit for fear it might connote an American tilt toward the Poles. Finally in early May William Castle, chief of the West European branch, informed Skrzyński's delegates that Washington would permit the foreign minister to tour the country unofficially and meet with American leaders in July and August in conjunction with an appearance to speak at the annual summer session of the prestigious Institute of Politics at Williams College in Massachusetts. Despite the obvious reluctance of the American authorities to receive him even under these reduced circumstances, Skrzyński snatched at this invitation to enter the country through the back door.[15]

Skrzyński accepted the American terms for his visit over the vehement objections of Wróblewski, who insisted that a ministerial journey sponsored by a provincial college was a humiliation to Poland that could only lower her repute in the United States. Wanting no part of the Skrzyński tour, Wróblewski asked permission to return home until after its completion. A piqued Skrzyński, who nursed other grievances against his envoy to Washington, was happy to oblige. "I gave [Wróblewski] permission to take his vacation at that time," he told Pearson in Warsaw, "and I hope to find a way to keep him here for good." Wróblewski departed not to return in June; Hipolit Gliwic assumed his duties temporarily, and Skrzyński dispatched Jan Ciechanowski, formerly counselor to the Polish legation in London, to take charge of preparations for the minister's pilgrimage to America.[16]

The decision to undertake the journey was Skrzyński's own, and he likewise kept his own counsel regarding his reasons for making the trip.

His publicly stated aim—to convey the gratitude of the Polish nation for past American contributions to his country—was transparent enough to prompt a variety of speculation on his true motive. The State Department guessed warily that Skrzyński would beseech American friendship as a counterweight to the Rhine pact and hoped they were mistaken.[17] The betting within Polish governmental ranks was that the foreign minister wanted both to open the doors of American capital to Poland—specifically to pry loose a second transfer of the stalled Dillon, Read loan—and simultaneously to score a personal coup.[18] While all of these considerations likely entered into Skrzyński's thinking, in originally devising his American visit he sought not so much to accomplish concrete objectives as simply to develop closer acquaintance with the United States in accordance with his high estimate of American importance in the postwar world. Viewing the journey as a means of laying the groundwork for possible future benefit, he saw it as his opportunity to establish rapport with American policymakers and arrest the decline of Poland's reputation in America with an individual and highly visible show of good will.[19]

Berlin also took notice of the impending Skrzyński visit to the United States as an interested third party. By mid-year of 1925 the German Auswärtiges Amt and its head, Stresemann, had resolved on a course of regaining all or part of the lost territories to the east by means of a diplomatic campaign to mobilize world opinion and foreign governments to apply appropriate pressure on the Poles. The denial of American credit to Poland played a central part in this strategy: believing that "whether Poland will receive further American loans will be decisive to her economic future," Stresemann foresaw the chance that Polish finances might deteriorate to the extent that Germany could dictate territorial concessions or impose conditions for an end to the trade war in return for bailing out the Polish economy.[20] The senior officials of the Wilhelmstrasse interpreted the Skrzyński journey as a Polish attempt to elude the net of financial and political isolation and directed their representatives in the United States to do their best to sabotage the visit, much as they had worked effectively against the success of the Dillon, Read loan. In the weeks before Skrzyński's arrival Ambassador Ago von Maltzan made the rounds of the State Department and leading New York banking houses to impart the message that the shaky Polish state was no place to invest either money or political capital.[21]

Among the financiers Maltzan needed to do little to cement the nearly unanimous opinion that Poland was a bad risk.[22] Polish exertions to win any sort of foreign monetary assistance resulted in June in receipt of a $6 million stopgap credit from Irving Bank of New York for defense of the beleaguered złoty, but the transaction—too small in itself to salvage Poland's currency—presented the only encouraging note in an otherwise dreary outlook on the American capital market. By summer the combined effects of the failure of the Dillon loan, the outbreak of the Polish-

German tariff war, and the suspense over the Rhine pact negotiations had closed American pocketbooks to Warsaw.

Politically as well as financially, American actions during the interlude preceding the Skrzyński visit developed in a fashion contrary to Polish wishes. Initially Wróblewski had predicted Washington would look askance at the German security proposal for the very reason that it would leave the Polish-German boundary an obvious sore point, and in response to his inquiries Kellogg answered that his government "could not in any way associate itself with a Security Pact and must maintain an entirely neutral position with regard to any boundary disputes arising in connection therewith."[23]

Before long, however, a pattern of quiet American support for the Rhine pact project began to emerge. Circumspect as usual, Coolidge allowed his ambassador in London, Alanson Houghton, to speak for Washington both privately and publicly in terms that admitted little ambiguity. Houghton himself had suggested a prototype of the German proposal in 1922, and he disapproved of the Versailles frontiers as provocatively unfair to Berlin; in June he told his German counterpart in London that the Americans favored the Rhine guarantee pact initiative.[24] On July 3 Coolidge himself announced his moral support for the measure. Speaking for the American financial community, Governor Strong of the Federal Reserve Bank of New York lobbied strenuously for the security treaty, attempting at one point to speed negotiations to a conclusion by threatening Stresemann with a cutoff of American loans.[25] Insistent as always on their freedom of abstention from European politics, the Americans nonetheless made plain their unofficial enthusiasm for a plan that held out the prospect of reconciliation among the leading powers of Western Europe.

As Polish fortunes dimmed during the summer, Skrzyński looked toward his imminent American visit with growing urgency and concentration of purpose. Conceived as an initial step in a general program of rapprochement with the United States, the journey gradually assumed for its author a more direct relevance to the current sources of Polish discomfort. Previewing the visit in a diplomatic circular of June 22, he identified as his primary goals the fostering of American "moral support for our aspirations and policies" and the creation of a climate of confidence in Poland within investing circles. A few days later he told Grabski—as if to justify his absence from Europe at a crucial moment—of the centrality of the United States in his immediate diplomatic strategies, insisting his voyages to America did not spring from "disregard for the present tension of the European situation, but precisely as a result of that tension."[26]

In the days before his departure, Skrzyński fretted over ways to increase his attractiveness as a guest. He engaged an instructor to polish his fluent but strongly accented English and sought a means to dispel the widespread American impression that Warsaw persecuted its minorities, a charge he feared particularly injurious among American Jewish financiers.[27] Not at all coincidentally, in late June the government reached an agreement with Jewish political factions, granting concessions in return for parliamentary support. The Poles trumpeted the compact as a turning point in the difficult course of the relations of the state with its Jewish minority, hoping to sway American sentiment favorably on the eve of the Skrzyński tour.

Skrzyński set out for America on July 2 amid a surge of Polish anticipation that his adventure might somehow open an avenue of escape from the predicament of Poland. The press applauded his enterprise and discoursed hopefully on the compatibility of Polish and American aims.[28] Skrzyński too yielded to the temptation to magnify the significance of his journey beyond realistic expectations. Pausing from his travels in Paris, he wrote Grabski that "the situation of the world is very difficult. . . . The key to the situation lies in the United States . . . which knows her vote [in European politics] is decisive." The foreign minister drew nearer his westerly destination excited by the conviction that his expedition represented "an epochal event in the history of Poland."[29]

Skrzyński prepared his American sojourn carefully, basing his approach on his analysis of the place of the United States in the postwar world. In his view, neither Europeans nor the Americans themselves fully comprehended the strength of the United States or understood the values she upheld. While a republic and nominally a champion of liberal tenets, America had been transformed by wealth into an instinctively cautious and conservative force but still responded viscerally to idealistic and crusading rhetoric that echoed her radical origins. Traditionally mistrustful of Europe, the American nation regarded isolation as an ideal and accepted foreign relations as an unpleasant fact of life to be conducted on its own terms or not at all.[30] Skrzyński hoped to manipulate these American attitudes to Polish benefit. Even so, he recognized the strictness of the limitations Washington imposed on its political activity in Europe. At most he sought to gain a token of American favor unaccompanied by diplomatic or military commitments, but even so modest a nod from the world's banker he considered sufficient to sway English policy and tip the European balance back in the direction of Warsaw.[31]

Specifically he wanted to elicit American approval of the principle that a European security arrangement should extend guarantees to all continental frontiers and not simply those in the west. Knowing that to reveal this objective openly would succeed only in alienating his American audience, Skrzyński chose to present his message in soothing and slyly neutral words. Anxious to disarm American suspicions that he had come to wheedle diplomatic and financial support, he disavowed such intentions[32] and posed instead not as an advocate of one country but as a spokesman for all of Europe, just as—in his thesis—Poland embodied all of the healthy attributes of European life. In the circumstances of 1925 this claim of Polish universality was plainly labored, but Skrzyński trusted in his own powers of charm and persuasiveness to carry the extravagant premise.

Skrzyński landed in New York on July 14, and during the following three weeks he barnstormed the country peddling his theories of Poland's kinship with the United States. He took as his forum the podium, the press, and the radio booth; in the course of his sojourn of twenty-three days he gave nineteen speeches and eighteen interviews. Everywhere he bestowed lavish praise on American achievements, lauding the United States as the source of modern economic genius and enlightened political virtues. He expressed his message in simple formulae designed to flatter both his country and his listeners. Skrzyński stressed the theme of a common Polish and American heritage of democracy and individual liberty, contrasting republican Poland favorably with Bolshevik Russia and "militaristic" Germany. Progressive Europe found itself under siege from the inimical forces of leftist totalitarianism and aggressive imperialism, and the peace and prosperity of the continent could be secured only through the perpetuation of the Versailles system, which favored the democratic and capitalist camp. Both out of self-interest and fidelity to her own ideals, the United States should lend a hand to strengthen the proponents of European moderation in their battle with extremist heresies.

Like Paderewski before him, Skrzyński asserted the logic of American patronage of Poland in defense of European political, economic, and social order. Conscious of postwar American sensibilities, he modified the argument of his predecessor by swaddling it in a calculated rhetorical appeal to the highmindedness and impartiality of his audience. While certain of the principles he espoused—fixed boundaries, the sanctity of treaties, implicit censure of Germany and Soviet Russia—obviously served the Polish *raison d'état*, he scrupulously shunned reference to parochial state interests and endeavored to present Poland as the exemplar of the qualities he praised. "Poland is the bulwark of the democratic world in Eastern Europe," Skrzyński declared to one gathering, "and she works in defense of private property and individual freedom."[33] When he spoke of Poland directly, he emphasized her peaceful intentions, made discreet note of her need for foreign developmental capital and offered to correct American misconceptions bred by unfamiliarity and malicious propaganda, lamenting that "most of what you know of us is to our disadvantage."[34]

From New York Skrzyński proceeded to a meeting with Coolidge on July 16 at the president's summer retreat at Swampscott, Massachusetts. The interview took place at the request of James C. White of the Republican National Committee, who obtained for the Polish pilgrim two hours in the midst of a presidential day.[35] After luncheon, Coolidge and his guest adjourned for a private conversation during which Skrzyński outlined his view of the state of the world and took up the problem of security. He likened the current situation to the World War, "which could not be won until after the entry of America." Warming to his motif of capitalism and civilization embattled, he urged Coolidge to "take the initiative instead of waiting for unpleasant developments" and employ the might of the United States on behalf of common values. In enumerating the cataclysmic consequences of American indifference, Skrzyński took care to "remind" the president of "the danger which the decline of Europe would pose to the civilization of the white race . . . and of the opportunity it would afford for the ascendancy of the yellow race."[36] Coolidge listened politely but noncommittally; undaunted, Skrzyński guessed that his arguments had hit their mark and retained his belief that Coolidge could be budged into an energetic foreign policy that could work to Polish profit in effect if not in overt purpose. Cabling his impressions to Grabski, he described the president as hopeful of pursuing "Wilsonian policies under the flag of Coolidge."[37]

Following his presidential conference, Skrzyński backtracked to Washington for a three-day round of informal talks in a similar vein with Kellogg and other officers of the State Department.[38] After a stopover in New York to address the Foreign Policy Association, he took temporary leave of the eastern seaboard to present himself in Chicago and Detroit, the midwestern centers of Polish-American settlement. Walking the thin line of American tolerance for foreign manipulation of ethnic ties, he exhorted the Polonia to combine loyalty to their new homeland with an abiding attachment to Poland. More than sentiment played a part in Skrzyński's call to the Polish emigration: one of the secondary goals of his journey was to rally the flagging affections of Polonia for the old country and restore its wartime effectiveness as a lobby for Polish interests.[39]

The Skrzyński caravan returned from the Great Lakes during the last week of July for his appearance at the Institute of Politics. The foreign minister devoted much preparation to his Williamstown speeches, which he considered the climax of his American tour, and he noted with satisfaction that his presence in the bucolic setting of the Berkshire hills was the talk of the seminar.[40] In a series of addresses delivered in the course of the program, Skrzyński elaborated his theme of the necessity of American help in the solution of the crises of the modern world. He invited the United States to construct a "Pax Americana" to shelter economic progress and republican government. Seeking a foundation in the American classics, he upended the Monroe Doctrine—the traditional touchstone of diplomatic quarantine from Europe—and argued that the democratic ideals inherent in the nineteenth-century theory of isolation now prescribed the intervention of the United States into the affairs of Europe to subdue the threats of Communism and militarism and ensure the preservation of "security, justice, peace and freedom."[41]

In spite of these oratorical flights, Skrzyński lost the Williamstown spotlight to another speaker, William Castle of the State Department, who overshadowed the Polish visitor with an exegesis of American policy toward Europe. Castle reaffirmed Washington's independence of European political commitments, restricting his country's true interests to the promotion of peace and commerce. He plainly endorsed the West European security pact and refused to vouch for the permanence of the Versailles frontiers. In short, Castle confirmed the main lines of the neotraditionalist policy of selective involvement that had been taking shape since the introduction of the Dawes Plan and in the process offered a prompt figurative rebuke to Skrzyński's conceptions of America's international mission.[42]

The final stop on the Skrzyński itinerary was Philadelphia, where on August 4 he met a congregation of financial luminaries gathered by Clarence Dillon. Extolling American capital as a potent instrument for peaceful global advancement, the guest of honor nominated Poland as an opportunity to do well by doing good through combining gainful foreign investment with backing for a mainstay of democracy and stability. Despite a sympathetic response he won no immediate converts and failed as well to pry loose a second loan issue from Dillon.[43] Skrzyński sailed from New York on his return voyage across the Atlantic the next day, proclaiming to the last his petition for an expanded American role in the world.

Skrzyński navigated home to an ovation of popular acclaim for his embassy to the New World. For his part, the foreign minister shared the sense that he had accomplished many of his goals. He basked in a feeling of personal triumph and congratulated himself that his insight into American attitudes had permitted him to plead his country's cause in the United States as no Polish representative before him.[44] In an interview with Polish journalists on August 15 he prophesied a foreseeable end to American seclusion, stating once more that "without American cooperation Europe cannot recover economic equilibrium or political health." Through its own miscalculations Europe had frightened off the United States in 1919 by demanding excessive and narrowly partisan commitments; only now had conditions altered sufficiently to permit the harnessing of American energies to the eventual solution of European problems.[45]

Skrzyński's assurance of future dividends only briefly obscured the fact that his American visit had yielded nothing to alleviate Poland's immediate financial and diplomatic plight. Under questioning from the press Skrzyński confessed his inability to coax an American loan, and the evidence of succeeding weeks demonstrated that he had made little impression in the United States and none at all in other capitals. Far from trumping Berlin, Skrzyński's expedition had played into the hands of German spokesmen by allowing them to cite the journey as evidence of Polish desperation.[46] Impatient for tangible results, a significant segment of Polish opinion soon turned on Skrzyński and chided him for junketeering at a time of true crisis. As disillusionment set in, the farsighted statesman of July became a frivolous seeker after "golden fleece" who subordinated wise policy to his taste for the international limelight.[47]

Certainly Skrzyński failed to persuade the United States to exchange her sympathy toward the Rhine guarantee project for his own version of a comprehensive security settlement. While appreciative of Skrzyński's flattery, the American press rejected his heretical reinterpretation of the Monroe Doctrine as a command for America to become the constable of the European beat.[48] Subsequent events soon dispelled Skrzyński's illusions of having influenced Coolidge and his administration. The Locarno conference adopted the security treaty in October, and American opinion hailed the news with near unanimity. Financial and governmental circles concurred with the *New York Times* that "the spirit of Locarno has descended like a blessing upon all Europe—in fact, upon all the world."[49] In the euphoria of the moment, few Americans cared that the Locarno accords withheld recognition of the permanence of Germany's eastern borders and so, by implication, sanctioned Berlin's revisionist suit against Poland.[50]

The treaties answered all that the United States requested of Europe: they provided evidence of growing harmony among the great powers, endorsed the principle of the peaceful settlement of disputes, improved the prospects for trade and investment, and asked nothing of America in the way of burdensome obligations. Locarno appeared to confirm the wisdom of American policy as enunciated by Castle at Williamstown; the design of Skrzyński, by contrast, offered the United States greater risks and uncertain benefits. Under a thin guise of evenhandedness, Skrzyński asked the Americans to serve as guarantors of Europe under conditions that amounted to the underwriting of Poland, as if to confirm Bismarck's dictum of half a century earlier that Europe was the favorite word of statesmen "who wanted something from other Powers which they dared not demand in their own name." Ironically, the American policy of stabilization came close to a literal fulfillment of Skrzyński's request for Washington and Wall Street jointly to exercise a benevolent guardianship over moderate Europe, lacking only the bias toward Warsaw and Versailles that had been his true—if concealed—goal.

Fruitless and in fact foredoomed, Skrzyński's overtures and journey to the United States in the spring and summer of 1925 represent nonetheless an interesting failure whose themes would reappear in the future. Skrzyński merits recognition for the cogency of the assumptions which underlay his foreign policy. He perceived the long-range threat to the Europe of Versailles posed by rightist imperialism and the Soviet Union and correctly forecast their collaboration in its demolition; as a corollary, he saw that the balance of the European state system now depended on the action of outside forces. He also stands as the first influential figure of postwar Poland to fathom the essential nature of American policy in Europe and to advance the idea that the Poles could win the support of the United States to the extent they managed to identify their interests with the overarching goals of European peace and stability. His conclusions went astray in presuming that America might allow itself to be talked into accepting Versailles as the indispensable charter of a stable Europe or establishing the Poland of 1925 as a model to which other

European countries should aspire. He erred further in supposing the Americans might rescue Warsaw from the Rhine security pact or eventually extend patronage over Poland, but the last point at least was not obvious in 1925.

Skrzyński cast his American policies with an eye to the long run. He believed justifiably that the infant Polish state stood a better chance of survival if nourished by the capital and friendly protection of the greatest power in the world. No Polish leader of the interwar era placed so high a value on America as Skrzyński, and none affected more the course of relations between the two countries. The brief phase of lively contact between Poland and the United States grew out of initiatives launched during Skrzyński's term of greatest eminence in the years 1924–1926, always with his approval and frequently at his inspiration. Unproductive of its original goals—except possibly as a vehicle for Skrzyński's vainglory—his American visit retains significance as the inauguration of a year of intensive Polish wooing of the United States, a year that ended with the fall of Skrzyński and the return to power of Józef Piłsudski.

Skrzyński was not the only Polish official to cross the Atlantic in search of assistance in 1925. The confluence of unfavorable economic trends and the resumption of inflation fed a decline of foreign and domestic confidence in the stability of the Polish currency. The Warsaw government compounded the problem by resorting to the issue of unsecured treasury notes. Unable to withstand the pressure, the złoty cracked at the end of July, falling from 5.18 to 6 to a dollar in the course of one day. In alarm Grabski once more dispatched emissaries to foreign money markets to beg for emergency short-term loans to tide the state over the latest crisis. To the United States he sent Vice-President Feliks Młynarski of the Bank Polski with instructions to implore Dillon, Read either to release the second transfer of the 8 percent loan or provide a stopgap credit to prop up the złoty. The stature of the envoy suggested the urgency of Grabski's request. During the postwar decade Młynarski served as Poland's principal financial spokesman to the outside world. Fittingly, he combined the traits that foreign moneymen generally found both most attractive and most unsettling in their Polish counterparts: charm and a seeming disregard for practicality that led them to doubt the Poles' professionalism. On this occasion Młynarski suspected that he had been charged with a hopeless errand, and his conviction hardened when he crossed paths with the departing Skrzyński in New York and learned of the foreign minister's own recent rebuff by Dillon. His mission frustrated before its beginning, Młynarski decided to try a new tack and obtained Skrzyński's permission to turn directly to the Federal Reserve Bank of New York for aid in the name of solidarity among central banks.[51]

During the postwar decade a loose directorate of leading national banks assumed responsibility for regulation of the world financial system. In 1925 this elite circle consisted of the Bank of England, the German Reichsbank and the New York Federal Reserve with their respective chiefs—Montagu Norman, Hjalmar Schacht, and Benjamin Strong—at the apex of the structure. The operation of this improvised confederation hinged on a cluster of shared assumptions on the duties and community of interest of the state banks. This triumvirate believed that the World War had disrupted a global financial arrangement of nearly perfect equilibrium and plunged Europe into a condition of undesirable and dangerous unsteadiness. They sought a restoration of the prewar financial order, which they equated with political and social health, and took for granted that the answer lay in loyalty to the conservative precepts of balanced budgets and sound currencies. Regarding the task as too vital and demanding to be left to governments dependent on popular favor, they gradually took up the work themselves and began to exert their combined influence on behalf of the panacea of monetary orthodoxy.[52]

Despite its common goals, the alliance of central bankers remained a delicate and conditional partnership among strong personalities, each dedicated to the pursuit of his own country's special interests. The Bank of England had slipped slightly from its prewar status of preeminence, but the enduring prestige of the institution permitted Norman to assume the rank of first among equals. Norman wished to preserve the international standing of his bank in a setting of European stability. He bore a strong antipathy to France and disapproved of the Versailles order as an instrument of French continental dominance. Hardly reticent to take a hand in diplomacy, Norman encouraged the recovery of German finance and sought ways to reduce French influence, particularly in the regions of Eastern Europe.[53]

His counterpart at the Reichsbank, Hjalmar Horace Greeley Schacht, was still more assertive of national political ends. Resentful of the losses imposed on Germany by the peace treaties, Schacht exceeded even his government in revisionist fervor and undisguisedly worked hand in glove with the Auswärtiges Amt. He would gain his greatest notoriety in the 1930s as the economic wizard of the Nazi regime. Even now, Schacht's obsession with the return of Germany to high estate occasionally unnerved American and British bankers, but they respected him for his contribution to the rehabilitation of German finances and deferred to his authority in Central and Eastern European questions.[54]

While nominally subordinate to the Federal Reserve Board, Benjamin Strong spoke for American finance in its relations with foreign central banks from its strategic post in New York. Strong yearned to conduct a vigorous policy abroad to consolidate American financial leadership and augment the international position of the Federal Reserve Bank. He considered the stabilization of Europe crucial to the affluence of his own country and wished to place his bank in the service of that objective. As he explained to officials of the Banque de France in 1926:

The United States had a real interest in . . . general monetary stabilization throughout the Continent of Europe. This interest was partly selfish. . . . So long as monetary unsoundness prevailed in Europe . . . Europe would remain a poor market for American products, most particularly for American farm products. . . . For this reason the Federal Reserve Bank of New York was interested in the question of stabilization, because it viewed stabilization as the only sure way of returning European markets to the normal purchasing power of prosperity.[55]

Strong restrained his activist impulses for fear of overstepping the boundaries of official American caution in dealing with Europe, for his known internationalist leanings made him a slightly suspect figure in the eyes of Congress and various executive departments. Herbert Hoover, for example, disparaged Strong as a "mental annex to Europe." His freedom of maneuver expanded after the establishment of the Dawes Plan, and the Coolidge government granted him a limited license to work inconspicuously in promotion of the reconstruction of Europe.[56] Unsure of the depth of his support at home and conscious of his inexperience on the world stage, Strong habitually took a back seat to his British and German colleagues, leaning especially on the guidance of his friend Norman.[57]

Upon the restoration of German finances in 1924, the concert of central bankers began to function as an informal agency of coordination of efforts at European stabilization. In its standard form of operation, the system allowed a supplicant state bank to appeal to its wealthier brethren, who would weigh the merits of the request, provide or arrange assistance and usually prescribe reforms intended to guarantee the management of the petitioner's finances along conservative lines. In 1925 the Federal Reserve and Morgan and Co. extended credits to the Bank of England itself to facilitate the return of the pound to the gold standard. During the same year the central bankers initiated a drive to bolster the Belgian currency. In electing to approach the Federal Reserve Bank, Młynarski hoped to procure similar relief for the Bank Polski.

To fulfill the courtesies due the acknowledged banker of Poland, Młynarski and Gliwic called on Dillon, Read on August 6 to obtain permission to address the Reserve Bank. Dillon consented to support the project and temporarily renounced his monopoly on Warsaw's credit in the United States in return for an extension of his option on the remainder of the 8 percent loan. The bankers ruled out an early realization of the second transfer but predicted better prospects in coming months.[58] The Poles also received token aid from another of their American creditors when Ulen and Co. advanced $750,000 as a demonstration of confidence in the złoty.[59]

Fortified with Dillon's blessing, Młynarski proceeded to the Federal Reserve Bank. In the absence of Strong, then on vacation in Europe, he placed his argument before Deputy Governor J. H. Case and Owen D. Young, one of the bank's directors. Over the course of several days Młynarski managed to impress Case, who wired Strong his recommendation that the Reserve Bank bestow an urgent credit of $10 million on the Bank Polski to uphold the złoty. Strong disputed the move, citing the current security pact negotiations and congressional criticism of his recent aid to the Bank of England, but Case persevered and won the grudging assent of his superior.[60] With that hurdle overcome, the contracting parties reached agreement on August 21. To Młynarski, the emergency credit represented the first step in the implementation of a broader program of central bank assistance for the Bank Polski. He raised the topic with Case, who hesitated to make a commitment in excess of his authority, and he advised Młynarski to return to Europe and present his petition directly to Strong and Norman.[61]

The receipt of the $10 million credit from the New York Federal Reserve constituted a significant gain for Poland in her financial relations with the United States. The American windfall temporarily slowed the degeneration of the złoty. The operation also performed the useful psychological service of demonstrating a prominent central bank's faith in the battered Polish currency and, by implication, in Poland herself at a time when American financial opinion had all but given her up for lost.[62] For his part, however, Młynarski pursued the credit not so much for its own sake as to get his foot in the door of the Reserve Bank. The most important consequence of Młynarski's conversations with Case and Young was the forging of a small but tangible link between the central banks of Poland and the United States. In granting the credit, the Reserve Bank took on the Bank Polski as a client and acquired a stake in Polish stability.

Młynarski caught up with Strong and Norman at the end of August and made his bid for a central bank stabilization credit for the Bank Polski in a series of meetings spanning three days. After exploratory encounters, the trio assembled at Norman's estate on August 31 and debated the proposition for five hours. Strong and Norman did not conceal their skepticism. Młynarski endured a number of pointed references to the Polish boundaries. Norman did not wonder that the Poles, saddled with the "monstrosity" of the Corridor, could find no lenders in foreign markets. Strong followed with a lecture on the futility of Grabski's habit of hunting for small foreign loans in an endless attempt to stay one jump ahead of the day of financial reckoning. According to the American, Poland should abandon Grabski's hand-to-mouth strategy for more reliable methods; the central banks would arrange a large stabilization loan in conjunction with a thorough overhaul of Polish financial practices. Strong held out the prospect of a loan from a consortium led by Dillon, Read on the condition that Poland would submit to a comprehensive plan of stabilization and agree to foreign supervision of its implementation. Only through such a scheme could Poland, situated geographically "between the hammer and the anvil," realistically expect to lure foreign investors. Norman seconded this view, and he and Strong charged Młynarski to return to Warsaw and place their offer before Grabski.[63]

Młynarski departed London confident that he had brought Norman and especially Strong closer to his own position in spite of the imperious tone of the interview,[64] but he failed to appreciate the extent of their misgivings regarding Poland. Norman disliked Warsaw for its French connection, while Strong shied away from the probable political complications of a Polish operation. Both men shared a reflexive distaste for Grabski's brash style of financial stewardship and questioned the ability of the Poles to master their difficulties. The governor of the Bank of England rated Poland as "financially the poorest land in Europe" and gibed that "it is the misfortune of Poland that she is populated by Poles."[65] In recounting to Case his talks with Młynarski, Strong declared that "Poles . . . are not very practical people, and . . . they do not know how to use their information along sound lines." Doubting the safety of further loans in the absence of basic reforms, he refused to commit the Federal Reserve Bank to aid for the Bank Polski beyond the $10 million credit of August.[66]

Upon arriving in Warsaw, Młynarski conferred with Grabski and outlined the embryonic proposal he had brought from England. The prime minister conceded the theoretical wisdom of the plan but balked at the provision for foreign control.[67] Opposed as always to the intrusion of outside influence into Polish affairs, Grabski resisted the accumulating evidence that any Polish loan would come with strings attached. In August he had received Sir William Goode, a British journalist and unofficial economic adviser to Hungary, who counseled him to secure a loan through the financial committee of the League of Nations in exchange for surrender to League financial oversight. This agency—in which Norman and the Bank of England enjoyed the principal voice— acted as a last resort for indigent states and already had accomplished the rehabilitation of Austria and Hungary, but League of Nations assistance exacted a heavy toll in pride and autonomy. Recourse to the League amounted to a virtual confession of national bankruptcy and placed the destitute country in a form of international receivership; such loans also bore the stigma of association with feeble states which had lost the World War. Anxious to avoid such humiliations along with the attendant risks of foreign influence, Grabski shunned the Geneva alternative and adhered to his stance in spite of growing pressure from Polish industrialists to scrape up a foreign loan even at the price of League control.[68]

While Grabski held out for miraculous deliverance from some quarter, Gliwic shuttled between Strong and Dillon during September and October in an effort to breathe life into the idea of a stabilization loan. The Poles already had compiled a long list of grievances against their American banker, but Strong's suggestion of a Dillon, Read syndicate represented their only current hope on Wall Street.[69] Gliwic met a chilly reception on both sides. At length a reluctant Dillon sketched an outline for a $25 million loan safeguarded by an appointed delegate of the banking group and presented the draft to Strong on October 6. After a thorough review of the problem the bankers agreed that Poland should invite an American expert to inspect Polish finances at first hand and settled on Dillon's nomination of Edwin W. Kemmerer, professor of economics at Princeton and consultant to the Dillon firm. They decided that until the Poles carried through this pledge of good faith, their best course was to "abstain from involvement" in Polish matters. A Dillon lieutenant disclosed the terms to Gliwic, who in turn relayed the news to Warsaw.[70]

Within weeks the health of the złoty grew more precarious, and Grabski summoned Młynarski late in October to convey his belated answer to Strong and Norman. Protesting that the institution of their conditions would take time and that Poland needed help immediately, the premier wanted the money first; he wished Strong to prevail upon Dillon to release the second transfer of the February loan. At the same time, he avoided definite commitment to the imposition of a foreign regime over Polish finances. Aware that this reply would not satisfy the bankers, Młynarski set out for London feeling "like a condemned man on the road to execution." Informed of Grabski's response, Norman retorted that Poland would obtain an American loan with foreign control or not at all. Arriving in New York in early November, Młynarski repeated his tidings to Strong, who dismissed Grabski's counterproposal out of hand. The Polish emissary made one final appeal to Dillon but received no more than an exasperated discourse on the dismal standing of Polish credit in light of the slide of the złoty. Inquiries at Irving Bank yielded the same result. Rebuffed on all sides, a glum Młynarski concluded that Poland had fallen into "complete isolation on the American market."[71]

The depreciation of the Polish currency sealed the fate of the cabinet whose claim to rule rested on its achievements in the realm of finance. As a peasant legislator defined the issue, "when the złoty falls, Grabski falls." In early November the Sejm erupted in denunciation of Grabski's leadership, including indictments of his loan policies. Socialist deputy Jędrzej Moraczewski, a member of the Piłsudski camp, scorned the premier's "naive" insistence that an American loan could be bought on terms short of outside control: "Gentlemen, any foreign loan, and particularly an American loan, must be expensive. . . . You will not find a kindhearted American capitalist who will not want to take our skin in return for a loan."[72]

His mandate rapidly dissolving, Grabski wired a telegram to America imploring Młynarski to work a wonder,[73] but his ministry had reached its end. On November 12 the złoty cracked, slipping from 6.2 to 6.9 to a dollar, and the Grabski coalition fell apart. Skrzyński picked up the pieces and added the premiership to his portfolio; Jerzy Zdziechowski, a rightist ally of industrial and financial interests, replaced Grabski at Finance in the new nonparty cabinet. Skrzyński promptly put a halt to his predecessor's frantic pleas for alms from abroad, admitting an inability to understand "how anyone in Poland is foolish enough to believe that a foreign loan for Poland in either England or America can be obtained at the present time."[74]

The distress in Warsaw led Berlin to sense that the "general economic breakdown of Poland" was imminent and that the time might be ripe to wring political concessions from the Poles. Working in tandem, the Reichsbank and the Wilhelmstrasse redoubled their efforts to link any program of international relief for Poland to the satisfaction of German claims against their eastern neighbor. The Skrzyński government found Germany unwilling to discuss a comprehensive economic reconciliation until the Poles agreed to return Upper Silesia and the Corridor.[75] These pressure tactics did not offend the governor of the Bank of England. The Polish malady troubled Norman, who feared the proverbially rebellious country might succumb to revolution and admit Bolshevism into the heart of Europe. To prevent this calamity he hoped to join forces with the Reichsbank to devise a plan for the rescue of Poland, and while territorial revision was not his highest priority, he saw no reason to object if Schacht named the eastern borderlands as the price of his participation.[76]

Although confident of Norman, Schacht worried that a handful of smaller American banks acting on sentiment might combine independently to prevent Poland from foundering. His anxieties were misplaced; in the autumn of 1925 the vaults of Wall Street had shut so tightly against Warsaw that some officials of the MSZ thought they detected a collusion of Anglo-American capital to deliver Poland up to the Germans.[77] What appeared conspiracy to the Poles was in reality the perception of American investors that Poland had not surmounted her chronic shortcomings of domestic stability and international security. The collapse of the złoty confirmed American disbelief in Polish financial prospects, and Grabski's desperate performance during his final months in office revived old apprehensions of Polish incompetence in administration.[78] Furthermore, the inclination of American capital to bypass Poland in favor of politically safer locales became more pronounced after the Locarno treaties stamped a mark of surety on West European ventures. The pace of American investment in Europe, subdued by the diplomatic suspense of the summer, skyrocketed after the conclusion of the security pact. The volume of trading in foreign loans for November 1925 exceeded all previous standards for the year. The stark contrast of Polish adversities on Wall Street with the general robustness of the bond market led Gliwic to predict that Poland would never make headway in the world's largest capital market until an Eastern Locarno validated her contested frontiers.[79]

Such diplomatic insurance clearly would not come from the United States. If they accomplished nothing else, Skrzyński's exertions of the summer revealed the vanity of that hope. In addition, the tone of the American press continued to suggest a revisionist cast of thought in European questions. A prominent American journalist advised the Polish envoy to prize Coolidge's retiring foreign policy, since the tenor of American opinion was such that "among the first fruits of [our] interference in European affairs would be calls for the dismantling of the Polish

Corridor and efforts to detach White Russia and Vilna from Poland."[80] This was an overstatement: the United States recognized no vital interest in refashioning European frontiers, but she was no more prepared to guarantee these boundaries than to modify them.

Encouraged by signs of the emergence of the United States as a leading actor in Europe, Poland reached out to America in the summer and autumn of 1925 in hopes, born more of wishful thinking than of fact, that the transatlantic giant might step in and restore the sagging Polish fortunes. As its spokesmen, Warsaw sent two emissaries: Skrzyński in pursuit of political favor and Młynarski in his footsteps hunting for loans. In the summation of a contemporary, "the quest of these Argonauts for the Golden Fleece ended in disappointment."[81] Skrzyński missed his aim of converting the United States to a defense of Poland in the guise of a defense of democracy, while the vice-president of the Bank Polski failed to mobilize American capital to maintain the level of the złoty. Of the journeys, Młynarski's was the more indicative of future developments. Neither Skrzyński nor any of his successors attempted a comparable bid for the diplomatic allegiance of Washington, while the germ of the stabilization plan implanted by Młynarski in his talks with Strong and Norman eventually bore fruit two years later. But in November 1925, checkmated on Wall Street, Młynarski felt helpless, "like a fish in sand."[82] The Polish voyages of rediscovery of the New World appeared to have run aground.

CHAPTER IV

Laying the Groundwork, 1925-1926

Yes, stabilizing the Poles seems to be a man size job and a perpetual one.
Edwin W. Kemmerer to William Hard, April 28, 1926

In his annual report of December 30, 1925, the German minister to Warsaw described the preceding twelve months as "the darkest in the history of the Polish state."[1] If this was an exaggerated estimate, then the magnitude of Poland's misfortunes also seemed hyperbolic. During the past year the Poles had absorbed a series of severe shocks—Locarno, the German tariff war, the withering of Polish credit, the resurgence of inflation and the related breakdowns of the złoty and the Grabski government. The succeeding Skrzyński cabinet took office in an atmosphere of political and economic exhaustion. The long-anticipated crisis of parliamentary Poland ended only with the Piłsudski coup d'état of May 1926, which marks the turning point of interwar Polish history. During its brief existence, however, the Skrzyński ministry finally managed to persuade the leading governmental and financial authorities of the United States to assume an interest in Poland as an element of stability in Eastern Europe. This achievement was both impressive and ironic, coming as it did at a time of demoralization and upheaval in Poland, and owed much both to the burgeoning confidence of Benjamin Strong and the diplomatic skill of the new Polish envoy to Washington.

Skrzyński recognized as his priorities the restoration of the economy and the adjustment of Polish foreign policies to the realities of the Europe of Locarno. In the realm of the treasury he and Finance Minister Zdziechowski discarded the strategies of Grabski for a traditional program of fiscal frugalities. On the other hand, Skrzyński reaffirmed the continuity of Polish diplomacy, including his fascination with the United States. Immediately upon the installation of his cabinet the authoritative *Messager Polonais* began to beckon to American money and influence, frequently echoing the themes Skrzyński had emphasized during his American tour.[2]

The high regard of the premier for the United States showed in his selection to occupy the vacant legation in Washington. After cutting his teeth as special operative of the MSZ for preparation of Skrzyński's American visit, Jan Ciechanowski replaced the banished Wróblewski as Polish minister. Ciechanowski was a natural choice for the post. Competent in diplomacy and conversant with matters of finance, he easily outshone his mediocre predecessors.[3] A protégé of Paderewski and a confidant of Skrzyński, he shared with his mentors a belief in the importance of the United States to Polish policies and made effective use of his access to the prime minister to gain a hearing for his views in Warsaw.

Above all Ciechanowski displayed a gift for endearing himself to powerful Americans. He parlayed an easy manner, a complete command of English and "a strain of appealing pathos" into an able and plausible sales pitch for Polish concerns, while his facility for tailoring his arguments to the taste of his listeners allowed him to speak to Americans in their own language in more than a literal sense. Previous Polish spokesmen, including even the much-admired Paderewski, had struck Americans as exotic, impractical, or incompetent; Ciechanowski, affable but businesslike, inspired their confidence, and it was this quality Warsaw wanted most in its American representative.[4]

Ciechanowski's mission was to solidify Polish credit in the United States in preparation for a substantial loan,[5] but the new leadership in Warsaw overturned Grabski's hand-to-mouth approach to foreign borrowing in favor of a more disciplined course. Accepting the need to reassure investors of Polish reliability, Skrzyński and Zdziechowski pledged to balance the budget and refrain from engaging the unproductive consumption loans Grabski had favored.[6] They adopted the position, long advanced by Clarence Dillon and other foreign bankers, that meaningful loans would only follow evidence of Polish recovery and resolved to postpone shopping for credit for a few months until their cure for the economy had taken hold.

Just as the Poles reconciled themselves to a stretch of credit isolation in the American market, they paradoxically encountered renewed stirrings of activity on Wall Street. Still hunting lenders in New York, Feliks Młynarski struck on the device of offering a lease on the state tobacco monopoly in exchange for a loan of $100 million. When Dillon, Read scorned Młynarski's asking price as "nonsense,"[7] he enlisted the aid of intermediaries who steered him in the direction of Bankers Trust Co., one of the premier American houses. Toward the end of November Młynarski obtained an interview with the chief officers of Bankers Trust, who professed their interest in the project subject to the recommendation of independent expert opinion. When notified of this development, Zdziechowski opposed the initiative as premature but relented at the urging of Ciechanowski. On November 30 the cabinet passed a motion to extend to Bankers Trust an option on the tobacco monopoly loan, and three weeks later Zdziechowski announced the parties had reached preliminary agreement.[8]

The emergence of the Bankers Trust business led to speedy fulfillment of Dillon, Read's standing suggestion that its consultant Edwin Kemmerer journey to Poland to inspect and report on Polish finances. Such an expedition was no novelty for Professor Kemmerer, whose services as an economic counselor to foreign countries were so much in demand that he became widely known as the "Money Doctor." During his frequent absences from the Princeton campus he had ministered to Germany, South Africa, and several Latin American states, acting most recently as currency and banking expert of the Dawes Commission in 1924. Rigorously orthodox in outlook, Kemmerer varied his remedies but little from patient to patient, consistently prescribing dosages of deflation, balanced budgets, and the gold standard. Because he approached economic problems with the mentality of an investment banker, his pronouncements carried weight on Wall Street, and it was precisely Kemmerer's intimacy with the New York capitalist fraternity that accounted for his special appeal to needy foreign governments, who hoped American money would follow in his wake.

The Poles tendered their invitation to Kemmerer by a circuitous route between Bankers Trust and Dillon, Read. Eager to furnish the expert testimony required by Bankers Trust, Młynarski proposed to Zdziechowski the engagement of Kemmerer. Less suspicious than Grabski of foreign interference, the Skrzyński government consented, but prudence and protocol demanded the acquisition of Kemmerer's assistance through the agency of Dillon, Read.[9] Possibly alarmed by the sudden entrance of a potential competitor for the title of banker to Poland, the Dillon firm completed the arrangements with dispatch and booked Kemmerer for a Christmastime passage to Poland.[10] To mitigate the effect of Kemmerer's ties to Dillon, Read and guard against the possibility that he might use his authority to sabotage the tobacco monopoly plan at Dillon's behest, Ciechanowski met with the economist before his departure and secured a pledge to honor the interests of Poland above those of individual banks.[11]

In playing off the two firms against each other the Poles were playing fast and loose with conventional banking etiquette, but the checkered history of their past dealings with foreign finance convinced them of the need to keep open as many options as possible. Nor could they decide their best course. Ciechanowski and Młynarski regarded the talks with Bankers Trust primarily as a lever to pry open the vaults of Dillon, Read, while Zdziechowski favored exactly the opposite approach.[12] Simultaneously Warsaw pursued the English avenues rejected by Grabski since the failure of the Hilton Young mission. Poland petitioned the Bank of England for a British adviser to the Bank Polski, but Norman scotched the idea, preferring to defer Polish questions until after the American investigation had completed its task.[13]

Kemmerer arrived in Warsaw on December 30 to conduct his whirlwind inquiry into Polish finances. He spent most of his visit of twelve days in consultation with officials of the government and the Bank

Polski, who accorded him red-carpet treatment. Kemmerer knew nothing of Poland and at first glance the extent of Polish economic dissaray appalled him, but at length his hosts brought him around to an "essentially optimistic" assessment. His original fear that Poland was ripe for revolution diminished. He approved the austerity plan of the Skrzyński cabinet as the prerequisite for recuperation and satisfied himself that the Poles, sobered by experience, had attained the level of maturity necessary to solve their problems. To assist the process of regeneration he favored an immediate stabilization loan of $15 million and promised Zdziechowski his help in procuring the money from Dillon, Read.[14]

Upon his departure on January 10 Kemmerer proclaimed his faith in Poland's future and issued a series of recommendations to facilitate Polish recovery. At the top of his agenda he placed the renewal of confidence in the battered currency and the attraction of foreign capital to quicken the pace of development. As the centerpiece of his program he advanced the prompt restoration of the złoty to par at 5.18 to the dollar coupled with a $15 million foreign loan dedicated to that purpose. The bulk of his supplementary suggestions hewed to the conventional wisdom of his day: the exaltation of the gold standard, the creation of a budgetary surplus, and the turning of a profit in foreign trade. Although he tactfully refrained from specifying how public spending might be cut to attain his ideal, privately he advocated reductions of expenditures for education, social services, and the military. In short, Kemmerer counseled the refashioning of Poland along the conservative lines that would appeal to investors abroad.[15]

Poland reacted to the Kemmerer findings with differing degrees of satisfaction and unease. Official circles embraced the report as an affirmation of Polish health even as they tried to ignore its insistence on rigorous overhaul of national finances, and they immediately began to ponder calling the author back for a return engagement in the near future.[16] At the same time a broad segment of Polish opinion dissented from the government view. Many distrusted Kemmerer as a foreigner and agent of the unpopular Dillon bank, while the left rejected his advice as reactionary. Some derided his formula as mere nonsense. To Maciej Rataj, the marshal of the Sejm, Kemmerer's words sounded like "the old song: 'reform, and then loans will follow,'" while a journalist likened the American expert to "a physician who would tell his patient that when the pains ceased he might be able to begin a cure."[17]

While Poles responded variously to the sudden attentions of American capital, Berlin viewed them with alarm as a threat to its hopes of linking Western loans to Poland with the satisfaction of its own grievances against Warsaw. The announcement of the Bankers Trust tobacco project already had startled the Auswärtiges Amt into a new round of oppositionist lobbying in England and the United States, and the emergence of the Kemmerer mission appeared still more dangerous. The Wilhelmstrasse feared rightly that Kemmerer had fallen under the sway of Polish persuasion, and Schacht worried that he might prevail upon Dillon, Read to issue a loan at minimal cost to the Poles.[18]

Kemmerer resisted German invitations to hear their arguments on the Polish question, but on January 11 Schacht buttonholed the returning American during a stop at the Berlin railroad station. Following an exchange of views on Poland, Schacht launched into a harangue on the eastern borderlands, pounding his fist and raising his voice in declaring Germany's determination to "fight for [the Corridor] diplomatically, legally, using all methods peaceful or otherwise."[19] Schacht had blundered, and his intemperate outburst returned to haunt him in coming months. Already rankled by tendentious German press accounts of his activities in Poland and inclined toward the Polish slant on the boundary question, Kemmerer left his impromptu meeting with Schacht certain that German motivations concerning the stabilization of Poland were neither disinterested nor welcome.[20]

While Kemmerer completed his investigations in Europe, the Poles moved to improve their standing with the Federal Reserve Bank of New York. Reporting on his sojourn in America, Młynarski convinced Zdziechowski that for all the attractions of the Bankers Trust transaction, the principal goal of Polish endeavors in the American capital market should be a large stabilization loan obtained through the mediation of the Reserve Bank. They decided to pursue negotiations with Bankers Trust as a means of testing the waters but concluded that a central bank loan stood a greater chance of establishing investor confidence in Poland and allowing her to compete for American capital on an equal footing with other borrowing countries. Zdziechowski accordingly instructed Ciechanowski to cultivate Strong and his superiors within the Federal Reserve hierarchy.[21]

Ciechanowski began by sounding out Treasury Secretary Mellon and Federal Reserve Board Governor Daniel Crissinger, who referred him to Strong. The Polish envoy met Strong for the first time in New York on January 6, 1926, and drew him into a discussion of the Polish problem. Recounting his country's efforts at recovery since the World War, Ciechanowski asked for the "moral . . . and material" assistance of the Federal Reserve Bank in furthering the consolidation of Poland as an essential element of the stabilization of Europe. Strong professed a lively interest in Poland and pledged his cooperation to the extent Warsaw acceded in "docile" fashion to the advice of the Reserve Bank and the Bank of England to adopt "a general program of reconstruction" on the Belgian model. At the same time the American discouraged the Bankers Trust venture as another Polish attempt to "plug holes" through sporadic and costly loans uncoordinated with any overall plan of development. Warming to Ciechanowski, Strong agreed to supply informal financial counsel to the Poles and tentatively proposed an exploratory visit to the Polish capital in the spring. Later that same day Strong summoned Ciechanowski to meet with Norman, then in New York to confer with his

American counterpart. Norman seconded Strong's earlier declarations, which repeated the conditions they had given Młynarski in London the previous autumn, and assured Ciechanowski of his genuine wish to see Poland placed on a firm footing. The central bankers concluded the conversation with requests for further evidence of Warsaw's resolve to reorder its finances.[22]

The interview pleased Ciechanowski enormously, not only for its substance but also for the quick rapport he had established with Strong. In the course of one afternoon he had neutralized much of the Reserve Bank chief's accumulated skepticism concerning Poland and won a commitment of friendly interest in Polish welfare. He detected as well a yearning on Strong's part to escape the tutelage of the Bank of England and sensed the possibility that Poland could exploit this opening to maneuver between Strong and Norman to advantage. In the meantime he asked Zdziechowski to respond favorably to the central bankers by drawing up "a comprehensive program of financial-economic policy for the coming few years," and within two weeks Warsaw provided Ciechanowski with a suitable memorandum for distribution to the Federal Reserve Bank and the departments of State and Treasury.[23]

While in New York to see Strong, Ciechanowski also attempted to clarify Polish relations with Dillon, Read in a pair of stiff conferences with the officers of the bank. Dillon chided the Poles for dealing with Bankers Trust behind his back and ignoring his advice on preparing the ground for future loans. In turn Ciechanowski shot back a critique of Dillon, Read's behavior toward Poland, attacking the bank's policy of "perpetual waiting" at a time of acute Polish need and accusing the firm of wishing "to obtain a monopolistic position in Poland in return for trifling aid." Following the recitation of mutual injuries, Dillon offered to take over the proposed tobacco monopoly loan at the price of $100 million if Warsaw in turn agreed to terminate relations with Bankers Trust.[24]

Not to be outdone, Bankers Trust pressed its suit to Poland on the strength of Kemmerer's preliminary reassurances. The bank sent a delegation to Warsaw to bargain with the government. After weighing the alternatives, Zdziechowski chose Bankers Trust over Dillon and on January 18 the Poles rewarded their visitors with an option to conclude a tobacco monopoly deal.[25] The agreement outlined a loan of $100 million at 7.5 percent interest payable in twenty years with provisions for oversight of the fund by a board appointed by the bank. Zdziechowski preferred these terms to Dillon's, but even so the announcement prompted grumbling in the press that the government had contracted a fool's bargain with Bankers Trust.[26]

Kemmerer returned to the United States in late January to report his Polish observations to his sponsors. He declared that while the Poles were suffering from a "nervous breakdown"—a national crisis of confidence—they were "going to pull through all right." He urged Dillon to lend the

Bank Polski $15 million, as he had promised Zdziechowski, and Ciecha-
nowski made him available to Bankers Trust and the New York Federal
Reserve Bank as well.[27] On January 29 Kemmerer met with Ciechanowski and Garrard Winston, the undersecretary of the treasury. The two
Americans argued against the tobacco loan as premature and secondary
to the need to stabilize the złoty and centralize Polish credit operations in
the United States within one bank—most advisedly, in Kemmerer's un-
surprising view, through his client Dillon, Read. Kemmerer also related
his stormy encounter with Schacht in Berlin. Ciechanowski hurried to
profit from the anecdote to discredit Schacht in the eyes of Winston, who
accepted the story as evidence of the dubious nature of German intentions
toward Poland.[28]

Meanwhile heavy pressure came to bear on Bankers Trust not to enact
its Polish loan in its anticipated form. Strong, a former president of the
bank, cautioned his old firm against the business altogether for fear it
would compromise an eventual stabilization loan.[29] By contrast, Montagu Norman believed the tobacco monopoly transaction could serve as
an acceptable vehicle on the condition that its control provisions might
be internationalized and extended over Polish finances as a whole, preferably through the League of Nations mechanism imposed on Austria and
Hungary. He and the Foreign Office impressed this reasoning on the
Poles and the bankers, and in early February Bankers Trust informed
Ciechanowski of its decision to adopt the viewpoint of the Bank of
England and insist on the attachment of a commission of experts empow-
ered to formulate and carry out a scheme of financial reorganization of
Poland.[30]

Confronted with such an "impossible" demand, Ciechanowski persuaded Warsaw to try to finesse Norman and appease Bankers Trust with
a hurried invitation to Kemmerer to lead an American investigatory team
later in the year. Not only did the Princeton professor constitute a known
and sympathetic quantity, contended Ciechanowski, but the gesture
would appeal to Strong and help to mollify Dillon. Upon ascertaining
the approval of the Federal Reserve Bank, Poland put the question to
Kemmerer, who readily accepted.[31]

The engagement of Kemmerer pleased the Reserve Bank greatly. Speaking for Strong, Deputy Governor Case restated his chief's interest in
Polish stabilization and, in a significant departure from previous policy,
told Ciechanowski that the bank might part company with the Bank of
England in the matter of Poland.[32] Strong confirmed this message in a
conversation of March 5, telling the Polish envoy that since their talk in
January he had come to oppose Norman's conceptions of League of
Nations control over Warsaw and concluded that "it would be sufficient
for Poland to agree to an advisory mission and eventually to the cooperation and counsel (in selected matters) of an American expert." As a bonus,
Ciechanowski gained from Strong acknowledgement of a "moral obligation" to obtain alternative funding for the Poles in the event of the

collapse of the Bankers Trust deal, which he had discouraged. The delighted Ciechanowski reported to Skrzyński that his spadework in America showed signs of bearing fruit and urged Warsaw to suspend direct dealings with Norman and "rely completely on Governor Strong."[33]

If the announcement of a second Kemmerer embassy gratified the American central bank, the British disliked the idea intensely. The Bank of England had no intention of ceding full responsibility for the Polish settlement to an exclusively American supervision. Sir Otto Niemeyer of the Treasury scoffed that "to put an isolated American expert . . . down in Poland and suppose that, by smiling at the Poles, he will enable them to behave properly, is complete nonsense."[34] In the British view the League possessed resources and experience no American body could match, and none doubted that English preferences stood a greater chance of acceptance if the road to the Bank Polski ran through Geneva, where Norman's words carried much weight, rather than New York.

Norman and the English also had their own reasons to mistrust Kemmerer, who had offended them on repeated occasions during his stints as counselor to South Africa and the Dawes Commission.[35] Kemmerer's association with Dillon, Read likewise disturbed Norman, who regarded Dillon as a maverick less likely than Bankers Trust to join a League of Nations combination.[36] At the same time, Norman grew increasingly receptive to German entreaties for the bankers to compel the Poles to swallow the loss of the Corridor as part of the price of assistance.[37] Determined not to allow Poland to substitute the appearance of controls for the reality, Norman quietly pressed Bankers Trust not to rise to the Kemmerer bait.

The exertions of the Bank of England paid off. On March 6 Ciechanowski spoke with Bankers Trust Chairman Seward Prosser, who notified him of the firm's decision not to exercise its option on the tobacco loan until Poland submitted her finances to "foreign control for an indefinite period of time." Citing Norman's recommendation, he demanded a "controlling body"—as distinct from a merely advisory panel—arranged most desirably through the League of Nations. Ciechanowski retorted that Bankers Trust had forgotten it was "dealing with a sovereign country and not with a commercial enterprise." He refused the proposal, and while the bank offered the Poles time to reconsider, Zdziechowski likewise concluded that the question of supervision had brought the tobacco loan to a dead end.[38]

The disruption of negotiations proved satisfactory to the interested onlookers of Berlin and London. By the end of March the Auswärtiges Amt and the Bank of England believed they had established the principle of the inclusion of stringent international controls in any Polish stabilization package and that in time Warsaw would give in to the joint regime of Bankers Trust and the League of Nations.[39] They next moved to break down the objections of Poland to Geneva. Bankers Trust tried to placate the Poles with assurances that it required no concessions of a political character, although Norman told the Germans that in fact he hoped a League solution would encompass the transfer of disputed Polish lands to their erstwhile owner.[40]

The Bankers Trust impasse left the Poles momentarily confused and uncertain of their best path through the increasingly tangled thicket of financial restoration. Contrary to the expectations of London and Berlin, Polish opinion rejected the League option out of pride and fear of— among other consequences—precisely the sort of exactions Norman had in mind. No other consensus formed within the ranks of decision makers. One school of thought, led by Młynarski, preferred an American connection and favored recourse to the Federal Reserve Bank or, as a last resort, the Bank of England. Some wanted no foreign loan at all. Zdziechowski retreated toward his earlier stance of a temporary withdrawal from the capital marketplace and trust in the methods of austerity, while Skrzyński's restive Socialist allies exhorted the government to stimulate the economy through greater public works spending and confiscatory taxation.[41]

At his post in Washington, Ciechanowski hoped to profit from adversity by calling on Governor Strong to make good his promise to provide a replacement for the miscarried Bankers Trust loan. Accompanied by Winston of the Treasury, Strong on March 9 paid a visit to the Polish legation, where he ruefully congratulated Ciechanowski on having "caught him in a trap." Pressing his advantage, the Polish minister restated the Skrzyński thesis that European order hinged on the fate of Poland, warning that:

> America's further indifference, her continued unwitting support of the anti-Polish campaign led by Germany and the continued lack of financial support of Poland by American capital eventually could result in a socially dangerous situation in all of Europe, hence a threat to world peace, for which the whole world—but America in particular, for she is most able to help—would bear responsibility.

Strong replied that Ciechanowski's observations, with their implicit references to the Bolshevik menace, were "very weighty" and announced his resolve "to aid Poland to the extent possible."[42] Finally after years of affirming a link between Polish welfare and global health, the Poles had found an influential American who seemed to agree.

Strong and Ciechanowski drew up a tentative outline of procedure at a meeting three days later in New York. The governor emphasized two points: that while Warsaw properly refused Norman's "politically motivated" League formula as "out of the question," the Bank of England should be included in any stabilization plan, and that the Poles had no choice but to accept some kind of benign control to win over wary investors. He suggested that Poland elaborate a preliminary program of recovery based on the findings of the second Kemmerer mission. He and

Norman would piece together a banking syndicate to issue an accompanying loan to be supervised by an apolitical American adviser. In the meantime, Warsaw should attempt both to satisfy its immediate credit needs and repair relations with its established American banker by appealing to Dillon, Read for the $15 million second transfer of the 1925 loan.[43]

When Zdziechowski relayed his assent,[44] Ciechanowski and Strong met again on April 11 in Washington to seal their bargain. Strong assumed responsibility for arranging the Polish matter with the European central banks. Already persuaded by Ciechanowski to limit the role of the Reichsbank as politically suspect, he proposed to procure the necessary cooperation of the Bank of England by telling Norman that the involvement of the League of Nations would discourage the participation of American capital in the venture and prompt the withdrawal of the Federal Reserve Bank. In May Strong would travel to Europe to meet with Zdziechowski and bring Norman around to the American scheme, and then all parties would await the conclusions of the Kemmerer commission before proceeding toward implementation of the plan.[45]

Strong's growing boldness in the question of Polish stabilization, so much at odds with his accustomed approach to international issues, stemmed from several sources. In the first place, the political implications of any Polish settlement that once had led him to give the Bank Polski a wide berth now persuaded him that only the Federal Reserve Bank could accomplish the work. Although not opposed in principle to the modification of the boundaries of Pomerania and Silesia, Strong gradually came to believe the imposition of political concessions on the Poles—the goal sought plainly by Schacht and to a lesser degree by Norman—would set a bad precedent. Notwithstanding the possible merits of the German case against Versailles, he worried that the injection of politics into the financial restoration of Europe might offend American investors and repel other candidates for rehabilitation, thereby jeopardizing the future utility of the method of central bank sponsorship of European stabilization he so favored. Encouraged by Ciechanowski's flattery, Strong concluded—perhaps naively—that only American leadership could ensure a politically nonpartisan and generally acceptable solution to the Polish financial crisis.[46]

In addition to his commitment to preserve the ideal of an apolitical central bank machinery for international stabilization, Strong seems to have regarded the case of Poland as significant in its own right. In the spring of 1926 one of his priorities was to discover ways to invigorate the U.S. agricultural sector by expanding its markets abroad, and he contended that a healthy Poland might import substantial stocks of American raw materials to feed her textile factories.[47] Aside from considerations of tangible benefits, the possibility exists that Ciechanowski's occasional lectures on the pivotal importance of Poland to the process of European stabilization hit their mark. Strong admitted as much to the Polish

diplomat, whether out of conviction or amiability; in any event, Ciechanowski's personal contribution to the evolution of Strong's Polish policy
cannot be overstated. A gregarious man, Strong liked and esteemed Ciechanowski, who in turn put his considerable charm to good use in
pleading the cause of his country.

In the last analysis, however, Strong's decision to strike an independent
posture on the issue of Poland grew out of his impatience to assert his
equality on the world scene with his friend and mentor Montagu Norman. As Ciechanowski had guessed, Strong longed to cease "playing
second fiddle to the Bank of England" and believed the magnitude of
American overseas investment entitled him to speak with greater authority in the councils of central bankers.[48] Quite apart from the merits of
Ciechanowski's arguments, the Polish dispute presented an opportune
vehicle for Strong's purposes. It afforded him the chance to advance
American conceptions by compelling the exclusion of the suspect League
of Nations from the mechanism of stabilization and preventing the overt
politicization of the system. Norman owed the Federal Reserve Bank a
number of recent favors, not least its aid in stabilizing the pound in 1925,
and Strong elected to call in his promissory notes to obtain English
compliance with his Polish program and demonstrate the arrival of his
bank as a leading force in financial diplomacy.[49]

Still apprehensive of criticism from within the American government,
Strong drew courage from the acquiescence of the Treasury in his efforts.
The subcabinet officers of the department, notably Garrard Winston, had
sympathetically observed the course of negotiations between Strong and
Ciechanowski since their inception. Like Strong, they desired the eman-
cipation of the New York Federal Reserve from London. Armed with
Winston's backing, Strong placed his Polish strategy before Secretary
Mellon, who assured him of the approval of the Coolidge administra-
tion.[50]

The replacement of the phlegmatic Alfred Pearson as U.S. minister to
Warsaw by a more energetic figure added another voice to the advocates
of American assistance to Poland. John B. Stetson, Jr., the scion of a
famous hatting concern, entered into his duties in August 1925, the first
of several diplomatic neophytes of commercial background to occupy the
Warsaw post during the interwar years. Although limited in capabilities,
he threw himself into his work with gusto, and a few months in his new
surroundings turned him into a zealous spokesman for Polish interests
and an increased American economic presence in the country.[51] Quickly
he announced his conversion to Skrzyński's view "that a strong Poland is
the greatest factor for the maintenance of peace in Europe." Obsessed
with the dangers of Soviet radicalism, German economic expansionism,
and British "trade aggression," Stetson called for a massive enlargement
of American influence in Poland to counteract these threats and
strengthen the position of the "reasonable" forces of the Polish right. He
exasperated his superiors by his inarticulateness, but his muddled and

rambling dispatches boiled down to a few basic points: that American financial involvement in Europe inevitably entailed political consequences, that the flood of American money into Germany imperilled the European balance and that "the best insurance against war is the equilibration of American investments" by increasing the share of dollars allotted to his host country. He fervently backed the idea of an American-sponsored stabilization loan and consistently pushed for the entry of American capital into various branches of Polish industry.[52]

Not only Stetson foresaw political benefits in the enlistment of American financial power in the economic restoration of Poland. From his vantage point, Ciechanowski described the Strong plan as a natural prelude to a diplomatic *entente* between Washington and Warsaw, applying the maxim that where American money went American governmental solicitude followed. In his view, the Poles had only to avoid antagonizing the Americans by admitting political intent and, once the financial link was established, allow events to take their course.[53] Other Polish observers agreed that the Skrzyński approach of solidarity with American stabilizing efforts in Europe had begun to pay dividends and that Poland, sheltered by a friendly United States and nourished by an influx of foreign cash, at last would escape from her paradoxical role as "Capitalism defender without capital."[54]

The forging of an alliance between Benjamin Strong and the Bank Polski took place against a backdrop of hopeful economic developments in Poland. In April the government announced the balancing of the budget in response to the Treasury's severities. Less committed than Grabski to keeping the złoty pegged at par, Zdziechowski also allowed the currency to depreciate slowly toward its natural level. This tacit devaluation made Polish goods more attractive in foreign markets, and the consequent growth of grade stimulated production and imparted a fresh bloom of health to the Polish economy.

Zdziechowski paid a price at home for the rigors of his cure in the form of mounting dissatisfaction on the left, but the resultant pickup of economic activity yielded immediate advantages on the international front. No longer expectant of impending Polish prostration, the Auswärtiges Amt in April conceded the futility of playing for the prompt restitution of the lost eastern territories in conjunction with a financial rescue package and fell back on a strategy of stalling international aid for Poland until a time more conducive to the fulfillment of German claims.[55] In the United States, the promising news from Poland stirred interest among merchants in search of fresh outlets. Emboldened by optimistic press accounts and the encouraging words of Kemmerer, several firms sent delegations to Poland in the spring of 1926 to inspect opportunities for commerce and investment.[56]

April also witnessed the closure of the largest American industrial transaction in interwar Poland. The partition of Upper Silesia had disrupted the extensive holdings of the Georg von Giesches Erben AG zinc foundries, and the hostility of Polish authorities toward German-owned enterprise rendered the position of the firm increasingly uncomfortable and unrewarding. Giesche placed its Polish possessions on the block, and in 1925 an American coalition of W. A. Harriman and Co. and the Anaconda Copper Mining Co. purchased majority control. For W. Averell Harriman, the future diplomat-politician and the more active of the American partners, the deal marked another in a string of European industrial acquisitions. After constituting themselves as the Silesian-American Corporation, the Americans turned to work out an acceptable arrangement with their Polish landlords. Happy to replace German tenants with Americans, Warsaw had encouraged Harriman in the course of his talks with Giesches Erben and was disposed to offer generous terms as an enticement to his compatriot entrepreneurs. Poland agreed to exempt Silesian-American from property taxes and export duties in return for guarantees that Americans would retain the controlling voice in the company and that within five years the new owners would double production and sink at least $10 million into plant improvements. The contract barely survived leftist opposition in the Sejm, but its ratification on April 30 sealed the bargain and cemented Harriman's hold on the largest American-owned zinc properties outside the United States.[57]

Meanwhile, the Poles attempted to revive their relations with Dillon, Read as Strong had advised Ciechanowski on March 12. That same day the Polish minister called on the bank and put in a request for a quick release of the $15 million second transfer. The firm and its Polish clients haggled over a multitude of formulae over the next two months, but accord proved elusive. Warsaw wanted the money instantaneously, wished to avoid tying its hands in dealings with other banks, and asked Dillon to take in the Banque Suisse as a partner in the venture. For its part, Dillon, Read objected that an immediate offering would certainly fail to sell—a judgment Ciechanowski secretly shared. Moreover, the bank demanded an end to Polish flirtations with Bankers Trust and refused to admit the Swiss into the picture. Finally at the end of April Dillon suggested a compromise: a prompt small loan followed at a favorable moment by the $15 million operation in exchange for a Polish promise not to treat with other American bankers for six weeks. Zdziechowski approved these terms, but not before the eruption of a political emergency within Poland persuaded the bankers to put their proposal on hold until the dust settled.[58]

The final crisis of parliamentary Poland arose out of the inability of the left to endure the government's drastic deflationary measures. Accusing Zdziechowski of trying to balance the budget on the backs of the working class, the Socialists boycotted his program in late April and defected from the ruling coalition. The shattered Skrzyński cabinet expired on May 5, giving way to a center-right combination headed by Wincenty Witos. The prospect of a third Witos government proved personally and politically intolerable to Marshal Piłsudski, who had retired from public office in 1923 in protest against the domination of the state apparatus by his enemies. Provoked to action by the reappearance of Witos, Piłsudski rallied his numerous adherents to topple the offensive cabinet. On May 12 he marched on Warsaw at the head of mutinous army units loyal to him. Intended as a peaceful show of force, Piłsudski's demonstration encountered unexpected resistance from government forces, and the collision plunged the capital into a brief but bloody civil war.[59]

The Polish upheavals stirred disquiet in Washington and Wall Street. The breakup of the Skrzyński coalition cast doubt on the permanence of Polish recovery and removed a government that had progressed toward winning the confidence of American finance. The explosion of the crisis into armed conflict raised temperatures at the State Department, where Secretary Kellogg worried that the struggle might tempt German or Lithuanian intervention and spark "a European war," and sent quotations of Polish bonds in New York diving toward new lows despite the efforts of Dillon, Read to calm the market.[60]

Among the first casualties of the turmoil was Governor Strong's European journey to iron out a Polish rehabilitation program in consultation with Zdziechowski and Norman. Strong already had reached London when Zdziechowski abruptly broke off their appointment to meet,[61] and the outbreak of the Piłsudski revolt a few days later ruined the American's bargaining position on the eve of his pivotal conferences with his British opposite number. Polish diplomats in London had doubted Strong's capacity to outplay Norman even under the best of circumstances, and the unresolved combat in the streets of Warsaw embarrassed and confused him. The news from Poland shook Strong's own faith in the future of the country, and the uncertainty of the outcome of the political contest called into question the adherence of the eventual winner to the commitments undertaken by Zdziechowski, including the Kemmerer mission.[62]

Capitalizing on Strong's disadvantage, Norman turned away his plan for an entirely American advisory machinery and held out for a League of Nations cure for Poland to be administered in the autumn. Protesting that "in the meantime . . . the patient might die," Strong recited his objections to the League, but his arguments lacked conviction and in the end he bent toward compromise. On May 14 he told the Polish minister to London, Konstanty Skirmunt, that he and Norman thus far had managed only to cancel each other out. The League remained a possible choice despite American misgivings, but the likely outcome was the broadening of the Kemmerer commission to include European experts; he commended this option as "rational" and capable of appealing to the Reichsbank and the Bank of England. Strong had emerged from his dickering with Norman with scarcely half a loaf.[63]

The fighting in Warsaw ended on May 15 with the victory of the insurgent forces and the consequent assumption of political mastery by Marshal Piłsudski. The coup d'état of 1926 stands as the watershed of interwar Polish history. A figure of outsize dimensions and prodigious personal magnetism, Piłsudski dominated the affairs of the country until his death nine years later, after which his disciples ruled in conscious imitation of his example. He used his authority to break with the patterns of the previous seven years, asserting the primacy of the executive power over the legislative and, in time, constructing an independent foreign policy that placed relatively greater reliance on Warsaw's own ability to regulate its relations with its dangerous neighbors than on the deterrent value of the French alliance.

Piłsudski's approach to government was singular and elusive of definition. While impatient with parliamentarism, he hesitated to replace it with outright despotism and only after a protracted legal battle subdued his opponents through a mixture of cajolery, intimidation and constitutional amendment. Cabinets served and disbanded at his pleasure, but he generally preferred to exert his influence through surrogates recruited largely from his coterie of fiercely devoted comrades and protégés from his days in the field. Despite his socialist background, Piłsudski's program of "regeneration," or *Sanacja*, eschewed ideological content and attempted to organize a national consensus about the person of the Marshal of Poland. For all its theoretical idiosyncrasies, the Piłsudski regime operated in practice as a safely centrist and technocratic government of moderately authoritarian bent.

In transferring power from Skrzyński to Piłsudski, the events of April and May replaced the outstanding advocate of close ties with the United States with a leader who ascribed far less importance to the American card. Unlike Skrzyński, now consigned to political oblivion, Piłsudski accepted the estrangement of the United States from Europe as natural. The Marshal conceived of Europe as an autonomous unit, and his policies relegated America to a distinctly marginal place in Polish calculations. In his first statement on relations with the United States, new Foreign Minister August Zaleski declared his understanding of the reasons that dictated to Washington a "certain reserve . . . [toward] problems of European politics" and asked only for the expansion of bilateral economic ties.[64]

In money matters as well the Piłsudskists showed a more equivocal attitude toward American influence. The Marshal and his followers wavered between acknowledgement of Poland's need for funding from abroad and instinctive distaste for the admission of foreign capital into the country. Piłsudski possessed at best an elementary grasp of economics and planned no innovations in that branch of statecraft. His interest in financial policy consisted primarily of a doctrinaire insistence on the soundness of the currency, stemming perhaps not so much from principle as from the memory that inflation had overthrown cabinets in 1923 and 1925.[65] While this concern for the health of the złoty pointed logically to a foreign stabilization loan, the Piłsudski camp was forced to weigh these considerations against its own strong nationalism and the sensibilities of its supporters on the left, who consistently had opposed the entry of alien capital on a large scale. More than once the *Sanacja* government would find itself compelled to choose between satisfying a hunger for American money or fulfilling the demands of domestic politics. The indications of their first days in power were that the new leaders intended to surpass their predecessors in skepticism toward foreign participation in the Polish economy. A Piłsudskist newspaper announced that Warsaw would refuse to buy loans at the price of outside controls, and the representative of Harriman and Co. departed the country when confronted with an official demand for renegotiation of the Giesche contract.[66]

Another incidental effect of the governmental transition in Poland was the diminution of the influence and autonomy of Skrzyński's handpicked American agent, Jan Ciechanowski, who not only lost his sponsor but nearly lost his job owing to his close identification with the old regime and his record of opposition to Piłsudski. Isolated at a stroke from the decision makers in his own government, Ciechanowski clung to his post only because his hosts valued him and Piłsudski was too distracted to get around to firing him.[67]

The United States reacted to the debut of the *Sanacja* regime with some misgivings. Since the World War, American observers of the Polish scene had tended to disapprove of Piłsudski as a military adventurer of socialist pedigree who might steer Poland toward social radicalism and diplomatic belligerence. At the same time they regretted the eclipse of Skrzyński, whose policies had impressed Washington as prudent and constructive. The State Department promptly recognized the new governors of Poland but privately urged the retention of Skrzyński at the MSZ as a token that the coup would not cause the abandonment of his conciliatory approach to European problems. A similar note of wariness characterized the response of the press, which generally withheld judgment on the insurrection while making no secret of its qualms concerning Piłsudski and his designs.[68]

The prospect of a Piłsudski government in Warsaw evoked particular discontent in the financial districts. The very fact of the revolt bore testimony to the persistence of the political volatility that was anathema to American investors, and the real or rumored attitudes of the victors toward economic questions aggravated the natural aversion of Wall Street to rebellions. False reports that the insurgents had seized the gold stocks of the Bank Polski frightened the Federal Reserve Bank, and the ultimatum to Harriman appeared to confirm the suspicion that the Piłsudskists harbored hostility toward American capital. Worried that the repercussions of the coup might jeopardize his accord with Strong, Ciechanowski warned the MSZ that unless the Poles took quick remedial action to dispel these poor first impressions, they risked forfeiture of the hard-won support of American financial authorities.[69]

Rather than risk the alienation of international finance, Warsaw curbed its autarkic impulses and set out to reassure foreign capital. Having made the point, at home as well as abroad, that Polish interests would be jealously protected in dealings with foreigners, the new government moved to demonstrate its receptivity to investors by ratifying the commitments of the Skrzyński cabinet. Over the course of succeeding weeks the Poles sealed the formation of a French-Polish consortium to build the port of Gdynia and took a series of steps to allay American doubts. Negotiations with Harriman resumed quickly, and by the beginning of July the government agreed to honor the contract of April 30 in return for minor adjustments leaving the company's privileges essentially intact. A few days later the Bank Gospodarstwa Krajowego came to terms with Ulen and Co. for a second set of small construction loans. American fears that Piłsudski might repudiate foreign debts evaporated as Poland delivered payment of its World War obligations on schedule, and the handing of the finance portfolio to Czesław Klarner, a former minister of industry and commerce, pleased Wall Street as an indication that Polish economic policies would remain well within the bounds of orthodoxy.[70]

From the American standpoint, the most meaningful of the Polish gestures of reassurance was the confirmation of the invitation to Kemmerer, whose advisory missions had become symbolic of Warsaw's willingness to carry out financial reforms in a manner acceptable to American capital. On May 28 the cabinet voted to reaffirm the plans to host the investigatory commission later in the summer and announced the decision with much fanfare in early June. The retention of Kemmerer provided genuine relief and satisfaction within the State Department and the Federal Reserve Bank, where the news was taken as proof that Piłsudski meant to honor the pledges of Skrzyński and Zdziechowski.[71]

Their apprehensions of Piłsudski largely neutralized by these measures, American onlookers began to reappraise the fledgling *Sanacja* regime as a worthy entrepreneurial partner. Strong threw off his shock at the coup and by June recovered his confidence in Poland.[72] Stetson lamented the loss of Skrzyński but rapidly adjusted to the advent of the Piłsudskists. Urging Strong to render all possible assistance to the new Polish rulers, he asserted that the turmoil of May had produced "a strong and honest government which will lean towards America and American ideas rather than towards France and French ideas as in the past."[73] The willingness of Harriman and Ulen to continue operations in Poland also helped to convince American finance that one could do business with Piłsudski. Six weeks after the coup the commercial attaché to the Polish legation in Washington, Witold Wańkowicz, reported that the official campaign to calm the nerves of American capital had succeeded.[74]

Germany meanwhile attempted to exploit the coup by offering again to aid in the economic restoration of Poland in return for territorial compensation. Having learned late in April of the budding collaboration of Ciechanowski and Strong, the Wilhelmstrasse sent Schacht to London to convince Norman to play an obstructionist part in the question of the

Bank Polski. Schacht hoped the Piłsudski revolt might disgust his fellow bankers and induce them to impose the detachment of the Corridor from Poland, but his efforts to sell the idea to Norman proved fruitless. If anything, the coup had deepened Norman's conviction of the urgent necessity to piece together an international plan of assistance for the Poles. He informed Schacht on May 27 that both the Federal Reserve Bank and the Bank of England were determined to stabilize Poland, and that Strong would not permit the dictation of territorial conditions to Warsaw; the most that could be hoped was to obtain the inclusion of the League of Nations to keep watch over Polish finances or, at least, to compel Strong to accept the international supervisory commission Norman had urged on him earlier in the month.[75]

Norman's plans ran afoul of Ciechanowski, who spent his summer deftly coaxing Strong back toward the conception of an American-sponsored stabilization program that had formed the heart of their gentlemen's agreement of April. Upon learning that Strong had given ground in his showdown with Norman, Ciechanowski guessed that he could put his foot down and prevail on the Reserve Bank to champion a purely American advisory board in spite of British opposition. In appeals to Strong and Deputy Governor George L. Harrison in June and July, the Polish envoy insistently combatted the alternative formulae of the League or an internationalized Kemmerer commission, stressing that a politically nonpartisan American mechanism would prove more palatable to Poland and American investors alike; furthermore, he added, the Bank of England would give way before a determined Federal Reserve Bank and accept American leadership.[76] Under Ciechanowski's coaching, Strong gradually regained his resolve. His reflexive distaste for a League solution reasserted itself, not least because he expected Dillon to withdraw from a Geneva project, and the logic of Ciechanowski's arguments against expansion of the Kemmerer panel impressed him as sound. In early August he assured Ciechanowski of his fidelity to their bargain of the spring and promised his resistance to any revision of the composition of the American advisory body, which in fact already had begun its labors.[77]

The initiative now shifted to the Kemmerer commission. Strong elected to await the pronouncements of the Princeton sage before taking further action toward completion of a Polish program, and interested American financiers postponed decisions on whether to launch Polish endeavors pending authoritative word from the "Money Doctor."[78] Ciechanowski for one did not doubt that the Poles would find the Kemmerer report both useful and flattering, and in a dispatch of August 25 he permitted himself to boast that:

> Concerning the Kemmerer mission, the Polish Government chose the less burdensome of two alternatives—submission to the temporary control of an international financial commission under League of Nations auspices,

which would bring in its train undesirable political consequences, or the engagement . . . of a completely dependent and apolitical mission of financial experts. Just such a mission is the Kemmerer mission.[79]

Not all Poles shared Ciechanowski's certainty of the benevolence and reliability of the American advisers. Elements of right as well as left warned of the perils posed by the investigatory commission and criticized the failure of the government to cancel the project. Socialist Herman Diamand bluntly called on Kemmerer to keep his "American nose" out of Polish affairs, and a leftist peasant deputy to the Sejm branded the Princetonian as "American capital's great huntsman . . . the true economic dictator of Poland, Governor Strong's viceroy in this youngest of colonies of the United States."[80] Many of the Piłsudski partisans themselves, more accustomed to belaboring than welcoming foreign capital and its representatives, adopted a defensive and apologetic tone in defending the decision of the state authorities to allow the opening of Polish finances to the scrutiny of outsiders.[81] Despite their discomfort, the Piłsudskists concluded that they could not afford to rescind the invitation. The Skrzyński government had wanted and promoted the Kemmerer mission; the post-May regime, which inherited the inquiry, merely tolerated it as a necessary embarrassment.

A buoyant Kemmerer sailed for Europe at the head of his delegation late in June. As in the previous December, he confidentially declared first loyalty to his Polish hosts rather than to his banking associates. Upon his departure he promised Wańkowicz to conduct himself "as if he were a Pole," stating further that "even should the United States adopt a stance which would be harmful to Poland, he would . . . defend the interests of Poland." Also as before, German representatives intercepted the American as his eastbound train passed through Berlin in hopes of tempering his Polish sympathies, and again he rebuffed their arguments as inimical to his clients in Poland.[82]

Kemmerer and his entourage arrived in Warsaw on July 3. Both in scope and duration the second Kemmerer mission constituted a far more ambitious undertaking than its abbreviated forerunner. During its sojourn of eleven weeks the panel conducted a comprehensive examination of the postwar Polish economy. The Americans gathered information from direct observation as well as consultation with state officials and business and banking leaders. In the course of one of these sessions the government presented a request for a stabilization loan of approximately $15 million.[83] When not at work in Warsaw, Kemmerer crisscrossed the country to partake of activities ranging from inspection of the construction of the port of Gdynia to negotiation of the rapids of the river Dunajec.

Although Kemmerer received a cordial greeting from his hosts, he met with continual evidence of the various resentments stirred by his presence in Poland. The Berlin press portrayed him as an "agent of American and

British capitalists," which did not prevent English newspapers from sniping at the Kemmerer committee as an inadequate substitute for the League of Nations. Within Poland as well the American visitors found themselves hardly sacrosanct. Unconvinced Socialists kept up a racket or protest against Kemmerer which the government, aside from Klarner, made no effort to rebut. Kemmerer also encountered resistance to his advice from the Bank Polski, which endorsed his suggestions for reorganization of the institution only after grudging hesitation.[84]

The Kemmerer mission departed on September 17 after submitting its report to Minister Klarner. The voluminous document applauded Polish progress toward economic rehabilitation while repeating its author's previous nostrums for improvement of the fiscal apparatus.[85] In certain specifics, Kemmerer revised his earlier views to the benefit of his hosts. For example, at Polish behest he discarded his opinion of the need to fix the złoty at original par of 5.18 to the dollar and settled for stabilization at 9.0, the prevailing value of the currency. In another switch, he refuted the common American belief that the Poles spent too much on armaments and, while mandating economy in military appropriations, openly endorsed the maintenance of a "strong army" and denied the necessity for deep cuts in the military budget.[86]

From the Polish perspective, the entire point of the American inquiry was to facilitate foreign borrowing, and the report devoted much attention to Polish credit needs and practices. Kemmerer endorsed Warsaw's petition for a pump-priming $15 million stabilization loan, although he admitted privately the money was "not entirely necessary" to secure the mending złoty; the primary function of the loan would be to stimulate confidence among Poles and investors. For the future he counseled Warsaw to borrow only for such productive purposes as public works construction and especially agricultural modernization, for he believed Poland's prosperity depended on her ability to supply industrial Europe with ever greater amounts of foodstuffs and raw materials. Reflecting the exasperation of American bankers with the Polish habit of shopping around from house to house, Kemmerer chided Warsaw for its dalliance with Bankers Trust and exhorted the government to settle on a single American banker and conduct most, though not necessarily all, of its foreign borrowing through that agent. Kemmerer carefully avoided speaking on behalf of any particular firm, but the clear implication of his argument was that Poland should remain a client of his sponsor, Clarence Dillon.[87]

Upon his return to the United States Kemmerer grumbled to the State Department that the Piłsudski coup had removed the officials most disposed to enact his recommendations, but for the most part he kept his complaints to himself and his report painted a distinctly rosy picture of Polish development. Even Młynarski found some of the American's conclusions "perhaps . . . a little overoptimistic."[88] Aside from its author's partiality toward Poland, the report owed its tone to its appearance at a time of unusual and, as it happened, largely artificial affluence. Production continued to rise, and the combination of a bountiful 1925 harvest and a British coal strike allowed exports to leap. The improving balance of trade staunched the drain of gold, and by autumn of 1926 the złoty had established itself firmly at the 9.0 level. The arrival of Piłsudski played no part in this process; the upward trend of the Polish economy had begun already under Skrzyński, and the coup coincided with a phase of general European prosperity, which saw many continental currencies achieve at least *de facto* stabilization in 1926. On the other hand, the prospect of a forceful and durable government after years of rickety and often ineffectual cabinets tended to fortify foreign and domestic confidence in the economic future of the country.

To be sure, Kemmerer hedged his observations with the qualification that Poland's momentary plenitude was partially illusory, but in his audiences with American bankers and businessmen he chose to accentuate the positive.[89] Toward the end of September he told Ciechanowski he would try to acquire loans for Warsaw from Dillon, Read and the New York Federal Reserve. A few days later he met with Dillon and urged him not only to issue the prescribed $15 million stabilization loan but to consider a full package of financing which would have the double effect of "securing Poland . . . and undoing Germany's designs for a new domination of markets." Dillon agreed to ponder the idea but hesitated to commit himself before allowing investors a chance to digest the Kemmerer report.[90]

The optimistic forecast of the American commission failed to convince all skeptics. Norman scoffed that if Kemmerer believed the Polish financial crisis was over, then "Kemmerer [was] greatly in error," and spokesmen for the Foreign Office and the Bank of England predicted the panel and its recommendations would sink into quick oblivion and make way for an inevitable League of Nations solution to the Polish problem.[91] Americans too stopped short of full acceptance of the report. Financiers and investors waited to see if events would confirm the Kemmerer verdict before putting their money on the line, and even so resolutely sympathetic an observer as Stetson anticipated an economic relapse in Poland before long.[92] The Poles meanwhile damaged their standing with Strong when Młynarski, in a moment of injudicious candor, told a British Treasury official that Warsaw took little stock in the Kemmerer commission except as a propaganda spectacular to persuade the world of Polish creditworthiness. The remark made its way back to Strong—who regarded Warsaw's compliance with Kemmerer's proposals as a precondition of his compact with Ciechanowski—and caused him to doubt the sincerity of Polish intentions.[93]

Nor had the Poles themselves reconciled their internal differences over the correct attitude toward foreign capital. Controversy continued to surround the questions of the usefulness and propriety of the Kemmerer mission and the necessity of an outside loan. Within the government

Klarner led a group of advocates for a large American stabilization loan, but the cabinet split on the issue and put off a decision for lack of consensus.[94] Having reluctantly carried the Kemmerer investigation through to a conclusion, the heirs of Skrzyński could not determine whether to follow the process to its logical end—an American loan in exchange for reforms—or abandon it for an alternative.

Arranged as a method of speeding the expansion of financial relations between Poland the United States, the Kemmerer commission and its recommendations left unanswered questions among Poles and investors alike. Nearly a year had passed since the fall of Grabski, and Warsaw found itself "still in a state of temporary credit isolation."[95] Outwardly little had changed, but the intervening months represented a crucial phase of Poland's long search for steady and generous access to American money. The chain of events set in motion by the emergence of Bankers Trust as a potential lender to Poland had led through the complexities of central bank rivalry to the formation of a coalition between Warsaw and the Federal Reserve Bank of New York, an alliance which survived—if barely—the violent seizure of power by Marshal Piłsudski. These various threads would unite in 1927 as components of the stabilization program that had taken its basic shape during the preceding year.

CHAPTER V

Mixing the
"Manhattan Cocktail,"
1926–1927

*The consummation of the loan begins a new epoch in Polish
history. Opportunity is calling Poland. I hope she will rise to
seize it.*

John B. Stetson, Jr., to William R. Castle, November 29, 1927

During the year following its introduction in the summer of 1925, the
proposal for a Polish stabilization loan organized by leading central
banks had advanced fitfully through the embryonic stages of development. Initially rejected as onerous by Grabski, the scheme won the
endorsement of the Skrzyński ministry when it discovered—nearly by
accident—a community of interest with the financial authorities of the
United States in joining forces against the Bank of England and the
Reichsbank. By submitting to the second Kemmerer inquiry, Warsaw
fulfilled the pledge of good faith stipulated by its gentlemen's agreement
with Benjamin Strong and brought the preliminary phase of the complicated operation to completion. Even so, a stabilization plan remained a
long way from achievement. Strong had yet to obtain the acquiescence of
his German and English counterparts. More importantly, the project still
lacked the most fundamental parts of the equation: the collaboration of
an American banking syndicate and—owing to the Piłsudski coup—the
consent of the newly skeptical Polish government. The fusion of these
missing elements would require another year of arduous negotiation.

In the lull that followed the Kemmerer investigation, the Poles scouted
for loans of any sort from Western bankers, whether connected with a
stabilization program or not. Even before the American commission left
Poland, Klarner directed Ciechanowski to resume his efforts to obtain
financing in New York at costs not to exceed 8.5 percent, attaching
priority to the second transfer of the Dillon, Read transaction of 1925.[1]
Midway through September Młynarski journeyed to London to meet
separately with Strong and Norman and elicit their thoughts on the
Polish question in the wake of the Kemmerer mission. To his surprise,

Strong appeared cool and reluctant to sponsor the Bank Polski over the opposition of London; Norman, on the other hand, seemed much surer of his mind. The chief of the Bank of England restated his consistent thesis that Poland had no option but to accept stabilization either through the League of Nations or an international supervisory committee invested with similarly broad powers of financial control. In other words, Strong's plan for exclusively American custody of the Polish matter would not do.

Młynarski deduced hastily from his interviews that Strong had lost his power play against Norman and that consequently the patronage of the New York Federal Reserve had come to nothing. He failed to perceive that Strong's aloofness stemmed not from "a mighty desire to be done with Europe once and for all" but from irritation at his own reported belittlement of the Kemmerer recommendations. Consoled by the promises of a Norman lieutenant that the restraints placed on the Poles would amount to *"financial control only* without any political admixtures," Młynarski advised Klarner to abandon the understanding with the Americans and resign himself to a choice between "Geneva or London."[2]

Scarcely had Klarner received this sobering news than he lost the finance portfolio as part of a cabinet shakeup. His dismissal had less to do with his policies than with the dynamics of the growing discord between the Piłsudskists and the recalcitrant Sejm, but the fall of a conspicuous proponent of alliance with American finance prompted Wall Street to jump to the conclusion that Warsaw had repudiated Kemmerer.[3]

Klarner's successor, Gabriel Czechowicz, moved hurriedly to dispel this impression. One of the few members of the Piłsudski camp with a genuine command of economics, Czechowicz regarded admission to foreign capital markets as essential to the future of Poland and advocated the engagement of a large American loan as the necessary certification of her creditworthiness. He understood clearly that failure to enact at least some of the suggestions of the Kemmerer panel would alienate New York bankers beyond recall. To guard against this possibility Czechowicz identified himself with Kemmerer's prescriptions of fiscal reform and proclaimed as his central goal the realization of an economic program conforming to the lines laid down by the American investigatory commission.[4] With most of his colleagues distracted by domestic politics, Czechowicz encountered little interference from within the cabinet.

While Czechowicz took Klarner's place as the strongest supporter of the stabilization plan within the Warsaw government, Minister Ciechanowski sought out his friends in Washington and New York to ascertain whether they meant to honor the accord he had reached with Strong in the spring. On October 20 Winston of the Treasury acknowledged that Norman was proving a stubborn opponent, but that the Reserve Bank remained determined to enforce its independent Polish policy as a demonstration of emancipation from the Bank of England. He added that

Strong enjoyed the full backing of the Treasury, which agreed that "a certain degree of planned activity by the Federal System in Europe is desirable and beneficial." He described the sponsorship of the Bank Polski as the opening move of a stealthy campaign to chip away at the shackles imposed on Strong by the potent American isolationist bloc and enjoined prudent silence on the Poles regarding the degree of Washington's complicity in the maneuver.[5]

Two weeks later Winston accompanied Ciechanowski to New York to receive confirmation of his message from George Harrison, then acting as Strong's stand-in during the governor's dangerous illness with pneumonia resulting from chronic tuberculosis. Alluding to Młynarski's pessimistic report, the Polish envoy expressed apprehension that Strong wished to "back off" from his commitments to Poland, whereupon Harrison in turn demanded an explanation for Młynarski's cavalier dismissals of Kemmerer. The cause of the Reserve Bank's reticence suddenly clear to him, Ciechanowski quickly applied a gloss to the incident and considerably exaggerated his government's readiness to carry out the Kemmerer reforms. Reassured by Ciechanowski's overstatements, Harrison joined Winston in affirming the validity of the bargain Strong had struck with the Poles. They advised Ciechanowski to give the Kemmerer report a chance to erode the shell of American disbelief in Poland before approaching a bank—preferably Dillon, Read—with an appeal for a stabilization loan.[6]

In his summary of the meeting, Ciechanowski told the MSZ that the Poles had reached a crossroads in the formulation of their foreign borrowing policy: either they could align themselves with Norman and accept stringent controls with possible political overtones or they could don the lighter burdens of Strong's plan and in the process establish their credit in the richest of capital markets. He exhorted Warsaw to resolve its doubts and throw in its lot unequivocally with the Americans. Perhaps hoping to check the decline of his influence since the advent of Piłsudski, he also proposed the concentration of responsibility for dealing with American banks within the Washington legation, claiming that to do otherwise would risk return to the haphazard and uncoordinated initiatives that had damaged Polish credibility on Wall Street in the past. As a case in point he protested the current endeavors of a representative of an organization of Polish contractors, Henryk Sztolcman, to procure a small loan from a New York concern, arguing that the operation might depress demand for a stabilization loan and needlessly complicate the pending negotiations with Dillon, Read.[7]

The flaw in Ciechanowski's reasoning was that the Dillon firm, favored by Strong and Kemmerer alike to lead the stabilization combine, refused for the moment to commit itself to participation in a Polish transaction. The tension that typified the relationship between Poland and her American banker had carried through the summer of 1926 when attempts to settle differences broke down into acerbic exchanges of mutual complaints. On the other hand, neither partner dared dissolve the loveless marriage, Warsaw for lack of another suitor and Dillon for fear of losing face in the banking world through divorce from a client government. When Kemmerer returned from Europe at the end of September and urged Dillon to resume lending to Poland, the bank agreed in principle but decided to wait for proof that Warsaw meant to follow the recommendations of the advisory commission. Ciechanowski objected to the requirement as yet another stalling tactic but yielded when Kemmerer sided with the bankers. The Polish minister returned to the Dillon, Read offices a month later only to hear the familiar homilies on the need for patience and time to build investor confidence in Poland.[8]

Aside from unhappy memories of the loan of 1925, the reasons for Dillon's hesitancy were substantially the same that had dogged Polish credit in the United States through the years. Chief among these was the republic's history of political and financial turmoil. The Piłsudski revolt in particular reminded Americans of the Polish reputation for instability, and they insisted on taking a long look to gauge whether the new regime could pacify the country and make it a safe haven for investment. Nearly six months after the coup not only Dillon but the entire banking fraternity of New York agreed that the domestic condition of Poland remained too tentative to permit flotation of a large Polish loan.[9]

As always, Poland's unfortunate geography compounded doubts of her internal soundness. Taking note of Warsaw's unsatisfactory relations with its neighbors, William Castle of the State Department, a sympathetic observer of Polish affairs, wrote that:

> if the Government really lives up to Kemmerer's recommendations . . . that will do a lot [to ingratiate investors], but there always remains in the background the fact of Russia on one side and Germany on the other, which fact does not seem to indicate the brightest possible future for Poland.

Owing to the entrapment of the country inside the German-Russian "nut cracker," Castle concluded that "so far as I am concerned personally, I should not want to invest much in Polish bonds unless I was so terrifically rich that I did not mind what happened to the money." So many of his compatriots agreed that even the highest-rated Polish securities available on the American market bore the stigma of speculative risks.[10]

The understandable desire of the bankers to apply special standards of precaution in business dealings with Poland provoked equally comprehensible expressions of annoyance from the Poles, who—already having endured examination by Kemmerer—began to wonder when the Americans would exhaust their list of preconditions. The disgruntled Młynarski outlined a financial program for the future based on the assumption that Poland would have to do without American capital. In December officers of the MSZ summoned Stetson to complain that American lending patterns discriminated against Warsaw and endangered the peace by favoring Germany and providing indirect encouragement to

German ambitions to extend economic and political dominion over East Europe.[11]

The first signs of a break in the tacit embargo of American capital shipments to Poland started to appear during the final weeks of 1926. The passage of several months lent a look of permanence to the new administration in Warsaw, and the *Sanacja* regime steadily convinced greater numbers of American onlookers of its competence and friendliness. In early December Stetson declared that "never since I have come to Poland has the spirit of the Polish Government towards American [investment] been as favorable and as reasonable as at the present moment."[12] As Harrison and Winston had predicted, the optimistic conclusions of the Kemmerer report gradually penetrated public consciousness and cast a new light on Polish enterprise. With much of Europe already saturated in foreign capital, buyers began to hunt other possibilities and sufficient numbers of them settled on Poland to create a modest bull market in Polish issues. Much of this activity represented a natural rebound from the artificial lows of the turbulent summer, but the upturn persuaded a reputable financial publication to nominate Polish bonds as an especially promising vehicle for investors.[13] By December the market showed enough strength to convince those American firms with an established interest in Poland that the time to act had arrived.

Anxious to prevent the loss of its Polish account to a competitor, Dillon initiated discussions with Ciechanowski in the first week of December in spite of threats from the Wilhelmstrasse to retaliate by cutting the bank out of an upcoming German loan.[14] Ciechanowski joined the talks in defiance of the wishes of his Finance Ministry. On November 30 Czechowicz had informed him of the government's decision to forgo negotiations for the second transfer of the 1925 loan "so as to have free hands and not be tied to the constantly insincere relations of [Dillon, Read]." Ciechanowski disingenuously interpreted the cable as an authorization to explore alternate credit projects with Dillon. At their encounter, the director of the bank's foreign department invited the Poles to draw up a schedule of long-term financing and informally offered to commence either by floating the unsold remainder of the first transfer of the 8 percent loan or staking $8 million for construction of a rail terminal in Warsaw. Aware of the Federal Reserve Bank's preference for Dillon and accustomed to broad latitude in dealings with American bankers, Ciechanowski agreed to consider the proposal and relayed it to Warsaw with a request for retroactive blessing of his freelance negotiation.[15]

Excluded from the process of decision at home, Ciechanowski did not know that the minister of finance already had elected to ally with another bank. Throughout the autumn Bankers Trust had kept open its lines of communication with the Poles, and at the end of November the firm sent a delegation to Warsaw armed with a proposition to resurrect the stillborn tobacco loan with notable dilutions of the stiff formula for external controls that had doomed the project in its earlier versions. Disenchanted with Dillon, Czechowicz leaped at the opportunity and at the same time moved to squelch Ciechanowski's unsanctioned foray into personal financial diplomacy. On December 17 he ordered Ciechanowski to "break off relations with the Dillon firm in a dexterous manner, utilizing his indecisiveness regarding the release of the second transfer."[16]

Polish representatives in the United States protested the rupture with Dillon as a rash departure from the wishes of the Federal Reserve Bank, but the legation in Washington had lost its battle for an autonomous role in the creation of foreign loan policy. Against his will, Ciechanowski told Dillon, Read that its service as banker to Poland had drawn to an end, but he could not resist leaving the door to reconciliation slightly ajar. Misreading the statement as a bargaining ploy, the bank dangled a more definite offer for the rail terminal loan in front of the touring businessman Henryk Sztolcman, who happily consented to talk about the idea and pursued discussions well into January 1927 in ignorance of the official fiat against further commerce with Dillon. The bankers concluded, as well they might, that the Polish threat of divorce was a mere exercise in coquetry.[17]

The confusion in America was more than duplicated in Warsaw. While the Finance Ministry labored to restrain Ciechanowski's independent instincts, it neglected to concert its actions with his superiors at the MSZ—a nearly fatal omission. Having eliminated Dillon from contention, Czechowicz granted the visiting Bankers Trust mission an option on the tobacco monopoly loan that included the standard promise not to deal with other banks during the life of the contract. The ink on the compact barely had dried before Foreign Minister Zaleski gave a similar and thus equally meaningless pledge to another American bank. Blair and Co. had first shown interest in Poland during the summer of 1926 through inquiries made by its Parisian agent Jean Monnet, then in the early years of an eminent career as a European statesman and financier. Monnet established contact with the MSZ through an intermediary and journeyed to the Polish capital in mid-December. Unaware of the simultaneous presence of the Bankers Trust negotiators, Zaleski and Monnet quickly agreed to a plan bestowing sole authority to organize a stabilization loan on a consortium led by Blair and Chase Securities Corporation.[18] American bankers had often bemoaned a chronic lack of coordination among the various departments of state in Poland, and now Czechowicz and Zaleski had contrived to commit the government to redundant and mutually exclusive obligations.

By the time they discovered their embarrassing and potentially devastating blunder, the Poles had little choice but to try to reach some accommodation between the rival banking groups. They divulged the existence of the awkward triangle to Monnet, who had lingered in Warsaw after the departure of the Bankers Trust contingent. After his angry astonishment wore off, he collaborated with the Finance Ministry in hunting an escape from the dilemma. Just before Christmas Monnet returned to Paris in hopes of persuading Bankers Trust to merge with the Blair-Chase partnership. After consultations the banks agreed to the compromise. Bankers Trust dropped the tobacco project and assumed leadership of the Blair syndicate, which adopted Dillon's lapsed title as American banker to Poland. As its first operation the coalition proposed a large stabilization loan in conjunction with a general program of fiscal reforms in Poland. In contrast to Kemmerer's figure of $15 million, the Bankers Trust outline envisaged a transaction of approximately $100 million devoted in equal shares to investment and support of the złoty.[19]

The bankers' proposition left the next move to the Poles. Czechowicz and Zaleski aside, the government had not made up its mind on foreign loan policy and reacted cautiously to the news from Paris, noting that the thorny issues—the cost of the money and the nature and scope of external regulation—remained an enigma.[20] In answer, Warsaw announced that a deputation consisting of Młynarski and Adam Krzyżanowski, a professor of economics at the Jagiellonian University of Cracow, would go to the United States ostensibly to discuss the implementation of the Kemmerer agenda with interested parties in New York. Official spokesmen transparently denied any direct connection with the Bankers Trust bid, but the MSZ quietly commanded Ciechanowski to relinquish responsibility for treating with the banks to the special emissaries.[21] Warsaw now had taken direct control over the negotiations. Młynarski and Krzyżanowski carried with them broad powers of discretion to strike a deal subject to subsequent approval by the Polish government. Before their departure they received an audience with Piłsudski, whose vague instructions authorized them to accept a loan even with League of Nations control "so long as the League appoints an American as financial adviser" to oversee the machinery.[22]

Młynarski and Krzyżanowski interrupted their pilgrimage at Paris to confer with Monnet and the leadership of the French central bank. Émile Moreau had become governor of the Banque de France in the summer of 1926 upon the installation of a cabinet pledged to restore the franc and mend French finances. Like Strong, he wished to extend his activity into the international arena and establish his bank as an equal of its English and German counterparts. As intensely as Schacht, Moreau identified his task with the fulfillment of the diplomatic goals of his government. Obsessed with the maintenance of French financial influence in the allied states of Eastern Europe and with the real or imagined plots of Montagu Norman to reduce these friendly countries to vassalage to the Bank of England, he had sympathized with Polish efforts to find funding in the United States as a means of thwarting Norman's "projects of domination" over Warsaw.[23]

Monnet too recognized a French political interest in the consummation of the Bankers Trust-Blair loan,[24] and he solicited the aid of the Banque de France; Moreau in turn laid the matter before Prime Minister Raymond Poincaré, who gave his assent. On February 1 the governor met with Młynarski, who requested French support in concluding the American stabilization loan. Appealing to Moreau's phobia for Norman, Młynarski contended that the French could buttress Strong and help to water down the controls, which as put forth by Kemmerer would prove "dangerous to the political independence of Poland." Moreau agreed handily and charged two deputies, Pierre Quesnay and Charles Rist, with surveillance of the Polish question.[25]

While Młynarski enlisted the Banque de France, at home the Polish government attempted to rally a nonexistent enthusiasm for the Kemmerer program within the parliament to convince the bankers of the imminence of reform. The debate made a curious spectacle. Even while chiding the Sejm for dragging its feet in evaluating the suggestions of the advisory panel, spokesmen for the regime hardly bothered to hide their resentment at having to appear as advocates of concessions to foreign interests. Czechowicz sounded the sole note of resolution. Lamenting that previous cabinets had "committed every possible error, and some impossible ones" in their dealings with foreign capital, he asserted his intention not to add to the list of mistakes by repudiating the American commission and alienating lenders; the government took Kemmerer's opinion "very seriously" and would introduce the reforms as extensively as possible. In the end Warsaw tried to strike a balance between the conflicting demands of the bankers and domestic opinion by proclaiming the right to modify or delete certain of the Kemmerer recommendations.[26]

Meanwhile, recognition slowly dawned on Dillon, Read that the Poles had switched their allegiance to Bankers Trust. Midway through January Warsaw caught up with Sztolcman and compelled him to break off talks with Dillon, and the bank realized belatedly that Ciechanowski's statement of separation had been genuine. Feeling abused, Dillon, Read accused the Poles of shifty conduct and angrily bade them good riddance.[27] After the bank recovered its temper, Strong attempted to heal the breach by offering to bring it into the Bankers Trust combination, but Dillon declined, citing reasons of prestige as the deterrent. All the same, the firm continued to hover on the margin, hoping for a hitch in the talks with the rival consortium that might permit it to reclaim Poland as an exclusive client.[28]

The chief of the Federal Reserve Bank likewise sought to reconcile differences with his colleagues Norman and Schacht, who reacted to the new Bankers Trust loan project with pronounced displeasure. As Młynarski and Krzyżanowski approached American shores, Strong wrote his old friend at the Bank of England a pair of "Dear Monty" notes, asking his cooperation in the Polish question and hinting he would be wise not to aid any "effort by Germany to 'torpedo' a sound settlement." The Europeans remained unimpressed. Norman spread the word in New York and Paris not to allow Poland to evade rigorous controls, and the German government and press intensified their propaganda war against Warsaw in a calculated endeavor to frighten off American lenders.[29]

While the central bankers maneuvered in the background, Młynarski and Krzyżanowski commenced their talks in New York midway through February. The Polish spokesmen first huddled with several former members of the Kemmerer commission, who gave their qualified endorsement of Warsaw's progress in fulfilling the prescribed reforms.[30] Having cleared this preliminary hurdle, the Poles proceeded to direct parleys with the Bankers Trust-Blair syndicate, represented by Monnet. For all his patriotic as well as commercial keenness to conclude the loan, Monnet opened the bidding for the bankers at a lofty level: an interest rate of 8 percent and an international advisory board to take the place of the League of Nations. The Poles balked at these conditions, most determinedly at the extent of the controlling apparatus, and the negotiations threatened to collapse practically before they had begun. To break the deadlock the contestants agreed to submit the problem to the ailing and absent Strong, and at the end of the month Harrison escorted Monnet, Młynarski and Ciechanowski to the governor's convalescent retreat at Asheville, North Carolina.[31]

The four-day conference at Asheville marked a prominent milestone on the path to the stabilization loan. For two days Młynarski and Monnet rehearsed their arguments for Strong's benefit, occasionally lapsing into heated exchanges. In the end Strong sided with Monnet, telling the Poles that the weakness of Polish credit in the United States dictated the inclusion of distasteful clauses to satisfy prospective American investors.[32] At the same time, he sweetened the pill with sugared assurances that the controls would prove more "symbolic" than real. Once Młynarski relented, Strong renewed his commitment to shepherd the project with or without the consent of Schacht and Norman, calling it a "test case" of the international influence of the Federal Reserve Bank. United around the program of the bankers, Strong's visitors—the "Four Gold Zlotys," as they styled themselves—returned to New York to apply the finishing touches to the package.[33]

The principles of a deal having been established, the Bankers Trust group formally submitted its offer to the Polish representatives two weeks later. The proposal called for a loan of approximately $50 million subject to the oversight of an American adviser and a committee of European experts appointed by the Poles. Młynarski and Krzyżanowski tentatively approved the terms in spite of misgivings that aspects of the agreement might fail to win favor in official Warsaw. Their decision stemmed in equal parts from apprehension that the government might otherwise reject out of hand a bargain they considered acceptable if not optimal and from recognition that their compact with the bankers constituted little more than a rough draft affording ample opportunity for further haggling.[34]

Even before Młynarski and Krzyżanowski affixed their signatures Strong decided to send Harrison to Europe later in the month to bring the other central banks into line with his Polish stabilization plan. Conscious as always of his domestic flanks, Strong first dispatched his deputy to Washington to make certain of official blessing of the scheme. On March 11 Harrison placed the question of his journey before the Federal Reserve Board. A lengthy debate produced no conclusion but left the impression that a majority of the body opposed the motion "lest we might inject ourselves into a delicate international situation." Five days later Harrison presented the Board with a potent ally in Secretary Mellon. Swayed by the presence of a cabinet member and by the argument that the rehabilitation of Poland would be "a direct help to every [American] cotton producer," the Reserve Board approved Harrison's trip on condition that he avoid entangling the United States in political matters.[35] In addition to Mellon and the Treasury, Harrison received support from the State Department and the Coolidge White House. The entire executive branch aligned itself with the Polish policy of the Federal Reserve Bank, and the endeavor became a government operation in all but name.[36]

In effect, Washington had chosen to employ Strong's Polish adventure as an instrument toward the attainment of desired goals: the enhancement of American financial prestige, the stimulation of agricultural exports and, to a lesser extent, the construction of a bulwark against Soviet Russia.[37] On the other hand, neither the government nor the Reserve Bank could afford to admit its involvement publicly for fear of transgressing the restrictions placed by postwar convention on official American activity in Europe. Because no Polish settlement could avoid impinging on the forbidden terrain of European politics, the authorities in Washington insisted that the undertaking proceed in strict confidence and under cover of the bogus but useful contention that it represented solely an arrangement of central banks acting independently of their governments. Taking caution a step further, Harrison admonished Ciechanowski that any Polish attribution of the stabilization program to the Reserve Bank would oblige it "immediately and completely to withdraw from the entire enterprise in view of the reaction such news would elicit from Congress."[38]

On March 18 the liner *Aquitania* embarked from New York bound for Europe, bearing Monnet and Harrison to Paris and Krzyżanowski and Młynarski toward Warsaw. Upon their arrival the Polish delegates deposited the accomplished fact of their accord with Monnet before Czechowicz and Kazimierz Bartel, the deputy prime minister. The quartet agreed to pass the formula on for the approval of "Belvedere"—meaning Piłsudski and his inner circle—with the recommendation that the government adopt it as a starting point for further dickering with the bankers.[39]

The proponents of the stabilization loan encountered heavy resistance in the councils of state. Of the cabinet ministers, Czechowicz and Zaleski defended the idea ardently and enrolled Bartel as a confederate. Their most adamant foe was President Ignacy Mościcki, who habitually opposed the entry of foreign capital into Poland on a large scale. Mościcki maintained that the loan was redundant, owing to the demonstrable health of the złoty, as well as inadmissibly stringent in its application of external controls. The final word, of course, belonged to Piłsudski, the prime minister of the day and unquestioned authority of the *Sanacja* regime, but for the moment he kept his counsel and permitted his subordinates to debate. Piłsudski's neutrality was more tactical than philosophical, for unlike Mościcki he accepted the necessity of finding a foreign loan; by the same token, he found much to dislike in the specific proposition brought home by Młynarski and Krzyżanowski, whom he cursed "in the most drastic words" after learning of the fruits of their sojourn in America.[40]

On the night of March 30 Piłsudski placed the Bankers Trust offer on the table of a meeting with Mościcki and Bartel that dragged past midnight while other concerned officials kept a vigil in an antechamber. Upon emerging, the Marshal delphically announced that since the loan constituted a long-term obligation he would leave the decision to President Mościcki in his capacity as head of state; premiers came and went, and not he but his daughters "Wandzia and Jadzia will have to pay the interest." This proclamation appeared to doom the measure, and an agitated Zaleski spoke of resignation, but the prime minister's deference to the president had not been all it seemed. Reviewing the session the next morning with an associate, Piłsudski asked playfully what verdict Mościcki might reach in view of the fact that "the entire Council of Ministers and I too favor the engagement of the loan. Who do you think will decide?"[41]

The answer clarified soon after Monnet arrived in Warsaw on April 2 to receive the reply of the Polish government to the Bankers Trust-Blair partnership. The discussions progressed smoothly, and on April 7 Monnet reported conclusion of an agreement with the cabinet. The harmony lasted but a few hours, for later that same day Piłsudski presented the banker with a demand for removal of the provisions for outside supervision. Professing amazement, Monnet declared Piłsudski's ploy "indecent" and demonstratively prepared to quit Warsaw. Before he could leave, the Poles tendered a second proposal to eliminate the European overseers and reduce the control mechanism to a single American adviser. Hopeful of keeping the negotiations alive, Monnet consented to submit the compromise to the collective judgment of the syndicate and entrained for Paris to set in motion another round of talks between the Bankers Trust group and their Polish clients.[42]

While Monnet and the Poles sparred in Warsaw, the Federal Reserve Bank shouldered the task of wrestling the dissident central banks into compliance with its Polish stabilization plan. The French presented no problem; both Poincaré and Moreau exceeded the Americans themselves in zeal for the program, and the principal worry of the Banque de France in anticipation of the conclave with Harrison was that its enthusiasm might betray too. baldly political a motive.[43] On the other hand, the English and Germans formed a potentially formidable bloc of opposition. Schacht no longer nursed illusions that he might extract boundary revision as an element of a solution to Polish fiscal woes, but he hoped with Norman's help to achieve the next best result: the prevention of international assistance to Poland until Warsaw settled its disputes with Berlin on German terms. Norman had started to vacillate, however, and at a private conference to synchronize positions on the Polish question Schacht found the Briton "truly dejected and annoying." In his more confident moments Norman declared himself ready to veto any design that excluded the League of Nations, but he interspersed these avowals with occasional hints that his desire to secure the stabilization of Poland by nearly any means had overtaken his insistence on the enlistment of Geneva.[44]

Strong sent Harrison to Europe with detailed instructions. Presuming that Schacht and Moreau would split their votes along predictable political lines, he identified Norman as the pivotal figure who might make or break an accord. Strong expected objections from his English colleague on the issue of control, and Harrison's delicate assignment was to prohibit the League without driving off its champion. The most likely way to accomplish this golden mean was to stress Strong's preparedness to enact his Polish agenda alone if need be, leaving Norman with a choice of bowing to New York or sacrificing the ideal of central bank solidarity. As Harrison steamed eastward, Strong attempted to soften Norman with another familiar letter, reminding his friend that "the 100% letter perfect program is only that rare bird when it suits everyone—and . . . no such plan ever exists. . . . After it is all behind us—and a success—we will forget the details and recall only the result!"[45]

Upon arriving in France, Harrison met separately with the central bankers to explain Strong's intentions and gauge their reactions before assembling them in a decisive summit. Responding according to form, Moreau pledged support and advocated the maintenance of a concerted front against the probable obstructions of the Reichsbank and the Bank of England. Norman gave a halfhearted pitch for the League but confessed an inclination to accept any Polish settlement compatible with central bank unity, which was "more important to him than this particular problem"; he required only the inclusion of a control mechanism satisfactory to Schacht. Now suddenly a crucial factor in the enterprise despite the efforts of the Americans to isolate him, the German proved surprisingly congenial, offering to cooperate as the representative of a neighbor holding a vital stake in the economic health of Poland. Although insistent that "ultimately the Danzig corridor must be changed," Schacht seconded Harrison's proposition that the banks banish political calculations from their deliberations.[46] The necessary elements of victory for the Federal Reserve Bank appeared to be falling into place.

The illusory concord of the pourparlers fragmented at the general meeting convened by Harrison at Calais on April 3. All parties assented in principle to collaborate in furtherance of the stabilization of Poland, but Norman and Schacht spoke as one in balking at the method of the Strong plan. They hoisted once more the banner of the League of Nations, and when Harrison and Moreau shot it down, Schacht complicated the proceedings by introducing a suggestion that the central banks issue a joint credit of their own to Poland without an accompanying program for overhaul of Polish finances. The parley broke up in disarray. Harrison attributed the Anglo-German performance to "pique" and a desire to test the sincerity of Strong's threat to ram his Polish policy through the wall of their disapproval, while Moreau interpreted their actions more gruffly as a bid "to torpedo the project of poor M. Harrison."[47]

After adjournment of the conference, Harrison and Moreau repaired to Paris to ponder their riposte to Norman and Schacht. His confidence shaken by the setback at Calais, the American received injections of courage from Moreau as well as from countrymen Mellon and Parker Gilbert. Advised by all hands to return the ball into his opponents' court, Harrison on April 6 cabled his chief that the Reserve Bank could select one of three options: abandonment of the Polish project owing to the antagonism of the Reichsbank and the Bank of England, making good the vow to push on with or without the sanction of the English and Germans, or adoption of the motion put forward by Schacht at Calais. Placed on the spot, Strong began to squirm. Intimations of his role as broker of the Polish stabilization effort had started to appear in the press, and he hesitated to assume full responsibility for the venture deprived of at least the protective covering of a collegial and relatively anonymous undertaking. Despite his qualms, Strong replied to Harrison the next day with directions to push ahead with the second alternative and hope for the best.[48]

Having salvaged the moral satisfaction of forcing Strong into a confession of paternity, Norman and Schacht agreed to stand aside and allow the Federal Reserve Bank to manage the Polish affair in its own fashion. At the same time they reserved the right to snipe at the activity from the sidelines. Norman reaffirmed to Schacht his displeasure with the American plan as heedless of "precautions which appeared essential." The outcome moved a disgusted Otto Niemeyer to grumble that:

> This scheme is actively supported by the Federal Reserve Bank (out of ignorance) and the Bank of France (for political reasons). . . . It is a kind of Manhattan cocktail of all former League schemes plus the Dawes plan with most of the alcohol left out. . . . The scheme religiously taboos the League: it does not provide any adequate control.

Rather than see the Bank of England and the Reichsbank dragged into the arrangement against their judgment, Niemeyer preferred to wait for the Americans to bow to reason and admit Geneva into the picture. Until then, the British and Germans should "do and say nothing leaving the Yanks and the Poles to make their own troubles."[49]

As Strong pocketed his slightly tarnished victory, the focus shifted once more to Poland and the Bankers Trust consortium, who resumed their dialogue in Paris on April 10. Młynarski acted as the principal delegate for Warsaw, while Monnet stood as first among equals on the negotiating team for the bankers. John Foster Dulles of the New York law firm Sullivan and Cromwell played a central part in the discussions, providing legal counsel to the banks and informally mediating the personal rivalry that cropped up between Monnet of Blair and his counterpart from Bankers Trust, Henri Fischer. Their collaboration on the Polish stabilization loan began a long friendship and professional association between Monnet and the future secretary of state.[50]

After opening smoothly, the session soon ground to a halt on the issue that had haunted the stabilization project since its inception: the question of foreign control. Taking their cue from Piłsudski, the Poles refused to retreat from their position of April 7 that the syndicate scrap its proposed international arbitration board and whittle the supervisory authority down to a resident American observer with strictly limited authority.[51] Loath to give ground on this point, the bankers dug in their heels and demanded both panel and adviser. Stalled at dead center, the talks protracted and dragged on fruitlessly into May.

While Młynarski grappled with Monnet and Fischer in Paris, his superiors in Warsaw continued their internal debate on the measure. The government shrouded its deliberations in secrecy, confining them largely to the triumvirate of Piłsudski, Mościcki, and Bartel.[52] Now that the prime minister had tipped his hand in favor of a loan, the arguments concentrated on the desirability of the Bankers Trust offer in particular. Mościcki still led the fight against the proposition, centering his attack on the vulnerable point of the controls. The president drew encouragement in this course from operatives of Dillon, who wooed him with promises of loans without strings in their effort to reclaim the Poles as clients. Piłsudski remained in the middle, favorably inclined toward the Bankers Trust deal but not sufficiently to override his unwillingness to swallow the international advisory committee.[53]

Variously intrigued or provoked by the droplets of information allotted them by the bankers and the regime, the Polish press and political world stirred a lively polemic on the question of the loan. Commercial and financial interests supplied the motion with its base of support, while the strongest dissension arose in the newspapers of the opposition of right and center, which seized on the issue as a cudgel with which to belabor Piłsudski.[54] The most visible adversary was Władysław Grabski, who declared that the stabilization plan would amount to "the command of foreign capital over Poland" and portrayed the American bankers as stalking horses for German influence. Accepting the challenge, Krzyżanowski retorted with a series of articles defending the loan and, for good measure, excusing the attendant controls as the unfortunate but inevitable price of Grabski's own economic maladministration.[55] The rigors of the Kemmerer reforms still presented an affront to national pride, but the

Bank Polski endorsed the program—not without trepidation—and at the beginning of May a quasi-official advisory board of financial experts pronounced its approval of the stabilization plan.[56]

Despite the discernible formation of a majority of Polish opinion in favor of the loan, Marshal Piłsudski persisted in withholding his consent out of dissatisfaction with the control apparatus required by the Bankers Trust group. Monnet and his colleagues declined Polish requests to relinquish the international panel and trim the powers of the American agent. Equally unwilling to relent, Piłsudski held firm and waited for the bankers to break the impasse by meeting his conditions. With no opening in sight, the Paris talks verged on collapse.[57]

Weary of the delays and out of sympathy with the Polish arguments, the Americans lectured the Poles on the perils of stubbornness and beseeched them to concede. Harrison and Strong reminded Ciechanowski that the application of meaningful controls was necessary to attract investors to the Polish bonds and warned that rejection of the Bankers Trust plan might scare world capital markets away from Poland for several years to come. Kept in the dark by Warsaw and anxious for the fate of his brainchild, Ciechanowski too urged the MSZ to swallow the bitter medicine for the sake of the benefits of the stabilization program, which he described as the chance to obtain "once and for all the political and financial confidence of the world, under American guarantee as it were."[58]

The Banque de France took the lead in seeking a compromise solution to the deadlock. During the first week in May Moreau gathered Monnet, Norman, and a shifting cast of leading American banking representatives for a round of informal talks in Paris to consider the Polish riddle. Suspected by Moreau of plotting to sabotage the American project, Norman in fact played a constructive part in the discussions, convinced at last of the urgent necessity to strengthen Polish finances with foreign aid and advice regardless of his personal disapproval of the Federal Reserve scheme. Operating with the quiet patronage of Poincaré, the sessions produced a series of proposals to reconcile the points of difference between the Poles and the bankers, most notably the immediate obstacle of the international commission. Reporting on the results of the Paris conclave to Strong, Norman expressed the hope that "a way out has been found."[59]

The intercession of the French central bank refreshed the stalemated loan negotiations and secured conclusion of a settlement between the Bankers Trust coalition and the Polish delegation. Charles Rist of the Banque de France entered the talks in the role of mediator. Desirous of salvaging the program he had done much to promote, Młynarski snatched gratefully at the proffered compromise and on May 16 notified Warsaw of an agreement in principle to meet halfway on the matter of supervision.[60] The formula abolished the international committee but endowed the American adviser with nearly all the powers sought by the bankers, including a seat on the board of the Bank Polski and extensive if incomplete dominion over Polish borrowing practices and allocation of the stabilization loan proceeds throughout the life of the plan. The additional panel of expert observers survived only in theory: serious disputes between Warsaw and the American agent would pass to an extraordinary council of arbitration jointly selected by the adversaries.

With the Bankers Trust accord in hand, Młynarski followed the script composed at Asheville and submitted the stabilization plan to the Federal Reserve Bank so that Strong might approve it and set about organizing a supplementary central bank credit of no less than $15 million.[61] Presented with the fruits of his yearlong campaign to establish American primacy in the financial restoration of Poland, Strong received another attack of cold feet and invited the Banque de France to assume sponsorship of the Polish program, pleading preoccupation with other pressing business. Fearful of identification as the progenitor of the scheme, the Reserve Bank had done its best to fade into the background since the Calais conference. Annoyed at Strong's abdication of responsibility for the Bank Polski during the difficult moments of April and May, Moreau fumed that "the American mentality includes scruples and complications which do not accord with action" and filled the vacuum of leadership as a stopgap. However, the Banque de France had no intention of occupying the bed Strong had made for himself. Moreau wanted as well to remain inconspicuous to avoid charges of political motivation, and the French firmly rebuffed New York's last-minute attempt to evade its duties to Poland.[62]

Forced to resume custody of the endeavor, Strong took under examination the stabilization plan elaborated by the Bank Polski as security for the Western lenders. Based on the Kemmerer recommendations, the scheme promised creation of a budgetary surplus and maintenance of the złoty at 8.9 to the dollar with gold backing. All of the provisions of the program were to be instituted over the course of a three-year span during which Warsaw would retain the American observer and exercise restraint in foreign borrowing. In return for these sacrifices, Poland would acquire a loan from the Bankers Trust syndicate of roughly $60 million intended principally to augment the gold reserves of the Bank Polski. On May 21 Strong informed Ciechanowski of his qualified acceptance of the design, noting only some misgivings that the position of the adviser lacked the full measure of proper jurisdiction.[63]

The governor then made an unsuccessful last try to enroll Clarence Dillon in the stabilization combine. Without consulting the bankers, Strong extended a personal invitation to Dillon to share in the loan. Out of pride, the erstwhile banker of Poland refused to take a back seat to the usurping Bankers Trust or make common cause with his bitter rival Blair and Co. Dillon, Read and Poland parted company after two years of uneasy association.[64]

On June 2 the Bank Polski formally adopted the plan, and four days later the Federal Reserve Board endorsed without controversy Strong's application to organize a short-term international central bank credit of $20 million for Poland, authorizing the Reserve Bank to commit as much as $10 million of its own funds to the venture. On June 7 Strong enlisted Moreau to assist in bringing the other European banks of issue into the fold, invoking—with unintentional irony—the maxim of central bank unity on behalf of the most divisive problem yet to confront the system.[65] The Reichsbank and the Bank of England received the most attention, for now that the Federal Reserve Bank had won its power play Strong badly wanted his beaten foes to take part and thereby legitimate his insurgency. Schacht already had obtained instructions in the matter from the Wilhelmstrasse, which wished to retain financial leverage on Poland and worried that repudiation of the credit might place Germany in a poor light and expose Schacht to the risk of isolation among his foreign peers. Stresemann decided that the Reichsbank must join in the central bank operation but that no German capital should share in the associated private loan engineered by Bankers Trust.[66] Norman climbed grudgingly on board once assured of Schacht's company, and the smaller banks automatically fell into line behind their larger brethren.[67] By June 17 Strong and Moreau completed arrangements for the transaction, which credited the Bank Polski with $20 million for one year. Participants included thirteen European central banks plus the New York Federal Reserve, whose donation of $5.25 million topped the list of contributors.

While Strong and Moreau prepared the central banks for their role, the Bankers Trust-Blair negotiating unit shifted to Warsaw to clinch the technical aspects of the contract and obtain the final consent of the Polish government. Foreseen as an anticlimactic settling of formalities, the end game lasted four more months and barely avoided stalemate. Monnet and his colleagues established headquarters at the Hotel Europejski, where they met frequently with a Polish deputation headed by Bartel, Czechowicz, and Stanisław Karpiński, president of the Bank Polski. These encounters soon came to resemble shadowboxing, for the crucial activity on the Polish side was taking place at the Belvedere palace, where Piłsudski painstakingly scrutinized the draft that had emerged from Paris. Młynarski and the Bank Polski had accepted the stabilization plan and the terms of the Bankers Trust loan, but as yet the prime minister hesitated to commit the Polish state. The parleys entered another period of suspense while the Marshal took his time deciding whether to ratify the action of the central bank.[68]

Piłsudski's principal reservations stemmed predictably from the provisions of oversight vouchsafed the American adviser. The agreement deemed too feeble by the Federal Reserve Bank offended Piłsudski as too strong. The delay embarrassed the representatives of the Bank Polski, who privately admitted the cogency of the bankers' arguments and recognized that the objections of the premier owed more to considerations of prestige than of business. Asking patience of Monnet, Młynarski clumsily explained that "as a dictator, Piłsudski could not agree to foreign control of his economy."[69] The negotiations seemed headed for another crisis, for Bankers Trust had forbidden its agents to grant further concessions on the powers of the observer, but at length Warsaw gave way. After receiving assurances that the Americans regarded the controls essentially as window dressing to catch the eye of cautious investors, Piłsudski examined the plan "word by word" for two days and finally gave assent on June 14. Mościcki and the cabinet confirmed the decision as a matter of course, and the road to agreement on the stabilization loan appeared clear at last.[70]

At this stage the bankers chose to interrupt the discussions for tactical reasons. The New York capital market was temporarily engorged with foreign securities, and the advent of the slack summer trading season held out little hope for an immediate increase in buyer receptivity. These factors aside, the assassination in Warsaw on June 7 of the Soviet envoy to Poland, Piotr Voikov, provoked a sudden crisis of relations with Moscow and gave unwelcome publicity to the latent political risk inherent in Polish bonds. Faced with this distinctly bearish climate, Bankers Trust elected to postpone conclusion and issue of the loan until autumn.[71] To forestall speculation that this latest snag betokened cancellation of the transaction, the bankers resorted to the sham of granting a superfluous short-term credit of $15 million as an advance on the larger operation. Piłsudski and the cabinet played along with the charade and approved the credit on July 6 in order to show the public of both countries a sign that the partnership of Poland and Bankers Trust was well on its way toward consolidation. Leaving only the financial details of the contract uncompleted, the banking representatives left Warsaw to await the fall.[72]

The stratagem of the bankers afforded time to prepare the ground for the loan before its release. The extension proved advantageous in the United States. Warsaw retained a noted publicity agent, Ivy Lee, to orchestrate an American press and advertising campaign to stimulate demand, and by September Wall Street opinion showed a moderately rosy outlook on Poland.[73] On the other hand, prospects in Europe failed to improve, particularly in the crucial markets of Germany and England. In Berlin, Schacht thwarted Strong's overtures to German investors, and the Foreign Ministry encouraged its missions to work against the success of the loan in small ways. Nor could British finance generate much enthusiasm for the Bankers Trust enterprise. The City of London still pined for the League of Nations, and the replacement of Geneva with the untested American mechanism reduced the already limited appetite of English capital for Poland.[74]

On September 23 the Bankers Trust delegation returned to Warsaw to dispose of the financial conditions of the loan. With the tender subject of control settled, Monnet and Fischer expected speedy agreement, but their judgment underestimated Piłsudski's tenacity and prickly sense of national honor. The bankers quoted an interest rate of 8 percent; for the sake of prestige Piłsudski demanded reduction by a point to equal the terms of the Belgian and German stabilization loans. The two sides debated the issue for several days without progress. After conferring with Bartel, Piłsudski decided to gamble and present the visitors with an ultimatum: "either agree to 7 percent or leave." The showdown took place in a face-to-face meeting with Monnet and his entourage, who offered to compromise at 7.5 percent. The Marshal vehemently refused, and the bankers made to depart. Changing tone abruptly, Piłsudski bade them stay, cheerfully imploring them to "let me have half a point for [my daughter] Wanda." With the tension broken, Piłsudski wheedled his way to 7 percent in return for some minor technical concessions.[75]

The tug of war over the interest rate only served as a prelude to the last of the seemingly endless string of deadlocks produced by the negotiations for the stabilization plan and loan. The discord this time centered on the issue price of the bonds, which Bankers Trust set at 90 percent of face value. The Poles objected, once more claiming entitlement to the same conditions given Germany in the Dawes loan of 1924 and correctly citing a preliminary quotation by the consortium of 92. The bankers replied that a recent sag in the bond market dictated the lower price; unsatisfied, Piłsudski "flatly refused" to step below 92. Warsaw broke off the talks on September 29, and once more Monnet and his fellows threatened to leave town. In the end, however, they chose to stay and try to iron out the problem rather than complete the rupture with their departure.[76]

The latest Polish demands exasperated both the bankers and the Federal Reserve Banks as unreasonable and unbusinesslike. The home office of Bankers Trust worried that even 90 was a risky price under prevailing market circumstances, a judgment Strong shared completely; to Harrison, "the whole thing [was] in a jolly good mess" and testified to a disheartening Polish "ineptness" and lack of sensitivity to the legitimate requirements of American investors. The negotiators for the banks likewise attributed Warsaw's stance to ignorance of the facts of financial life and adopted a tutorial pose in their sessions with the Poles, administering basic "lessons in economics and especially in the technique of placing a loan of this nature on the New York market."[77]

The bankers' patronizing justifications of the lower emission price failed to move Belvedere because they missed the core of the Polish objections. As Czechowicz frankly admitted to them, the government granted the strength of their arguments from a purely commercial standpoint but declined to yield for reasons of "dignity." More to the point, the advantage of negotiation had shifted to Warsaw. Always before in her dealings with American capital Poland had acted the supplicant, incapable of driving a sharp bargain for fear of losing the infrequent customer; now for the first time the tables had turned. One step away from a contract that would gain a major new client and open an untapped and potentially significant field of investment, the Americans desired more to lend than the Poles desired to borrow. Convinced that his country would prosper no matter the fate of the loan, Piłsudski possessed freedom to dicker without the nagging dread of economic breakdown that had inhibited Grabski. As for the possible domestic repercussions of the defection of Bankers Trust, the prime minister contended he could "make political capital either way" by posing as opener of the vaults of the West or as stalwart defender of national honor. On the other hand, Bankers Trust had been hooked, and its agents pleaded with headquarters in New York for some last concession that would nail down the elusive deal.[78]

Bankers Trust held firm and the war of wills continued through the first week of October. In the interim Warsaw hopped with activity as various figures tried to push events in one direction or another. The French ambassador, Jules Laroche, lobbied the MSZ in favor of the bankers' proposal, while the British minister, Sir William Max Muller, countered him in hopes that a League of Nations scheme would take its place. Rumors alleged that Piłsudski's immovability had driven Czechowicz to the brink of resignation. The imminent and irrevocable collapse of negotiations was widely predicted.[79]

The breakthrough arrived on October 8. After consulting with Monnet, Młynarski persuaded Czechowicz to present the bankers with a counterproposal to raise the issue price to 92 in exchange for a contraction of the period of amortization from thirty to twenty years.[80] Monnet and Fischer forwarded the formula to New York with their endorsement, and the syndicate responded with approval on October 10. The Polish government hurriedly reviewed the compromise, and the next day the cabinet adopted the motion and announced its final acceptance of the loan and the plan for financial reform of which it was an element.[81] After more than two years of laborious haggling enmeshing the Polish authorities with a host of fractious partners—American bankers, central bankers, the Kemmerer commission, and four foreign governments—the stabilization program at last had come to realization.

The formal signature of the contract took place on October 13, and Monnet and his associates discovered that Piłsudski had yet one more surprise in store for them. Following the ceremony the Marshal handed the bankers a note embodying his demands for numerous restrictions on the involvement of the plan's American adviser in Polish domestic life. Among other points, Piłsudski stipulated that the observer should:

> refrain from reading Polish and German newspapers. . . . In this way the Adviser will avoid poor and erroneous information. . . . Furthermore, I desire that the Adviser should endeavor to avoid mixing to any extent in the internal affairs of the State by coming to the defense of any party or clique, and that in the realm of economy and finance he should never come into opposition to the Minister of Finance and the President of the Cabinet.

The document amounted to a request that the overseer would exist as a virtual figurehead bereft of any real authority to enforce his will and that of the banking group on the economic practices of the debtor country. The foreigners were "astounded and indignant" at Piłsudski's performance, but with the hard-earned covenant already in hand they swallowed their vexation and promised to select a "responsible man and give him instructions to attend only to the implementaiton of the stabilization plan and not to meddle in other matters."[82]

The accord reached on October 13 called for a loan of $62 million at 7 percent interest payable in 1947, of which $47 million would originate in the United States. Bankers Trust and Chase assumed the tasks of fiscal agents in liaison with Blair and Guaranty Trust. A separate but related English issue of £2 million placed through Lazard Bros. and Co. brought the total of the transaction to $71.7 million, by far the largest loan ever granted interwar Poland. The agreement earmarked roughly two-thirds of this sum for strengthening of the złoty, freeing most of the balance for investment. Simultaneously the central bank credit of $20 million went into effect, further bolstering the reserves of the Bank Polski. On the same day Mościcki promulgated a pair of decrees bringing the stabilization plan into force and officially adopting the gold standard and pegging the currency at the prescribed 8.9 to the dollar. Robust in fact for longer than a year, the złoty was now certified as healthy in name as well.[83]

Foreign reaction to the news from Poland covered a broad range of sentiment. American commentators predictably applauded the loan for the same reasons that had prompted U.S. sponsorship of the undertaking: the encouragement of European reconstruction, the expansion of American exports and economic sway, the creation of a barrier against the spread of radicalism.[84] Not all onlookers shared the enthusiasm of the Americans. Opinion in Germany feared that the agreement might hurt German business through the diversion of foreign investments to a more attractive Poland or embolden the Poles to take a harder diplomatic line toward Berlin. For his part, Norman could not bring himself to believe in the ability of the American plan to satisfy investors without the respected trademark of a League of Nations guarantee. As he wrote to Strong, "I think the Prospectus reads very well. . . . But what you are up against . . . is *feeling*—deep-rooted: to which figures are an inadequate answer." Despite its discontent, the Bank of England took defeat gracefully and declared its readiness to contribute to the success of the program.[85]

Within Poland the conclusion of the loan excited much comment. A clear majority greeted the development happily. Spokesmen for the regime quickly claimed the pact as a vote of international confidence in the *Sanacja* government.[86] Business and financial circles looked forward to a stimulating influx of scarce capital from abroad while most of the press hailed the accord with Bankers Trust as not only an economic success but a tribute to Polish status in the world—a confirmation, in the words of the *Messager Polonais,* of "the elevation of our national prestige, of the rank Poland occupies among the nations."[87] Even Grabski, who had expended much ink in condemnation of the loan throughout the past year, embraced the stabilization plan in its final form as a vindication of his own philosophies of relations with foreign finance.[88]

An outnumbered but vocal alliance of rival ends of the political spectrum dissented from the approving chorus on the grounds that the government had conceded too much to the bankers. The shrillest opposition came from the rightist National Democrats, who berated Piłsudski for striking essentially the same bargain they had urged on his predecessors before the coup. On the other side of the aisle, the Socialists moderated their initial criticisms in expectation that the loan would provide indirect benefits to labor. As details of the stabilization plan became public, the terms of the contract—especially the weak but symbolically sovereign American adviser—provoked a partial backlash against the loan and aggravated the customary suspicion of the Polish left for alien capital. The Socialist organ *Robotnik* charged that under the arrangement with Bankers Trust "practically every problem of our financial policy is potentially a matter for arbitration in which the arbiter will be a foreigner."[89]

Not only Poles commented that the conditions of the loan exacted a heavy toll of national pride. To Austen Chamberlain the deal constituted "hard terms" for the borrowers, and an officer of the Auswärtiges Amt sneered that Poland had managed to obtain the loan only at the cost of "partial renunciation of her financial independence."[90] To some extent, the Poles indeed had taken a loss on monetary clauses in order to avoid the potential dangers of submission to a League of Nations framework. Even Strong and Monnet, the architects of the American plan, concurred in the view of Norman that Warsaw could have negotiated a cheaper package through Geneva if not for its insurmountable political objections to League oversight. Taken as a whole, said a leading Swedish banker to a Polish diplomat, "the conditions of the loan are so burdensome" that he could not understand "how [your] government could agree to them." By the same token, he went on, the familiar and largely intrinsic impediments to Poland's credit were so formidable that the deal probably represented the best attainable.[91]

This statement contained much truth and, in fact, judgment of the severity of the loan depended on the standard chosen as the basis of measurement. Certainly when contrasted to the conditions of contemporaneous American transactions with Germany and Western Europe—countries with established credit, solid reputations, and uncontested frontiers—the Polish loan of 1927 took on an aspect of costliness and rigor. Lacking these advantages, Poland paid more for her money in accordance with the rules of the capital market game.[92] On the positive side of the ledger, the financial sections of the Bankers Trust contract significantly bettered those of the Dillon, Read issue of 1925. Furthermore, when matched against previous European stabilization schemes the Polish plan ranked among the more lenient, particularly in the relative weakness of its supervisory authority. Considering their handicaps and the naturally stringent nature of loans designed for stabilization of currencies deemed feeble, the Poles did well for themselves.[93]

That the terms of the deal emerged relatively favorable for the Polish side owed largely to the work of Marshal Piłsudski, whose innocence of economics and banking had not prevented him from wringing a series of concessions from Bankers Trust. Occupied until the spring of 1927 with other official business, Piłsudski took personal command of the management of the bargaining in its later stages. Ciechanowski and Młynarski had tended to defer to the bankers, but the prime minister adopted an aggressive style of negotiation which did not shrink from unorthodox and occasionally shifty methods. His deft and characteristic oscillation between ultimata and charm kept the bankers off balance and on the defensive, and by calculating and shrewdly capitalizing on their eagerness to close the deal he won capitulations on the contested points of issue price, interest rate, and the extent of foreign control—the visible matters of prestige that were his principal concern. Piłsudski savored his cat-and-mouse game with a worthy opponent like Monnet;[94] free of the paralyzing fear that his economy would collapse without the largesse of Bankers Trust, he could afford to take the chances that appealed to this lifelong political gambler, and his audacity paid dividends. In many ways the loan negotiations posed the first meaningful test of Piłsudski's diplomatic abilities since his seizure of state power, and he passed the challenge in impressive fashion.

The Polish stabilization project also marked a turning point in the course of interwar finance. In the first place it was, as contemporaries recognized, the "first such operation to be realized under distinctively American leadership in all of its phases."[95] Ultimately traceable to the ambition of Benjamin Strong, the effort generated durable tensions among his foreign peers. The Polish issue disrupted the traditional partnership between the Federal Reserve Bank and the Bank of England, overturned Norman's preference for achieving European stabilization through the agency of the League of Nations and hastened the end of the central bankers' collegial and harmonious approach to currency salvage operations. Following on the Polish precedent, the Banque de France assumed the lead in stabilizing the Romanian leu in a fashion similarly distasteful to the Bank of England.[96]

Inside the country most intimately affected by it, the Polish stabilization plan stirred high and even extravagant hopes in many quarters. Judged by most criteria, Poland did not need a stabilization loan in 1927. The national economy was flourishing, and the złoty required no buttressing from outside to maintain its balance. In a strict sense, Mościcki's objection to the program as superfluous contained much validity, but concern for the złoty played no part in the decision to enact the plan. As viewed from the Polish perspective, the true utility of the loan lay not in its immediate effects but in its promise of future benefits. By engaging the stabilization plan and its attendant obligations, Warsaw wished to capture the attention and elusive confidence of foreign investors in emulation of the example set by Germany in 1924. The Poles regarded the Bankers Trust loan as the long-awaited entry into the elite circle of borrowers that would lead to the replenishment of their meager stocks of capital and ensure development and prosperity.[97] Nor did they limit their aspirations to economic aims. Many picked up the theme Ciechanowski had emphasized from the outset of his deliberations with Strong in 1926: that the forging of a link with the financial might of the United States would increase the political and diplomatic stature of Poland as well. A Polish treasury official who had acted as a principal in the springtime negotiations in Paris predicted that the realization of the stabilization plan left "nothing to prevent Poland from becoming a truly great country."[98] Only the passage of time would prove the accuracy of this forecast and reveal whether the value of the American loan justified its cost and the effort expended in its accomplishment.

CHAPTER VI

The Failure of
Stabilization, 1927–1930

When you decide to take a foreign loan, you must not imagine that you will get it because of your good looks, but because it lies in the interest of the creditors, and you must expect them to wish to capitalize. But it is necessary to enlarge the scope of our independence and avoid subjection to the creditors: the Government is a party to the transaction, so the Government has its rights as well.

Józef Piłsudski, June 8, 1929

With the engagement of the stabilization loan of 1927 under American patronage Poland appeared at last on the brink of realization of her aspiration of breaking into the front ranks of capital-importing countries. The expectation prevailed at home and abroad that the contract with the Bankers Trust consortium marked the inauguration of a wave of foreign investment in the country. In the flush of the moment, no less a source than Jean Monnet rhapsodized that "the cash boxes of the world are now opened to Poland . . . and [she] will be able to get as many loans as she wishes."[1] Such rosy forecasts rested on the assumption that Wall Street would continue to buy into Europe at the unprecedented rate of the past three years; unfortunately for Polish hopes, a more accurate augury of the future lay in the contemporaneous warnings of Parker Gilbert and the State Department that Germany had reached the point of saturation in foreign loans.[2] The great boom of American overseas investment had begun to play out just when the Poles seemed next in line to reap its rewards. Instead of cementing the financial partnership between Warsaw and New York, the three-year period of execution of the stabilization plan observed the blighting of the economic relationship whose expansion had been a central aim of Polish policy since 1924.

The plan unfolded smoothly through its first weeks. The 7 percent bond opened to subscription on October 18, 1927 and sold out its American quota within two weeks. The issue also showed strength on the French market. Midway through November the Bank Polski proclaimed that the sudden influx of foreign exchange had rendered the Polish gold reserve proportionately the largest in the world, a phenomenal 111 percent of coverage for each paper złoty. A bevy of intrigued American and European bankers, "all with their noses to the wind," flocked to Poland to explore her commercial possibilities in light of the successful debut of the Bankers Trust loan.[3]

While the Polish stabilization drive started strongly in his absence, the nominee for the post of American adviser to the Bank Polski made preparations for his extended residency in Warsaw. The selection of a suitable financial overseer for Poland had posed a thorny problem for Strong. The Reserve Bank had ruled out the natural candidate, Edwin Kemmerer, for the reason that an experienced banker would inspire more confidence among investors than an academic.[4] After some hesitation the choice fell on Charles S. Dewey, an assistant secretary of the treasury and former vice-president of the North Trust Co. of Chicago. Dewey had monitored the evolution of the Polish stabilization initiative from his perch in Washington and began to lobby strenuously for appointment as financial adviser to Poland practically from the moment the outlines of the plan took definite shape in the summer of 1927.[5] Strong disputed the volunteer's qualifications, citing his unfamiliarity with European conditions, but Dewey persisted and enrolled his chief, Secretary Mellon, as his sponsor. In the end Dewey won the job nearly by default as other contenders removed themselves from consideration for the remote and largely ceremonial office. Strong reluctantly settled for Dewey in September, and in October the Poles announced the identity of their American financial supervisor for the coming three years.[6]

The post for which Dewey had fought so hotly had been tailored carefully to combine high visibility with a minimum of true authority. At the insistence of Warsaw the American bankers had agreed during the course of the loan negotiations that the adviser would serve essentially as a token to reassure the buying public. Forced to relinquish his Treasury connection and accountable ultimately to the Bank Polski, Dewey possessed scarcely more than recommendatory powers over Polish fiscal and borrowing practices, and both his new employers and the Federal Reserve Bank expressly admonished him not to trespass the bounds of his narrowly defined jurisdiction.[7]

Aside from his command over a special account designed as security for the lenders and the ability to veto certain types of loans, the American agent's principal means of leverage on Warsaw derived from his mandate to issue quarterly statements on the progress of stabilization in Poland. Even so, this right of reportage by itself endowed the observer with a potentially formidable check on Polish policies; to the extent the Poles opposed the wishes and counsel of the adviser, they ran the risk that his rebuke might damage Polish credit and negate the purpose for which his position had been created. Precisely this consideration had persuaded the bankers that their representative could protect their interests without resort to the type of formal controls intolerable to Polish sensibilities.[8] In other words, the American observer to a limited degree could make of his position what he wished, depending on his own willingness and ability to use the abbreviated powers at his disposal.

Simple in theory, the job of the financial adviser was both delicate and difficult. Suspended in a limbo between the Poles and the bankers and armed with little more than moral influence, he was expected to attract money to Poland while imposing discipline and austerity on a government for which he was a natural target of resentment. To accomplish these goals he would need to win the confidence of both of his masters—a feat requiring considerable dexterity and balance. In this situation the precise theoretical powers of the supervisor counted for less than his skills of tact and judgment.

As it happened, vanity and not diplomacy was the definitive trait of the adviser-designate. A compulsive self-promoter who craved a brilliant political career, Dewey saw himself as much more than the passive figurehead for whom the job had been molded. In the weeks before his departure, he described his function grandly as that of a "Financial Ambassador" of the United States to Poland and developed a penchant for blurring the distinction between his past affiliation with the Treasury and his impending service in Warsaw, much to the discomfort of the State Department, which winced at any suggestion of a link between the American government and the Polish stabilization program. Assistant Secretary Castle feared that Dewey's energy, ambition, and exalted conception of his task would lead to trouble, and he warned Minister Stetson to brace himself for the appearance of the newcomer.[9]

Dewey arrived in Warsaw on November 21 just as the stabilization plan encountered its first setback. After its robust opening, the 7 percent loan had sold poorly in London since the early days of November, and a sudden scare of war between Poland and Lithuania further depressed the desirability of the bond in all markets.[10] Feeling the pinch, the Bankers Trust coalition requested Poland to join in a move to maintain the prices of the loan by absorbing the excess issues. When Warsaw declined to bear a portion of what it considered the bankers' responsibility, the syndicate likewise ceased to intervene in the marketplace as of December 6. In response, quotations of the Bankers Trust loan sagged overnight from 92 to 89 and carried other Polish bonds downward with them. This episode set an inauspicious tone for the future association of Poland and the Bankers Trust group. The banks regarded the stabilization loan as a test case to use in calculation of public demand for Polish transactions, and the inability of the venture to sustain its early momentum dampened their enthusiasm for subsequent operations. At the same time, the dispute over price supports strained the tenuous accord between Warsaw and Bankers Trust and introduced into the partnership the same elements of wariness and mutual annoyance that had poisoned the Polish alliance with Dillon, Read.[11]

Dewey received a mixed reception from his Polish hosts, whose expectations of the adviser divided sharply. Optimists saw in him the catalyst of a fruitful "Americanization" of the national economy, but to the unreconciled opponents of the stabilization plan he arrived as the "New Sovereign in Poland," an offensive manifestation of outside interference in Polish affairs. However, the popular mind regarded Dewey simply as the figure responsible for luring foreign capital to Poland, and he quickly acquired the nickname *Dawaj*—"Hand it over!"—a punning reference to his supposed function as provider of money to Warsaw.[12] Governmental as well as public opinion showed ambivalence toward Dewey's presence in the country; the American observer received a lavish official welcome, but Piłsudski pointedly snubbed the agent he considered a nuisance at best and avoided him as much as possible throughout his residency.[13]

Dewey adjusted rapidly and effortlessly to his new regimen. He found Warsaw an agreeable and lively locale, and his first contacts with the state authorities convinced him that the Poles meant to honor the provisions of the stabilization program and merited the sympathetic assistance of the outside world. Like Stetson before him, he became a staunch partisan of the *Sanacja* regime as a businesslike and conservative government receptive to cooperation with American interests.[14] Persuaded of the reliability of Polish fiscal policy, he made no attempt to alter its basic course and scrupulously avoided conflict with the Finance Ministry and the Bank Polski. In fact, the work of the economic administration appeared to bore him, and he paid it little attention apart from routinely endorsing the actions of the national financial organs.[15] Dewey's passive approach to his supervisory chores both gratified the government and freed him to concentrate on pursuits more to his liking—the cultivation of Warsaw society and the promotion of the enrichment of Poland in tandem with American and European investors.

Early in his tenure Dewey decided that the Poles needed someone to manage their integration into international commerce and that he was the man for the job. The American delegate believed that the key to Polish prosperity lay in the expansion of the agricultural production of the country. While Dewey encouraged a moderate degree of industrialization, at heart he shared Kemmerer's vision of Poland as a supplier of huge amounts of raw materials to the factories of the West. Accordingly, he advised Warsaw and foreign finance alike to pump money into the agrarian sector of the economy in order to build for a mutually beneficial future. As a corollary, Dewey opposed the breakup of the large estates as a threat to the entrepreneurial capacity of the great landowners, whom he saw as the pillars of his development plan. His consistent antipathy to land reform—a chronic and sensitive issue in interwar Polish politics—confirmed the hostility of the left for the alien adviser. In the meantime he urged the Poles to embark on a crash program to increase the acreage of land under cultivation as the quickest way to stimulate production and reduce rural overpopulation, and he brimmed with suggestions ranging from wholesale deforestation to drainage of the Pripet marshes.[16]

To spur and supplement the growth of Poland into an agrarian giant, Dewey proposed a massive infusion of Western capital in the form of trade and investments. Unlike Stetson, who regarded British economic influence in Poland as inimical to U.S. business interests, he saw sufficient opportunities for all comers and dreamed of a condominium of English and American finance in the country.[17] Nor did he wish to exclude the Germans, whom he considered Poland's natural trading partners. Deploring the Polish-German tariff war as a senseless waste of a valuable commercial relationship for the sake of a petty political vendetta, Dewey used his influence in the spring of 1928 in an attempt to mediate the dispute and resolve it by compromise. Dewey's well-intentioned if ineffectual efforts at reconciliation between Warsaw and Berlin reflected both his typically American belief in the healing power of trade and his restless inability to confine himself to his prescribed duties, a quality which caused his sponsors in New York no little anxiety. Undaunted even by the taboo subject of the Pomeranian boundaries, he unofficially commended to his Polish acquaintances the wisdom of offering Germany a readjustment of the Corridor in return for economic concessions until Strong learned of his indiscretions and put a stop to them.[18]

Dewey imagined his part in swelling the trickle of foreign capital into Poland as that of broker and chief publicist for the country, bringing into play the boosterish "methods of the President of the . . . Kiwanis Club" in a campaign to build enthusiasm for his client. He adopted a straightforward and twofold approach. On the one hand he enjoined the Poles to practice the frugality and orthodoxy that Wall Street took as proof of creditworthiness; on the other, he turned his periodic reports into a forum for advertisement of Polish achievements and prospects.[19] Invariably optimistic, Dewey's pronouncements took care to place Poland in a complimentary light and to point out to his Western readers the most likely areas of profitable investment in Polish enterprises. The American observer threw himself into advocacy with such zeal that he soon came to identify completely with his hosts. Meeting with Dewey in France in the summer of 1928, Strong was dismayed "to hear him so frequently refer to Polish matters as 'our' problem or 'our' affair. He seems to consider himself just as much a Pole as though he were born there."[20]

Widely disseminated by Polish spokesmen, Dewey's first reports contributed to an emerging sense of American opinion that Poland at last had shaken off the difficulties of her infancy and entered into a period of abundance and tranquility. Added to the favorable impressions created by the enactment of the stabilization plan, Dewey's bouquets to the virtues of Piłsudskist government and the vigor of the Polish economy—taken for the moment at face value—fostered a discernible if fleeting mood of confidence in Poland. Ciechanowski informed the MSZ that the comments of the adviser evoked a "gratifying response" within the Coolidge administration, while the American press suspended its habitually somber reportage of Polish matters in favor of upbeat stories under such headlines as "Poland Definitely Stabilized, Happier and More Prosperous."[21]

Profiting from their greater attractiveness in the afterglow of the stabilization loan, the Poles obtained a series of short-term foreign municipal loans during the first semester of 1928. Two of these transactions bore American trademarks. A coalition of Boston firms signed contracts totalling $21.2 million with the city of Warsaw and the province of Silesia. Intended for the construction of public works, the bonds carried identical price tags of 7 percent.

These modest successes provided ammunition for the Polish defenders of the stabilization package and momentarily disarmed its enemies. Crowing at the expense of the "numerous" critics of Dewey and the program he represented, Czechowicz on March 11 confidently predicted to the Sejm an imminent flood of foreign money in return for the minimal sacrifices imposed on Warsaw. Other government spokesmen in the legislature followed the lead of the minister of finance, pointing to the municipalities loans as proof that "the road to the international market lies open to us."[22] Both in their public and private statements, officials of Poland and the United States alike expressed satisfaction that the stabilization loan had invigorated relations between the two countries and improved the outlook for bilateral economic intercourse. On May 17 the minister of industry and commerce, Eugeniusz Kwiatkowski, marveled to Stetson that "the results already visible of American participation in Polish affairs was (*sic*) truly astounding and exceeded anything that could possibly have been imagined a few years ago."[23]

All the same, not all observers viewed the future of ties between Poland and Wall Street with such enthusiasm. On the western shores of the Atlantic, the Bankers Trust deal of 1927 aided Polish credit but did not establish it beyond question. As the journalist Frank Simonds told the counselor of the British legation in Warsaw, the stabilization loan represented less "a sign of American confidence in Poland" than a reflection of the fact that "there was a superfluity of money in America and with superfluous money one enjoyed the privilege of a gamble."[24] While New York remained mindful of the risks of Polish business, a significant segment of opinion in Poland worried that the costs of the American connection might outweigh its advantages. A visiting financier from Warsaw confided to Moreau that "the Poles are a little uneasy at the economic influence that the Americans wield in their country," and Piłsudski harbored suspicions that the natural covetousness of the foreign bankers posed dangers to the higher moral and political interests of the nation.[25]

Despite its reservations concerning outside capital, Warsaw counted on the Bankers Trust group to provide the money necessary to finance the development of Poland and counterbalance her chronic trade deficit. During the negotiations for the 7 percent issue of 1927, the stabilization combine had avoided commitment to a definite schedule of subsequent loans; nevertheless, both the syndicate and the Poles expected the partnership to endure and produce further transactions insofar "as the American market could absorb them." The coalition had adopted Poland as a permanent client, claiming general rights of priority in Polish credit operations in the United States, and sketched its intention to stake the building of railroads and other public works. With good reason, Warsaw interpreted these statements as the equivalent of a pledge "that the bankers would give other loans at fairly regular intervals"—in fact, this understanding alone had persuaded Poland to assume the obligations of the stabilization plan. In addition to the projected series of construction loans, which it took for granted, the government entertained hopes that Bankers Trust might capitalize such enterprises as the exploitation of Silesian mineral resources.[26]

The anticipated torrent of dollars into Poland never materialized. Among the variety of causes of this unwelcome result was simple bad luck: the fact that the great bull market in American foreign lending had run its course by the spring of 1928. The year of the Polish stabilization loan marked the high point both of the postwar European economic recovery and of the exodus of American money to the Old World. The wave of general prosperity had borne Eastern and Central Europe on its crest, and not only Poland but several other countries in the region received an unprecedented degree of attention from Wall Street in 1927. At that moment buyers began to pull out of the crowded international field in favor of the lures of the stock exchange. Fearful that a continuation of the breakneck pace of lending abroad might deplete American gold supplies, Strong and the Federal Reserve increased the cost of money in order to reduce the volume of loans and discourage stock speculation. Predictably, during the second half of 1928 levels of foreign lending in New York plunged 42 percent from the standards of the previous year.[27] In a tighter market, the countries most likely to be left out in the cold on Wall Street were those that—like Poland—lacked credit of long standing and a deep reserve of buyer confidence.

The exertions of the governor of the Federal Reserve Bank to redirect American entrepreneurial energies inward also reflected his waning interest in the cause of European stabilization. His health failing, Strong had come to believe by 1928 that the intervention of the Reserve Bank in the outside world had accomplished its goal and that the time had come "to keep out of any complications of the sort which the European banks of issue are likely to encounter."[28] He drafted a similarly narrow definition of his obligations to Poland, the foremost beneficiary of his activist phase of the recent past. In March he told his deputy that their "moral responsibility" in the Polish case was to keep a protective eye on the Bank Polski so long as the central bank credits remained in force; upon the expiration of this account in autumn of 1928, Poland would become a matter of no special interest to the Federal Reserve. In contrast to his expansive mood of 1926, Strong advised his friend Ciechanowski in

August not to "look on America as [Warsaw's] sole source of capital," counseling the Poles to align themselves with "the French market, which . . . in the near future might become the best natural loan market for Poland."[29] This constituted Strong's last word on Poland; within two months he was dead, and Harrison had assumed management of the Reserve Bank.

As always, Polish credit in the United States suffered from memories of internal turmoil and apprehension of international complications. Even in the relatively tranquil diplomatic atmosphere of 1928 the cautious world of investment regarded Polish bonds as a gambler's game. On New Year's Day of 1929 the financial counselor to the Polish mission in Washington, Aleksander Woytkiewicz, lamented that "even the intelligent American" thought of Poland as a country known for only two things:

> 1*st*, that . . . she has for the ten years of her existence struggled with problems she has not always combatted successfully; 2*nd*, that . . . she represents a population of 30 million wedged between two enemies who number, respectively, 60 million and 120–150 million, and that a collision with either of them could lead easily . . . not to her downfall—no one expects that!— but to a suspension of her payments. Therefore it is necessary to be exceedingly wary of Polish issues and, at the most, to invest only very small amounts of capital in them, but the most prudent course is to avoid Polish issues altogether.[30]

As Woytkiewicz wrote, the 7 percent stabilization loan—the bellwether of the Polish portfolio—stood at 87½ on the New York exchange, several notches below its original price of 92. Within six months the issue had slumped to 85, illustrating the weakness of Polish bonds in an inhospitable market.

The curdling of business prospects spoiled the appetite of the Bankers Trust consortium for dealings with Poland. At the outset of 1928 the stabilization group reaffirmed its willingness to underwrite a series of investment loans to its client and agreed to send a delegation to Warsaw to elaborate a program of borrowing in consultation with Polish authorities.[31] When the bankers arrived in April, Czechowicz greeted them with a shopping list amounting to $57 million in credit spread over three years. The visitors took the proposal home with them after renewing their expressions of interest in rail construction. Upon returning to New York, however, the bankers—made hesitant by tight money and the indifferent performance of the 1927 loan—proclaimed the government's package "too ambitious" and out of proportion to the meager American demand for Polish business. Pointing to the lagging sales of their first venture as proof that Warsaw had not yet established its credit in the public mind, Bankers Trust instructed the Poles to wait a few months for a more likely moment and to prepare the ground for future operations through scrupulous adherence to the stabilization plan.[32]

To appease their disappointed clients, the Americans investigated the possibilities of financing the consolidation of a multitude of Polish agrarian credit organizations into a central land bank to simplify and focus the entrance of foreign capital into the agricultural pursuits of the country. Neither party to the talks regarded the project highly: the syndicate preferred to postpone all Polish transactions until better times, and while the Poles welcomed the scheme if it prompted an injection of foreign cash, they considered the land bank vehicle deficient in intrinsic merit. Even Dewey, the champion of agricultural development, questioned the creation of the bank on the grounds that it would duplicate the functions of other credit institutions or somehow divert its resources toward smallholders and reform efforts and away from "the large landholders who really produce the exportable surplus." Dewey reversed his opinion once he realized the land bank represented Poland's only hope for a major loan, but in September Harrison and Bankers Trust informed Polish operatives that the enterprise could not thrive in the inclement market climate and that they had no choice but to put it off.[33]

The reluctance of the stabilization group to part with its money tempted the Poles to look for other sources of funding, notably their former banking agent in the United States. Despite the loss of its Polish account to Bankers Trust, Dillon, Read maintained contact with the Poles and in the fall of 1927 suggested the revival of the Warsaw rail terminal loan, which had fallen through with the rupture of their alliance at the end of 1926. Poland agreed readily and in January 1928 won permission from Bankers Trust to conclude the deal.[34] In short order the Dillon firm, with Warsaw's approval, requested admission into the stabilization combine as an equal partner. Bankers Trust accepted Dillon's candidacy for membership, but in August Blair blackballed the application of its bitterest rival within the financial world. This intrusion of cutthroat commercial politics into the workings of the consortium enraged the Poles. Woytkiewicz asked an officer of Bankers Trust:

> if he did not think that Blair's conduct would impede the group in the attainment of the goal for which it was formed, namely to fulfill the borrowing needs of Poland and to develop her credit. . . . Such a state of affairs . . . could lead to the question whether a group had the right to exist that could not fulfill the task for which it came into being.

The incident led Ciechanowski to ask Strong to contrive the ouster of Blair from the coalition in favor of Dillon. The dying chief of the Reserve Bank declined, arguing that Monnet's firm represented Poland's link to French capital and noting that Dillon could participate in some Polish business independently. Strong's reasoning prevailed, but the episode aggravated the growing suspicions of the Poles that the stabilization combine hindered more than helped their credit.[35]

Polish diplomats in the United States accorded Dewey a trust they withheld from the banks, but the American financial adviser likewise played a prominent if inadvertent part in the frustration of Poland's borrowing during the first year of his tenure. The Bankers Trust consortium never had demanded an absolute monopoly over Polish credit in America and specifically granted Warsaw license to contract with competitors for certain loans so long as Dewey affixed his imprimatur to the transactions. The handful of municipal bonds Warsaw obtained in the spring of 1928 fell into this category. Intent on exploiting this loophole to the fullest, Polish agents descended on New York hunting for similar opportunities in a haphazard and uncoordinated manner reminiscent of the period of hyperinflation.[36] This scattershot approach displeased Dewey, who agreed with the Reserve Bank that Poland should seek only issues "of first quality, handled through first grade concerns" and worried that "the constant appearance of these small loans every two or three months" might jeopardize her chances to win greater prizes on Wall Street. The adviser accordingly used his influence to curb Warsaw and compel it to give up fishing for financial small fry. Dewey believed the imposition of this discipline served the credit interests of his clients in the long run, but his Polish detractors charged, with some justice, that the effect of his policy was to deny Poland the only money available to her for the sake of hypothetical and increasingly uncertain benefits in the future.[37]

The stagnation of Polish business in New York began to trouble Dewey during the later stages of 1928. In September he persuaded the Federal Reserve Bank to arrange renewal of the $20 million central bank credit to the Bank Polski for another year, not because he doubted the strength of the złoty but solely to appease a Polish public made impatient for results of the stabilization plan. At the same time he urged the American banking group to chart a definite program of lending to Poland even if the time to act was not at hand. Along with Harrison, Dewey trusted that the credit market would rebound within a few months and rekindle interest in Polish bonds, and he hoped to make the best of the slump by laying the groundwork in anticipation of the recovery.[38]

In an attempt to break the impasse Warsaw turned once more to Dillon, Read and the rail terminal loan. Responding to Polish overtures, Dillon offered in October to bankroll the project through release of the remainder of the 8 percent bond of 1925. The proposal intrigued the Poles not only for its own virtues but also as a way to thumb their noses at the Bankers Trust syndicate. However, the negotiations never reached beyond preliminaries. Talks with Dillon's lieutenants revealed that the terms of an agreement inevitably would reflect the depressed condition of the securities market; furthermore, Woytkiewicz warned that even a loan bearing steep interest might prove a "disaster" and end only by inflicting more damage on Polish credit in the United States. In view of these unappealing prospects, Warsaw broke off the dalliance with Dillon in the early days of the new year.[39] Although nothing resulted from the discussions on the Warsaw rail terminal, they represented a milestone of sorts as the final serious attempt to resume business relations between Poland and her first American banker. After a stormy four-year relationship that produced but one loan, Dillon, Read passed out of Polish affairs for the last time.

The inability of the stabilization plan to swell Polish coffers with meaningful amounts of foreign capital disappointed the Poles and distressed the *Sanacja* regime, all the more for its contribution to a general national economic slowdown. The frustration of Polish credit expectations invalidated a vital assumption underlying fiscal policy and produced in the country—in the words of Stetson—"a shortage of money which verges on a crisis." Aside from its concrete effects, the borrowing drought embarrassed the government and played into the hands of its domestic antagonists. Official spokesmen publicly upheld the line that the dry spell was no more than a temporary setback, but these wan assertions failed to impress the critics of the stabilization scheme, who scorned them as unconvincing justifications of a miscarried policy. Attacks on the crippled plan began to appear with greater frequency in the newspapers and parliamentary statements of the opposition. Originally hailed as a triumph by a clear majority of Polish opinion, the stabilization loan had become a source of reproach against the government in the space of a year.[40]

In the meantime, the visible symbol of American financial influence in Poland had established himself as a conspicuous presence in the country. Dewey's routine mixed business with large measures of recreation: his residence at the Sobański palace became a fixture of the social circuit in the Polish capital, and he grew so fond of one of the city's restaurants that he expressed interest in buying it.[41] During his working hours Dewey became a constant irritant to the American diplomatic mission through his incessant upstaging of the legation. He stayed continually in the spotlight by means of interviews and public appearances and used his access to official circles to curry favor with his hosts and gradually eclipse Stetson in their eyes as the chief representative of the United States. The disgruntled American minister in turn complained to the State Department that Dewey was not only frivolous and meddlesome but ineffective, alleging—with but slight overstatement—that he had allowed the Poles to capture and turn him into a glorified propagandist whose rosy pronouncements no one took seriously outside Poland.[42]

Dewey's essential aim—to enhance Polish credit through his optimistic reports—remained the same, but the passage of time altered some of his opinions and led him to branch out into new activities. In particular, his deepening fondness for the Poles caused him to abandon neutrality in their chronic feud with Germany. The adviser still hoped for the achievement of a trade treaty that would provide an outlet for Polish foodstuffs and raw materials and perhaps even "help in due time solve other questions pertaining to frontiers," but by the close of 1928 he concluded that the trade war was a deliberate German provocation cloaking a campaign of diplomatic aggression in economic guise. Like Kemmerer before him, Dewey took umbrage at the treatment accorded him by the German press and decided that Berlin harbored improper political designs against Warsaw.[43] In response, he began to use his position to promote Polish independence of German economic influence that might be translated into a means of diplomatic pressure. He lent support to a nationalist drive to boycott imported luxury items—a move directed primarily against German goods—and angered Berlin by publicly refuting its case in the commercial treaty controversy.[44]

As he grew disenchanted with Germany, Dewey turned to investigate Poland's neighbor to the east. The potential of the enormous and largely untapped market of Russia fascinated many American traders in the later years of the postwar decade. More than one entrepreneur had followed the lead of Baldwin Locomotive and acquired an interest in Poland as a stepping-stone to eventual entry into the Soviet Union, and from time to time Polish representatives employed their adjacency to Russia as their trump card in enticing American capital to their own country.[45] Inspired both by curiosity to inspect the Soviet experiment and a sense of being the eyes and ears of U.S. finance in Eastern Europe, Dewey arranged to visit Moscow for several days in November 1928. The adviser's private junket irked Stetson. Dewey neglected to clear his trip with the legation, and the circumstances of the journey stirred a rash of embarrassing speculation among Poles—rumors fed by his own habitual exaggeration of his intimacy with the elite of Washington—that Herbert Hoover, then president-elect, had entrusted him with a secret mission to open lines of direct communication with the Bolshevik state.[46]

His Moscow itinerary consisted of little more than a few uneventful interviews with lesser Soviet bureaucrats, but he saw enough to excite his imagination. Upon his return to Warsaw Dewey related to a British diplomat that "his strong personal desire was that England and America should work together in Poland and should eventually through Poland enter Russia" and confessed his dream of establishing a holding company composed of English, American, and Polish capital in equal shares to operate in Poland "with a view to the Russian market in the future."[47] Nothing came of this reverie, but the idea of developing Poland as a gateway to the vast hinterlands to her south and east stuck in Dewey's mind and became a central element of his vision for the enrichment of the country.

In January 1929 Dewey returned to the United States for several weeks to confer with the stabilization bankers and drum up business for Poland. He timed his expedition to coincide with the transition to the Hoover administration so that he might gain the ears of its leaders, but he succeeded only in obtaining an audience with the lame duck Coolidge. Dewey proved more fortunate in a speaking tour which took him from Washington to New York and Chicago. Much in the manner of Skrzyński in 1925, he spread the gospel of Polish achievements on the banquet circuit and lauded the country as a prime target for investors. His reassurances of Polish stability concealed his own inner qualms that the rancorous quarrel between Piłsudski and his parliamentary opponents was building to a new internal crisis, but his enthusiastic testimony to the health of the Polish economy impressed his audiences and won praise from the press that "Mr. Dewey has made good."[48]

Effective at the podium, Dewey fared worse with the bankers who comprised his essential public. During the past year his stock had declined sharply in the eyes of the stabilization group, which completely discounted his glowing reports. The bankers mocked him privately as "Pan Deweski" for his obvious affection for the Poles and dismissed him as a dilettante who uttered "nothing but superlatives" of his hosts. A meeting with the visiting agent merely confirmed the syndicate in its opinion. Dewey entered the conclave nervous and poorly prepared, and when he suggested issue of loans the bankers rejected the proposal out of hand. Dewey's shaky performance so displeased the consortium that a representative of Blair wished aloud that he could be sacked.[49] Aside from its limited publicity value, his American pilgrimage accomplished nothing. Dewey returned to Warsaw empty-handed and so lacking in credibility with the stabilization combine that his utility as a mediator between Bankers Trust and the Polish treasury had evaporated.

Other efforts to attract American capital to Poland in the early months of 1929 proved equally fruitless. Unwilling to hazard their money in a sluggish market, the stabilization bankers likewise exercised their veto power to shut out other entrants for fear that rival Polish issues would devalue the 1927 bond and ruin the chances that Bankers Trust might eventually place a successful loan. Following the precedent established with the exclusion of Dillon, Read in 1928, the group turned down a bid by Stone, Webster, and Blodgett to join the coalition for the purpose of floating the central land bank business.[50] Another aspirant for the land bank contract—Paine, Webber and Co.—dropped out of the running largely owing to exasperation with Dewey. With his customary inattention to detail the adviser had neglected to acquaint himself thoroughly with the land bank project, and Paine, Webber found him of no help in resolving the practical difficulties of a business proposition.[51]

Relations between the stabilization group and Poland deteriorated from bad to worse. For its part, the syndicate regarded its Polish account as a failed venture that was turning rapidly into a fiasco. The worldwide credit slump persisted and demand for Polish bonds continued to lag behind the expectations of 1927. In addition, the bankers grew weary of Warsaw as a nettlesome partner not worth the headaches it cost. The coalition decided that the state of the market prohibited a large Polish operation for at least another year and became irked that its clients would not concede the logic of this position. Visiting in New York in March, Stetson warned the chairman of Bankers Trust, Albert Tilney, that if he did not release a loan soon the Poles would turn to Paris for money instead; Tilney replied that "so far as he was concerned he would much prefer to see the French bankers do it." Angered at its inaction, Dewey in May sent the consortium a vehement protest against its "indifference" to Poland. This impolitic step completed the estrangement of Dewey from Bankers Trust and, if anything, further reduced the concern's interest in Polish matters. In effect, the adviser had written off the stabilization bankers as a source of assistance to Warsaw and decided that his hosts could do better looking for other benefactors.[52]

The Poles had reached the same conclusion ahead of Dewey. The basic assumption of Piłsudski's policy toward the banks had been that foreign finance was inherently an exploitative and even dangerous force, which might be permitted to operate in Poland only if held tightly in check. From its inception the *Sanacja* regime had combined deep-seated mistrust of foreign capital with grudging recognition of its essential function in the invigoration of the Polish economy. The compact of 1927 with Bankers Trust by no means signified the resolution of this philosophical conflict within the Piłsudski camp, but rather an attempt to solve the dilemma by reaping the benefits of outside investment while neutralizing its dangers. The government expected the stabilization plan to pay quick dividends, and when it did not Warsaw's instinctive reaction was to blame the banks. The accumulation of grievances against their American fiscal agents over the past months convinced the Piłsudskists that the syndicate was dealing in bad faith, and by the end of 1928 they relinquished serious hope that the combine would follow the 7 percent loan with a successor. The Poles also chafed under the restrictions of the consortium's priority clause, which they regarded as an unfair brake on their freedom to negotiate with other firms. As the usefulness of the connection with Bankers Trust shrank in Polish eyes, official attention focused less on maintaining good relations with the group than on circumventing the "banker-sharks" to hunt for funds elsewhere.[53]

Marshal Piłsudski had made the decision to commit Poland to the stabilization plan, and his disenchantment with the program likewise inclined the government to allow the alliance with Bankers Trust to lapse. Gradually the Polish strongman's apprehensions of the alien observer and the domineering intent of the consortium overcame his appetite for American capital, and his imagination conjured threats where none existed. Dewey never won his confidence, and Piłsudski criticized as unduly gloomy the advisory reports that struck American financiers as impossibly optimistic. He also worried that Dewey wished to "unite Poland with Germany in an economic sense," a goal directly contrary to the revised intentions of the adviser. As for the banks, the Marshal fancied that they sought to take control over the national purse strings when in fact the consortium would have preferred to wash its hands of the Poles.[54]

Piłsudski's displeasure with the stabilization experiment swung the balance in governmental circles toward those elements which had opposed the plan from the beginning as an intolerable insult to Polish sovereignty. As in 1927, President Mościcki championed this view. In the spring of 1929 Jean Monnet attempted to organize a European loan for the central land bank under the leadership of Blair, and when the arrangements neared completion in June Mościcki intervened to spike the deal. Arguing that Warsaw should offer the contract instead to an interested Italian firm, the president contended that to perpetuate the link with the Bankers Trust coalition would risk falling into "financial slavery to the [stabilization] group." His warnings against monopolization by the Americans struck a responsive chord. With resentment against the syndicate running high, the cabinet agreed to reject the Blair proposal, and this time Piłsudski did not override Mościcki as in 1927.[55] After two years of unhappy experience with the stabilization plan, Warsaw had turned its back both on the Bankers Trust consortium and, by extension, the idea of a predominant role for American capital in the development of Poland.

With fitting symbolism, the unraveling of the Polish liaison with the American bankers coincided with and probably precipitated the ouster of Jan Ciechanowski as minister to the United States. Ciechanowski's job had hung by a thread since the coup of 1926, but so long as Warsaw nourished aspirations on Wall Street his excellent connections in Washington and New York made his presence in America indispensable. When this justification for his retention vanished, Piłsudski purged the envoy whom he accounted a personal and political foe of long standing. Late in 1928 the Marshal ordered the Foreign Ministry to recall Ciechanowski on the grounds that "he was to blame for our credit difficulties in the United States and payment of usurious interest." The MSZ opposed the move, but in January 1929 Ciechanowski was compelled to step down.[56]

The Washington appointment went in turn to Tytus Filipowicz, a well-traveled diplomat of decidedly modest talents, as a reward for his long allegiance to Piłsudski. The distinguishing characteristic of Ciechanowski's successor was his indolence, and Zaleski privately considered him incompetent to fill his new post, but Filipowicz desired and obtained the honor as the culmination of his lengthy career.[57] Aside from its other effects, the selection of a loyal mediocrity for the Washington vacancy clearly reflected the low priority Piłsudski assigned to Polish relations with the United States.

As Warsaw quietly allowed its ties with Bankers Trust to fall into disrepair, the forces of the Polish opposition sharpened their attack on the government for its foreign financial policies. The parliamentary foes of Piłsudski ascribed the failure of Polish credit to the shortcomings of *Sanacja* and the stabilization program it had accepted. As the embodiment of the plan, Dewey became a prime target of abuse. Mention of his name in the Sejm prompted derision from the opposition benches, and a peasant deputy lampooned him as less an adviser than a "financial watchman, for he sits here and stands guard over the Polish economy, fearing that somehow that 70 million dollars might get lost." Socialist Herman Diamand called the regime to account for the fact that Dewey "has disappointed . . . for he did not establish our credit, the building of which was his mission."[58]

Divided by personal rivalry, the principal American representatives in Warsaw united in disputing the mounting evidence that the financial collaboration foreseen in the stabilization plan had broken down irremediably. Unsettled by indications that the Poles were switching their attention to English and Italian capital markets, Stetson in May assured Premier Kazimierz Świtalski that Polish misfortunes on Wall Street were temporary. Even the relentlessly hopeful Dewey acknowledged that Poland had slid from prosperity into a phase of recession, but true to form he professed to spy a hidden advantage in the economic decline. Reasoning that the slump would compel Warsaw to practice frugality and offer tempting concessions to foreign creditors, he argued that Poland would cut a good figure in New York once buyers tired of stocks and shifted back to overseas enterprise. In the summer he told his parents that "Poland is now on the verge of real popularity" with American investors.[59]

As before, Dewey's forecast substituted hope for reality. Not only loans but all types of economic contact with the United States failed to match, let alone surpass, the standards of 1927. Hobbled by poor organization, uncompetitive pricing and a bad reputation as unreliable businessmen, Polish exporters found the American market an unprofitable locale. U.S. demand for a limited range of Polish products—mainly foodstuffs and raw materials—remained at token levels, and as Polish imports from the New World climbed, Warsaw's balance of trade with the Americans grew outlandishly lopsided. Excepting commerce handled through German middlemen, in 1928 Poland sold $2.1 million of goods to the United States, or roughly 4 percent of her purchases in America.[60]

Direct American investment in Polish enterprises also fell short of the predictions of the architects of the stabilization package. In 1929 foreigners controlled approximately 20 percent of Polish industry. American holdings in Poland ranked third behind French and German properties and clustered in the mining and petroleum fields. If subordinate, the U.S. share in Poland was strategic: American interests dominated zinc and steel production within the country and figured heavily in the extraction of oil and coal.[61] American participation in Polish industry registered a nominal rise in the period following stabilization but for a variety of reasons never achieved the commanding position that Dewey and Stetson, among others, had prophesied and encouraged. While Poland offered buyers the attractions of abundant natural resources and cheap labor, these attributes were negated by the turn toward tighter money in the United States and the perpetual deterrent fear that any Polish ventures depended in the end on the fragile diplomatic and political tranquility of Eastern Europe.

While these impediments to American investment lay outside Warsaw's control, the policies and tendencies of the Sanacja government also dissuaded outside capital despite the outwardly welcoming posture of the authorities. Not a few financiers avoided Poland out of distaste for her advanced labor legislation and bewilderment at her complex and jerry-built tax structure. Suspicious of foreign enterprise, the Piłsudskists adhered as well to étatist principles and professed—and exercised—the right to close supervision over alien economic activity within their boundaries. Commercial negotiations with Poland proved invariably laborious, and most entrepreneurs who finally contracted with the Poles complained afterward of "constant Government interference" in their operations through regulation, tax manipulation, and the overt application of pressure to bring company practices into harmony with official goals. Domestic political considerations often lay at the root of this harassment. Labor spokesmen hectored the regime not to allow the Americans a free hand to run factories in their accustomed and allegedly oppressive fashion, and foreign managers of Silesian industries found themselves subjected to continual and unwelcome Polish demands to abet the nationalization of the region.[62] Accustomed to broad autonomy in the management of their overseas plants, American businessmen commonly found their experiences in Poland wearisome and ultimately unsatisfactory, and their difficulties in turn discouraged other investors.

The frustrations generally encountered by American companies active in Poland showed most clearly in the case of their most prominent representative, Harriman and Co. Since his acquisition of the Giesche zinc concern in 1926, Harriman had consolidated his position in the Silesian mining industry and branched out into porcelain and steel works. He extended his Polish holdings primarily at the expense of German proprietors left over from prewar days, a development that chagrined the Wilhelmstrasse.[63]

In spite of its practical utility in reducing German ownership in Silesia, the American firm never gained the full acceptance of its Polish hosts. Persistent if unfounded rumors that Harriman was a tool of Berlin circulated widely, prompted by his heavy investment in industries of the *Reich* and the fact that his Polish possessions still bore much of the character of the old German administration. Germans sat on the board of Giesche as minority stockholders and filled many of the managerial posts in his factories. For business reasons, Giesche retained membership in an association of German producers that openly deplored Polish ascendancy in Silesia. Harriman innocently supposed that his plants could stand aloof from ethnic politics, and by choosing to stay neutral in the clash of rival nationalisms in the borderlands, he lent unwitting plausibility to the charge that his presence retarded rather than advanced the diminution of German influence in Polish Silesia.[64]

Above all, Harriman's refusal to purge German overseers from Giesche for the sake of the polonization of Silesia hampered his relations with Polish authority. Upon its entry into Poland the firm had pledged gradually to replace German supervisory personnel with Poles, but the turnover progressed too slowly to please Warsaw or the provincial governor Michał Grażyński, a zealous exponent of the Polish nationalization campaign. The Americans protested official importunities to accelerate the process as bad business, affirming—quite rightly—that the government was asking them to place political and national considerations ahead of personal merit as criteria for hiring. The manager of Giesche, G. S. Brooks, argued that he could not afford to dismiss the Germans for the reason that "today there simply are not enough trained and experienced Poles in the country to run the plants. It will be years before they can be developed." Poland refused to yield. What Harriman saw as a question of efficiency the Poles viewed, so Grażyński told Stetson, as a crucial battleground of "a hidden war [with] the German minority" in which Warsaw had no choice but to impose its will on Giesche in the name of *raison d'état*. Because it involved a fundamental clash of contradictory interests, the dispute over the polonization of the Harriman properties became a permanent sore point between the Poles and the American firm.[65]

In spite of these frictions, in 1929 Harriman launched the most ambitious undertaking ever attempted by an American corporation in interwar Poland. Since 1926 the Poles had sought to enlist a foreign firm to plan and install a system of electric power in much of the countryside. Harriman became the leading aspirant to the contract. Negotiations started in earnest in 1928, and by the spring of the next year the company submitted a scheme to electrify Silesia and southwestern Poland—one-fifth of the total area of the country including one-third of its population—at a cost of $100 million spread over the life of a concession of sixty years. The minister for public works, Jędrzej Moraczewski, received the proposal favorably as a useful stimulus to modernization that native capital could not provide. The government privately notified Harriman of its endorsement of the project in principle and during the summer took the offer under consideration for formal approval, binding itself in the meantime not to treat with competitors.[66]

While the regime deliberated the Harriman electrification concession, the measure provoked a furor of antagonism within the country from an unlikely coalition of left, right, and special interests. Socialists decried the initiative as a monopolistic invasion of foreign and private capital into a function properly belonging to the state, warning that its acceptance would make Harriman "nearly the economic dictator of Poland." The right protested the American plan as a setback to the polonization of the national economy and joined with industrialists in arguing that the task should be entrusted to Poles. All of these elements agreed that the draft proposal promised too much to Harriman in profits and tax breaks, and all expressed to varying degrees the fear that—in the words of Stetson—"the Harriman project is a purely German one, with American financial interests as mere figure heads." A few centrist voices defended the Harriman concession, but they hardly matched in number or volume the congeries of forces which found the issue a useful weapon in the sharpening partisan warfare of the day.[67]

As the opposition pounded away at the Harriman concession, second thoughts on the venture started to appear in official ranks as well.

Mościcki predictably led the fight against the electrification scheme within the inner circle, but even the proponents of the contract hedged their endorsements with mounting reservations. Most of these objections centered on financial provisions, but neither could the Piłsudskists ignore the allegations of Harriman's German sympathies. Polish opinion lent sufficient credence to these stories to make the project politically hazardous for *Sanacja*; furthermore, some members of the government themselves suspected that the Harriman company was a front for the admission of unwelcome German influence under American auspices.[68]

Nor did the conviction that the Harriman offer constituted a potential threat to Polish security depend on the belief that it was a Trojan horse. With its military cast of mind, the Piłsudski regime worried that the consolidation of so much of the economy of Silesia—a likely enemy target in any future war—into the hands of a foreign owner represented a strategic liability no matter what the loyalties of the firm. Consequently in August the War Ministry forbade the construction of any central electric station within 250 kilometers of the German border, forcing the company to redraw its blueprints.[69] Confronted with rising inner doubts and clamorous public dissent, Warsaw put off a final verdict on the electrification proposition.

The postponement of an answer to Harriman also owed much to the intensification of the Polish internal political wars, which commanded the attention of the government during the period 1929-1930. Once more the question of the competence of the regime in dealing with foreign capital played an incidental part in the polemic. Speakers in the Sejm pointed to the reticence of American lenders as evidence of the outside world's lack of confidence in Piłsudski, whose supporters retorted that blame for the country's credit predicament belonged not to *Sanacja* but to its irresponsibly defamatory critics. The simmering feud between the regime and its legislative enemies assumed the dimensions of a constitutional crisis in the summer of 1929 when the Sejm brought impeachment proceedings against Czechowicz for his refusal to answer parliamentary charges that the Piłsudskists had misappropriated state funds for partisan purposes. In making the case against the defendant—and by extension the government he stood for—one of his accusers cited the low quotations of Polish bonds in New York as refutation of the assertion by the erstwhile minister that his administration had stabilized national finances.[70]

Responding to his opponents in kind, Piłsudski prepared for a showdown and threw down the gauntlet by packing successive cabinets with his military protégés, the so-called "Colonels"; their advent reflected the increasingly authoritarian leanings of a government whose patience with parliamentarism had worn thin. Despite the standing ban against his involvement in domestic politics, Financial Adviser Dewey wholeheartedly took the side of the Marshal. In April 1929 Dewey warned Mościcki that foreign opinion would frown on any strengthening of the "Colonel" element, but within three months he changed his mind and praised the new generation of ministers as a distinct improvement on their predecessors.[71] Dewey made little effort to hide his preference for Piłsudski over the Sejm, which he considered an obstructive body perhaps best done without. Toward the end of his tour in Poland he rhapsodized the Marshal as "a fond but severe school master [who] enforces discipline . . . when his pupils do not behave."[72] Proclamations of this sort enraged the opposition, but in this instance at least the government understandably saw no cause for objection to advisory commentary on internal matters.

In the meantime, Dewey's pipe dream of transforming Poland into a base for future American expansion into the Russian and East European market swelled to grandiose proportions. During June and July of 1929 he undertook a second personal reconnaissance mission to the Soviet Union. Intrigued by what he had seen during his first visit, Dewey wished to take a closer look at Russia on the grounds that the inevitable reintegration of the country into world commerce required the creation of "a group of people who can interpret back home just what the whole situation is about, its possibilities and its dangers."[73] In fact, his sojourn in Moscow proved no more substantial than its forerunner. He managed to speak with a handful of taciturn Soviet officials of second rank but never progressed beyond superficial exchanges and failed to perceive that the onset of the Stalinist epoch boded extremely ill for the expansion of Western commercial intercourse with the Soviet Union. The adviser returned to Poland full of enthusiasm but no closer to realization of his Russian chimera.[74]

During the same summer Dewey began to develop a new theme that became the pet concern of his last year of service in Warsaw. Building on his faith in the potential of world commerce with the expanses of Eastern Europe, he argued that a happy accident of postwar political geography permitted the revival of an ancient and natural trade route stretching from the Baltic to the Black Sea to shuttle goods between east and west through a minimum of frontiers and customs barriers. The conduit he described traced a network of railroads and riverways running through Poland and Romania. In truth, his hypothesis rested on faulty history and shaky commercial logic; no such passageway had existed in the past, and the practical obstacles to its creation were all but insuperable. Nevertheless, Dewey seized on the idea as a chance to turn Poland into the principal distribution center of European trade. The adviser constructed his plan on a gigantic scale. It foresaw the fusion of Eastern Europe into an economic unit to be nurtured and drained by an artery of traffic between the Polish port of Gdynia and the mouth of the Danube.

The design contained a political angle as well. Since the theory called for the route to pass through the fewest possible borders for the sake of thrift and convenience, Dewey explicitly declared that Poland should retain her disputed Baltic littoral and full sovereignty over the entire course of the Vistula in contradiction of German revisionist claims to the

Corridor.[75] In furtherance of this proposal he inaugurated a series of exploratory visits in the Danubian states. In June he journeyed to Bucharest to lay the groundwork for his scheme. He urged Romanian officials to expand commercial ties with Poland and streamline customs regulations, but he scored his greatest success in an audience with the boy-king Michael, whom he delighted with the symbolic gift of a toy cargo ship.[76]

A month later he asked Hoover for a personal interview so that he might introduce his Russian stratagems to American officialdom, but by this time the State Department had its fill of Dewey and squelched the meeting. The reports of the Warsaw legation continued to portray him as an incapable busybody, and the policymakers in Washington absorbed much of this view. In ruling on the request, Undersecretary Castle disparaged the adviser as a publicity-monger trying to make the front pages with a presidential audience. Judging from Dewey's past performance, Castle concluded he could "imagine nothing more unfortunate because he would pass thereafter as being in the closest confidence of the administration and with his well-known tactlessness might get us into serious difficulties." Under the circumstances the department decided the best course was to ignore Dewey and accordingly prevailed on the White House to avoid him.[77]

Soon afterward the definitive end of the postwar boom arrived with the Wall Street crash of October 1929, which foreshadowed the great world depression of the 1930s. Like many contemporaries, Dewey underestimated the implications of the collapse and even welcomed it as a portent of renewed investment in Poland. Since 1928 he had awaited a break in stock prices that would draw buyers back into foreign markets, and he reasoned that his fiscally conservative client stood to gain from the bust in New York. With characteristic reference to Poland in the first person, he predicted to a British diplomat "we will begin to receive first short term and then long term credits . . . and as our slate is very clean the results should be immediately apparent."[78]

Animated by this prospect, Dewey set sail for the United States at the end of the year to spend two months in his familiar role as sales representative for Poland. A New York journal greeted his arrival in port with snickers that his scheduled address on the condition of the Polish economy promised to furnish "a highly hilarious evening," but the visitor soon made plain his disagreement with such skepticism. In a series of talks in New York and Chicago Dewey contended that a stable Poland possessed every prerequisite for affluence except the tonic of foreign capital. Expounding his theory that the Poles were destined to dominate Western trade with Russia and the Near East, he advised his listeners to steal a jump on the future and invest in the country while advantageous terms were still available. The speaker added his opinion that the existence of the much-maligned Polish Corridor served the "interests of the world" by providing a direct commercial outlet from the Baltic to Romania, belittling Germany's revisionist stance as no more than "a sentimental point of view." Dewey's outspoken defense of the Polish frontiers gladdened Warsaw but earned him rebukes from the German press as an abuse of his advisory function.[79]

Upon concluding his lecture tour Dewey spent the final month of his sojourn conferring on Polish matters with financiers and government officials on the east coast. He approached numerous New York bankers with pleas to issue loans to Poland but significantly omitted the stabilization group from his circuit. In the capital he buttonholed every secondary bureaucrat who would receive him and through persistence obtained private if perfunctory séances with Hoover and Mellon. All the while Dewey's Polish associates marveled at the diligence and ardor of his labors in behalf of Warsaw. Wańkowicz reported with admiration that the American adviser's meetings occupied nearly his every waking hour, and the Polish chargé, Wacław Podoski, averred that his sentiments for Poland had ripened from sympathy into virtual "patriotism."[80]

Dewey's exertions in the United States yielded a commitment from the Standard Steel Car Corp. to extend a credit line of $20 million to a Polish firm for construction of rolling stock but made no impression on the bankers, who were his primary target. In fact, even Dewey privately admitted that Poland seemed headed inexorably toward political and economic crisis, and he conceded the futility of hunting for loans in such conditions. Nevertheless he maintained that the depression represented no more than "a perfectly normal cycle of dull times following good times" and held that lending would resume eventually; in the meantime he energetically if fruitlessly attempted to persuade American businesses—notably General Electric Co.—to open operations in Poland and gain a foothold in preparation for the inevitable rebound.[81]

While Dewey attempted to drum up American corporate activity in Poland, Warsaw gradually made up its mind to reject the one major firm that showed real interest in Polish investment. Feeling the pressure of public opinion, the cabinet decided to spurn the Harriman electrification offer in the fall of 1929. To avoid charges that the government had reneged on its word or shown weakness before the domestic opposition, Premier Świtalski resolved to provoke the company into withdrawal through insistence on revision of the contract. This gambit misfired when Harriman unexpectedly accepted the modified terms and left the Piłsudskists with no easy escape from their dilemma. As the critics of the deal kept up a din against the electrification concession, the regime bought time by referring the question to a plethora of committees and departments in an effort to postpone action as long as possible.[82]

Polish procrastination ended in the spring of 1930 when competing firms tendered bids on the electrification project which Warsaw could not entertain until it had settled with Harriman. On May 26 a special cabinet session produced a recommendation "to refuse Harriman's offer without delay," and on June 4 the government notified the Americans of its unconditional repudiation of their proposal. The Poles cited dissatisfaction with the terms of the contract as the official rationale for their decision, but privately they mentioned a variety of motives, including their qualms at the extent of Harriman's German connections.[83] Polish denials to the contrary, the rupture with the Americans probably had much to do with the simultaneous announcement of the formation of a joint Polish-French company for the purpose of completing the electrification of southwestern Poland. The coincidence led Harriman to infer reasonably that Warsaw had violated the ban on negotiations with rivals pending a verdict on his bid, and the concern enlisted the aid of the State Department in seeking redress from the Poles.[84]

Unable either to induce American firms to make direct investments in Poland or to persuade the government to assent to the Harriman concession, Dewey reverted to hunting for loans in the last months of his advisory duty, but without notable success. The climate for international lending grew steadily worse, and petitions to French finance and the newly-established Bank for International Settlements miscarried. The best the Poles could manage by the autumn of 1930 was a $3 million short-term credit from Irving Trust of New York for repurchase of 7 percent 1927 bonds at the depressed price of 78.5.[85]

For lack of anything better to do, Dewey continued to toy as well with his favorite hobbyhorse, the integration of Eastern Europe into a huge market for Western capital. In 1930 two developments—French Foreign Minister Aristide Briand's call for creation of a "United States of Europe" and the staging of an International Agricultural Congress in Warsaw— convinced the adviser that his own idea had become timely. In the spring he obtained an invitation to journey to Paris to confer with Briand, and during June and July he added Yugoslavia to the list of his travels. While in Belgrade he met with leading officials, including King Alexander, and raised eyebrows by issuing a public call to the countries of the region to encourage foreign investment and protect national minorities—a sensitive topic in the tensely heterogeneous South Slavic kingdom. In the course of his stay he intimated to the Polish legation the existence of a link between his East European junkets and "a whole series of financial transactions" he had in mind for the future.[86] Dewey also paid a return visit to Romania, the southern terminus of his imaginary Baltic-to-Black Sea trade channel, where his globetrotting in the service of his project embroiled him in misadventure. One night highwaymen robbed him at gunpoint of two thousand dollars. The incident embarrassed the Romanians, but the victim of the holdup laughed it off to his hosts as "an attempt on their part to make me feel very much at home as being a Chicagoan I was quite used to such situations."[87]

Dewey's advisory service in Warsaw ended with a flurry of fanfare and a general recapitulation of the main themes of his Polish stewardship. His final report admitted the severity of Poland's economic malaise and regretted her lack of success in world money markets during his residency but ended on the characteristically cheerful note that Poland was merely "in a period of rest but ready to respond to the first signs of an awakening business activity." He extolled the Poles for the sobriety of their fiscal policies and stressed his conviction of their country's coming greatness as a conveyer of international commerce.[88]

Dewey also discovered opportunities to fire parting shots at some old antagonists. He assisted another nationalist drive to boycott German imports in support of native industries and, in a last affront to the Polish opposition, acquiesced in the transfer of part of the reserve fund of the Bank Polski to permit the Piłsudskist forces to cover their partisan expenses of a parliamentary election campaign in which the government resorted to intimidation and repression to subdue the political factions of the right and center-left.[89] For the most part, however, the adviser spent his valedictory days in Poland in a succession of fetes, decorations, and fulsome—if perhaps not entirely sincere—testimonials from the Poles, whose opinions of the American expert imposed on them by the foreign financiers remained ambiguous to the end.

Proclaiming the past three years as "the happiest period of his life," Dewey departed for home on November 20, 1930, the expiration date of the stabilization plan. Conforming to ingrained habit, he punctuated his return trip to private life in Chicago with speeches and appearances lauding Poland, Piłsudski, and the benefits of American investment in Eastern Europe.[90] Dewey's almost paternal affection for his adopted homeland endured long after the severance of his ties to the Bank Polski. He paid annual visits to Poland until the outbreak of the Second World War and continued to comment sympathetically on her affairs, styling himself virtually as an unofficial Polish envoy to the United States.[91]

The financial adviser left to mixed appraisals of his work. His farewell came none too soon for John N. Willys, the new American ambassador, who like his predecessor found Dewey an overbearing nuisance and took a personal dislike to him. On the whole, the evaluations of the State Department anointed him with commendations heavily diluted with references to his clumsiness and shallowness.[92] The response of Polish opinion to Dewey ranged from cold to lukewarm. Oppositionist elements on both ends of the spectrum deplored him for his attachment to *Sanacja*, his status as a foreigner and—in the instance of the left—his social and fiscal conservatism. Governmental and financial circles found his views more agreeable, but even they depreciated his abilities and defined his accomplishments in patronizing terms. Of all Dewey's attributes, Poles praised most highly his inclination to let them run the financial adminis-tration of the country as they pleased, and his defenders asserted that even if the American agent had not managed to do Poland much good, then at least he had done no particular harm.[93]

Dewey was the last of the American financial counselors of the 1920s who, like Gilbert in Germany and Jeremiah Smith in Hungary, personi-fied the joint efforts of Washington and Wall Street to stabilize postwar

Europe; by all odds he was also the least effective. The paucity of his achievements in Poland had little to do with his many mistakes and shortcomings, although he might have proved marginally more successful had he not alienated the American bankers and diplomats with whom he dealt, embraced the Poles so openly, and expended most of his time chasing personal notoriety and concocting outsize and impractical schemes. The most skillful of advisers would have found the credit squeeze of 1928–1929 and the subsequent depression insuperable handicaps to the amplification of Polish ties with American capital. In a narrow sense, Dewey might even—as indeed he did—claim to have fulfilled his essential purpose, for upon his departure, as in 1927, the złoty ranked among the strongest of European currencies. Yet the fact remained that Dewey attained none of his principal objectives: the improvement of Polish credit in New York, the introduction of Anglo-American finance into the country on a broad scale, the development of Poland into an agricultural exporter and commercial middleman of first rank, and the unlocking of Russia and Eastern Europe to Western enterprise. Measured against his own aspirations, Dewey's mission in Warsaw ended in almost unqualified failure.

Much the same verdict applied to the stabilization loan and program Dewey symbolized. The loan provided a transitory stimulus for the national economy, but the attached provisions of financial discipline exerted little effect beyond the dubious benefit of reinforcing an already stabilized currency.[94] Of course, Warsaw had agreed to shoulder the superfluous plan in the first place only for the purpose of attracting money from abroad, and in this decisive respect as well the calculations of 1927 went awry. The year following the accord with Bankers Trust represented the peak of Poland's appeal as an importer of capital, but the subsequent souring of business and credit ruined her ambitions in world markets. By 1930 the net influx of foreign funds amounted to less than 3 percent of the corresponding figure for 1928, and Warsaw took in less in new American loans than it paid in amortization of previous debts.[95] In Polish reckoning the stabilization plan fell short of success in every way, and in the process the budding financial association between Warsaw and Wall Street simply withered away—a break hastened by the *Sanacja* government, which in effect repudiated the alliance with New York out of disappointment and growing suspicion of the political consequences of American economic influence. Intended at its inception as the first of many such transactions, the Bankers Trust loan of 1927—itself only a "drop in the ocean of Polish needs," in a contemporary estimate—ended not as the vanguard of American investment in Poland but its climax.[96]

CHAPTER VII

The Conduct of
Political Relations,
1927–1932

In the eyes of American opinion it is axiomatic that Central Europe is indisposed, and on the basis of that judgment one finds many quack prescriptions to heal it. . . . In this situation our best course is to prepare for the moment when it will be necessary to explain why [revision] cannot be applied to Central Europe.

Tytus Filipowicz to August Zaleski, November 19, 1929

The decision of the United States to restrict her activities in the affairs of postwar Europe spoiled the Polish hopes of 1919 to enroll the Americans as protectors of the independence and integrity of reconstructed Poland. Rejecting the alternatives of isolation and full participation in European diplomacy, Washington chose a middle course of promotion of the recovery of Europe through economic intervention and encouragement of the peaceful resolution of international controversies. As a consequence, relations between Poland and the United States existed primarily on the financial plane, and for the most part neutral America remained irrelevant to Warsaw's obsessive search for security against its potential enemies to east and west. On the other hand, Washington reserved the right to enter into European politics at its discretion, and the growing assertiveness of American policy makers as the presidency passed from Coolidge to Herbert Hoover caused the actions of the United States to intersect more frequently with Polish interests. With paradoxical irony, however, the advent of a more vigorous American foreign policy under the stewardship of a figure renowned for his humanitarian service to Poland coincided with the growth of Polish misgivings concerning the effects of U.S. diplomatic efforts in Europe. Six years after Skrzyński crossed the Atlantic in 1925 in hopes of rallying the United States to assume guardianship over his country, the Poles found themselves forced to address stern and well-founded admonitions to Washington not to conspire with other powers to contract the Polish frontiers.

In spite of the failure of the Skrzyński mission of 1925, the idea that Warsaw might turn American policies to its advantage retained an appeal in Polish opinion. The unswerving aim of Polish diplomacy in the 1920s was to preserve the balance of international forces codified in the peace treaties and protected by the network of alliances constructed by France. Just as consistently, the United States refused to align with any European state or bloc, preferring to employ her wealth as her chief instrument of foreign policy. However, the Poles widely expected the Americans sooner or later to throw off their inhibitions against political involvement in Europe and to bestow their favor in direct proportion to the magnitude of their financial investment in particular countries. Such deterministic arguments accounted for the eagerness of many Polish observers to hail each real or rumored American transaction in Poland as an omen of Washington's partiality toward Warsaw, and calculations of diplomatic benefit had animated the endeavors of Jan Ciechanowski to institute a stabilization program under sponsorship of the central bank of the United States.

Of course, the contention that American sympathies followed the dollar cut both ways, and the logical conclusion to this line of reasoning was that the United States would gravitate irresistibly to the side of Germany, by far her largest European customer and debtor. Fear of an eventual *entente* between Washington and Berlin nagged at the Poles, and by the later period of the Coolidge presidency the MSZ began to worry openly that "a series of circumstances has inclined the U.S. to a favorable disposition" toward Poland's traditional rival to the west.[1]

This observation contained some justice, even though Washington's good relations with the Weimar Republic represented a natural outgrowth of certain basic American attitudes rather than a conscious choice of allegiance. The policy of the United States coincided with German interest—and diverged from that of Poland—in its rejection of the Treaty of Versailles and in its unwillingness to recognize the French alliance system as a satisfactory framework of European security, and American sentiment generally applauded the pacific and ostensibly conciliatory strategies of Stresemann that the Poles regarded as the wolf of the *Drang nach Osten* in lamb's clothing. Warsaw especially feared the prejudicial potential of the American economic stake in the *Reich*, and to a great extent Poland's financial diplomacy toward the United States during these years stemmed from a desire to neutralize the political danger she perceived in the growing intimacy of Wall Street with German enterprise.

The benevolence of the United States toward Berlin troubled the Poles largely out of concern that one day Washington might lend its support to the advocates of boundary revision in Central Europe. Interwar Germany never accepted her eastern border as final, and Poland never admitted the possibility of its modification. A substantial share of world opinion adopted the German viewpoint, and the Polish Corridor of Pomerania especially gained popular currency as a symbol of the supposed short-

comings and inequities of the peace treaties. The established policy of the
United States toward the question was, in essence, to have no policy at all
on the grounds that it was of solely European significance and, as such,
not a legitimate interest of a country which had resigned responsibility
for the security of that continent. When Polish diplomats occasionally
raised the issue to rehearse their arguments, the formulary American
response was that—as Kellogg told Ciechanowski in 1928—Washington
"must maintain an entirely neutral position with regard to any boundary
disputes" in Europe.[2]

Although the United States neither endorsed nor deplored the Polish
frontiers in an official sense, the State Department monitored the running feud from a distance, and individual American diplomats formed
private opinions and expressed them with varying degrees of candor.
Frequently an envoy's judgment reflected the standpoint of his host
government. From Warsaw, for instance, John Stetson consistently upheld the Polish case for retention of the borderlands, while Alanson
Houghton and Jacob G. Schurman, successive chiefs of the Berlin embassy between 1922 and 1929, made little effort to conceal their revisionist
leanings.[3] During the regimes of Hughes and Kellogg, however, the
makers of foreign policy in Washington never strayed from their bland
proclamations of disinterest in the contested western borders of Poland.

Despite its equivocal nature, the American practice of abstention from
European territorial questions inadvertently worked to Polish advantage
in certain respects. To the United States such matters as dominion over
Pomerania appeared provincial and subordinate to the overriding problems of the general pacification and economic revitalization of Europe.
Washington saw no reason to object to treaty revision on principle, but it
urged the Europeans to defer consideration of these contentious issues
lest they should divert attention from the more essential tasks of reconstruction.

In the specific instance of the German-Polish dispute, the Americans
asked the contestants to avoid war at all costs and hoped that time and
trade would heal the rift. Visiting Warsaw in 1927, Schurman told Józef
Lipski of the MSZ that in attempting to ameliorate the differences between Germany and Poland "it is necessary to put off into the future the
questions of a political nature, *like the boundary dispute, and concentrate for the present on a settlement of economic questions.* That is the
only way to stabilize relations between the two countries." The ambassador also admitted the need to "uphold" the Versailles frontiers for several
years until Europe recovered its economic health.[4] The Poles derived two
distinct, if indirect, benefits from this stance: so long as the Americans
withheld support from the revisionists, their neutrality tacitly facilitated
the perpetuation of the territorial status quo, while the likely practical
effect of Washington's advice to put off adjudication of border grievances
into an uncertain future would have been to permit the current owners to
strengthen their grasp on the disputed lands by means of natural demo-
graphic shifts and policies of nationalization.

On the other hand, the Poles suspected that the trend of U.S. policy in Europe might work against them in the long run, and during the Coolidge years the MSZ watched anxiously for signs—a hostile editorial, or an ambiguous diplomatic remark—that American opinion had swung in favor of the German territorial claims.[5] To prevent the United States from drifting into the revisionist camp, Warsaw attempted to exploit the deepseated American fear of a renewal of European war. In their conversations with State Department operatives, Polish diplomats bluntly identified the maintenance of their country's frontiers with the preservation of peace and warned that any attempt to detach the Corridor or other contested regions would meet armed resistance from Poland. Given this resolve, they contended, the German revisionist campaign amounted to a provocation which endangered the basic goals of American policy in Europe. As Foreign Minister Zaleski told the U.S. chargé in Warsaw in 1927, "fixed boundaries . . . and Poland's determination to have them remain so fixed, would never bring a war, whereas . . . an attempt to change any boundaries would logically tend to the opposite result."[6]

The fate of the Polish Corridor, however, was far removed from the agenda of the Kellogg State Department. The characteristic theme of European diplomacy of the later 1920s—the so-called era of Locarno—was the search for a peaceful resolution of the tensions and controversies left over from the World War and its aftermath. The principal quandary of American policy in the region was to foster international tranquility and stability with a minimum of political means and risk. Recognizing the urgency of the French hunger for protection against the possibility of German *revanche*, the United States sought ways to reassure Paris while still avoiding commitment or alliance, hoping above all to wean France away from reliance on military coercion.

This mixture of caution and conciliatory intent found expression in the most conspicuous American diplomatic initiative undertaken in postwar Europe. When French Foreign Minister Briand publicly called on the United States in 1927 to agree to outlaw war between the two countries, Washington correctly read the offer as a veiled ploy to compromise its neutrality. The Americans deftly sidestepped the dilemma by suggesting the admission of other states into the antiwar covenant, at one stroke reducing the role of the United States from partner to disintereseted broker and eliminating any hint of a privileged place for France in U.S. policy. Caught in their own trap, the French reluctantly took up the American counterproposal, which contained the germ of the Kellogg-Briand Pact of the next year.

Kellogg unveiled the Franco-American draft treaty in April 1928, simultaneously inviting the adherence of England, Germany, Italy, and Japan. Initial Polish reaction to the announcement fell far short of enthusiasm. The press of all factions dismissed the Kellogg plan, bereft as it was of provision for enforcement, as a naive and inadequate solution to the problem of European security. Official opinion regarded the American formula as potentially worse than merely useless; Zaleski alerted his missions to the hazard that a strict interpretation of the pacifistic injunction of the accord might undermine "the practical value of our defensive alliances." In Washington, Ciechanowski made a point of stressing to the State Department his government's anxiety that Berlin would seek somehow to transform the pact into a revisionist device.[7]

In spite of their distaste for the Kellogg proposition, the Poles' strongest objection to it was, paradoxically, that it made no room for them. The American overture wounded Polish sensibilities on several counts. In the first place, the Poles bore a certain resentment against the Kellogg plan as a derivative but inferior substitute for their own European security scheme of the previous year, which had drawn heavy criticism from other states before its passage in adulterated form by the League of Nations. Worse, the restriction of membership offers to a select few implied an arbitrary division of countries into greater and lesser powers, with Warsaw relegated to the junior ranks. Poland habitually bridled at any suggestion of her secondary importance among the nations, not only out of pride but from an ingrained determination based on unhappy historical memory not to allow the formation of an elite club of powers that might assert the right to decide questions touching on her interests without her participation. The Poles especially demanded to be treated as an equal of their German adversary, and they took offense at Kellogg's implicit if unconscious snub even as they worried about exclusion from the diplomatic councils of the great.[8]

For these reasons Zaleski resolved to persuade the United States to offer Poland admission among the original signatories of the treaty. On May 14 the foreign minister conferred with Stetson and conveyed his regret that the Kellogg initiative had neglected to number Warsaw among the chosen. He contended that Poland merited invitation in acknowledgement both of her own past sponsorship of a prototypical accord and of her pivotal geographical and political significance, at the same time complaining frankly that the American proposal threatened the Poles with loss of face in relation to Berlin. In the meantime, the French had notified Washington through various channels of their desire to admit their East European allies into the pact. Seeing no point in opposing the request, Kellogg promptly informed Stetson of his approval of the Polish application for charter membership in his antiwar association; Zaleski received the news with satisfaction and agreed to submit it to the judgment of Piłsudski and the other state authorities.[9]

The Poles formed their response over the course of the succeeding weeks. For his part, Marshal Piłsudski removed himself from the debate in choleric and unequivocal fashion. When the deputy foreign minister broached the matter of the pact, the premier snarled that the MSZ was "taking up his time with foolishness" and submitted imaginative, if anatomically improbable, suggestions of what Kellogg could do with his parchments.[10] Within the Foreign Ministry discussion proceeded at a more measured level. Warsaw decided to join the treaty subject to a number of conditions designed to ensure that it would not interfere with the existing Polish security arrangements, a stance that approximated the French position. On May 30 Zaleski advised Stetson of his country's acceptance of the antiwar covenant with the understanding that it neither compromised the Polish alliances nor forbade recourse to self-defense or collective action in the face of aggression. Both in official communications and informal presentations the representatives of the MSZ stressed Poland's insistence on recognition as an original signatory to the pact with full rights of consultation on any subsequent modification of its provisions. The emphasis given this theme led Stetson to observe correctly that the Poles considered the Kellogg plan more a test of their prestige than a real contribution to European peace.[11]

On June 23 the State Department extended invitations to fourteen capitals, including Warsaw, to approve a revised draft of the treaty that explicitly sanctioned defensive uses of military power; that same day Kellogg assured Ciechanowski that the amendment legitimated all of the Polish reservations. In the first week of July the directors of the MSZ gathered to ratify the foregone conclusion that if Poland saw little of value in the Kellogg pact, she at least had "no basic objection" to it in light of the American clarifications. Zaleski endorsed the verdict as a matter of course, and on July 18 Poland joined seven other countries in acceptance of the antiwar agreement.[12]

The negotiations for the Kellogg accord culminated in Paris in a spectacular signing ceremony on August 27. Most of the delegates present shared the Polish opinion of the innocuous pact as little more than a gesture of international piety; such was not the view of Kellogg himself, who shed grateful tears when Zaleski bestowed a few platitudinous tributes on his invention in a private conversation.[13] On the whole, Polish observers greeted the conclusion of the treaty with faint praise. The insertion of Poland among the signatory powers moved the centrist and goverment press to confer lukewarm blessings on the American project, although the left and right wings denounced it respectively as a piece of bourgeois hypocrisy and a sop to Germany. Meanwhile, the Foreign Ministry hid its inner conviction of the insignificance of the agreement behind a front of complimentary rhetoric, while the insult of the belated invitation to participate lingered in official memory.[14]

In spite of their original reserve toward the pact, the Poles gradually warmed to the treaty as the realization dawned on them that its prohibition against offensive war might be invoked in support of the existing order of frontiers and power relationships. Zaleski occasionally made public citation of the American pact as an integral component of the European security system, and even Piłsudski came to admit that adherence to the antiwar covenant placed a "great moral obstacle" before a potential aggressor.[15] The Kellogg accord served as the model for the Litvinov Protocol of 1929, a regional nonaggression compact binding Poland, Romania, the Soviet Union, and the Baltic states.

In particular, Warsaw eagerly advanced the thesis that the Paris agreement exerted a stabilizing effect on relations between Poland and Germany and placed the weight of international opinion against any attempt to alter the Polish boundaries by force. To the extent that the pact supplemented the Versailles system, it also permitted the interpretation that American neutrality benefited the forces of equilibrium in Europe. This self-serving rationale received the surprisingly emphatic confirmation of none other than the namesake of the measure. In late summer of 1928 Kellogg told Ciechanowski that Washington's sponsorship of the antiwar treaty "must have opened the eyes of the Wilhelmstrasse to the fact that the American Government does not intend to be drawn into any revision of the existing 'status quo.'"[16]

The year of the Kellogg pact brought to an end the term of the Coolidge administration, and the presidential election of 1928 commanded an unusual degree of interest both in Poland and within the Polish-American colony in the United States. The contest matched Secretary of Commerce Hoover, famed as a benefactor of the Polish state in its infancy, against the first serious Roman Catholic aspirant to the presidency, the Democrat Alfred E. Smith, a figure of special appeal to immigrant voters. Hoover overwhelmed his opponent, and political analysts agreed that sentiments of gratitude for service to the ancestral homeland had induced Polonia to abandon its traditional Democratic allegiance in favor of the Republican candidate.[17]

Warsaw proclaimed satisfaction with the election of Hoover but doubted that his advent would affect the conduct of American policy in Europe. If anything, the MSZ braced itself for the unwelcome possibility that the technocrat in the White House might tilt slightly toward Germany as the key to European economic prosperity. At the same time, Ciechanowski applauded the choice of Henry L. Stimson to succeed Kellogg at the helm of the State Department, noting that the new secretary showed no signs of prejudice against basic Polish interests.[18]

The new administration maintained the general line of the Coolidge European policy, including its profession of platonic good will toward Poland. During its first year in office the Hoover government paid a symbolic compliment to Warsaw by granting the Polish request of long standing to exchange ambassadors. In the first semester of 1929 England and Italy decided to install embassies in the Polish capital, and the Poles and Minister Stetson bade Washington follow suit. The State Department perceived no compelling diplomatic necessity to elevate its representation in Poland, but it approved the step principally for the reason that "it would undoubtedly please the Poles in the United States."[19] In December Hoover accordingly revealed his intention to raise relations with Poland to the ambassadorial level, and a joint congressional resolution completed the formalities in January 1930.

The promotion of the U.S. mission in Warsaw also afforded Washington a convenient opportunity to dispose of Stetson, who long since had forfeited the confidence of his superiors. In his four years of service the American minister had worn thin on the Poles and nettled his British counterparts through his personal crusade to reduce English economic influence in Poland as a boost to traders from his own country. For its part, the State Department wrote him off as a failure and trusted that a more capable replacement might bring the Warsaw mission out of the shadow of the presumptuous financial adviser Dewey. Upon announcement of the plans to establish an embassy in Poland, Stetson resigned from the Foreign Service under pressure[20] to make way for Alexander P. Moore, the current ambassador to Peru. A journalist by trade and notable as the widower of the famed vaudevillian Lillian Russell, Moore was a respected personality, but he died after a short illness in February 1930 before he could assume his duties.

To fill the vacancy as the first American ambassador to Poland, Hoover selected John N. Willys, the wealthy chairman of the automobile concern that bore his name. Unlike Moore, Willys was a novice at diplomacy and his appointment owed less to merit than to his Republican credentials and the sponsorship of an influential homestate senator. The new envoy quickly proved a dismal choice for the Warsaw post. Clerical-nationalist circles in Poland railed at Willys—a Protestant enthusiast—as an "active enemy of Catholicism," the religion of the great majority of the Polish nation, and upon his arrival in May 1930 the Poles found him deficient in ability and preparation. Willys impressed his hosts by leasing one of the grandest palaces of Warsaw as his residence, but throughout most of his tenure the building remained empty while the absentee ambassador stayed at home nursing his business through the rigors of the depression. In midyear of 1931 the disgruntled Hoover drily noted that Willys "apparently does not like living in Warsaw" and complained that he spent more than half his time as a truant from his diplomatic responsibilities.[21]

Meanwhile, Minister Filipowicz stayed on in Washington to assume command of the newly-created Polish embassy. The lackadaisical pace set by the ambassador accorded with the gradually diminishing importance of the United States to Polish policy. Piłsudski always had considered the United States a marginal element in European affairs, and with the decline of American overseas investment his government lost interest in maintaining close relations with Wall Street. The graduation of the Washington mission to ambassadorial dignity conflicted ironically with the steady trivialization of its function since the days of Ciechanowski's barely restricted freedom to conduct financial diplomacy.

The principal task of the embassy in the Piłsudskist scheme of things was to unify the American Polonia in support of Poland in general and the *Sanacja* regime in particular. Abetted by social pressures and tight American controls on immigration, the natural process of assimilation had estranged the mass of Polish-Americans from the affairs of the old country since the end of the World War, while the coup of 1926 had intensified the factional strife that kept the politically active segment of

Polonia in a state of fragmentation. Perhaps a majority of American Poles sympathized with Piłsudski,[22] but the entrenched leadership of their principal organizations and publications—the so-called "Old Guard" that had admired Paderewski and the Polish right—regarded the *Sanacja* government in Warsaw with indifference or outright hostility. The new rulers of Poland determined that a mobilized and pacified Polonia might prove an asset to the homeland and directed their diplomats in Washington to pursue that objective.

Aided by the legation, an insurgency of Piłsudskist leaning wrested control of the Polish National Alliance from the Old Guard in 1928 and committed the largest of the Polonian fraternal groups to a program of solidarity with the aims of *Sanacja*. The rebel capture of the P.N.A. touched off a virtual war of words in Polish-American circles between the backers of Piłsudski and their antagonists, represented mainly by the staunchly conservative Polish Roman Catholic Union.[23] By no means a champion of *Sanacja*, Ciechanowski displeased Piłsudski as less than a reliable missionary to Polonia, and upon the envoy's removal from Washington the Marshal took care to replace him with a loyalist whom he could trust to reward or combat Polish-American elements according to their opinion of the authorities in Poland. Filipowicz threw himself into the fray with alacrity, seeking especially to restrain the vituperative criticisms of Piłsudski that appeared regularly in the organs of the P.R.C.U. and its allies.[24]

The plan to transform Polonia into a cohesive bloc of support both for the interests of Poland and its embattled government faltered after its initial successes. After three years of ascendancy the Piłsudskist vanguard alienated the membership of the P.N.A. by the militancy and open partisanship of its platform; in 1931 the traditionalists regained domination over the body, restored their customary agenda of abstention from Polish affairs and on that basis achieved an armistice with the rest of organized Polonia.[25]

Warsaw's campaign to rally its diaspora in the United States had proceeded from a false estimate of the devotion of the Polish-American to his original homeland. Polish representatives found—occasionally to their astonishment—that the great majority of the immigrants regarded themselves as Americans, retaining only a sentimental tie to Poland.[26] Preoccupied with the struggle to improve its social and economic standing and blend into American life, Polonia considered Poland far removed from its immediate concerns, especially as the postwar prosperity gave way to depression. After their passing absorption in the sectarian battles of the old country, Polish-Americans once more retreated within their own ranks to tend to matters closer to home.

The overall tenor or relations between Poland and the United States during the Hoover years maintained the note of bland amity sounded in the exchange of ambassadors. In confirmation of their cordiality the two states reached agreement on a treaty of friendship, commerce, and consular rights on June 15, 1931, after six years of sporadic negotiation. Modeled after similar accords Washington had contracted with other European governments, the document promised to strengthen "the bond of peace which happily prevails" between Poles and Americans through codification of bilateral trade and travel while eschewing any hint of mutual political obligation or association.[27]

These public proclamations of good will did not prevent the growth of fears in Warsaw that the tug of American financial interests would tempt the Hoover administration to adopt the German position on boundary revision. Soon after the inauguration of the new president in 1929 the issue of the Polish western frontiers confronted American spokesmen, albeit in unofficial fashion, in the course of international talks held in Paris for the purpose of modifying the schedule of German reparations payments as set forth in the Dawes Plan.

Although the United States took no direct part in the conference, Owen Young of General Electric and the new York Federal Reserve Bank presided over its deliberations in a private capacity. Hjalmar Schacht of the Reichsbank served as chief representative of Berlin. During pourparlers in February Schacht, still an ardent revisionist, confidentially imparted to the American experts his conviction that Germany could pay her indemnities only in tandem with political concessions including recovery of the Polish Corridor; uncomfortable with the sensitive topic, Young and his colleagues appealed to the German banker to omit it from his formal statements in return for a vague pledge to take his grievances into account in calculating a final reparations total. Unable to take the hint, Schacht rocked the conference—and surprised his own government—on April 17 by submitting a motion that suggested the retrocession to Germany of her former colonies and the lands lost to Poland through the Treaty of Versailles.[28]

The introduction of politics into a forum ostensibly reserved for consideration of financial questions irked U.S. as well as European opinion. The American delegates in Paris resented Schacht's allusion to revision as offensive and gratuitous. The State Department likewise expressed its disapproval of the German proposal. Stimson quietly scolded Berlin for permitting the commission of such an unseemly gesture in its name, while Assistant Secretary Castle "did not spare critical words" in his observations on the Schacht memorandum. Envoys of the Auswärtiges Amt nervously reported from Washington that the Paris episode had damaged German standing in the United States.[29]

The indignation over Schacht's indiscretion blew over and did not impede the conclusion of the Young Plan, but the incident aggravated a raw nerve within Polish officialdom. Notwithstanding the annoyed reaction of the United States against the revisionist gambit at Paris, the mere mention of the Corridor issue in the presence of U.S. bankers at an international conclave on reparations hardened suspicions in Poland that Berlin was using its financial leverage on Wall Street to foster and manipulate an "almost involuntary American support" for its territorial ambitions in the east.[30] Coinciding with the ripening of Polish disenchantment with American capital as represented by the Bankers Trust stabilization consortium, the Schacht note alarmed the Warsaw government at its highest levels.

The appearance of the memorandum prompted Marshal Piłsudski to warn his lieutenants that Washington might someday ask Poland to make "a payment of a political nature" to her western neighbor to forestall a German economic breakdown with its consequent ruination of American investments. The Polish commander-in-chief told Mościcki and Premier Świtalski that if such a request came to pass, "he would proclaim when necessary that if anyone tries to tamper with our borders, he will declare a defensive war and announce the intention to destroy foreign territory." Such a demonstration, he maintained, would convince the world that "there can be no question of any bartering of our lands."[31]

Polish diplomats in Washington assured the Foreign Ministry that the Schacht note in no way reflected the views of the United States,[32] but as the world slipped into depression over the next two years American opinion took a decided turn against Poland and her policies. The economic slump hastened the disintegration of the uneasy diplomatic truce embodied in the Dawes Plan and the Locarno agreements. Relations among the European powers became visibly more strained, and war no longer seemed an unlikely result of the mounting international tensions. Beset by financial stress and beleaguered by extremists of left and right, the unstable government of Heinrich Brüning in Germany pressed its claim for redress of its complaints against the treaties of 1919 with waxing impatience and stridency. The boundary dispute between Berlin and Warsaw reached new heights of shrillness, and many accounted the Polish Corridor the greatest of all threats to the peace.

Fed both by a concerted German propaganda campaign aimed at winning Western sympathies and an instinctive aversion to European war, American sentiment crystallized around positions distasteful to the Poles.[33] Never kindly disposed toward interwar Poland, liberal circles in the United States censured the authoritarian evolution of the Piłsudski regime and portrayed Warsaw as an oppressor of Jews, Ukrainians, Belorussians, and resident Germans.[34] A consensus formed about the proposition that France and her allies contributed to the European turbulence by seeking to imprison Germany within a net of punitive and divisive checks. Above all, Americans associated Poland with the Danzig Corridor, which they deemed a root cause of the turmoil in Europe. A flood of newspaper articles and polemical literature devoted to the Corridor appeared in the United States during the Hoover years, as elsewhere in the West. A majority of these commentators upheld the justice of the revisionist point of view and many of them prescribed peaceful modification of the Polish boundaries as a cure. The issue spawned headlines on the order of "Europe's Sorest Spot" and "Poland Courts a New War," and in 1931 one widely-read journalist wrote that the discord over the Corridor represented "for Europe, and even America . . . the most tragic circumstance in contemporary life."[35]

Skepticism of the durability and equity of the Polish frontier with Germany likewise reached to the core of the Hoover government. The State Department preserved its policy of noninterference in the quarrel over Pomerania, but a growing number of American diplomats privately concluded that abolition of the Corridor was only a matter of time.[36] Both Hoover and Secretary of State Stimson faulted the Versailles treaty for having "set up these separate little countries" in Europe. Stimson intimated his leanings to Ambassador Filipowicz in January 1931, telling the Polish envoy "one thing [was] sure, that the Germans had succeeded in establishing in public opinion a just case for the revision of the Corridor."[37]

As the year 1931 opened, Stimson's foremost diplomatic aim was not to redraw the European map but to ensure the success of the Geneva disarmament conference scheduled for the following year. He and Hoover began discussing American disarmament policy in January and discovered they disagreed—a not uncommon occurrence. Hoover wished to propose a worldwide reduction in naval arms. By nature more adventurous than his chief, Stimson believed the achievement of disarmament required greater imagination. The secretary of state held that armaments were not the cause but the result of international insecurity; for this reason, disarmament would only follow the solution of the European disputes that prompted the proliferation of weaponry. As an impartial but interested observer, the United States could best prepare for the conference by urging the Europeans to arrive at amicable settlements of the feuds that perpetuated a spirit of rancor. With Hoover distracted by an ailing domestic economy, Stimson found himself free to pursue his idea. Throughout the early months of 1931 he industriously pressed his disarmament strategy upon the governments of Western Europe.[38]

As spring turned to summer, international anxieties grew more acute when Central Europe plunged into financial crisis and Germany wavered on the edge of bankruptcy. The United States took special interest in preventing a German collapse. Apart from the huge American economic stake in Germany, Hoover and Stimson accounted the hard-pressed cabinet of Brüning the only alternative to a dangerous Communist or chauvinist successor regime.[39] Seeking to relieve the pressure on Berlin, Hoover on June 20 called for suspension of payment on all intergovernmental debts for one year. Although the French hesitated to give the Germans something for nothing, the Hoover moratorium obtained approval from all major creditors within three weeks.

Poland concurred in assent to the American initiative but inwardly nursed a sense of chagrin at the measure. Warsaw grumbled that Germany should pay for her reprieve with a pledge to forsake her revisionist demands, and Hoover's largesse galled the Poles all the more in view of their belief that America easily could—if she would—force such a change in German policy by using her leverage as creditor. At the same time, the moratorium persuaded the MSZ that the United States had begun to take a more active interest in European affairs and would bear watching in coming months.[40]

During the same summer of 1931 Stimson crossed the Atlantic to take part in a round of consultations among West European leaders on the subjects of disarmament and the financial emergency. Despite intensive diplomatic labors, all attempts to ease the crisis splintered on the rocks of Franco-German friction. Both Brüning and the French premier of the day, Pierre Laval, favored a rapprochement between Paris and Berlin, but neither could discover a formula for solution of the political issues that separated them. The question of the peace treaties presented the foremost obstacle. France as well as Poland counseled the imposition of a "political moratorium" on revisionist agitation—including the matter of the Corridor—in return for financial assistance to Germany. Seeking to convert his country's relative prosperity to advantage, Laval in July dangled a loan on these terms in front of the Germans, but Brüning rejected the offer. For their part, the British and Americans frowned upon the French stance as shortsighted and unproductive, and the impasse deepened Stimson's suspicion that the enmity of France and Germany prevented an effective attack on the conditions that threatened European equilibrium.[41]

At this time the American secretary of state's effort to produce disarmament through encouragement of peaceful resolution of the outstanding political problems of Europe came to concentrate on the Polish Corridor. Before his European sojourn he had regarded the Corridor as a matter of no special urgency. His opinion changed instantly as the result of a casual remark dropped in conversation by the French prime minister. On the morning of July 24 Stimson conferred privately in London with Laval. During the meeting Laval commented that in the realm of Franco-German relations, "the underlying problem which could solve everything else was the question of the Polish corridor. If that could be solved France would have no other real trouble with Germany." This statement made a powerful impression on Stimson, who had come to believe the reconciliation of Paris and Berlin was the key to the relaxation of world tensions—"everything depended on that."[42] In fact, Laval's expression of impatience with the Corridor reflected merely his personal observation and not the policy of the French government, which dutifully, if somewhat grudgingly, supported its Polish ally's right to her existing boundaries.

From London Stimson proceeded to Berlin, where he was struck by the unanimity of German opinion in demanding the readjustment of the Polish frontier. His encounters with Brüning confirmed his esteem for the German leader and reinforced his desire to see the chancellor's shaky regime maintained.[43] Intrigued by his interview with Laval, Stimson may have concluded that a revision of the Corridor in favor of Germany might strengthen Brüning's hand at home even as it removed the greatest impediment to Franco-German harmony and improved the outlook for disarmament.

In any case, the Corridor began to assume a central place in Stimson's calculations. From Berlin he journeyed to Sciberscross, Scotland, to spend August on vacation. While awaiting a visit from British Prime Minister Ramsay MacDonald, Stimson read a newly-published popular account of European affairs—*Thunder Over Europe* by E. Alexander Powell—that called the Corridor "the most perilous [threat] which confronts the world today" and urged its liquidation.[44] The argument impressed him; MacDonald arrived August 6, and that evening the American told his guest of the book and its "indictment against Poland," which the caller agreed was "well taken."[45]

Continuing their talks the next day, they concurred in the judgment that the Europe of Versailles required peaceful alteration: the treaty established an unnatural and potentially explosive preponderance of French power on the continent. MacDonald said the time had come to get the controversial provisions of the Versailles order "up for discussion" and identified German territorial grievances against Poland as a case in point. Stimson affirmed his interest in the idea and asked MacDonald to keep him abreast of developments by means of personal correspondence.[46]

Heartened by what he took as signs of headway toward a European settlement, Stimson returned to the United States in early September eager to promote further progress. At the same time he began to drop broad hints that Washington would welcome a speedy resolution of the Corridor issue. The secretary held press briefings on September 9–10 at which he stated confidentially that the United States was "interested in having [the German-Polish] boundary and its problems settled in a peaceful way." On the day of his second session with the journalists, Stimson also held a "long and important" talk with the French chargé d'affaires, Jules Henry, in which he made clear his concern over the Corridor and recommended that Europe grant a prompt hearing of revisionist claims to clear the diplomatic air.[47]

While Stimson went out of his way to discuss the Corridor with the West European powers, he did not broach the sensitive topic with representatives of the state that held title to the contested lands. He excluded the Poles from his calendar not only for the obvious reason of Warsaw's unbending opposition to revision, but even more out of the conviction that at bottom the Corridor dispute was a matter of German-French relations—a function of great-power politics and general European interest—in which parochial Polish concerns were of little consequence.

His apprehensions aroused by leaks of Stimson's press-conference allusions to Pomerania, Polish chargé Władysław Sokołowski cornered him in mid-September and extracted a pledge of American *désintéressement* in the frontier imbroglio.[48] If evasive, Stimson's denial was technically correct: he hoped to see the Europeans compose their differences without the direct involvement of the United States. Stimson conceived of America's role in the process as that of a high-minded mediator among disputants who, once coaxed to the bargaining table, would make their own decisions. He did not believe his advocacy of a peaceful solution of a dangerous European issue violated Washington's policy of evenhandedness, even if that solution inevitably entailed major Polish concessions to Germany.

Later that same month the United States tendered an invitation to Laval to pay a state visit in late October, and Stimson glimpsed his chance to bring his disarmament policies closer to fruition. On September 30 he startled Hoover with the observation that the Laval talks represented:

> a great opportunity . . . to put in a good stroke on what are really the underlying and fundamental problems in the European question. . . . The only way we can get at the question of European peace with disarmament, is to get at the underlying problems which lie between France and Germany. These are the real problems of a general disarmament conference, the question of the revision of the Versailles Treaty.

Stimson wanted no less than to transform the Geneva forum into a European peace conference empowered to redefine the Versailles system, the sort of revisionist parley implied in MacDonald's musings at Sciberscross. The necessary precondition of such a congress was an accommodation between Paris and Berlin, and he saw the Laval visit as an ideal occasion to advance toward that end. Although taken aback, Hoover agreed to Stimson's request for permission to talk over his idea with Senator Dwight Morrow, whom the secretary wished to designate the head of the American delegation to Geneva.[49]

During the following week Stimson met several times with Morrow and a small group of advisers to review American policy toward Europe and concoct a plan to persuade Laval to forswear French insistence on maintenance of the Versailles status quo. They dusted off a proposal that had long attracted Stimson, the proffer of a "consultative pact" with France in hopes of buttressing her security with a vague promise of American benevolence and simultaneously inducing Paris to compromise its differences with Germany.[50]

Stimson's desire to win Laval over to the cause of revision for the sake of disarmament survived the shock of Morrow's sudden death on October 5. He continued to gather with his coterie of State Department intimates and sharpened his focus on the Polish Corridor as the key to the European puzzle. On October 12 he met with Hoover again and told the president that "the political questions of the Eastern boundary of Germany underlay the whole question, not only of disarmament but of the economic rehabilitation of Europe; and . . . we might just as well dig into them all with Laval."[51] Stimson received quiet encouragement in this direction from several prominent American bankers who regarded the suspense over the Corridor as an impediment to the economic stabilization of Europe; from one of the financiers, Paul M. Warburg of the International Acceptance Bank and the Manhattan Company, he borrowed the idea of spanning the Corridor with an international highway linking the separated German territories.[52] Enlisting the aid of Robert Kelley, the head of the East European desk of the State Department, Stimson elicited suggestions of "frontier rectifications" and other concessions the Poles might grant in return for an "Eastern Locarno" that would provide a comprehensive guarantee of their modified borders.[53] Although the secretary of state assured the uneasy French ambassador, Paul Claudel, that he had no intention of imposing an agenda on the Laval talks, he was resolved not to allow the Corridor to pass unnoticed.[54]

The goal of attaining peace through revision had captured Stimson's imagination, and he persisted in the face of overwhelming evidence that the Laval summit was neither the time nor the place to address the Corridor. Laval's personal views notwithstanding, France upheld her policy of support for the Polish frontiers and made known her preference to avoid the subject during the American visit.[55] Stimson's eagerness to grant priority to the eastern boundaries also ran counter to the advice of the State Department's European hands, who thought the subject too hot to handle and generally endorsed the French arguments for a temporary "political moratorium."[56] More importantly, he faced an uphill battle to convince the president of the wisdom of his thesis that the pacification of Europe demanded an unprecedented peacetime commitment to French security from the United States in return for reconsideration of the Polish Corridor and other issues stemming from the treaties.[57]

These dismal prospects of success to the contrary, Stimson was fired with an almost missionary zeal to break the European logjam. Attracted by nature to personal diplomacy, he believed he could appeal directly to Laval, whom he considered a reasonable and flexible sort, and set in motion the creation of a European coalition united in adherence to his own views of disarmament and peaceable revision. The secretary of state felt it lay within his power personally to resolve the difficulties that beset Europe, and so he persevered despite the odds against him.[58]

In the meantime, Laval's impending journey to America stirred a bad case of nerves in Poland. Whispers of Stimson's intentions to raise the Corridor with the French filtered into the *Baltimore Sun* and the German Wolff press agency in early October. Sokołowski in Washington disputed the significance of the stories, but Warsaw—sensitive as always to suggestions of American revisionist leanings—took the rumors seriously.[59] The Poles accordingly launched a vigorous effort to ensure that their interests would not suffer harm from the Washington parleys. Zaleski sought and obtained Laval's assurances that he would give no ground on the Corridor during the conference.[60] Anxious inquiries made of Willys and the

State Department complained of the offending newspaper accounts and hinted at the suspicion they were not pure journalistic fancy.[61] The foreign minister directed Skirmunt, the Polish ambassador in London, to inform his American counterpart that German irredentism was a threat to the peace and to see that this pointed message reached the State Department in advance of Laval's arrival.[62] Summoned from leave in Poland to consult with Zaleski and Piłsudski, Filipowicz cut short his vacation to return without delay to Washington, cabling ahead to his subordinates at the embassy to procure an interview with Hoover before the president met with the French visitor.[63]

Granted his audience with Hoover on October 21, the Polish envoy used the occasion to deliver the strongest blow of Warsaw's diplomatic campaign to remove the Corridor from the arena of the Franco-American summit. Speaking "on the authority of Marshal Piłsudski," Filipowicz bluntly declared that Poland would not tolerate the contraction of her western boundary by any means: "Poland wants peace, but only on the basis of the maintenance of existing treaties. Revision means war." He also warned that continued German provocation would tempt a Polish invasion "to settle the thing once and for all." Filipowicz repeated his pugnacious statement to Undersecretary Castle, who considered the message so inflammatory that he wondered whether the best thing to do with his record of the conversation was not "to burn it up."[64]

Piłsudski had played the trump he had held in reserve since 1929 for possible use against a revisionist bid from Washington. Hoover and Stimson both found Piłsudski's curt admonition infuriating, but the belligerent reputation of the Polish strongman dissuaded the Americans from dismissing it as empty bluster. Castle advised Stimson that the proclamation from Warsaw rendered "any solution of the political questions of the eastern frontier of Germany . . . almost impossible short of war."[65]

Even before the Poles dramatically asserted themselves, Stimson's high expectations of the Laval summit had given way to pessimism. He feared rightly that Hoover considered the visit "just a nuisance" and lamented that "our ideas have not gotten together." In particular he had failed to win presidential acceptance of the consultative pact, which had formed the heart of his project to obtain French concessions. In fact, Hoover agreed with Stimson's overall diagnosis of the European malaise, but he drew entirely different conclusions. Figuratively throwing up his hands in impatience with European quarrels, Hoover wanted to put Europe on notice that the United States would offer no new initiatives on the order of the debt moratorium until the Old World had patched up its discords.[66] This clashed fundamentally with Stimson's readiness to assist in a European settlement and ensured that the Franco-American conference would make no substantial contribution toward that end.

Beginning his American tour in these inauspicious circumstances, Laval landed in New York on October 22 amid a swirl of speculation that the United States meant to depart from its established policy and suggest the placement of the Corridor on the international agenda—even though, in the words of the *New York Times*, merely to imagine the possibility seemed "almost fantastic."[67]

The French premier arrived in Washington the next day and closeted himself with Hoover and Stimson at the White House. The talks rambled over various topics, but the German-Polish rivalry held center stage. Hoover began by deploring the instability of Central Europe, and Laval promptly recommended the "political moratorium" as a solution. Protesting this as an "immoral suggestion," Stimson reminded Laval of his admission of July that the Polish Corridor constituted the only barrier to a French-German reconciliation and proposed that the dispute was "remediable." Uncomfortable, the visitor replied that the Corridor was inexcusable—"anyone could look at the map and and see that it was an absurdity"—but insisted that Polish intransigence made its modification impossible. Contradicting Stimson's claim that Berlin confined its territorial ambitions to the east, he asserted that revision of the Corridor would only whet German appetites for Alsace-Lorraine. Alarmed at Laval's unexpected inflexibility toward Germany and disappointed with Hoover's seeming acquiescence in the argument for putting talk of revision on ice, Stimson allowed the subject to drop, finding some consolation in the fact that he had "brought the matter up and shown what we felt about it."[68]

As the leaders huddled at the White House, a more public drama unfolded at the other end of Pennsylvania Avenue on Capitol Hill. A large party of French journalists in Laval's retinue secured an interview with Senator William E. Borah of Idaho, the powerful and voluble chairman of the Senate Foreign Relations Committee. Equally renowned as a critic of the Versailles order and as a man of independent and quotable opinion, Borah was asked his view of the European issues presumed to occupy the Hoover-Laval discussions. Claiming to speak only for himself, Borah delivered a sharp critique of French policy that emphasized the need for drastic overhaul of the peace treaties:

> If I had my way about it . . . I would change the Polish Corridor if it was possible to do so; and I would change the situation with reference to Upper Silesia if I could. . . . It could be done . . . peacefully by the nations interested coming together and making the change. . . . If you were going to deal with a specific subject like the Polish Corridor . . . you would call together the three or four nations that are particularly interested.[69]

When a messenger hurriedly reported Borah's words to the conferees at the White House, Laval broke into a horrified laugh and blurted, "Why, the man lives in Mars!" Meanwhile, the putatively extraterrestrial legislator ruefully told a friend, "I suppose I have likely started something." The senator's statement was hardly newsworthy in itself—he had said much the same thing for years—but the startling timing of his endorsement of treaty revision electrified a capital already abuzz with rumors that the Corridor lay on the table of the Hoover-Laval conversations. The Borah interview caused a sensation and understandably excited a flurry of speculation abroad on the true nature of Washington's attitude toward the Polish boundaries.[70]

By next morning Borah's pronouncement clearly had upstaged the summit talks and prompted the widespread, if mistaken, impression that he had spoken with official imprimatur, especially in light of the common knowledge that the senator had conferred with the president on the eve of the Hoover-Laval meeting.[71] At the least, the episode had cast an embarrassing spotlight on the sensitive issue of revision. Facing the press on October 24, Stimson denied complicity in the interview and insisted the United States took "no direct interest" in the Corridor. Fearing that the newspapers had blown the incident out of proportion, Stimson that night entertained a party at his estate with a good-natured "debate" between Borah and Laval, who mulled over the topics of disarmament and treaty revision in a spirit of amiable disagreement. The publicity stirred by the Borah interview compelled the White House as well to deny that Hoover had proposed the dismantling of the Corridor.[72]

On October 25 Stimson met privately with his French guest and took up the Polish frontiers once more, persuaded that an informal setting might encourage Laval to moderate his unyielding stance against Berlin. Stimson impressed upon his interlocutor the need to make some attempt to mollify German resentment in order to start the process of European reconciliation, suggesting at the least the simplification of transit across the Corridor between the *Reich* and the East Prussian enclave. Laval agreed that the Corridor was a "monstrosity" but nonetheless avoided any relaxation of his insistence on the political moratorium. Stimson found Laval more accommodating in Hoover's absence, as he had hoped, but personal diplomacy had failed to melt French resistance.[73]

The Laval sojourn ended that night with a reception at the French embassy for the diplomatic corps. Seizing on the presence of Borah, Filipowicz approached the senator and conspicuously reproached him for his interview, charging that his words would incite the German Nazis. Borah retorted that the best way to neutralize Hitler was to liquidate the Corridor and provide fair treatment for the German minority in Poland. The tense if polite exchange amused the capital considerably, and even the disputants recognized the comic overtones in this drawing-room altercation. An official of the Polish embassy drolly assured the press that Borah and Filipowicz "could make it up without resorting either to pistols or rapiers."[74]

The Hoover-Laval summit and its meager accomplishments quickly receded from the headlines, but the furor aroused by the Borah news conference persisted for weeks. When Italian Foreign Minister Dino Grandi called on the United States in November, he made a point of avoiding the subject of treaty revision for fear of repeating the discomfort encountered by Laval.[75] The interview of October 23 enhanced Borah's already legendary reputation for speaking frankly and out of turn, and journalistic parodists lampooned his latest indiscretion with relish.[76] The episode inspired public protests in Poland and demonstrations of support in Germany, whose diplomats regarded it hopefully as an oblique American endorsement of German territorial aspirations.[77]

Aside from Filipowicz's energetic personal objection, official Polish response to the interview was mild. Beyond *pro forma* expressions of indignation, Warsaw paid little heed to Borah, who in Zaleski's estimation "merely repeated his well-known views." At the same time, the incident afforded Poland an opportunity to restate her insistence on the inviolability of the peace treaties and indirectly to renew her warning to the United States not to dabble in horsetrading over the Corridor.[78]

European observers generally interpreted Borah's words as representative of American sentiment, and Washington did little to invalidate this impression. Although they disclaimed responsibility for the interview, neither the White House nor the State Department rebuked Borah or repudiated his statements, so inviting the conclusion that the senator from Idaho had—as Walter Lippmann put it—provided "the kind of insight into significant American opinion, inside and outside the Administration, which could have been conveyed in no other way."[79]

Stimson's failure to win Laval over to revisionism marked an abrupt end to his exploratory effort to commit the influence of the United States toward arrangement of a settlement of the Polish boundary dispute. In short order the secretary of state turned his attention away from the problems of Central Europe owing to his increasing absorption with the Japanese encroachment into Manchuria as well as a growing despondency over the European impasse. He lost confidence that the Polish Corridor controversy could be solved peacefully, and he glumly wrote to MacDonald that "this is a bad time for those constructive advances in foreign relations which you and I talked over together at Sciberscross."[80]

While the secretary of state lost interest in the Polish boundaries, the problem occupied the thoughts of several of the European specialists within the American diplomatic corps for several more months. Their consensus was that the tension over the Corridor—the "protruding sore thumb of Europe"—was rapidly reaching the breaking point,[81] but Poland's categorical rejection of any amendment of her frontiers persuaded the State Department not to put Warsaw's words to the test. As Castle saw it, Piłsudski's threat of force provided convincing evidence of the need to "do what we can to prevent any agitation of that question. Certainly nobody would feel that a settlement of the question was worth a war."[82]

One enduring effect of the fiasco of the Laval visit was to cause Washington to put aside the temptation to intercede, however unobtrusively, in the Corridor dispute. The passing sense of some American diplomats that their government could assist in the resolution of the conflict over Pomerania gave way to a resigned acknowledgement that the matter lay beyond the power or will of the United States to act in Europe. The counselor of the Warsaw embassy, John C. Wiley, reported early in 1932 that "as for American policy in the premises, there can, I fear, be only a negative one: to hope for the best. The Eastern frontiers of Prussia have been changing almost constantly since the Xth century. They probably will continue to do so."[83]

Stimson's flirtation with revision of the Polish Corridor passed without a lasting effect on European politics and, in fact, produced only a momentary disturbance in relations between Poland and the United States. The brisk exchanges of October had left a few bruises, but these healed relatively quickly. Home for consultations in November, Willys found Hoover still smarting from Filipowicz's announcement of Polish readiness to take up arms. Willys managed to soothe the president, but he noted a residue of bitterness in official American circles.[84] Another feud ended a few weeks later when the Polish embassy in Washington gave a breakfast in honor of Senator Borah. The gesture moved a local journalistic wit to report that "Poland and Idaho have apparently buried the hatchet."[85]

In itself an aberration in the generally amicable and uneventful pattern of political relations between the United States and Poland, the Stimson revisionist plan of 1931—the one venture of interwar American diplomacy into the thicket of European boundary questions—nonetheless represented a logical product of the inclinations of U.S. policy in Europe. Washington recognized the central importance of a healthy Germany to its goal of European recovery and agreed to wield its influence selectively as a nonpartisan patron of concord and the general interest according to its lights. As often as not, as in the examples of the Dawes Plan and Locarno, American diplomatic intercession worked to amend the peace settlement of 1919, which the United States had repudiated. Washington conducted its policies in Europe independently and in pursuit of its own objectives—peace and its own version of stabilization—rather than out of alliance or sympathy with individual states or blocs, and so their effects might vary with changing conditions. This rule applied as well in the particular issue of the Polish western boundary, which the United States upheld for the sake of stability and calm during the Coolidge years and sought to redraw in 1931 once the conviction took hold that to maintain the Corridor was more dangerous than to alter it. Only the Polish threat to resort to war for the sake of the Corridor persuaded the United States to retract its suggestion. Perceiving this shift in American opinion, Warsaw adjusted its expectations of the United States accordingly. Having once counted on Washington's protection of their interests, the Poles now asked only for its indifference.

CHAPTER VIII

Conclusion: Depression, Debts, and Estrangement, 1932–1933

Poland had thought the role of the United States in Europe could only be beneficent. Not directly involved in continental disputes, possessing enormous financial resources and great economic influence, surrounded by an aura of impartiality, she had the power to exert a salutary force in the pacification of Europe. Alas, it appears that America's statesmen are ignorant of the continent, that they harbor false impressions of the European situation and . . . that they do not care to practice a policy of world solidarity.

Kurjer Warszawski, December 11, 1932

The great global depression dominated the Western world of the early 1930s and profoundly altered the character of international relations in Europe. Unprecedented in severity or duration, the universal economic affliction dispelled the prosperity upon which the relative calm of the Locarno period ultimately depended. The slump abetted the rise of German Nazism and other forces hostile to the established European order even as it introverted and demoralized governments and diminished their ability to contend with the new economic and political challenges. The attendant constriction of world commerce likewise prompted a fundamental shift in American foreign policy. No longer able to fulfill its accustomed postwar role of banker to Europe, Washington gradually reverted to a position approaching true isolation, not to emerge until 1940 with the decision to aid Britain in the Second World War. The depression, then, marked the definitive end of a decade of relatively lively financial and political contact between Poland and the United States.

Until 1932 Polish leaders pointed with pride to their country as a model of comparative economic health amid the chaos of Eastern and Central Europe. Speaking with the American chargé in Warsaw in the autumn of 1931, the deputy minister for foreign affairs, Józef Beck, serenely likened Poland to "an island about which turbulent waters whirled but which was not in danger of being submerged."[1] Such boasts contained more bluster than accuracy, for Poland was no exception to the extreme privation that gripped the agrarian countries of the Baltic and Danubian regions. Dependent as their neighbors on exports of foodstuffs and raw materials, the Poles suffered from the drastic fall of agricultural prices and the reduced trading capacity of their foreign customers. The devastation of agriculture wiped out the earning power of the state, brought the problem of rural overpopulation to calamitous dimensions and crippled industry as well. Polish national income declined by 25 percent between 1929 and 1933, while during the same period industrial production slumped by one-third and unemployment quadrupled to 17 percent.[2]

More than ever Poland required the stimulus of foreign credit to revive a paralyzed economy,[3] but the depression dried up the sources of capital and diverted the remaining trickle of loans away from Germany and the countries to her east. The collapse of agricultural markets discouraged lending to the agrarian states, and the conspicuous increase of economic distress and political tension in Central Europe gave investors fresh reason not to hazard their money in a troubled area. Far from adding to the national treasury from abroad, Warsaw could not manage even to hold its own. Already by 1931 the effects of debt service had turned Poland into a net exporter of capital, and the subsequent recall of short-term credits that followed in the wake of the Central European financial crisis of the same year threatened to bleed the country of foreign exchange.[4]

At the same time the depression accelerated and confirmed the deterioration of economic ties between Poland and the United States that had begun with the break in the lending boom in 1928. Choked by the protective Hawley-Smoot tariff of 1930, the volume of trade between the two countries fell fourfold within three years. Poland's exports to America dwindled nearly to a halt, characteristically amounting to a bare 10 percent of her imports from across the Atlantic. The American share of holdings in Polish joint stock companies remained at approximately 20 percent of total foreign investment—roughly equivalent to the French and German portfolios—but registered a modest decline in absolute terms.[5]

Meanwhile, Warsaw's standing as a borrower on Wall Street hit bottom. The combination of flagging American lending ability with minimal public confidence in the Polish republic rendered new issues out of the question, while by 1932 the prices of the country's existing securities on the New York market had slipped to half their original value.[6] With the American avenue foreclosed, the Poles turned elsewhere for the meager amounts of foreign capital they could find in their reduced circumstances, notably to France, which succumbed to the economic disease relatively late. A French firm contracted to stake construction of the Silesian-Baltic railway in 1931, the same year that Warsaw procured a $30 million loan from the doomed financial empire of Ivar Kreuger, the

Swedish "Match King." These transactions took up some of the budgetary slack in the short run, but as the depression hit its nadir in 1932 the influx of foreign currency into Poland virtually ceased.

The world crisis sealed the failure of the stabilization plan of 1927 to swell Polish coffers with the anticipated reward of American loans and investments. In 1931 a despondent Governor Harrison of the New York Federal Reserve acknowledged the miscarriage of Benjamin Strong's Polish adventure in a melancholy conversation with Filipowicz and Woytkiewicz, blaming the disappointment of "the justified hopes of Poland" on the depression, "which cannot be brought under control by any conscious efforts." The American helplessly advised the Poles to wait out the bad times and attempted to point out a silver lining in the fact that the very inability of Warsaw to attract foreign capital had spared it the disaster that had befallen oversaturated Germany. As a paradoxical result of her relative economic isolation, Harrison claimed, "Poland, while admittedly hungry, is not sick."[7]

In an ironic postscript to the stabilization program, the Polish government doggedly—and perhaps unwisely—upheld the banner of fiscal orthodoxy long after the evident invalidation of its original purpose as a lure for foreign investors. Inexpert in economics, Piłsudski and his henchmen prized the rehabilitation of the złoty as their chief financial achievement and resolved to defend the currency at all costs, largely for the sake of international prestige and domestic political gain, not to mention an ingrained dread of renewed inflation. Poland accordingly responded to the depression with a conservatism unsurpassed in Europe, pursuing a path of spartan austerity and painfully maintaining the gold standard as other states abandoned it. Aside from satisfying official notions of monetary rectitude, this course of action yielded scant benefit for Warsaw. In an era of devaluation, the high worth of the złoty priced Polish goods out of the world market, while the government's doctrinaire approach to solution of the emergency probably delayed the eventual recovery of the country.[8]

The depression upset the established system for discharge of intergovernmental obligations and brought pleas for relief from hard-pressed debtors. The Hoover moratorium provided a respite of one year, but the United States—by far the leading world creditor—refused to consider readjustment or outright cancellation, in keeping with her fixed postwar policy. In December 1931 the American Congress, heeding the call of public opinion, forbade renegotiation of the European war debt arrangements despite the warnings of the president that some governments could not meet their scheduled payments. During the course of 1932, however, the Europeans began to take unilateral action for release from their liabilities. As the creditors' principal means of leverage on their debtors—the threat to cut off future lending—ceased to have any meaning, the resort to sovereign default beckoned as an avenue of escape. In January Chancellor Brüning announced Berlin's inability to furnish reparations any longer, and as the year drew on seven governments ended payment on private loans. On July 1 Greece became the first country to avail itself of the standard provision for postponement of its American war debt increment.

For its part, Warsaw always had made a point of diligence in settling its bills as a proof of its reliability as a borrower, but as the economic doldrums persisted the satisfaction of lenders became an increasingly onerous burden. The Polish debt service gradually ate away at the national gold reserves, which provided the guarantee of the stability of the currency. For Poland, as for many borrowers, the key to an alleviation of the problem lay with the United States, which ranked first among the country's creditors and commanded 69 percent of Polish state indebtedness; amortization of American obligations alone drained fifteen million dollars from the treasury annually. While maintaining an outward display of equanimity, Polish officials discreetly started to hunt for a reprieve from the debt quandary. In November 1931 the minister of finance publicly recommended an extension of the Hoover moratorium as the best way to erase a projected budget deficit for the coming year, and the following April Zaleski pressed the French to devise a comprehensive plan for European recovery encompassing partial or complete liquidation of the foreign debt claims of the American government.[9]

The first signs of serious divergence between Polish and American views of the war debt question appeared during negotiations for rescheduling of the payments put off by the Hoover moratorium. Displeased with the terms offered by Washington, the Poles ignored a series of U.S. reminders extending into the final weeks of the "Hoover year." Finally in May 1932 Ambassador Willys called on the MSZ to convey the message that the State Department would construe further delay as tantamount to repudiation, leading to a "grave situation" that would "create an unfavorable attitude concerning all debt matters."[10] Faced with this unwelcome prospect, Warsaw relented quickly. On June 10 the two governments reached agreement on a revised timetable for refunding Polish obligations for 1931–1932 totalling $7.5 million.

The problem of the war liabilities grew more acute through the summer of 1932. American diplomats in Warsaw quietly predicted that Polish default was only a matter of time, and after the Lausanne Conference all but eliminated German reparations in July an expanding segment of Polish opinion called for annulment of intergovernmental debts as a matter of balance and justice.[11] In the company of Latvia and Estonia, Poland notified the United States on September 14 of her decision to defer settlement for two years of the $1.1 million installment on principal falling due on December 15, as provided in the debt funding accord of 1924. Washington received the unsurprising news equably but firmly reminded the Poles that the suspension did not embrace the $3.3 million in interest charges also scheduled for payment in December.[12]

While indications of an impending collision over the debts gathered during the spring and summer of 1932, contacts between the United States and Poland continued in other forums. After years of preparation, the Geneva disarmament conference opened in February. The conclave droned on uneventfully for four months, stuck on the issue of German claims to military equality with potential adversaries, before Hoover electrified the proceedings with a proposal to abolish offensive weapons and substantially reduce stores of defensive arms. The American plan excited the intense opposition of France and Poland, among others, because the president's formula could have no effect other than to narrow their military edge over Berlin precisely when the advantage appeared most necessary to cow an increasingly truculent Germany. In his capacity as chief Polish spokesman, Zaleski sought to derail the Hoover project by delaying debate until after the American election in November, reasoning that the president either would suffer defeat at the polls or abandon his brainchild in the event that victory removed his need to make a diplomatic splash.[13] In the end, the U.S. initiative met a quicker death. Few delegations saw merit in the vague and sweeping proposition, and the conference relegated the Hoover plan to the dustbin before the close of the summer.

Although cured of its fleeting temptation of 1931 to take a direct hand in the matter, the State Department continued to keep a wary eye on the discord between Warsaw and Berlin centering on the boundary dispute in Pomerania. Tensions reached a peak in June when Poland sent the destroyer *Wicher* into Danzig harbor to emphasize her determination to defend her contested rights in the free city. Reverting to their earlier stance as passive advocates of peace in the borderlands, American officials took pains during the summer to commend to Filipowicz and his lieutenants the desirability of "keeping cool" and avoiding unnecessary provocation that might swell the rising Nazi tide in Germany.[14]

In September the American chief of staff, General Douglas MacArthur, stopped for five days in Poland as part of a tour of inspection of East European armies intended to acquaint U.S. leaders with the practical difficulties of disarmament in the region. The visitor observed Polish maneuvers near the Soviet frontier and engaged in genial conversations with Marshal Piłsudski on the military predicament of a state wedged between two larger enemies. With respect to Germany, Piłsudski said that Warsaw was "playing for time," calculating that each passing year of peace brought Poland nearer her western neighbor in manpower and so lessened the danger of attack from that quarter. Upon his return to the United States, MacArthur gave Stimson a relatively sanguine estimate of Poland's chances to escape her strategic dilemma, noting that the Red Army was "sunk" as a fighting force owing to the upheavals of the Soviet Five-Year Plan.[15]

Toward the end of the year the American embassy in Warsaw gained a new occupant. To the surprise of none and the relief of many, Ambassador Willys resigned his post in the spring to devote full time to his personal fortune and ailing business. The position remained vacant for six months before Hoover, in the last stages of an uphill battle for reelection, urgently thrust the appointment upon F. Lammot Belin, a retired career diplomat and erstwhile manager of the White House social calendar. The choice was entirely political; Belin was related by marriage to the wealthy and influential du Pont family, and his nomination coincided with an endorsement of the underdog incumbent by the president of the giant industrial firm.[16] None of Hoover's exertions could stave off defeat at the hands of his Democratic challenger, Franklin D. Roosevelt, but Belin received confirmation and took up his duties in Warsaw in December.[17]

The electoral campaign turned exclusively on the issue of the shattered American economy, and Polish diplomats in Washington paid the contest little heed except to note that Polonia had cast its ballots heavily for Roosevelt and his party. Apart from occasional stirrings of hope that a Democratic president might mold a foreign policy in the spirit of "the great Wilson," meaning openly sympathetic to the Poles, Warsaw's agents recognized that the end of twelve years of Republican rule in America held little likelihood of fundamental changes in U.S. attitudes toward Europe and their consequent impact on Poland.[18] On a more modest scale, the representatives of the MSZ debated what effect the election might have on the unsolved problem of the war debts, which—amid growing signs that a number of countries planned to default their December payments—appeared likely to assume critical proportions during the awkward phase of transition between administrations.[19]

Soon after the election Warsaw began to sound out the lame duck Hoover government for signs of flexibility on the debts. On November 10 Filipowicz called on Stimson and limned the Polish economic plight in dire words. The ambassador concluded his exposition with the observation that "the main thing troubling [the Poles] was their debt payment on December fifteenth" but made no proposal for remedial action, stating that "they were waiting for Great Britain and France to shoot first on that question." Within days, as expected, London and Paris requested postponement of their indemnities for December, and Poland quickly made known her desire to share the benefits of any relief accorded other debtors.[20]

On November 22 Filipowicz formally presented the Polish case for deferment of the December 15 installment to an impassive Stimson. Acting on the advice of American lawyers, the MSZ based its appeal on the grounds that payment on time was literally impossible. Contending that the depression had rendered the original debt amortization schedule of 1924 unworkable, the envoy also called for the initiation of proceedings for renegotiation of the agreement.[21] These suggestions failed to impress the Americans any more than the analogous and simultaneous petitions of several other European states. Standing on the position that the executive lacked the power to authorize such changes in refunding procedure in opposition to the express will of Congress, Washington rejected the Polish request and demanded payment in full and on time of the $3.3 million transfer, bending only to the extent of pledging that Hoover would ask the legislature to establish an agency to reopen the war debts settlements.[22]

Disappointed but undeterred, the Poles tried again a week in advance of the December 15 deadline. On December 8 the Polish embassy delivered to the State Department a note setting forth a long list of reasons why Warsaw had no choice but to withhold payment. In many ways, the letter provided a jaundiced official commentary on the entire past decade of financial dealings between Poland and the United States. The Poles took aim at the war debt agreement of 1924, charging that its interest rate was excessive and out of proportion to the country's ability to pay. Pointedly outlining the enervating effect of Warsaw's balance of payments deficit with the United States, the document slyly asserted that Poland could not settle the debt without undermining the złoty and abandoning fiscal conservatism—without jettisoning, in other words, the policies imposed on her by a succession of American counselors. For good measure, the brief described suspension of the war debt as necessary to permit Warsaw to discharge its private loans, "in the first place those contracted in the American market."[23] Again the answer from Washington afforded little comfort. Meeting with Filipowicz the next day, Stimson repeated his government's insistence on receipt of the December installment, adding wanly that Congress might accept the alternative of payment into a blocked account.[24]

The deadlock over the war debts inflamed Polish opinion and placed the *Sanacja* regime in a painful dilemma. The press—particularly the mouthpieces of the right—rose in protest against the United States as a grasping creditor bent on collecting her bills even if it caused the ruination of Europe. The government papers were more restrained, but even the Piłsudskist journals sported such defiant headlines as "Only One Reasonable Solution: Do Not Pay."[25] The arousal of patriotic indignation complicated the already delicate situation of the authorities in Warsaw and forced them to factor domestic political considerations into their decision. On the one hand, default would entail loss of face for *Sanacja* and forfeiture of the hard-won Polish reputation as a conscientious debtor; on the other, compliance with the American dictum meant swimming against the tide of public sentiment and exposing the government to accusations from the right of knuckling under to foreign pressures at the sacrifice of national interests. Uncomfortable in its quandary, Warsaw vacillated as the due date drew near, one day leaning toward repudiation, another day hoping for a last-minute bargain involving partial satisfaction of the December obligations as a token of good faith. Impatient for an answer, Filipowicz telephoned Warsaw on December 12 and finally received definitive word from the Finance Ministry that Poland had decided not to pay.[26]

Unaware that Poland had resolved to reject any solution short of full postponement, Hoover struggled to reach a compromise formula on the eve of the deadline. On the morning of December 14 the president telephoned Stimson to ask if some special allowance might be made for the Poles, as they were "in a very difficult position and have been making a brave fight." Hoover recommended handing Warsaw the option of discharging one million dollars immediately and arranging for payment of the remainder within thirty days. The secretary of state pondered the idea, and when Filipowicz arrived for consultation later in the day he offered the package to the ambassador, explaining that "we felt sympathy with his government." In light of his orders, Filipowicz now hoped for no more than to put the best face on Polish default; even so, for the sake of appearances he agreed to discuss the matter that afternoon with Ogden Mills, the secretary of the treasury.[27]

Filipowicz returned to the State Department the next morning to tell Stimson what he already knew: that Poland, along with several other European states, had elected to decline fulfillment of the debt increments due that day. The ambassador had gone through the motions of meeting with Mills but reported that subsequently he had received telephonic instructions from Colonel Beck, recently appointed as successor to Zaleski at the MSZ, that Poland could afford payment of no amount for fear of endangering the gold cover of the złoty. Filipowicz asked if his interlocutor had any further suggestions; Stimson answered curtly in the negative, and the interview came to an abrupt end.[28]

In all, Poland and three other countries—Belgium, Hungary and Estonia—followed the example of the French in defaulting their war debt obligations on December 15. Added to the $1.1 million suspension announced in September, the delinquent interest installment left Warsaw $4.4 million in arrears to the United States. At the same time, not every state chose the road of repudiation; England led a list of six debtors which punctually, if unwillingly, settled their accounts with Washington.

The choice of Warsaw to enter the ranks of the defaulters elicited strong reactions on both sides of the Atlantic. American opinion focused on France as the leading European culprit, but—swayed by popular notions that the Polish republic owed its existence in large part to Washington and U.S. charity—regarded the actions of the Poles as evidence of particular ingratitude. As one outraged headline spluttered, "U.S. Made Poland, Yet Poland Defaults."[29] Predictably, Polish sentiment ran in opposite directions. The newspapers applauded the decision of the government and praised Paris for having led the way in foiling the American attempts to block the only logical outcome of the tangle of intergovernmental debts. Seeking security in numbers, spokesmen for Sanacja asserted that if relatively solvent France and Belgium could not afford their debt charges, stricken Poland possessed all the more reason to request a period of grace.[30]

However, the government did not escape unscathed by domestic critics of its handling of the debt issue. Polish financial circles questioned the wisdom of the default and read it as a virtual admission of failure to manage the economy on the part of the Piłsudskists.[31] This impression provided grist for the partisan mills of the rightist opposition, which exploited the opportunity with relish in spite of its own advocacy of repudiation. On the morrow of the lapsed deadline the National Democratic bloc of the Sejm introduced a motion of inquiry into the financial competence of the regime. The measure fell before the Piłsudskist majority, but not before its sponsors gained the satisfaction of making the taunting point that had the government's humiliating declaration of destitution to the United States "not been part of an official statement, those words would have caused the confiscation of any paper that printed them."[32]

Chagrined that the American noncancellationist stance had forced him into an unhappy decision affording embarrassment at home and abroad, the ultimate target of these barbs resorted to bitter humor in assessing the events of the past few weeks. Shortly before Christmas Piłsudski convened a meeting of his general staff. Upon completion of the agenda, the assemblage bestowed holiday blessings on their chief. As he made to depart, the Marshal jocularly pleaded with his colleagues to append the wish "that I should not be sucked dry by America. That would not pay." "It never pays to pay," one of them called after him, to the amusement of all.[33]

Its annoyance aside, Warsaw still hoped to salvage its credit by reaching an accommodation with the United States, guessing that the breakdown of the established schedule of amortization might make the Americans more receptive to Polish arguments for renegotiation so as to obtain partial restitution rather than none at all. On December 20 Colonel Beck identified his government's objective as modification rather than annulment of the debt and announced that Poland was prepared immediately to begin talks toward resumption of payments on a reduced scale, contending that the sums at stake were "too small" to justify a breach in relations.[34] These overtures drew a chilly response from the State Department. When Filipowicz laid the proposition before him two days later, Stimson brushed it aside with studied finality. The secretary retorted that Washington had no intention of revising the war debts, adding to boot that in the event of a change of policy, preferential consideration "naturally" would go to those states which had made a "distinct sacrifice" in meeting their obligations for December.[35]

After his fruitless meeting with Stimson, Filipowicz relinquished the task of hunting for a reconciliation of the war debt dispute to his recently-appointed replacement, Stanisław Patek. Like Filipowicz, the incoming ambassador brought to the United States a record of long association with Piłsudski and extensive diplomatic experience, having served a stint as foreign minister before heading the Tokyo and Moscow missions.[36] Patek spent his first months in his new post shuttling almost constantly between Washington and Warsaw as a glorified courier. Following a preliminary audience with Undersecretary Castle at the State Department just before the New Year, he departed for Poland to confer on debt policy with Piłsudski, who imparted his instructions and promptly sent him on the return voyage westward. Granted a séance with Stimson on January 18, Patek essentially repeated the Polish formula of December 22 for an abatement of the debts; unsurprisingly, the American followed suit, insisting on the inviolability of the schedule of 1924. With the contestants still at loggerheads, Patek broke off the discussions and set sail for Europe on January 20.[37]

The ambassador's deputies attributed his absence from Washington to heart trouble and his need for a vacation from overwork;[38] the more likely explanation was that the Poles had given up on the Republicans and resolved to wait for the entrance into power of Roosevelt and the Democrats before resuming the war debt parleys. During the intervening lull, American diplomats in Warsaw paused to analyze the Polish default and arrived at differing judgments. While stopping shy of urging abolition of the liabilities, Ambassador Belin wrote sympathetically of the plight of his hosts, affirming that they were doing their utmost to economize in unenviable circumstances. A more acerbic tone dominated the report of the consul general, J. Klahr Huddle, who maintained that Poland in fact could have paid without jeopardizing the stability of the złoty and defined the question principally as a test of the country's "national honesty and . . . of its . . . right to a place among nations." If the Poles could not refund at least half their debt, he sniffed, their "capacity to undertake the international obligations of a sovereign state may be seriously questioned."[39]

By the same token, the war debt imbroglio did much to confirm a growing sense of Polish disillusionment with the United States and resentment of her financial sway. In large part this tendency arose out of the disappointed expectations of the early years of independence, when Poles had nurtured a virtual cult of America. The experiences of the World War, and especially memories of Woodrow Wilson and the Hoover relief, had won for the United States an unrivalled place in Polish affections, while postwar Poland looked to America—modern, vibrant, fantastically rich—as a model for her own development. Since that time Washington had renounced the Wilsonian legacy and the economic crisis had tarnished the allure of the American example. Many Polish commentators on the United States of the depression era cast a cold eye on the "new Rome," deploring its materialism and cultural poverty and warning of its insatiable drive to bring the globe under the domination of the dollar.[40]

Angered by the trend of U.S. actions in Europe, the political right pointed to the Hoover moratorium and the clash over the war debts as proof that Washington had aligned itself with forces inimical to Polish interests. Writing in the National Democratic *Gazeta Warszawska* in 1933, Roman Dmowski, the ranking theoretician and publicist of the

Polish right, linked the United States to such standard bugbears as Germany and international Jewish finance. Predicting that the depression would diminish American influence in Europe, Dmowski concluded "one should not be surprised if that does not cause sorrow in Poland."[41]

Impatience with the American demands for repayment stirred animosities within official circles as well, and the standoff prodded the ill and aging Piłsudski into caustic reminiscence of his past dealings with the United States. In early March he told Świtalski that he had concocted the idea of celebrating an "America day" to shame Washington into moderation of its stance on the war debt but lately had abandoned the project. The Marshal went on to state that "he had very bad experiences with the American [stabilization] loan some time ago" and regaled his listener with angry recollections of 1927, leaving Świtalski impressed that "the Commander's ire remains so animated despite the passage of years."[42]

Upon the installation of the new regime in Washington, Ambassador Patek crossed the Atlantic for the fifth time in three months in a final attempt to find a mutually acceptable adjustment of the war debts. Arriving in New York on March 16, the envoy found himself besieged by reporters imploring a statement on the Polish Corridor in light of the recent arrival of Hitler to power in Germany and a related increase in tension over the question of Danzig.[43] After making his escape from the unwelcome attentions of the journalists, Patek proceeded to the capital. Within two weeks he met on separate occasions with the president and his secretary of state, Cordell Hull, but achieved no progress toward a settlement of the principal irritant in American-Polish relations.[44] If anything, the Democrats proved less accommodating on the question of the war debts than their Republican predecessors. Roosevelt as candidate had endorsed the popular noncancellationist line, and once in office the New Deal government assigned low priority to the recovery of the obligations, and even lower to their revision, in its absorption with its crash program for revival of the domestic economy.

With both countries locked into irreconcilable positions, the Polish default of American war debts protracted and gradually became permanent. When the time came for the next semiannual payment in June 1933, the pattern of the previous winter repeated itself: Washington called in its dues, and Warsaw responded with pleas of insolvency and suggestions of renegotiation, which in turn brought a frosty refusal from the United States. By the following December the procedure had turned ritualistic and automatic, and in short order the liabilities became a dead letter.[45] The Hoover moratorium of 1931 represented for Poland, as for France and a number of other countries, the effective termination of payment of her war debt to the United States. In all, the Poles had refunded $22.7 million since 1925, leaving an unpaid balance of $461.1 million.

The collapse of the war debt accord of 1924—the document that had initiated and largely governed the conduct of financial relations between Poland and the United States—marked the end, in fact as well as symbol, of significant contact between the countries during the remaining years of peace. Turning its back on the measured internationalism of the Republicans, the Roosevelt administration treated involvement in the affairs of the outside world as an unwelcome distraction from American recovery and took scant interest in Poland once it overcame early apprehensions that the advent of Hitler meant the outbreak of European war over Pomerania. During the anxious spring of 1933 the president wondered aloud to foreign diplomats if some "mechanical arrangement" to ease German communication with East Prussia across Polish territory might not defuse the problem, and a suspicious Patek forced Hull into a denial of "any purpose of our Government . . . to discuss the Polish Corridor with any government at present, and especially without the presence of Poland."[46]

To universal surprise, however, the Nazi assumption of control in Berlin produced a speedy rapprochement between Poland and Germany which culminated in a declaration of nonaggression in January 1934. Mindful of German diplomatic isolation and military vulnerability, Hitler sought to reduce tensions on his eastern flank while he consolidated his dictatorship and began a program of massive rearmament. The agreement left the Polish alliances intact and appeared to institute Warsaw's long-sought "political moratorium" by tabling discussion of bilateral disputes for ten years; by complementing a nonaggression accord of 1932 with Moscow it also seemed to solve the problem of encirclement that had been the historic bane of Poland. The turnabout delighted the United States and persuaded Washington temporarily that the crisis of Central Europe had broken. In the flush of the moment the American ambassador in Warsaw, John Cudahy, declared that "the Polish-German pact . . . has relieved the situation here of any tension and this post has now resolved itself into a function of long distance reporting."[47]

As political ties languished, so also the economic links connecting Poland to the United States loosened to the point of separation. In 1934 Congress prohibited further American lending to war debt delinquents through the Johnson Act, which caught the Poles in its net. The legal proscription of new issues to Poland was redundant, for it merely duplicated the collective judgment of the banking and investment fraternity. In fact, the holders of Polish securities from the 1920s tried to unload them before they too went the way of the war debts, driving their prices so low that they became favorites of speculators on the Warsaw exchange.[48] The Poles managed to scrape up two minor credits in England before the doors of foreign vaults slammed shut to stay, compelling the government to resort to such devices as internal subscription loans to make ends meet.

More out of pride and habit than any realistic expectation of reward, Poland continued to service her private American debts long after default had become the rule rather than the exception in international transactions. Finally in 1936, with the stability of the złoty at stake, the Poles began to abandon payment of their dollar loans one by one; within the year the repudiations embraced the entire portfolio of American holdings in Polish bonds. Warsaw quickly despatched Adam Krzyżanowski, a veteran of the stabilization loan talks of a decade earlier, to parley with its creditors on the other side of the Atlantic, and by 1937 Poland had come to terms for a resumption of payment at lower interest and spread over a more leisurely timetable.[49] This modifed plan remained in effect barely a year before the German and Soviet invasions of September 1939 jointly overran the Polish state and cast its foreign securities into renewed and seemingly permanent limbo.

Eventually, however, the socialist successor to the vanished Poland of the interwar epoch added a belated footnote to the history of the private American loans dating from the era of Paderewski, Piłsudski, and their counterparts. In the latter stages of the 1960s the Polish People's Republic, apparently hoping to improve its reputation within the realm of international commerce by making good the obligations of its bourgeois forerunner, began to intimate its readiness to make partial restitution of these old claims. After entering into negotiations with the Foreign Bond-holders Protective Council of New York in 1972, Warsaw consented three years later to reimburse owners of these venerable securities at 40 percent of original face value. The deadline for redemption of the coupons expired in the tumultuous summer of 1980,[50] the season of the birth of Solidarity, six decades after conclusion of the first of the loans and four years before the scheduled completion of payment of the Polish World War debts.

During the postwar era of Republican predominance extending from 1921 to 1933 the United States followed a course of selective participation in the affairs of Europe. In its most distinctive phase, corresponding approximately to the presidency of Coolidge, the policy sought to advance American interests by encouraging prosperity, tranquility, and political moderation in Europe, chiefly through the device of massive overseas investment and secondarily through a sparing exercise of governmental power operating as an avowedly neutral influence on the continent. Initially disappointed by the withdrawal of Washington from the coalition of World War victors whose continued support she coveted in peacetime, reconstituted Poland gradually developed a strategy to put the American desire for European stability to use in her own constant struggle for economic viability and diplomatic security. This theme dominated relations between Poland and the United States during the decade spanning the Dawes Plan and the depths of the world depression, and the history of that association in turn sheds light on the nature and bounds of American activity in interwar Europe.

The first serious Polish attempt to adapt to the postwar American policy of stabilization occurred in 1924 after a five-year eclipse of ties with the transatlantic republic. In that year the government of Władysław Grabski responded to the inauguration of a surge of U.S. investment in the Old World by taking steps toward making his needy country an attractive recipient of loans. His foreign minister and eventual successor as premier, Aleksander Skrzyński, broadened these efforts and added a political dimension to them, asking for American financial and diplomatic support for Poland not as an ally but as a bastion of democracy, peace and social conservatism which might further accomplishment of U.S. aims in Europe. Skrzyński dramatized his appeals with a tour of the United States in 1925, and upon his elevation to leadership his ministry placed the strengthening of Polish credit on Wall Street near the top of its agenda.

These initial explorations yielded scanty results, but in 1926 the Poles unexpectedly found themselves adopted by Governor Benjamin Strong of the Federal Reserve Bank of New York—with the covert backing of the Coolidge administration—as a vehicle toward the promotion of the American central bank to a commanding position in international finance. In exchange for Warsaw's submission to an economic recovery program elaborated and supervised by American advisers, the Reserve Bank agreed to sponsor a large loan designed to prime the pump for a steady flow of foreign capital into Poland. The accord was largely the handiwork of Jan Ciechanowski, the capable Polish minister to Washington, who conceived of the arrangement as a means of realization of Skrzyński's goal of financial and subsequent diplomatic partnership with the United States. This strategy rested on the theory that—as one Polish diplomat characterized the American attitude—"Poland and her fate do not concern us; but if 300 million of our dollars should become engaged there, and if the fate of those dollars should depend on the fate of Poland, well—then things would be different."[51]

Ironically, Ciechanowski's patron fell from office soon after the forging of the alliance with Strong and the unfinished American project devolved as an unwanted bequest upon the strongman regime of Piłsudski, which held no special place for the United States in its platform and grudgingly assented to the rehabilitation scheme in 1927. Intended as prologue, the installation of the stabilization plan in fact marked the zenith of American-Polish collaboration, which thereupon went into decline as economic conditions worsened and Warsaw found itself increasingly at odds with Washington on such international political questions as debts and reparations, disarmament, and revision of the Polish frontiers. The prolonged anticlimax dragged on until the depression caused the virtual withdrawal of the American presence in Europe and obliterated the conditions that had permitted the brief invigoration of relations between the United States and Poland in the middle years of the postwar decade.

The Polish courtship of Wall Street did not fail entirely. Before the depression Americans invested significantly more money in Poland than in any other state of Eastern Europe, and in the four-year space between Locarno and the stock market crash the country trailed only Germany and Italy among European net importers of dollar loans. Yet these achievements scarcely satisfied Polish aspirations to compete successfully with the West European borrowers who found ready buyers on the American market, and particularly with the Germans, who attracted eight dollars for every one that made its way to the Poles. Had not some Americans, like Clarence Dillon and Charles Dewey, dreamed of using Poland as a springboard into the Russian trade, the disparity would have been greater still.

The reasons for the relative scarcity of American investment in Poland were no mystery even to contemporaries. Public distaste for Polish policies, so pronounced among American liberals, played no great part in the equation; while Warsaw labored under the weight of a reputation for anti-Semitism, oppressiveness and militarism, this appears to have little influenced the behavior of buyers and still less that of the hardheaded Yankee bankers. Some responsibility may be attributed to the advent of *Sanacja*, which looked upon the attentions of foreign capital as a distinctly mixed blessing, and even more to a general recession of international lending which followed the stabilization agreement of 1927. However, ultimate accountability for the sluggish Polish performance on Wall Street rests with the ineradicable perception of U.S. finance that Warsaw was a poor risk.

Simply put, American banks refused to lend to Poland because they regarded such ventures as unprofitable and dangerous, and both houses that went against the grain of opinion and took the chance—Dillon, Read and Bankers Trust—ended by regretting their decision to open Polish accounts. In each case the same pattern prevailed: the bond sold poorly, the bank lost interest in Poland as a client, Warsaw grew impatient and dismissed the firm after an unhappy association that produced but one loan. Not only Poles concluded that the banks had been derelict in their duty toward Warsaw; in 1929 the Polish financial counselor in Washington approvingly quoted a U.S. banking representative who told him "you have the right *to blame us, the American bankers,* for the fact that you have not attained the economic level that is rightfully yours. Twice you have entrusted to American finance your program of economic development . . . and twice you have been disappointed."[52] Using Wall Street as a scapegoat might have eased Polish frustration, but it missed the essential point that the banks were not charitable organizations but private businesses seeking profit and persuaded by instinct and experience that loans to Poland did not pay. Cautious and ill-acquainted with Europe, the American foreign investor sought the safest possible location for his money[53] and consistently found the Poles wanting by this standard.

American finance never relinquished the fear that Polish investments would fall victim to internal upset or catastrophe visited from without. Similar anxieties bedeviled the credit of all the countries of Eastern Europe,[54] but perhaps none felt their effect so much as Poland. Only the consolidation of the Piłsudski government in the latter years of the 1920s convinced outsiders that the state had seen the last of inflation, financial irresponsibility, and political turmoil, and it was then that Warsaw scored its largest successes on the American market. In a sense, this confirmed a major weakness of the interwar international financial system: that private investors would not lend to a country at the time of its greatest need, but only after the emergency had already been weathered. As the old joke had it, a banker would offer an umbrella when the sun shone and snatch it back at the first sign of rain.

Nevertheless, the Poles could not repeal geography, and so their foremost handicap in dealing with Wall Street remained irremediable. In the eyes of the world, no other European country appeared more vulnerable to its enemies or less likely to live at peace with them, and a question mark hung perpetually over its existence. Consequently, Polish attempts to strengthen ties with the United States faltered in the face of an insoluble dilemma: the Poles sought U.S. loans and investments to arouse friendly American interest in their security and well-being, but the financiers balked precisely because the Polish state was so visibly insecure. Americans would not invest in Poland because at bottom they believed that in time Germany and Russia would crush her as before, and the future was to prove them correct.

Avoidance of precisely that destiny was the cardinal objective of interwar Polish diplomacy, and if Warsaw regarded the United States primarily as a potential source of capital, it also expended much effort in attempting to ensure at least the friendly neutrality of Washington in political questions. Despite the general amity that prevailed between the two countries, their foreign policies occasionally worked at cross purposes as demonstrated most dramatically in the events surrounding the endeavors of Henry Stimson to pave the way for revision of the Polish Corridor in 1931. That episode furnishes a ready insight into certain fundamental differences of outlook that made Poland and the United States an unlikely diplomatic match.

In its conception, American policy in Europe neither favored nor opposed Polish interests; rather it ignored them. Throughout the postwar decade the Poles tried and largely failed to win U.S. recognition of the right of their state to be taken seriously as an independent and important factor in European affairs. Given the size, the military capability, and the strategic significance of Poland—a country roughly comparable in population and resources to Italy—theirs was not an outlandish request. Washington, however, acknowledged few peers on the continent. To the Americans, England, France, Germany, and Italy ranked as meaningful powers and other lands, excepting the special case of the Soviet recluse, fell into the categories of diplomatic ciphers or dependents of the great.[55] In American calculations, Poland figured less prominently as a state than as a problem. Stimson, for instance, conceived of the Polish Corridor essentially as a controversy between Berlin and Paris in which the Poles played an incidental if inconvenient part. In common with many of his countrymen, he believed France possessed the ability and the right to make a deal with Germany on the Corridor and enforce it on her Polish ally.[56] The French could have told Stimson—as in fact they did—that Warsaw was no one's puppet, but the Americans viewed Poland more as a pawn than a protagonist of international politics, and the idea of making common cause with her simply never occurred to them.

A mighty state that conducted policy on a global scale, the United States scarcely comprehended the outlook of a distant, impoverished, and insecure Central European country whose history had taught it to beware partition and dictation from greater powers. As outside observers, the Americans claimed to hold a uniquely broad and nonpartisan perspective on European problems, and Washington assumed reflexively that its voice, because neutral, was therefore that of reason. The United States approached Polish questions in the same olympian manner which to her seemed impartial and to the Poles seemed unsatisfactorily heedless of their rights and needs. Polish officials responsible for dealings with the United States were painfully aware that Warsaw's political relations with the Americans were in large measure but a function of "a whole series of factors . . . over which we have no control," such as U.S. policy toward France, Germany, or Russia.[57] Even the readjustment of the Polish Corridor meant nothing to Stimson except as part of a general European settlement. Whether Germany or Poland gained or lost a small amount of land was of no account; all that mattered was that the dispute should be "settled in some fashion" and removed as a barrier to the pacification of Europe.[58]

Much like the English, the Americans saw nothing sacrosanct in the peace treaties of 1919 and accordingly objected to the diplomacy of France and her allies as unwisely dogmatic and pugnacious. In the same view, a course of judicious concessions to Germany—as in the instances of the Dawes Plan or Locarno—represented the best hope of healing and calming Europe. By extension, Stimson regarded the Polish refusal to permit revision of the Corridor as a triumph of narrow nationalism over the requirements of European and world peace: it was not only selfish, but ultimately a shortsighted contradiction of the best interest of Poland, which too would share the benefits of continental tranquility. Warsaw was fated to appear in the unsympathetic guise of an obstinate opponent of a compromise solution of international discord, a formula that appealed to Americans as the ideal resolution of disputes to which the United States was not a party. The distaste Hoover and Stimson felt for the shrill Polish warnings of 1931 that revision meant war symbolized American displeasure with policies which, as they saw it, held a gun to Europe's head rather than submit the gains of Versailles to arbitration.

In many ways, Washington had no settled policy for dealing with Poland because it felt the need for none. "Warsaw [is] so damned far away," Walter Lippmann wrote to Hugh Gibson in 1919,[59] and such was the perception of Americans throughout the interwar years. The United States recognized no vital interest in the security or well-being of Poland. The Poles frequently attempted to persuade them otherwise, but the Americans paid attention to the Polish republic only intermittently and solely as it fit within the context of their search for a stable Europe. The paradoxical result was that problems associated with Poland coaxed the United States to the limits of her willingness to intervene in European affairs. The Polish stabilization operation of 1926–1927 was perhaps the most ambitious undertaking of interwar U.S. financial diplomacy, while the Stimson revisionist project of 1931 formed its political counterpart as Washington's single serious foray into the complex of European boundary questions. In both instances American initiatives proceeded from the correct, if only dimly understood, assumption that Europe would not be pacified without solution of the troubles of the eastern sector of the continent, and in both as well representatives of the United States were forced to decide how far they were willing and able to go to achieve this objective. In a sense, then, Poland provides a test for measurement of the range and means of Republican policy in Europe. American diplomacy embraced Polish issues only in its most expansive and activist moments; during its more reticent phases, Poland again receded beyond the horizon of U.S. concerns.

For their part, the Poles accurately comprehended the nature of the postwar American presence in the Old World, with its emphasis on the search for stability, but never fully came to grips with its restricted relevance to their problems. Persuaded of their own importance in the European balance, they expected the United States someday to come to the same realization and to act decisively on it one way or another. Consequently Warsaw viewed the American attitude toward Poland as constantly in a process of evolution in which the present was never as significant as the future and the past hardly counted at all as a guide. This propensity inclined the Poles toward excesses of optimism or pessimism regarding America. In such as Skrzyński, it bred inflated and unrealistic visions of the United States as a benefactor, while Piłsudski leaned in the opposite direction and tended to exaggerate the ability and desire of America to employ its influence and economic strength in a manner injurious to Poland. In either case, the authors of these differing conceptions based their American policies on the assumption that the U.S. posture of relative indifference toward their country was anomalous and transitory and so prepared, each in his own fashion, for the day it would change.

That expectant quality typified the relationship between the United States and Poland during the era of dollar diplomacy in Europe. To the Poles, America represented a potential that failed to mature. The idea that Poland might derive material and diplomatic benefit from collaboration with the United States was a doctrine for optimists who worked to construct artificial bonds of interest where none existed naturally. The leading advocates of expansion of relations between the two states looked beyond the realities of the moment and sought to plant the seeds that would bear fruit in the long run. Given other circumstances, they might have succeeded, but the conditions of the interwar years did not permit such a result. In the end, they pursued a dream that never came true.

Notes

ABBREVIATIONS

AAN	Archiwum Akt Nowych, Warsaw
AAN-AB	Ambasada RP w Berlinie, AAN
AAN-AL	Ambasada RP w Londynie, AAN
AAN-AW	Ambasada RP w Waszyngtonie, AAN
AAN-KŠ	Kazimierz Świtalski, AAN
AAN-LN	Delegacja RP przy Lidze Narodów w Genewie, AAN
AAN-MSZ	Ministerstwo Spraw Zagranicznych, AAN
AAN-PPRM	Protokoły posiedzeń Rady Ministrów, AAN
ADAP	Germany, Auswärtiges Amt, *Akten zur deutschen auswärtigen Politik 1918–1945*
AGND	Archiwum Adiutantury Generalnej Naczelnego Dowództwa (Archiwum Belwederskie)
APIP	Polska Akademia Nauk, Instytut Historii, *Archiwum polityczne Ignacego Paderewskiego*, 4 vols. (Wrocław, 1973–1974)
BPPP	France, Ministère des Affaires Étrangères, *Bulletin périodique de la presse polonaise*
DBFP	Great Britain, Foreign Office, *Documents on British Foreign Policy, 1919–1939*
FRB	Federal Reserve Bank of New York records, Federal Reserve Bank of New York
FRUS	United States, Department of State, *Foreign Relations of the United States*
GFMR	German Foreign Ministry records, R. G. 242
HHCP	Commerce Papers, Herbert Hoover Presidential Library, West Branch, Iowa
HHPP	Presidential Papers, Herbert Hoover Presidential Library, West Branch, Iowa
HIA	Hoover Institution Archives, Hoover Institution on War, Revolution and Peace, Stanford University
HIA-US	Poland, Ambasada (U.S.), HIA
IHGS	Archiwum Instytutu Historycznego im. Generała Sikorskiego, London
IHGS-AL	Kolekcja Ambasady RP w Londynie, IHGS

LC	Library of Congress, Washington, D.C.
PIA	Joseph Piłsudski Institute of America, New York
PIA-AL	Ambasada RP w Londynie, PIA
PRO	Foreign Office Papers, F.O. 371, Public Record Office, London
SDNA	State Department Decimal File, R. G. 59, National Archives, Washington, D.C.

CHAPTER I

1. Instructions for chiefs of Polish diplomatic missions, July 7, 1919, APIP, v. 2, p. 256.
2. Lester V. Chandler, *Benjamin Strong, Central Banker* (Washington, 1958), pp. 145–146.
3. Ibid., p. 144.
4. Untitled lecture by R. H. Lord [*ca.* 1920-1921], Edward M. House Papers, Sterling Library, Yale University.
5. The oft-quoted words of French Foreign Minister Stephen Pichon. For treatment of Polish issues at the peace conference, see Kay Lundgreen-Nielsen, *The Polish Problem at the Paris Peace Conference: A Study of the Policies of the Great Powers and the Poles, 1918–1919* (Odense, 1979), and Piotr S. Wandycz, *France and Her Eastern Allies, 1919–1925: French-Czechoslovak-Polish Relations from the Paris Peace Conference to Locarno* (Minneapolis, 1962).
6. In 1919 Herbert Hoover declared: "I know of no other nation that commands such undivided good will among Americans as the Poles" (Adam Olszewski, *Historia Związku Narodowego Polskiego*, 6 vols. [Chicago, 1957-1968], v. 3, p. 294). For an indication of Polish sentiment, see Poland, Sejm, *Sprawozdanie stenograficzne z posiedzenia Sejmu Rzeczypospolitej*, January 8, 1920, p. 5.
7. Władysław Skrzyński to Polish Legation, Washington, October 8, 1919, AAN-AW n. 208.
8. *Sprawozdanie*, March 26, 1919, p. 1096.
9. *Zniszczenia wojenne i odbudowa Polski* (Warsaw, 1929).
10. V. N. Bandera, *Foreign Capital as an Instrument of National Economic Policy: A Study Based on the Experience of East European Countries Between the World Wars* (The Hague, 1964), pp. 4–5; Leopold Wellisz, *Foreign Capital in Poland* (London, 1938), p. 41.
11. Zbigniew Landau and Jerzy Tomaszewski, *Anonimowi władcy: z dziejów kapitału obcego w Polsce, 1918–1939* (Warsaw, 1968), p. 33.
12. For example, see Józef Piłsudski, *Pisma zbiorowe*, 10 vols. (Warsaw, 1937-1938), v. 5, p. 49.
13. "The engagement of American capital in Poland should be considered the strongest possible guarantee [of America's continued interest in Poland]. In the first place, American capital is not politically dangerous to Poland, and once interested in Poland, American capital will of necessity support her" (Władysław Skrzyński to Polish Legation, Washington, October 3, 1919, AAN-AW n. 208).
14. Address to the American-Polish Chamber of Commerce and Industry, May 27, 1920, AAN-AW n. 597.
15. On May 22, 1919, Paderewski told the Sejm that without the aid of Wilson and House, "Poland doubtless would remain an internal question of Germany and Russia" (*Sprawozdanie*, p. 25). Also Paderewski to Eustachy Sapieha, December 6, 1920, APIP, v. 2, pp. 594–595.
16. Piłsudski to Komitet Obrony Narodowej, December 15, 1919, AGND 64/1998.
17. Note these items in the House Papers: Paderewski to House, January 12, 1919 and March 7, 1919; House to Wilson and Robert Lansing, September 19, 1919.
18. R. H. Lord's "Report on Poland," 1918, and "The Problem of East Galicia,"

April 23, 1918, Inquiry Papers, Sterling Library, Yale University; United States, Congress, *Congressional Record*, v. 57, p. 725 and v. 58, pp. 5969–5970; *New York Times*, November 24, 1919; *New Orleans Times-Picayune*, March 23, 1919.

19. In the House Papers: "Notes on the Russian Situation" [February 1919?]; House to Wilson, February 23, 1919; Council of Ten meetings, January 12, 1919, and February 25, 1919. See likewise the record of meeting of David Lloyd George and Georges Clemenceau with Italian and American representatives, December 12, 1919, DBFP, ser. I, v. 2, pp. 744–748.

20. Paderewski to House, January 1, 1919, January 12, 1919, and March 7, 1919, House Papers; Frank Polk Diary, October 2, 1919, Frank Polk Papers, Sterling Library, Yale University. For an American view, Allen W. Dulles, "Lithuania and Poland—The Last Barrier between Germany and the Bolsheviki," December 30, 1918, FRUS: Paris Peace Conference, v. 2, pp. 481–483.

21. Counts of Polish-Americans varied considerably depending on the criteria used for definition. Other contemporary estimates ranged up to four million (Prince Albert Radziwiłł, "Polish Emigration," April 4, 1923, AAN-AW n. 908). For the political activities of Polonia during the war, see M. B. Biskupski, "The United States and the Rebirth of Poland, 1914–1918" (Ph.D. dissertation, Yale University, 1981); Stanley R. Pliszka, "The Polish-American Community and the Rebirth of Poland," *Polish American Studies* 26 (1969), pp. 41–60; Jacek Ryszard Wędrowski, *Stany Zjednoczone a odrodzenie Polski: polityka Stanów Zjednoczonych wobec sprawy polskiej i Polski w latach 1916–1919* (Wrocław, 1980).

22. Władysław Skrzyński to Polish Legation, Washington, October 3, 1919, AAN-AW n. 208; Konstanty Buszczyński to MSZ, February 8, 1919, Konstanty Buszczyński: Korespondencja i Papiery, Biblioteka Narodowa, Warsaw; Buszczyński to MSZ, September 21, 1919, APIP, v. 2, p. 338.

23. Henry Morgenthau to Paderewski, August 10, 1919, and Polk Diary, September 17, 1919, Polk Papers; House Diary, April 8, 1919, and House to Hugh Gibson, May 3, 1919, House Papers. See the concurring *New York Times* editorials of August 23, October 30, and December 24, 1919.

24. Wilson to Joseph P. Tumulty, January 11, 1919, in Suda Lorena Bane and Ralph Haswell Lutz, eds., *Organization of American Relief in Europe, 1918–1919* (Stanford, 1943), p. 177. Hoover's views are set forth in his memoranda of February 19 and April 18, 1919, House Papers, and Hoover to Edwin B. Parker, September 3, 1919, Hugh S. Gibson Papers, HIA. See also Teresa Małecka, "Pomoc rządowa Stanów Zjednoczonych Ameryki dla państwa polskiego po I wojnie światowej," *Przegląd Historyczny* 70 (1979), pp. 73–88, and Frank Costigliola, *Awkward Dominion: American Political, Economic, and Cultural Relations with Europe, 1919–1933* (Ithaca, N.Y., and London, 1984), pp. 39–54.

25. H. H. Fisher, *America and the New Poland* (New York, 1928), pp. 267–271, 278–279; A. B. Barber, *Report of European Technical Advisers Mission to Poland, 1919–1922* (New York, 1923), pp. 3–4; Hugh Gibson Diary, April 23, 1919, Gibson Papers.

26. Władysław Wróblewski to Maurycy Zamoyski, January 25, 1924, AAN-AW n. 1804; Nancy Harvison Hooker, ed., *The Moffat Papers: Selections from the Diplomatic Journals of Jay Pierrepont Moffat, 1919–1943* (Cambridge, Mass., 1956), pp. 10–11. William R. Castle of the State Department later described Gibson to Hoover as "undoubtedly the most brilliant man in [the Foreign Service]" (January 21, 1929, HHPP). Gibson figures heavily in Martin Weil's study of the formation of the modern U.S. diplomatic corps, *A Pretty Good Club: The Founding Fathers of the U.S. Foreign Service* (New York, 1978).

27. Gibson Diary, April 15, 1919. See also Gibson to Lansing, January 22, 1920, SDNA 860.00/3, and Ronald E. Swerczek, "The Diplomatic Career of Hugh Gibson, 1908–1938" (Ph.D. dissertation, University of Iowa, 1972), pp. 138–148.

28. House Diary, June 25 and 26, 1919; Hoover to Wilson, June 2, 1919, Herbert Hoover Papers, HIA. Morgenthau's account of the mission is included in his autobiography *All in a Life-Time* (Garden City, N.Y., 1922), and the text of his report appears on pp. 405–437. Also consult William Phillips to Morgenthau [December 1919?], Henry Morgenthau, Jr., Papers, Franklin D. Roosevelt Presidential Library, Hyde Park, N.Y.; Morgenthau to Hoover,

August 12, 1919, Gibson Papers; Jan Ciechanowski to Paderewski, June 30, 1919, APIP, v. 2, pp. 230-232; Polk to Lansing, September 22, 1919, Polk Papers. Gibson and his colleagues at the Warsaw legation shared in the "genteel" anti-Semitism common among American diplomats of the time, and they tended to regard Polish Jews with distaste and contempt, believing their goal was to promote Zionism and disrupt Poland. See Robert D. Schulzinger, *The Making of the Diplomatic Mind: The Training, Outlook, and Style of United States Foreign Service Officers, 1908-1931* (Middletown, Conn., 1975), pp. 131-132, and Castle to Bainbridge Colby, November 6, 1920, SDNA 860c.00/217.

29. In the House Papers, Gibson to House, April 29, 1919, House to Gibson, May 3, 1919, and House Diary, May 5, 1919. Also Hooker, p. 14, and Henry L. Stimson Diary, March 9, 1920, Henry L. Stimson Papers, Sterling Library, Yale University. Paderewski encouraged the view that he was the sole alternative to rule of Poland by radicals (Paderewski to House, January 12, 1919, House Papers).

30. June 2, 1919, Walter Lippmann Papers, Sterling Library, Yale University. The criticisms of American liberals are exemplified in the *New Republic*, May 3, 1919, pp. 10-13, and June 14, 1919, pp. 199-200. See also Major T. R. Ryan to General Tasker Bliss, July 23, 1919, Tasker Bliss Papers, LC.

31. In SDNA, William Dawson to Lansing, January 8, 1920, 860.00/2, and Dawson to Gibson, February 25, 1920, 860.00/4; Frederick Palmer, *Bliss, Peacemaker: The Life and Letters of General Tasker Howard Bliss* (New York, 1934), pp. 368, 411, 416.

32. *New York Times*, February 8, 1920. A State Department operative described Piłsudski as "not particularly well balanced" (Castle to Colby, November 6, 1920, SDNA 860c.00/217). See the *Washington Post* of March 28, 1920, and Zygmunt J. Gasiorowski, "Joseph Piłsudski in the Light of American Reports, 1919-1922," *Slavonic and East European Review* 49 (1971), pp. 425-436.

33. Lubomirski to MSZ, November 20, 1919, AAN-AW n. 226. In addition, report to Leon Biliński, December 9, 1919, HIA-US.

34. For an outstanding treatment of Poland's Russian policy and its consequences see Piotr S. Wandycz, *Soviet-Polish Relations, 1917-1921* (Cambridge, Mass., 1969).

35. In SDNA, Gibson to Lansing, January 17, 1920, SDNA 760c.61/-, and February 19, 1920, 860c.51/73; Gibson to Jay Pierrepont Moffat, June 23, 1920, Jay Pierrepont Moffat Papers, Houghton Library, Harvard University. On September 17, 1919, Undersecretary of State Polk warned Paderewski that the Poles "would certainly get no economic help from the United States as long as they were fighting in all directions" (Polk Diary). Also in the Polk collection, Bliss to Polk [before November 15, 1919], and Polk's reply, November 15, 1919.

36. Lubomirski to MSZ, January 24, 1920, AGND 65a/2362; in SDNA, Lansing to U.S. Legation, Warsaw, February 5, 1920, 760c.61/8, and Colby to U.S. Legation, Warsaw, March 25, 1920, 760c.61/34; Polk Diary, April 2, 1920.

37. Hoover told Polish representatives that "no good can come to Poland from this war" (Landau and Tomaszewski, *Anonimowi*, p. 42). Consult William H. Hawkins's memorandum of interview with Wilson held September 27, 1920 [1933?], Bainbridge Colby Papers, LC. On the other hand, the U.S. Legation in Warsaw applauded the Polish advance (Moffat to Gibson, May 29, 1920, Moffat Papers).

38. In the Colby Papers, Gibson to Colby, July 17, 1920; Colby to Wilson, July 18, 1920; Wilson to Colby, July 20, 1920. Also Gibson to Moffat, July 23, 1920, Moffat Papers; Colby to U.S. Embassy, London, August 6, 1920, SDNA 760c.61/135; Lubomirski to MSZ, July 27, 1920, AGND 68b/5085.

39. The text of the Colby Note is in FRUS 1920, v. 3, pp. 463-468. The document did not cite the Curzon Line, but the clear tendency of American policy was to adopt it as a model for a final boundary.

40. Colby to Wilson, August 9, 1920, Colby Papers. Also Lubomirski to MSZ, August 9, 1920, AGND 68a/4691. Colby told a group of Polish-American petitioners that "we cannot go to the aid even of Poland, provided the view prevails in this country that we have no concern with anything beyond our national borders" (*New York Times*, August 19, 1920).

Colby misled his listeners to the extent his remarks implied that a willing government was restrained by public opinion; rather the State Department gratefully accepted this "view" as a justification for inaction in a difficult spot.

41. In SDNA, Colby to U.S. Legation, Warsaw, August 21, 1920, 760c.61/224A; Lubomirski to Colby, August 30, 1920, 760c.61/273; Norman Davis to U.S. Embassy, Paris, August 31, 1920, 760c.61/257; Colby to U.S. Legation, Warsaw, September 23, 1920, 760c.61/326. See also Warren Robbins memorandum, August 24, 1920, AAN-AW n. 226.

42. Sapieha to Lubomirski, September 10, 1920, AAN-AW n. 208.

43. In AGND, Major Kazimierz Mach to Army Command, January 9, 1921, 72b/6631 and an unattributed report on American foreign policy, May 17, 1921, 74a/7294.

44. Lubomirski to MSZ, January 17, 1921, Ambasada RP w Paryżu, n. 22, AAN (the emphases are Lubomirski's). Also Mach to Army Command, January 3 and January 9, 1921, AGND 72b/6631; protocol of meeting of directors of political departments of MSZ, April 30, 1921, AAN-AW n. 42.

45. Protocol of meeting of directors of political departments of MSZ, January 18, 1921, AAN-AW n. 42; Franciszek Pułaski to MSZ, March 29, 1921, Ambasada RP w Paryżu, n. 30, AAN.

46. RWB [Robert W. Bliss] memorandum of interview with Lubomirski, April 9, 1921, SDNA 760c.6215/298; Lubomirski to MSZ, October 17, 1921, AAN-AW n. 228; Polish Legation, Washington, to Piltz, January 17, 1921, HIA-US. Compare the vastly differing accounts of the same meeting: Lubomirski record of conversation with Hughes, April 14, 1921, AAN-AW n. 228, and Hughes memorandum of conversation with Lubomirski, April 14, 1921, Charles Evans Hughes Papers, LC.

47. Hughes to George Harvey, May 18, 1921, FRUS 1921, v. 1, p. 16. Also Castle to Gibson, May 12, 1921, William R. Castle Papers, Herbert Hoover Presidential Library, West Branch, Iowa; Lubomirski record of conversation with Hughes, May 5, 1921, AAN-AW n. 228; MSZ to Lubomirski, May 27, 1921, HIA-US; Hughes memorandum of conversation with Lubomirski, May 12, 1921, Hughes Papers; Castle to Hughes, May 19, 1921, SDNA 760c.6215/52.

48. Lubomirski records of conversations with Hughes, May 12 and June 2, 1921, AAN-AW n. 228; Hughes to Lubomirski, May 14, 1921, SDNA 760c.6215/40. Of one of Lubomirski's stiff petitions to Hughes, Gibson snorted that "it appears to be about as foolish a document as even he is capable of turning out. . . . How anybody with the brains of a linnet could have written such a note is beyond me" (Gibson to Moffat, May 24, 1921, Moffat Papers).

49. Sir Auckland Geddes to Lord George Nathaniel Curzon, May 18, 1921, DBFP, ser. I, v. 16, p. 106.

50. British notes of Allied conferences at the Quai d'Orsay, August 12, 1921, DBFP, ser. I, v. 15, pp. 703–704.

51. MSZ to Polish Legation, Washington, May 4, 1920, AAN-AW n. 525; Leon Berenson to MSZ, May 28, 1920, AGND 67a/3627; Lubomirski to MSZ, March 22 and March 24, 1920, AGND 66/3095; Polish record of meeting of Gibson with officers of Polish Legation, Washington, May 26, 1920, AAN-AW n. 226.

52. "Memorandum for the Minister on Loan Questions" [after 1927], AAN-AW n. 470; Biliński to Paderewski, November 12, 1919, APIP, v. 2, pp. 367–70; Leon Biliński, *Wspomnienia i dokumenty*, 2 vols. (Warsaw, 1924–1925), v. 2, pp. 284, 440–441; Zbigniew Landau, "Pierwsza polska pożyczka emisyjna w Stanach Zjednoczonych," *Zeszyty Naukowe Szkoły Głównej Planowania i Statystyki* 15 (1959), pp. 59–76; Alexander Janta, "Conrad's 'Famous Cablegram' in Support of a Polish Loan," *Polish Review* 17 (1972), pp. 69–77.

53. *New York Times*, June 5 and June 14, 1920; Władysław Grabski, *Dwa lata pracy u podstaw państwowości naszej* (Warsaw, 1927), p. 9; Polish Legation, Washington, to MSZ, April 2, 1920, HIA-US.

54. Hoover to Lubomirski, October 25, 1920, AAN-AW n. 437; Lubomirski to MSZ, November 15, 1920, AGND 71/6217; Stanisław Arct, *Projekt odbudowy Polski przy pomocy*

amerykańskiej (Warsaw, 1920), pp. 4–6. American loans to Poland totaled $29.9 million by the end of 1920 (Cleona Lewis, *America's Stake in International Investments* [Washington, 1938], p. 622).

55. In AAN-AW: Konstanty Skirmunt to Lubomirski, August 3, 1921, n. 208; H. B. Smith memorandum of conversation with Jerzy Michalski, November 5, 1921, n. 263. In other AAN collections, see "From the Report of Vice-Minister Rybarski" [ca. November 1920], Ignacy Jan Paderewski (archiwum), n. 989, and MSZ circular "Economic Review: The Economic Relations of Poland with Foreign Countries," January 20, 1922, Konsulat RP w Buffalo, n. 34.

56. Memorandum of Polish Embassy, Paris, January 15, 1921, AAN-AL n. 331; unattributed report to Army Command, May 20, 1921, AGND 74a/7567.

57. Polish General Staff report on the United States, October 30, 1920, AAN-MSZ n. 226; MSZ circular "Economic Review: The Economic Relations of Poland with Foreign Countries," January 20, 1922, Konsulat RP w Buffalo, n. 34, AAN; Wróblewski to MSZ, March 7, 1923, HIA-US.

58. Samuel M. Vauclain and Earl C. May, *Steaming Up! The Autobiography of Samuel M. Vauclain* (New York, 1930), pp. 264–265. Also Vauclain's address to American-Polish Chamber of Commerce and Industry, May 18, 1922, AAN-AW n. 600; *Poland*, May 1923, p. 180; *New York Sun*, February 21, 1922.

59. Address to American-Polish Chamber of Commerce and Industry, May 27, 1920, AAN-AW n. 597. Baldwin was the mainstay of the Chamber, which functioned as the principal American lobby for Poland in the 1920s. Operating under close supervision by the Polish diplomatic mission in Washington, the APCC published *Poland* magazine and exhorted American business to invest in the country. Never able to make much of an impression on its intended audience, the APCC declined into uselessness after Vauclain's enthusiasm flagged in the later years of the decade.

60. Castle to Colby, November 6, 1920, SDNA 860c.00/217.

61. Hipolit Gliwic to Michalski, January 26, 1922, AAN-AW n. 572; Hugh Wallace to Colby, February 12, 1921, SDNA 760c.61/452. Note also Prince Casimir Lubomirski, "The Prospect for Peace in Poland," *Journal of the American-Polish Chamber of Commerce and Industry*, March 1921, p. 5.

62. *New York Times* editorials of November 14, December 12, and December 21, 1922, and June 6, 1923.

63. June 22, 1921. Another contemporary view of Polish inflation written by a former ARA adviser is E. Dana Durand, "Currency Inflation in Eastern Europe," *American Economic Review* 13 (1923), pp. 593–608. Likewise see H. B. Smith report, September 19, 1921, H. B. Smith Papers, HIA.

64. Lubomirski to MSZ, January 21, 1921, Ambasada RP w Paryżu, n. 22, AAN; in AAN-AW, U.S. Legation, Warsaw, "Memorandum for Conversation with the Minister for Foreign Affairs," August 1, 1921, n. 400, and Zygmunt Jastrzębski to Gliwic, November 24, 1922, n. 262.

65. Gibson to Castle, March 14, 1921, Castle Papers; in SDNA, Gibson to Hughes, March 9, 1921, 860c.51/126, and Gibson to Henry Fletcher, March 19, 1921, 860c.51/140. A reputation for dishonesty dogged the Poles in these years. An internal memorandum of the Commerce Department charged Warsaw with habitually "playing fast and loose with business matters" (Durand to Grosvenor Jones, July 10, 1922, n. 262).

66. One American bank declared that Poland's financial associates in the United States had "neither standing nor money, nor even an honest name" ("Information Received from the National City Bank" [1921], AAN-AW, n. 441). Also Wacław Walter to Ministry of Finance, September 28, 1922, AAN-AW n. 473.

67. In AAN-AW, Arct to Polish Official Purchasing Bureau, Warsaw, April 18, 1921, n. 297, and J. W. Krauze to Lubomirski, June 10, 1921, n. 473.

68. Gibson to Colby, December 17, 1920, SDNA 860c.50/8. In AAN-AW n. 571, E. C. Morse to Gliwic, March 17, 1922, and Paul Klopstock to Gliwic, July 1, 1922. Likewise

176 / Notes

A. B. Barber to Leopold Skulski, January 3, 1920, in Zbigniew Landau and Jerzy Tomaszewski, ed., *Kapitały obce w Polsce, 1918-1939: materiały i dokumenty* (Warsaw, 1964), pp. 63-64.

69. Stefan Grotowski to Gliwic, January 27, 1922, AAN-AW n. 271; Jerzy Barthel-Weydenthal, "Polish Exports to the United States 1920-21 and their Outlook for the Future," May 1, 1923, Konsulat RP w Buffalo, n. 34, AAN.

70. Conrad Lesley to Z. Kurnikowski, February 20, 1924, AAN-AW n. 602. During the early 1920s the United States provided between 12 and 16 percent of Polish imports annually, second to Germany. On the other hand, Polish sales to the United States invariably accounted for less than 1 percent of the Polish export trade in the same period. For example, in 1925 Poland imported goods from the United States in excess of twenty-three times the value of her exports to America. See the publications of Poland, Główny Urząd Statystyczny, *Annuaire du commerce extérieur de la République Polonaise, années 1922 et 1923* (Warsaw, 1924), p. xi, and *Rocznik handlu zagranicznego Rzeczypospolitej Polskiej 1924-1925* (Warsaw, 1926), p. 3.

71. Chandler, p. 253. Also see Frank Costigliola, "The Politics of Financial Stabilization: American Reconstruction Policy in Europe, 1924-30" (Ph.D. dissertation, Cornell University, 1973), pp. 49-50, and Michael J. Hogan, *Informal Entente: The Private Structure of Cooperation in Anglo-American Economic Diplomacy, 1918-1928* (Columbia, Mo., 1977), pp. 42, 62-63.

72. In FRUS 1922, v. 1, Eliot Wadsworth to Hughes, April 18, 1922, pp. 397-398, and Hughes to Myron Herrick, April 22 and June 3, 1922, pp. 399-401.

73. In AAN-AW, record of meeting between Gibson and Michalski, January 13, 1922, n. 258, Gliwic to Michalski, March 1 and May 25, 1922, n. 298, and record of conference of economic personnel of Credit Department, Polish Ministry of Finance, October 18, 1922, n. 262; Durand to Hoover, February 24, 1922, HHCP.

74. In AAN-AW, Merrill, Lynch and Co. to Gliwic, April 25, 1921, n. 446, and Gliwic to Minister of Industry and Commerce, March 6, 1922, n. 262. Also record of meeting of Council of Ministers, April 21, 1922, AAN-PPRM n. 18; *New York Times*, April 26, 1922. The loan was to be placed through White, Weld and Co. at 8 percent interest (Durand to Hoover, May 4, 1922, HHCP).

75. H. B. Smith memorandum of conversation with Jastrzębski, August 17, 1922, SDNA 860c.51/264. Likewise record of conference of economic personnel of Credit Department, Polish Ministry of Finance, October 18, 1922, AAN-AW n. 262.

76. Polska Akademia Nauk, Instytut Historii, *Historia Polski* (Warsaw, 1978), v. 4, part 2, p. 208.

77. *New York American*, August 21, 1923. Also Sir William Max Muller to Curzon, August 29, 1923, PRO N7359/29/55; Pierre de L. Boal to Hughes, August 23, 1923, Gibson Papers; *New York Times*, August 25 and August 29, 1923; Maciej Rataj, *Pamiętniki 1918-1927* (Warsaw, 1965), p. 168; Wincenty Witos, *Moje wspomnienia*, 3 vols. (Paris, 1965), v. 3, pp. 47-48; Pierre Robin, *La réforme monétaire en Pologne* (Paris, 1932), p. 19.

78. Gliwic to Hubert Linde, August 30, 1923, AAN-AW n. 437. Already eighteen months earlier Gliwic had asked for a transfer, lamenting that economic relations with the United States had been mishandled beyond hope of correction (Gliwic to Minister of Industry and Commerce, March 6, 1922, AAN-AW n. 262). For the insistence of American opinion that Polish financial reform must precede borrowing, see Durand, "Currency Inflation," p. 607, and "Finance and Currency Situation in Poland," *Annals of the American Academy of Political and Social Science* 102 (1922), pp. 32-39.

79. Stanisław Stroński to Witos, November 10, 1923, Stanisław Kauzik, n. 18, AAN; Paderewski to Grabski [between April 1 and May 13, 1924], APIP, v. 3, pp. 78-80; Christian A. Herter to Durand, December 26, 1923, HHCP.

80. MSZ circular, June 11, 1921, IHGS-AL A.12.53/4; in AAN-AW, Lubomirski to MSZ, June 5, 1921, n. 228, and Michał Kwapiszewski record of conversation with Castle, July 20, 1921, n. 260.

81. In the Castle Papers, Gibson to Castle, June 3, 1921, and Castle to Gibson, July 13,

1922. Likewise Gibson to Hughes, September 30, 1922, SDNA 711.60c/2; report of H. B. Smith, November 22, 1921, AAN-AW n. 263; H. B. Smith to Julius Klein, June 30, 1922, Smith Papers.

82. Gibson memorandum of conversation with Wróblewski, September 27, 1922, Castle Papers. For examples of American complaints against Lubomirski, see Castle to Benjamin Thaw, February 14, 1922, Castle Papers, and Hughes to U.S. Legation, Warsaw, May 24, 1922, SDNA 701.60c11/72. When Foreign Minister Narutowicz informed the State Department that Lubomirski would be recalled, he termed the envoy's conduct "disgraceful and very harmful to Poland" (Gibson to Castle, August 11, 1922, Castle Papers). Lubomirski had met with severe criticism from various quarters in Poland as well, accused of indolence and incompetence (*Sprawozdanie*, January 27, 1921, p. 48; Paderewski to Lubomirski, April 27, 1921, APIP, v. 2, pp. 644-645; Ellis Dresel to Hughes, November 20, 1921, SDNA 701.60c11/60).

83. Gibson to Castle, November 23, 1922, Castle Papers; FRUS 1923, v. 2, pp. 738-751.

84. Such instances abound in the Castle Papers: Gibson to Castle, October 16, 1921, January 3, 1922 and July 16, 1923; Thaw to Castle, April 13, 1922. At one point Gibson fumed at the difficulty of saving "the Polish Government from utter collapse and prevent-[ing] this mass of thirty millions of people from becoming a menace to civilization" (Gibson to Hughes and Fletcher, August 25, 1921, SDNA 860c.00/88). In the Gibson Papers, Gibson's memorandum for conversation with Polish foreign minister [1923], and Gibson to Hughes, April 12, 1923. Substantive differences were aggravated by those of temperament as well, for American officials regarded Poles as "diplomats in the oriental tradition," meaning sly and deceitful (Gliwic to Stefan Przanowski, September 21, 1921, AAN-AW n. 266).

85. Gibson to Hughes and Fletcher, December 1, 1921, SDNA 860c.00/104. The *New York Times*, which favored Poland, deplored the rise of this line of thought in editorials of November 11 and December 4, 1923. Gliwic told Henryk Strasburger in a dispatch of August 18, 1922, that America considered Poland "an exotic creature of France" (AAN-AW n. 228).

86. The Poles despised this term, which implied that the region they called *Pomorze*, or Pomerania, was properly German land wrested from the *Reich*. In fact, the extension of a neck of land to the Baltic Sea separating East Prussia from the other German territories conformed to the outline of the ancient Polish state, and Poles formed a solid majority of the population of the Corridor. Tendentious or not, the appellation quickly gained currency and became standard parlance outside Poland. Although it lay beyond the boundaries of Poland, the Free City of Danzig, designated an independent entity under League of Nations auspices to serve as a port for the Polish state, was generally included in the popular conception of the Polish Corridor.

87. Gibson to Castle, May 26, 1922, Castle Papers. Even so, Gibson denied the charges of Polish imperialism (Gibson to Hughes, February 15, 1923, Gibson Papers). An article in the *Washington Star*, October 23, 1921, bore the headline "Poland, With Fantastic Dreams of Empire, Draws Daily Nearer Abyss of Utter Ruin."

88. For example, Henryk Arctowski, "Poland and the Political Balance of Power in Europe," lecture delivered at Columbia University, January 7, 1921, AAN-AW n. 1270.

89. Unattributed report on American foreign policy, May 17, 1921, AGND 74a/7294; Ignacy Matuszewski memorandum, April 1921, in Polska Akademia Nauk, Pracownia Historii Stosunków Polsko-Radzieckich, *Dokumenty i materiały do historii stosunków polsko-radzieckich*, 9 vols. (Warsaw, 1962-1974), v. 4, p. 15; in AAN-AW, Gliwic to Jan Dąbski, October 19, 1921, n. 764, and Gliwic to Strasburger, August 18, 1922, n. 228.

90. For example, Paul Super, *Twenty-Five Years with the Poles* (Trenton, N.J., 1947), p. 31. For reflections of this view in the press, *New York Times*, August 16, 1926; *New York Tribune*, March 12, 1921; *Outlook*, February 18, 1925, pp. 255-256, and April 22, 1925, pp. 607-608.

91. In the Gibson Papers, Gibson to Harvey, May 22, 1921, and Gibson to Hughes, August 18, 1921; John C. White memorandum, February 21, 1921, SDNA 860c.00/210.

92. In AGND, report of Komitet Obrony Narodowej to Piłsudski, August 18, 1919, 63/

1667, and report of American Department, MSZ, January 17, 1921, 72a/6483; Polish Consulate, New York, to MSZ, June 9, 1922, AAN-AW n. 971. For Polonia in the immediate postwar years, see Olszewski; Pliszka; and Mieczysław Haiman, *Zjednoczenie Polskie Rzymsko-Katolickie w Ameryce 1873-1948* (Chicago, 1948).

93. Barthel-Weydenthal to MSZ, October 1, 1919, Ambasada RP w Paryżu, n. 22, AAN; Edward R. Kantowicz, *Polish-American Politics in Chicago, 1888-1940* (Chicago, 1975), p. 123.

94. Gliwic memorandum, July 11, 1925, AAN-AW n. 34; I. Morawski, "Emigration Report for 1928" [1929], Konsulat Generalny RP w Nowym Jorku, n. 128, AAN.

95. Protocol of meeting of directors of political departments of MSZ, June 15, 1921, AAN-AW n. 42.

96. MSZ to Polish Legation, Washington, December 13, 1923, Konsulat RP w Buffalo, n. 58, AAN; unattributed report, May 23, 1921, AGND 74a/7569. In 1921 Hoover sent a message to the congress of the Polish National Alliance, praising the PNA for its devotion to Poland but stressing that the time had arrived to "turn our attention to our own home, for we are all Americans and America must be first in our hearts" (Olszewski, v. 3, p. 362).

97. Kantowicz, p. 122.

98. In AAN-AW n. 228, Gliwic, "Principles of Polish-American Relations," and Gliwic to Stefan Ossowski, both dated July 19, 1922.

99. Swerczek, pp. 153-154.

CHAPTER II

1. *Rzeczpospolita*, April 23, 1923.

2. Gibson to Colby, October 5, 1920, SDNA 860c.00/72.

3. "Conservative opinion at the time was somewhat aghast" (Lawrence Smith, "The Zloty, 1924-1935," *Journal of Political Economy* 44 [1936], p. 150). However, see the approving views in Frank Kellogg to Hughes, March 5, 1924, Calvin Coolidge Presidential Papers, microfilm edition, and William J. Kelley memorandum December 6, 1924, William J. Kelley Collection, HIA.

4. "Foreign loans are for Poland a greater danger than for many other countries. In the realm of foreign credit there is always much room for international political intrigue. We have dangerous enemies. If we wish them not to harm us, we must avoid foreign loans" (Grabski, *Dwa lata*, p. 118).

5. *Sprawozdanie*, October 22, 1924, p. 21.

6. Grabski, *Dwa lata*, p. 118. Also Zbigniew Landau, "Władysław Grabski a pożyczki zagraniczne," *Kwartalnik Historyczny* 66 (1959), pp. 1185-1205; Teresa Małecka, *Kredyty i pożyczki Stanów Zjednoczonych Ameryki dla rządu polskiego w latach 1918-1939* (Warsaw, 1982), pp. 80-81; Jerzy Tomaszewski, *Stabilizacja waluty w Polsce: z badań nad polityką gospodarczą rządu polskiego przed przewrotem majowym* (Warsaw, 1961), p. 59.

7. Henryk Jabłoński, "Z tajnej dyplomacji Władysława Grabskiego w roku 1924," *Kwartalnik Historyczny* 63 (1956), pp. 446-451; Tomaszewski, pp. 44-45.

8. Hilton Young to Grabski [1924], AAN-MSZ n. 43; Konstanty Skirmunt, "Wspomnienia" (typescript memoir), p. 140, Biblioteka Jagiellońska, Cracow; Boal to Hughes, February 14, 1924, Gibson Papers. The Young mission is documented in Landau and Tomaszewski, *Kapitały*, pp. 145-207.

9. Georges Soutou, "L'impérialisme du pauvre: la politique économique du gouvernement Français en Europe Centrale et Orientale de 1918 à 1929," *Relations Internationales* 7 (1976), pp. 219-239.

10. Grabski report to Council of Ministers, October 8, 1920, in Landau and Tomaszewski, *Kapitały*, p. 68.

11. For discussion of the Dawes Plan and its evolution, Costigliola, *Awkward*; Costigliola, "Stabilization"; and Stephen A. Schuker, *The End of French Predominance in Europe:*

The Financial Crisis of 1924 and the Adoption of the Dawes Plan (Chapel Hill, N.C., 1976).

12. The American policy of stabilization in Europe is cogently outlined in Melvyn P. Leffler, "American Policy Making and European Stability, 1921–1933," *Pacific Historical Review* 46 (1977), pp. 207–228. Also Costigliola, "Stabilization," Costigliola, *Awkward,* and Werner Link, *Die amerikanische Stabilisierungspolitik in Deutschland 1921–1932* (Düsseldorf, 1970).

13. Costigliola, "Stabilization," p. 146; Joan Hoff Wilson, *American Business and Foreign Policy, 1920–1933* (Lexington, Ky., 1971), pp. 117, 121; Lewis, p. 620. In 1923 Americans lent $92 million to Europe, less than a quarter of their total foreign lending. In the next year, American loans to Europe jumped to $580 million and remained near that level through 1928. During this period European securities accounted for roughly half of American lending abroad, Lewis, pp. 628–629.

14. Grabski, *Dwa lata*, pp. 116, 118–119. The fear that foreign lenders might attach political strings to their money was common throughout Eastern Europe, with the result that American capital was generally preferred in the region, Elmer Davis, "Character of American Influence on Eastern Europe in the Near Future," *Annals of the American Academy of Political and Social Science* 102 (1922), pp. 123–124.

15. *Sprawozdanie*, December 2, 1924, pp. 4–15; Aleksander Szczepański to MSZ [1925?], in Barbara Ratyńska, *Stosunki polsko-niemieckie w okresie wojny gospodarczej, 1919–1930* (Warsaw, 1968), pp. 84–85.

16. For example, Wacław Fabierkiewicz, *O konsekwensjach gospodarczych Planu Dawesa* (Warsaw, 1925), p. 28. On the other hand, one of Poland's most prominent economists, Adam Krzyżanowski, argued in 1926 that American capital flow to Germany indirectly stimulated Poland and that "the economic future of Poland depends in large measure on the degree to which Germany is aided by American investors" (*Polityka i gospodarstwo: pisma pomniejsze oraz przemówienia, 1920–1931* [Cracow, 1931], p. 270.

17. Rataj, p. 282. Also *Sprawozdanie*, October 22, 1924, p. 21.

18. Klopstock to Gliwic, May 2, 1924, AAN-AW n. 476; Barber to J. Eberhardt, January 19, 1924, Stanisław Kauzik, n. 18, AAN; Grabski to Paderewski, February 23, 1924, and Wróblewski to Paderewski, March 31, 1924, APIP, v. 3, pp. 75–76, 78.

19. Grabski, *Dwa lata*, pp. 113–114.

20. In AAN-AW n. 298, Economic Section, MSZ, to Polish Legation, Washington, October 14, 1922; Gliwic to Grabski, February 6, 1923; MSZ circular, May 15, 1923.

21. In AAN-AW n. 298, Gliwic to Kucharski, September 14, 1923, and Wróblewski to Roman Dmowski, November 12, 1923; Wadsworth to Hughes, September 26, 1923, SDNA 800.51 W 89 Poland/14.

22. Gliwic to Grabski, February 12, 1924, AAN-AW n. 298.

23. Hughes memorandum of conversation with Wróblewski, June 10, 1924, Hughes Papers; in AAN-AW n. 299, Wróblewski to Andrew Mellon, June 19, 1924, and Polish memorandum of meeting of Wróblewski and Gliwic with World War Foreign Debt Commission, June 23, 1924; Minutes of meeting of World War Foreign Debt Commission, June 23, 1924, HHCP.

24. Grabski, *Dwa lata*, pp. 113–114; Western Department, MSZ, to Wróblewski, September 1, 1924, AAN-AW n. 299.

25. J. Grzymała-Grabowiecki, *Polityka zagraniczna Polski w roku 1924* (Warsaw, 1925), pp. 52–53; *New York Times*, January 24, 1925.

26. Wróblewski to Grabski, November 12, 1924, Stanisław Kauzik, n. 18, AAN.

27. Wróblewski to MSZ, December 2, 1924, AAN-AW n. 299.

28. Some years later a senior State Department official summarized Pearson's work in Poland: "He was anxious to leave [Warsaw] . . . and the Department was very glad to have him leave. . . . Pearson is in no way an effective minister" (Castle to Hoover, January 21, 1929, HHPP). See also Lesley to Gliwic, June 11, 1924, AAN-AW n. 1804, and Eberhardt to Kauzik, July 5, 1924, in Landau and Tomaszewski, *Kapitały*, p. 90. For his part, Gibson was more than ready to take on his new assignment in Bern: "We are lucky to go there now

because the bottom has dropped out of this place," meaning Poland (Gibson to Hugh Wilson, April 16, 1924, Hugh Wilson Papers, Herbert Hoover Presidential Library, West Branch, Iowa).

29. Hiram Barney to C. Bascom Slemp, August 4, 1924; Joseph C. Grew to Slemp, August 7, 1924; and Slemp to Barney, August 12, 1924, Coolidge Papers.

30. MSZ to Wróblewski, October 3, 1924, AAN-AW n. 506. The connection with Ulen was not satisfactory, as the company's work suffered inadequacies and cost overruns (Landau and Tomaszewski, *Anonimowi*, pp. 86–114). Also see Zbigniew Landau, "Pożyczki ulenowskie," *Najnowsze Dzieje Polski: Materiały i Studia z Okresu 1914-1939* 1 (1958), pp. 123–160.

31. *Sprawozdanie*, October 22, 1924, p. 19, and November 7, 1924, p. 24.

32. Rataj, p. 238.

33. *New York Times*, October 21, 1924.

34. Grabski to Wróblewski, November 13, 1924, in Landau and Tomaszewski, *Kapitały*, p. 208.

35. January 10, 1926.

36. Ibid.; *New York Times*, April 12, 1925; Frank J. Williams, "A New Leader in Finance: Clarence Dillon," *Review of Reviews*, February 1926, pp. 147–148; Ciechanowski to Aleksander Skrzyński, January 9 and January 12, 1926, AAN-AL n. 84. Dillon lived well into his nineties, dying in 1979. His son, C. Douglas Dillon, succeeded him as head of Dillon, Read and served as secretary of the treasury in the cabinet of John F. Kennedy.

37. Costigliola, "Stabilization," pp. 133, 143; *New York Times*, February 4, 1925; James A. Logan to Hoover, September 5, 1924, HHCP.

38. Gliwic to Grabski, December 8, 1924, in Landau and Tomaszewski, *Kapitały*, p. 210.

39. In Landau and Tomaszewski, *Kapitały*, Wróblewski to Grabski, November 21, 1924, Gliwic to Grabski, December 8, 1924, Grabski to Wróblewski, December 10, 1924, and Czesław Klarner to Wróblewski, December 17, 1924, pp. 208–215.

40. In AAN-AW, Robert Hayward to Gliwic, December 22, 1924, n. 476 and "Memorandum for the Minister on Loan Questions" [after 1927], n. 470; in Landau and Tomaszewski, *Kapitały*, Grabski to Callaway, December 12, 1924, Klarner to Wróblewski, December 17, 1924, Grabski to Polish Legation, Washington, January [1-3?], 1925, Wróblewski to Grabski, January 5, 1925, and Grabski to Wróblewski [after January 5, 1925], pp. 212–218.

41. Hayward to Gliwic, February 9, 1925, AAN-AW n. 506; Rataj, pp. 262–264; Wróblewski to Grabski, January 5, 1925, and Grabski to Wróblewski [after January 5, 1925], in Landau and Tomaszewski, *Kapitały*, pp. 215–218.

42. Auswärtiges Amt to German Embassy, Washington, January 27, 1925, in Ratyńska, *Stosunki*, p. 197; Pearson to Hughes, February 6, 1925, SDNA 860c.51 D 58/14; Wróblewski to Grabski, February 21, 1925, AAN-AW n. 477.

43. In AAN-AW, Callaway to Wróblewski, January 16, 1925, n. 476 and Wróblewski to Grabski, March 30, 1925, n. 478. Grabski implies in *Dwa lata*, p. 117, that the press reports were inspired by hostile German sources. The Poles regularly complained of prejudicial German influence in American newspapers. There was a kernel of truth in this charge; most dispatches of Polish news originated from correspondents stationed in Berlin who obtained their information from German sources. These tended to place Poland in a bad light. In this case, however, the stories were not plants, but arose out of a coincident increase in Polish-German tension over territorial and minority issues.

44. Witold Wańkowicz to Gabriel Czechowicz, December 22, 1926, AAN-AW n. 470. In the same collection, Wróblewski to Grabski, March 30, 1925, n. 478.

45. Wróblewski to Grabski, March 30, 1925, AAN-AW n. 478; Wróblewski to Grabski, February 5, 1925, and Grabski to Polish Legation, Washington, February 9, 1925, in Landau and Tomaszewski, *Kapitały*, pp. 222–223.

46. In AAN-AW, Grabski to Wróblewski, February 14, 1925, n. 277; Wróblewski to Grabski, March 30, 1925, and Wróblewski to Dillon, April 9, 1925, n. 478. Also Wróblewski to Grabski, February 13, 1925, in Landau and Tomaszewski, *Kapitały*, p. 225. Wróblewski

described the new conditions as "brutal" (Wróblewski to MSZ, March 3, 1925, also in *Kapitały*, pp. 233-234).

47. German Consulate, New York, to Auswärtiges Amt, March 22, 1927, GFMR K161 K020748. In 1925 the prevailing rates of interest for European loans ranged from 6.5 to 7.5 percent in Western Europe to 7.5 to 8 percent for clients east of Germany. No European loan of 1925 bore higher interest than the Dillon, Read 8 percent.

48. For example, Krzyżanowski, *Polityka*, p. 130; *Przemysł i Handel*, May 9, 1925, p. 644; "Memorandum for the Minister on Loan Questions" [after 1927], AAN-AW n. 470.

49. *New York Times*, February 25, 1925.

50. Grabski, *Dwa lata*, pp. 117-118.

51. *Kurjer Warszawski*, March 14, 1926; Rataj, p. 325.

52. Feliks Młynarski, *Wspomnienia* (Warsaw, 1971), p. 256; Ciechanowski to August Zaleski, December 9, 1926, AAN-AL n. 85.

53. Wróblewski to Grabski, March 30, 1925, AAN-AW n. 478 and Wróblewski to Grabski, May 22, 1925, in Landau and Tomaszewski, *Kapitały*, p. 237. For Dillon's rivalry with Morgan for influence in Europe, Costigliola, "Stabilization," pp. 267-268, 275-276, and Herbert von Dirksen memorandum of conversation with Hjalmar Schacht, January 5, 1926, ADAP, ser. B, v. 2:1, pp. 86-89.

54. *Public Ledger* (Philadelphia), February 16, 1925.

55. BPPP, n. 152; *Sprawozdanie*, February 27, 1925, pp. 16-17, 19.

56. *Głos Narodu*, February 18, 1925. Writing in the respected *Czas*, March 6, 1925, Krzyżanowski called procurement of the loan "a great political, economic and financial success," *Polityka*, pp. 129-130.

57. Gliwic to "Józiu," February 25, 1925, AAN-AW n. 1942. In the same collection, Wróblewski to Grabski, March 30, 1925, n. 478.

58. *New York Times*, February 14, 1925. They were not alone. Moody's, the noted securities analysts, reported talk in New York of several Polish loan prospects, Jones to Hoover, February 24, 1925, HHCP. See as well Herbert Feis, "The Export of American Capital," *Foreign Affairs* 3 (1925), pp. 679-680.

59. Wróblewski to Grabski, March 30, 1925, AAN-AW n. 478.

60. Pearson to Hughes, February 6, 1925, SDNA 860c.51 D 58/14; Wróblewski to Grabski, March 30, 1925, AAN-AW n. 478; Leland Harrison to Harold P. Stokes, February 13, 1925, HHCP. In accordance with State Department policy, the contract stipulated that no proceeds of the loan would be applied to military purposes (Hayward to Hughes, February 5, 1925, HHCP).

61. Zbigniew Landau, *Polskie zagraniczne pożyczki państwowe 1918-1926* (Warsaw, 1961), p. 188. The exchange of notes between Hughes and Wróblewski is printed in FRUS 1925, v. 2, pp. 692-696. The course of discussions leading to the agreement is illustrated in Hughes's memoranda of conversations with Wróblewski of February 28 [*ca.* June-November] and November 6, 1924, Hughes Papers.

62. Wróblewski to Grabski, March 30, 1925, AAN-AW n. 478. The slump in American lending to Europe in the spring of 1925 is documented in the Federal Reserve Bank of New York's *Monthly Review of Credit and Business Conditions*, May 1, 1925, p. 3, and October 1, 1926, p. 5.

63. A. Gostomski, *Pozycja polska na amerykańskim rynku kapitału* (Warsaw, 1926), p. 4.

64. Sylwester Gruszka to Ciechanowski, October 4, 1927, AAN-AW n. 492.

65. For instance, a *New York Times* editorial of May 12, 1925, observed that the German initiative, if realized, would cause "the frontiers of Poland [to] become an immediate subject of debate and the cause of a perpetual nervous crisis in Central Europe."

66. "Memorandum of Conversation between Mr. Gliwic and Mr. Hayward," April 21, 1925, AAN-AW n. 478. Polish officials agreed that uncertainty over the embryonic security pact accounted more than any other reason for the unpopularity of the 8 percent loan (Wróblewski to Grabski, April 24, 1925, AAN-AW n. 479, and Feliks Młynarski, *The*

International Significance of the Depreciation of the Zloty in 1925 [Warsaw, 1926], p. 48). The security pact talks exerted a depressing effect on all American loan activity in Europe (Federal Reserve Bank of New York, *Monthly Review*, November 1, 1925, p. 3).

67. Stanisław Karpiński to Wróblewski, May 4, 1925, in Landau and Tomaszewski, *Kapitały*, p. 91.

68. Max Winkler to Gliwic, March 26, 1925, AAN-AW n. 652. The Dillon loan's ranking of "Baa" placed it within the speculative category of the Moody ratings, reflecting—according to Moody—not the intrinsic value of the bond, but recognition that it would be subject to "fear over possible difficulties on the Continent."

69. Dillon to Wróblewski, April 21, 1925, AAN-AW n. 479.

70. *New York Times*, March 25, 1925; Rataj, p. 312; Grabski, *Dwa lata*, p. 135.

71. "Memorandum of Conversation between Mr. Gliwic and Mr. Hayward," April 21, 1925, AAN-AW n. 478. In the same collection, Dillon to Wróblewski, April 21, 1925, n. 479.

72. Wróblewski to Grabski, May 22, 1925, in Landau and Tomaszewski, *Kapitały*, p. 237.

73. "Memorandum of Conversation between Mr. Gliwic and Mr. Hayward," April 21, 1925, AAN-AW n. 478; Wiesław Balcerak, *Polityka zagraniczna Polski w dobie Locarna* (Wrocław, 1967), p. 101.

74. Wróblewski to Grabski, April 24, 1925, AAN-AW n. 479; *Sprawozdanie*, April 28, 1925, p. 70.

75. Zbigniew Landau, "Bank Dillon, Read and Co. a Polska," *Sprawy Międzynarodowe* 12 (1960), pp. 70-71. Possibly Dillon was less than categorical in his rebuff; some Polish officials maintained that during his visit the banker made a vague pledge to float $7.5 million in the near future, memorandum prepared for Młynarski on the Dillon, Read loan [October 1925], in Landau and Tomaszewski, *Kapitały*, p. 238.

76. Ago von Maltzan to Auswärtiges Amt, June 17, 1925, GFMR L591 L188820. Some Poles remarked bitterly that American finance indirectly facilitated the German blockade by lending large sums to Berlin (Młynarski, *International*, p. 82).

77. John B. Stetson, Jr., to Kellogg, March 1, 1927, SDNA 860c51/616. Also see Grabski, *Dwa lata*, p. 181, and Hayward to Gliwic, July 28, 1925, AAN-AW n. 480.

78. Ulrich Rauscher to Auswärtiges Amt, December 30, 1925, ADAP, ser. B, v. 2:1, pp. 77-79; Krzyżanowski, *Polityka*, p. 553.

79. Krzyżanowski, *Polityka*, pp. 552-553.

80. The term "rotten loan" (pożyczka parszywa) is taken from Witos, v. 3, p. 59. After Piłsudski seized power in 1926, his followers criticized Grabski for contracting loans that were "outright injurious," citing the Dillon transaction as one of the "most vivid" examples of the type (A. Sapieha, "Zaufanie kapitałów zagranicznych do Polski," in Instytut Gospodarstwa Społecznego, *Na froncie gospodarczym: w dziesiątą rocznicę odzyskania niepodległości 1918-1928* (Warsaw, 1928), p. 150). Also note Grabski, *Dwa lata*, p. 258; *Kurjer Warszawski*, March 14, 1926; *Sprawozdanie*, November 10, 1925, pp. 5-14.

81. Grabski, *Dwa lata*, pp. 118-119. In addition, Stetson to Kellogg, May 11, 1927, SDNA 860c.51/629 and Adam Krzyżanowski, *Dwa programy finansowe* (Cracow, 1927), pp. 34-36. The bank knew of these charges, which it denied emphatically (Ciechanowski to Zaleski, October 8, 1926, AAN-AL n. 85).

82. This reading of the motive of Dillon, Read became the standard interpretation of contemporary Polish historical writing, stemming from the conclusions of Zbigniew Landau. As summarized in "The Foreign Loans of the Polish State in years 1918-1939," *Studia Historiae Oeconomicae* 9 (1974), pp. 289-290, his view is that "it was the objective of [Dillon, Read] to make it impossible for Poland to obtain any further loans in the U.S.A. and thus to force her to succumb to the dictates of the German Reich. It was hoped in Germany that the expected breakdown of the Grabski reforms would force Poland to look for loans at any price to save her economy. If Poland would be unable to find it (*sic*) in Paris . . . in London . . . and in the U.S.A. . . . then, willy-nilly, she would have to make economic and territorial concessions to Germany." Earlier in "Pożyczka dillonowska. Przyczynek do działalności kapitałów amerykańskich w Polsce," *Kwartalnik Historyczny* 65

(1957), Landau had registered the opinion that "in contracting the loan in 1925 Dillon acted in the interest of Germany" (p. 84) and set forth his arguments (pp. 79-85)—most of them highly speculative.

Landau's position does not stand up to scrutiny, and it has been challenged persuasively in Małecka, *Kredyty*, pp. 87-91. Furthermore, nothing in the documentary evidence supports the thesis that Dillon's actions toward Poland were swayed by such considerations. That the banker acquired financial interests in Germany is hardly exceptional given the attractiveness of German opportunities to American investors, but he operated in numerous European countries, including Poland's French ally. German documents give no hint of collusion with Dillon; indeed, far from accounting Dillon their confederate, German officials regarded him with suspicion for his connection with Poland. While Dillon on at least one occasion privately suggested the return of the Polish Corridor to Germany as a contribution to European harmony—and then withdrew the proposal upon hearing the Polish arguments in opposition to it—this does not appear to have been an important question to him (Ciechanowski to Zaleski, October 8, 1926, AAN-AL n. 85). To uphold the contrary requires explanation why Dillon should have subsidized through his loan the construction of a rail line linking the new port of Gdynia to the Polish mainland, an act that could only further the integration of Pomerania into the Polish state and bolster its independence of German economic influence. Dillon's option clause—the device by which he is alleged to have sought to choke off Polish credit—was but a conventional practice of international banking. If Dillon truly had desired to drive Poland into the arms of Germany, then his simplest, most direct course would have been not to lend to Warsaw at all. Neither does such a conspiratorial view of Dillon's motives fit his subsequent actions. To assert that the efforts of the bank to promote Polish credit in the United States through management of publicity, sponsoring of symposia and public functions on behalf of Warsaw, and funding the visits of Polish officials to America were all part of an elaborate sham strains credibility. For what it is worth, those Polish representatives who dealt directly with Dillon, Read consistently defended the bank against charges of bad faith, as exemplified by Ciechanowski to Skrzyński, March 29, 1926, AAN-AL n. 641, Wańkowicz to Czechowicz, December 22, 1926, AAN-AW n. 470 and Wańkowicz to Ciechanowski, February 15, 1927, HIA-US.

83. Strong to Owen Young, March 3, 1927, FRB C261.1.

84. Młynarski, *International*, p. 53. However, Młynarski contended otherwise in his memorandum "The Polish Currency and the Problem of Free Trade," November 1926, AAN-AW n. 694, where he stated that the withholding of the second transfer demonstrated that Poland "cannot always count on foreign help *even under normal circumstances*" (the emphases are Młynarski's).

85. Grabski, *Dwa lata*, p. 273.

CHAPTER III

1. Alfred Wysocki, "Dzieje mej służby" (typescript memoir), v. 1, p. 263, Biblioteka Ossolineum, Wrocław.

2. Rataj, p. 298; Chamberlain to Sir Eyre Crowe, March 14, 1925, PRO C3753/459/18. Also in PRO, Max Muller to J. Ramsay MacDonald, July 28, 1924, N6329/112/55, and Sir Eric Phipps to Victor Wellesley, August 17, 1925, C10882/459/18. For these references from PRO I am indebted to Dr. Thomas S. Dyman.

3. *Czas*, August 1, 1924.

4. Skrzyński elaborates this aim in his *Poland and Peace* (London, 1923), especially pp. 146-151, and in the *Czas* interview of August 1, 1924.

5. *Sprawozdanie*, February 6, 1923, pp. 11-12.

6. For example, the memorandum "On the Foreign Policy of the United States" prepared by Gliwic, June 30, 1925, AAN-AW n. 34, and the editorial of the quasi-official *Le Messager Polonais*, January 19, 1925.

7. Report of Szczepański [1925?], quoted in Balcerak, p. 46. Similar sentiments appear in a dispatch by Tadeusz Romer, July 27, 1925, AAN-LN n. 122.

8. "America in the rebuilding of Europe shows a certain onesidedness in her granting of credit. In connection with the Dawes plan the opinion seems to prevail that for the reconstruction of Europe it is sufficient to oil the industrial machinery of Germany. . . . It may follow that America in desiring to finance peace will in reality finance a new preparation for war" (Dr. Felix Młynarski, "American Credit for Poland," *Poland*, August 1925, p. 461).

9. For examples of official attitudes, Wróblewski to Skrzyński, June 1, 1925, AAN-AW n. 68, and report by Theodore Jaeckel, "The Danzig Corridor and Upper Silesia," April 16, 1925, SDNA 760c.6215/413. For the press, *New York World*, August 14, 1925, *New York Times*, June 28, 1925, and William Martin, "Treaty Revision," *Atlantic Monthly*, July 1925, pp. 117-127.

10. Wróblewski to MSZ, March 3, 1925, AAN-AW n. 228.

11. *Sprawozdanie*, April 28, 1925, p. 95.

12. Max Muller to Chamberlain, June 3, 1925, PRO N3169/3169/55. See the references to Skrzyński's views of America in Skirmunt, "Wspomnienia," pp. 132-133.

13. Wróblewski memorandum for Hughes, February 3, 1925, SDNA 860c.01/409. At the time, exchanges of embassies were less common than in later days and attainment of ambassadorial rank counted for more as a measure of prestige. In 1925 the United States maintained embassies in six European countries—England, France, Germany, Italy, Spain, and Belgium.

14. Pearson to Kellogg, April 18, 1925, SDNA 760c.6215/415.

15. In AAN-MSZ n. 101, Wróblewski to Skrzyński, May 9, 1925, and Skrzyński to Wróblewski, May 11, 1925; Wysocki, "Dzieje," v. 1, pp. 268-269. Costigliola describes the Institute in *Awkward*, pp. 71-72. For general treatment of the Skrzyński visit to America see Piotr S. Wandycz, *The United States and Poland* (Cambridge, Mass., and London, 1980), and Balcerak.

16. Pearson to Evan Young, May 14, 1925, SDNA 701.60c11/110. Warsaw was not pleased with Wróblewski's performance in Washington and faulted him for his supposedly clumsy negotiation of the Dillon, Read loan (Pearson to Kellogg, June 26, 1925, SDNA 701.60c11/112; also Wysocki, "Dzieje," v. 1, pp. 269-270, and Skrzyński to Polish Legation, Washington, May 15, 1925, AAN-MSZ n. 101).

17. In SDNA, Kellogg to U.S. Legation, Warsaw, May 1, 1925, 033.60c11/8, and Pearson to Kellogg, May 2, 1925, 033.60c11/9.

18. Wysocki, "Dzieje," v. 1, pp. 263, 268-269; Grabski, *Dwa lata*, p. 174; Juliusz Łukasiewicz, *Aleksander Skrzyński* (Warsaw, 1932), p. 15.

19. Max Muller to Chamberlain, June 3, 1925, PRO N3169/3169/55; Skirmunt, "Wspomnienia," p. 133.

20. See Stresemann's memorandum of June 30, 1925, in Christoph M. Kimmich, "The Weimar Republic and the German-Polish Borders," in *Essays on Poland's Foreign Policy, 1918-1939*, ed. Thaddeus V. Gromada (New York, 1970), pp. 41-45.

21. In GFMR, Erich Zechlin to Maltzan, June 9, 1925, L591 L188827-39, and June 27, 1925, L591 L188824-25. In addition, Janusz Sobczak, *Propaganda zagraniczna Niemiec weimarskich wobec Polski* (Poznań, 1973), p. 286, and Pearson to Kellogg, May 26, 1925, SDNA 860c.00/285.

22. Maltzan to Auswärtiges Amt, June 17, 1925, GFMR L591 L188820. Wysocki relates a contemporary conversation with "Rockefeller"—presumably John D. Rockefeller, Jr.—who told him that American capital shied away from Poland out of unfamiliarity and lack of confidence in Polish business practices. "Under these circumstances," stated the American, "Poland cannot expect a substantial loan offered at better terms" ("Dzieje," v. 1, p. 264).

23. Kellogg to Pearson, June 5, 1925, FRUS 1925, v. 1, pp. 23-24. See as well Polish Legation, Washington, to Department of State, May 28, 1925, FRUS 1925, v. 1, pp. 24-26 and Wróblewski to Skrzyński, April 30, 1925, AAN-AL n. 83.

24. Ratyńska, *Stosunki*, pp. 147–148. Houghton had served as American ambassador in Berlin for 1922–1925. His version of a "Rhine pact" is presented in Houghton to Hughes, October 23, 1922, FRUS 1922, v. 2, pp. 171–175. The Poles considered Houghton their most decided antagonist within the State Department (Ciechanowski to Skrzyński, March 30, 1926, AAN-AL n. 3).

25. Stresemann to Dr. Walther Jänecke, November 4, 1925, in Stresemann's *Vermächtnis*, 3 vols. (Berlin, 1932–1933), v. 2, p. 222.

26. AAN-AW n. 227; Balcerak, p. 108.

27. Max Muller to Chamberlain, June 3, 1925, PRO N3169/3169/55. In fact, American bankers cared very little about Polish internal practices aside from those which, like economic and financial policy, bore directly on the prospects for business profit or loss.

28. BPPP, nos. 155–156.

29. Balcerak, p. 106; Wysocki, "Dzieje," v. 1, p. 270.

30. These thoughts are outlined in the MSZ circular "Analyse politique du séjour du Comte Alexandre Skrzyński . . . aux États-Unis," August 1925, AAN-MSZ n. 101. While anonymous, this document clearly was prepared by Skrzyński or someone privy to his thinking. The MSZ instructed its personnel to regard the report as "our internal and confidential analysis" of the ministerial sojourn (Wysocki to Skirmunt, September 1, 1925, AAN-AL n. 1166).

31. Skrzyński diplomatic circular, June 22, 1925, AAN-AW n. 227.

32. *New York Times*, July 8 and July 15, 1925.

33. *Le Temps*, July 23, 1925. After his journey Skrzyński laid down in his report a series of "rules" for dealing with the United States, one of which was always to "present questions in their broadest aspect, to speak of them as the interests of all humanity and not just of certain States" ("Analyse politique du séjour du Comte Alexandre Skrzyński . . . aux États-Unis," August 1925, AAN-MSZ n. 101).

34. *New York Times*, July 22, 1925.

35. James C. White to Everett Sanders, June 27, 1925, Coolidge Papers. An associate of Paderewski during the World War, White maintained a friendly interest in Poland in peacetime; he knew Skrzyński and told presidential aide Sanders, "I am anxious to help him in every way possible not only for personal but for political reasons." He did not identify these "political reasons," but one might guess that he wished to use a presidential audience for Skrzyński as a means of currying favor for the Republican Party among Polonia.

36. "Analyse politique du séjour du Comte Alexandre Skrzyński . . . aux États-Unis," August 1925, AAN-MSZ n. 101. The warning of submersion in an Asian tide was a pet theme of Skrzyński; see his similar pronouncements in *Le Messager Polonais*, August 20, 1925, and the *New York Times*, August 16, 1925. He held that the white race formed two territorial blocs in Europe and North America and that a lack of solidarity between them would tempt inundation from the east. Such ideas circulated fairly widely at the time, and there seems no reason to dismiss out of hand Skrzyński's claim that the argument appealed to Coolidge. The contention combines an implicit anti-Soviet message with elements of the traditional Polish claim for recognition as the shield of Western civilization against Oriental onslaughts.

37. Skrzyński to Grabski, July 17, 1925, AAN-MSZ n. 101.

38. In AAN-AW n. 227, Polish Legation, Washington, to MSZ [July 17, 1925] and [July 18, 1925]. Note also *Le Temps*, July 20, 1925.

39. Skrzyński diplomatic circular, June 22, 1925, AAN-AW n. 227; Ciechanowski to Skrzyński, February 11, 1926, AAN-AL n. 84.

40. Official MSZ summary of Skrzyński journey [1925], AAN-MSZ n. 101.

41. His speeches were reprinted under the titles *American and Polish Democracy* (Washington, 1925) and *American Policy Toward Europe as Viewed by a European* (Washington, 1925). The citation is from the latter, p. 12.

42. The text of the Castle address, entitled "America and Europe," apears in Kolekcja Jana Ciechanowskiego, 82/13, IHGS.

43. See AAN-AW n. 227 for the text of his address, dated August 4, 1925. Also note

Młynarski, *Wspomnienia*, p. 255. According to the German embassy in Washington, Dillon, Read largely paid the expenses of Skrzyński's tour (Maltzan to Auswärtiges Amt, August 19, 1925, GFMR L591 L188887).

44. "Analyse politique du séjour du Comte Alexandre Skrzyński . . . aux États-Unis," August 1925, AAN-MSZ n. 101. Skrzyński claimed that Coolidge congratulated him for his statesmanlike qualities (Phipps to Wellesley, August 17, 1925, PRO C10882/459/18). The British minister to Warsaw commented sarcastically on Skrzyński's "childish" satisfaction with his visit (Max Muller to Chamberlain, August 26, 1925, PRO N4938/3169/55). Likewise see Tadeusz G. Jackowski, *W walce o polskość* (Cracow, 1972), pp. 318–319.

45. *New York Times*, August 16, 1925.

46. In GFMR, Rauscher to Auswärtiges Amt, August 22, 1925, L591 L188871-72, and Maltzan to Auswärtiges Amt, August 19, 1925, L591 L188886-93; Max Muller to Chamberlain, August 6, 1925, PRO N4680/3169/55; Frederick Cunliffe-Owen to Paderewski, August 17, 1925, APIP, v. 3, pp. 104–105; Jackowski, pp. 318–319; Harald von Riekhoff, *German-Polish Relations, 1918-1933* (Baltimore, 1971), p. 256.

47. Allusion to the myth of Jason was a common method of belittlement of the Skrzyński voyage to America. References to "golden fleece" appear in Rataj, p. 334, and *Sprawozdanie*, March 2, 1926, pp. 17–18. The journalist Bernard Singer portrayed the journey as typical of Skrzyński's hunger for praise in a piece reprinted in his *Od Witosa do Sławka* (Paris, 1962), p. 98. The newspaper *Warszawianka* took the foreign minister to task for "lecturing America on world history" (Max Muller to Chamberlain, August 26, 1925, PRO N4938/3169/55).

48. For example, see the *Washington Post*, August 10, 1925.

49. November 11, 1925. Dillon, Read greeted the treaties as a boon to foreign investment (*New York Times*, November 9, 1925). Coolidge saluted Locarno in his message to Congress of December 8, 1925, FRUS 1925, v. 1, pp. xii–xiii.

50. The American ambassador in Berlin, Jacob G. Schurman, believed that Locarno "ought to establish peace in Western Europe for a generation at least" while setting a precedent for eventual liquidation of remaining European issues (Barbara Ann Welter, "The United States and Weimar Germany, 1919-1929" [Ph.D. dissertation, University of Wisconsin-Madison, 1960], pp. 241–242). The same argument persuaded the *New York Times* to drop its previous objection to an exclusively West European pact, July 22, 1925. Alanson Houghton, on the other hand, accepted with *sang-froid* the conclusion that Locarno would "of course ensure a relatively longer period of peace and at the same time tend to fix the point where the next great war will begin, i.e., the German-Polish frontier" (Houghton to Coolidge, August 19, 1925, Coolidge Papers).

51. Młynarski, *Wspomnienia*, pp. 247–248, 252–255.

52. For studies of the relations of the major central banks, see Chandler; Hogan; Stephen V. O. Clarke, *Central Bank Cooperation, 1924-1931* (New York, 1967), and Richard Hemmig Meyer, *Bankers' Diplomacy: Monetary Stabilization in the Twenties* (New York and London, 1970). For the effects of central bank policies in reinforcing social and political conservatism, Charles S. Maier, *Recasting Bourgeois Europe: Stabilization in France, Germany, and Italy in the Decade after World War I* (Princeton, 1975), pp. 589–590.

53. On Norman, consult Andrew Boyle, *Montagu Norman: A Biography* (New York, 1967) and Sir Henry Clay, *Lord Norman* (London and New York, 1957). In his *Mémoires* (Paris, 1976), p. 111, Jean Monnet recalls the stature of Norman and his bank in the postwar decade: the Bank of England was "the citadel of citadels. . . . It is difficult today to imagine the prestige and strength of that institution in the early part of the century. It more or less regulated credit throughout the entire world. . . . Montagu Norman was the man who governed the citadel. He was redoubtable." Norman's animus to France was well-known. In *Souvenirs d'un gouverneur de la Banque de France, histoire de la stabilisation du franc, 1926-28* (Paris, 1954), pp. 48–49, Émile Moreau reports the Briton's declaration of hatred for the policies of the French government.

54. For Schacht, Helmut Müller, *Die Zentralbank, eine Nebenregierung: Reichsbankpräsident Hjalmar Schacht als Politiker der Weimarer Republik* (Opladen, 1973), and the

autobiographical Hjalmar Schacht, *My First Seventy-Six Years* (London, 1955). For his high repute within American financial circles, Ciechanowski to MSZ, January 30, 1926, AAN-AW n. 72. Strong's reservations on Schacht's political aims appear in his letter to Pierre Jay, July 20, 1925, in Chandler, p. 334.

55. Memorandum of Strong's meeting with Pierre Quesnay and Charles Rist, August 24, 1926, Benjamin Strong Papers, Federal Reserve Bank of New York. Chandler remains the principal study of Strong's career.

56. Chandler, pp. 250-252, 254-255. Also Schuker, pp. 162-163 and Costigliola, "Stabilization," pp. 15-16.

57. In speaking to Młynarski of Strong's relations with Norman, a Federal Reserve lieutenant "crossed two fingers and said Strong and Norman were just that close" (Młynarski, *Wspomnienia*, p. 259).

58. Ibid., p. 256; Gliwic to Grabski, September 1, 1925, AAN-AW, n. 480. Gliwic described Dillon's reaction as "helpful" (Gliwic to Skrzyński, September 1, 1925, AAN-AW n. 2586).

59. Résumé of the life of Henry C. Ulen [October 24, 1931], AAN-AW n. 574; Stetson to Kellogg, September 17, 1925, SDNA 860c.51/523.

60. Młynarski, *Wspomnienia*, pp. 256-259; Strong to Case, August 15 and August 18, 1925, Strong Papers. Strong's word was final, as the Treasury Department assured the Poles it would leave the decision to the Federal Reserve Bank (Gliwic to MSZ, August 27, 1925, IHGS-AL A.12.53/8). Still uncertain of the wisdom of the venture, Strong wrote to Norman that "apparently [the Poles] are a bit pressed with their exchange, and we have agreed to assume our share of the yellow man's burden"—meaning, presumably, the obligations of gold-rich banks—"and make them a loan" (August 23, 1925, Strong Papers).

61. Młynarski, *Wspomnienia*, pp. 257-259; Case to Strong, August 21, 1925, Strong Papers; Młynarski to Grabski, August 20, 1925, Stanisław Kauzik, n. 18, AAN.

62. Gliwic to MSZ, August 20, 1925, Stanisław Kauzik, n. 18, AAN; *New York Times*, August 29, 1925; *Journal of Commerce*, August 19, 1925.

63. Młynarski, *Wspomnienia*, pp. 263, 265-268. See also Strong to Case, September 1, 1925, Strong Papers; and in IHGS-AL A.12.53/8, Młynarski to Grabski, August [31?], 1925, and Polish Legation, London, to Polish Legation, Washington, September [9?], 1925.

64. Młynarski to Grabski, August [31?], 1925, IHGS-AL A.12.53/8.

65. Friedrich Sthamer to Auswärtiges Amt, October 7, 1925, GFMR K161 K020173-75.

66. Strong to Case, September 1, 1925 and September 2, 1925, Strong Papers. Gliwic blamed the influence of Norman for inciting Strong's skepticism toward Poland (Gliwic to Skrzyński, September 1, 1925, AAN-AW n. 2586). Strong made no secret of the fact that had he been in the United States at the time of Młynarski's call on the Federal Reserve Bank, he would not have approved the emergency credit (Młynarski, *Wspomnienia*, p. 267, and Gliwic to Skrzyński, October 12, 1925, in Landau and Tomaszewski, *Kapitały*, p. 240).

67. Młynarski, *Wspomnienia*, pp. 271-272.

68. Grabski, *Dwa lata*, pp. 216-218; Landau, *Polskie*, pp. 166-168. Goode told German diplomats in London that aid for Poland should depend on internal financial reorganization and frontier concessions to Germany (Albert Dufour-Feronce to Auswärtiges Amt, December 17, 1925, ADAP, ser. B, v. 2:1, pp. 33-37).

69. Polish officials blamed Dillon for not acting to prevent the fall of the złoty in the summer of 1925, for not supporting the price of the 8 percent loan and, of course, for his reluctance to issue a second transfer. In addition, Warsaw disapproved of its banker's growing portfolio of German investments. See Młynarski, *International*, pp. 61-62; Grabski, *Dwa lata*, p. 180; Stetson to Kellogg, April 19, 1927, SDNA 860c.51/626; and in AAN-AW, Leon Orłowski to Gliwic, July 30, 1925, n. 227, and Władysław Sokołowski to Western Department, MSZ, February 16, 1926, n. 74.

70. Gliwic to Skrzyński, October 12, 1925, in Landau and Tomaszewski, *Kapitały*, pp. 240-241; in AAN-AW n. 480, Gliwic to Hayward, October 2, 1925, and Hayward to Gliwic, October 5, 1925.

71. Młynarski, *Wspomnienia*, pp. 272-276. See as well Młynarski to Grabski, No-

vember 4, 1925, IHGS-AL A.12.53/8, and Hayward to Gliwic, November 5, 1925, AAN-AW n. 481.

72. *Sprawozdanie*, November 10, 1925, pp. 5–14, 39–41. Note likewise Grabski, *Dwa lata*, pp. 29–31.

73. Finance Ministry to Western Department, MSZ, November 12, 1925, AAN-MSZ n. 5004.

74. Stetson to Kellogg, November 11, 1925, SDNA 860c.51/533. Also in SDNA, Stetson to Kellogg, November 25, 1925, 860c.00/298.

75. Dirksen to Zechlin, December 15, 1925, GFMR K161 K020149-50. See also Dirksen memorandum of December 29, 1925, ADAP, ser. B, v. 2:1, pp. 69–74; Zygmunt J. Gasiorowski, "Stresemann and Poland After Locarno," *Journal of Central European Affairs* 18 (1958), pp. 293–294; Rataj, p. 347.

76. Sthamer to Auswärtiges Amt, October 7, 1925, GFMR K161 K020173-75.

77. Maltzan to Auswärtiges Amt, October 31, 1925, GFMR K161 K020235; Jackowski to Skrzyński, September 25, 1925, AAN-AW n. 223; Kazimierz Olszowski to MSZ, November 18, 1925, in Landau and Tomaszewski, *Kapitały*, p. 95. Jackowski repeats his indictment of "Anglo-Saxon merchants" in *W walce*, p. 319. The rumors stemmed largely from German sources who broadcast tales of a tacit understanding between American and German finance to carve out spheres of economic influence in the world and assign Eastern Europe to Germany. The theory gained credence in the autumn of 1925 when Schacht visited the United States to consult with American financial leaders. The stories came to the notice of the *New York Times*, which reported they were "ridiculed as absurd in all serious financial circles" (November 9, 1925).

78. Młynarski to Grabski, November 3, 1925, IHGS-AL A.12.53/8; Jaeckel to Kellogg, September 17, 1925, SDNA 660c.50/34; stenographic report of Schacht to German government and provincial officials, December 5, 1925, ADAP, ser. B, v. 1:1, pp. 18–31.

79. Gliwic to Skrzyński, October 12, 1925, in Landau and Tomaszewski, *Kapitały*, p. 241.

80. Ciechanowski to Skrzyński, March 18, 1926, AAN-AL n. 84. For examples of contemporary journalistic criticism of the Polish boundaries, see Charles H. Sherrill, "The Danzig Corridor: Is It a New War Breeder?" *Review of Reviews*, September 1925, pp. 387–388, and Frederick Palmer, "Where the Next European War Will Start," *Harper's Monthly*, November 1925, pp. 739–746. Oddly, a study of ten major American newspapers by the Polish legation in Washington found a majority of them generally "friendly" to Poland and only one—the Hearst *New York American*—consistently hostile (Orłowski to Political Department, MSZ, November 4, 1925, AAN-AW n. 1272).

81. Krzyżanowski, *Polityka*, p. 553.

82. Młynarski, *Wspomnienia*, p. 286.

CHAPTER IV

1. Rauscher to Auswärtiges Amt, ADAP, ser. B, v. 2:1, p. 77.

2. See the issues for November 22, November 29, and December 10, 1925.

3. The contemporary tributes to Ciechanowski are legion. Stetson called him "one of the best men in Polish service" in a dispatch to Kellogg, September 4, 1925, SDNA 701.60c11/115, while an anonymous White House memorandum for Coolidge praised his "wide and brilliant Diplomatic (*sic*) experience" (December 2, 1925, Coolidge Papers). On the Polish side, Skirmunt to Skrzyński, August 5, 1924, IHGS-AL A.12.53/6; Skirmunt, "Wspomnienia," p. 133; and Młynarski, *Wspomnienia*, p. 280. A dissenting opinion appears in Jan Drohojowski, *Jana Drohojowskiego wspomnienia dyplomatyczne* (Cracow, 1970), pp. 148–149.

4. *Boston Globe*, June 27, 1926. In addition, Castle to Stetson, May 21, 1926, Castle Papers; George L. Harrison to Strong, June 18, 1926, Strong Papers; Ronald Campbell to Arthur Henderson, March 19, 1930, PRO A2394/943/45; Garrard Winston to Charles Dewey, October 18, 1927, Charles S. Dewey Papers, HIA.

5. Stetson to Castle, June 8, 1926, Castle Papers.

6. *Le Messager Polonais*, November 29, 1925; Jerzy Zdziechowski, *Sytuacja gospodarczo-skarbowa Polski i drogi naprawy* (Warsaw, 1925), p. 9.

7. Hans Heinrich Dieckhoff to Auswärtiges Amt, November 7, 1925, GFMR K161 K020238.

8. Młynarski, *Wspomnienia*, pp. 275–278; record of meeting of Council of Ministers, November 30, 1925, AAN-PPRM n. 31; *Le Messager Polonais*, December 20, 1925; Ciechanowski to Skrzyński, November 29, 1925, AAN-AW n. 505, and the following in IHGS-AL A.12.53/8: Ciechanowski to Skrzyński, November 29, 1925, Skirmunt to Polish Legation, Washington, November 30, 1925, and Zdziechowski to Skrzyński, November 30, 1925.

9. Młynarski, *Wspomnienia*, pp. 278–279; Młynarski to Kemmerer, December 15, 1925, Edwin W. Kemmerer Papers, Mudd Library, Princeton University. At the time of Grabski's collapse, Skrzyński offered the British minister a sharp critique of the financial policies of his erstwhile chief, "especially his short-sighted refusal to accept a foreign adviser when it was the only condition on which a foreign loan was obtainable" (Max Muller to Chamberlain, November 13, 1925, PRO C14541/459/18; for this citation from PRO I am indebted to Dr. Thomas S. Dyman).

10. Młynarski, *Wspomnienia*, p. 279; Edwin W. Kemmerer Diary, December 17, 1925, Kemmerer Papers.

11. Ciechanowski's dispatches to Skrzyński of December 20, 1925 in AAN-AW n. 518 and AAN-MSZ n. 5004. Dillon, Read promised Kemmerer a "free hand" in Poland (Kemmerer Diary, December 19, 1925). Bankers Trust worried that Kemmerer would be "somewhat a tool of Dill.[on] and could injure or discourage the market from [their] business" (Ciechanowski note of conversation with Adam Faterson, December 21, 1925, AAN-AW n. 505).

12. In AAN-AW n. 505, Młynarski to Zdziechowski, December 5, 1925, and Ciechanowski to Młynarski, December 12, 1925. Zdziechowski seems to have wanted to liquidate Polish ties with Dillon as soon as possible (Zdziechowski to Société de Banque Suisse, December 30, 1925, AAN-AW n. 482). In a telephone conversation with an unidentified partner, Młynarski noted the marked preference of the finance minister for the "new banker" over the "old banker" (December 7, 1925, AAN-AW n. 505).

13. In PRO N41/41/55, Sir Frederick W. Leith-Ross to Alan G. Anderson, December 23, 1925, and Anderson to Skirmunt, December 29, 1925.

14. Kemmerer to Stetson, February 17, 1926, Kemmerer Papers. Also Stetson to Kellogg, January 20, 1926, SDNA 860c.51/550; Zdziechowski to Skirmunt, January 17, 1926, AAN-AL n. 641; *New York Times*, January 13, 1926.

15. Edwin W. Kemmerer, *Reports Submitted by the Commission of the American Financial Experts* (Warsaw, 1926), pp. 553–555; Kemmerer's memorandum of conversation with Wacław Wiślicki [January 1926], Kemmerer Papers.

16. Stetson to Kellogg, January 20, 1926, SDNA 860c.51/550; *Le Messager Polonais*, January 12 and February 10, 1926; Kemmerer Diary, January 29, 1926; in AAN-AW n. 518, Ciechanowski to Skrzyński and Zdziechowski, January 14, 1926, and Ciechanowski to Kemmerer, February 1, 1926.

17. Rataj, p. 348; Edwin C. Kemp to Kellogg, January 21, 1926, SDNA 860c.51/551.

18. In ADAP, ser. B, v. 2:1, Wilhelm Wallroth to German Legation, Warsaw, December 21, 1925, pp. 80–81, and Dirksen memorandum of conversation with Schacht, January 5, 1926, pp. 86–89; in GFMR, Wallroth to German Embassy, London, December 24, 1925, K161 K020362, Maltzan to Auswärtiges Amt, December 29, 1925, K161 K020374, and Carl Theodor Conrad von Schubert to German Legation, Warsaw, January 6, 1926, K161 K020347.

19. Ciechanowski to Skrzyński, February 3, 1926, AAN-AL n. 84. Also Młynarski, *Wspomnienia*, p. 283. The incident delighted the MSZ, which instructed its representatives to mention it freely in diplomatic conversations, Juliusz Łukasiewicz to Skirmunt, February 27, 1926, AAN-AL n. 84. British sources noted at the time that Schacht seemed more than usually impatient to settle the boundary dispute with Poland (Lord Edgar Vincent D'Abernon to Chamberlain, January 23, 1926, DBFP, ser. 1A, v. 1, pp. 347–348).

20. In the Kemmerer Papers, Kemmerer to Case, January 26, 1926, and Kemmerer to Stetson, February 17, 1926; in AAN-AW, Faterson and Charles Law to Młynarski, January 9, 1926, n. 505, Ciechanowski to MSZ, January 9, 1926, n. 518, and Zdziechowski to Ciechanowski, January 10, 1926, n. 518.

21. Młynarski, *Wspomnienia*, pp. 280–281; Zdziechowski to Skirmunt, January 17, 1926, AAN-AL n. 641; Skirmunt, "Wspomnienia," p. 141.

22. Ciechanowski to Skrzyński, January 12, 1926, AAN-AL n. 84; Ciechanowski to Zdziechowski, January 8, 1926, IHGS-AL A.12.53/8.

23. Ciechanowski to Zdziechowski, January 8, 1926, IHGS-AL A.12.53/8. Also Ciechanowski to Skrzyński, January 12, 1926, and March 4, 1926, AAN-AL n. 84. The undated memorandum is in Kolekcja Jana Ciechanowskiego, 82/12 n. 4.

24. Ciechanowski to Skrzyński, January 11, 1926, AAN-AL n. 84.

25. Ciechanowski to Skrzyński, January 11, 1926, AAN-AL n. 84; Zdziechowski to Skirmunt, January 17, 1926, AAN-AL n. 641; Henry Cochran to Kemmerer, January 21, 1926, Kemmerer Papers.

26. Zdziechowski to Skirmunt, January 17, 1926, AAN-AL n. 641; Stetson to Kellogg, January 20, 1926, SDNA 860c.00/307; BPPP, n. 162; Zdziechowski to Ciechanowski, January 21, 1926, HIA-US.

27. *Newark Evening News*, February 6, 1926; *New York Times*, January 21, 1926. Also Kemmerer Diary, January 28, 1926; Ciechanowski to Skrzyński, February 3, 1926, AAN-AL n. 84; and in AAN-AW n. 518, Seward Prosser to Ciechanowski, January 28, 1926, Ciechanowski to Kemmerer, January 30, 1926, and Ciechanowski to Prosser, January 30, 1926.

28. Ciechanowski to Skrzyński, February 2, 1926, AAN-AW n. 518, and February 3, 1926, AAN-AL n. 84. Within the latter Ciechanowski included the comment "aside from all other benefits of Prof. Kemmerer's stay in Poland, his conversation with Undersecretary Winston (who until now has looked on Poland rather skeptically), and particularly that part of the conversation dealing with the activities of Germany and the declaration of Schacht, has repaid the cost of the journey."

29. Ciechanowski to Skrzyński, March 8, 1926, AAN-AL n. 641.

30. Ciechanowski to Skrzyński, February 11, 1926, AAN-AL n. 84; Skirmunt to MSZ, February 10, 1926, IHGS-AL A.12.53/8; Max Muller to Chamberlain, January 27, 1926, PRO N452/41/55; Costigliola, "Stabilization," pp. 337–339.

31. Ciechanowski to Skrzyński, February 11, 1926, AAN-AL n. 84. Also Kemmerer Diary, March 1, 1926; Ciechanowski to Skrzyński, March 3, 1926, AAN-AL n. 84; in AAN-AW n. 518, Ciechanowski to Skrzyński, February 11, 1926, Ciechanowski to Case, February 18, 1926, and Kemmerer to Ciechanowski, March 8, 1926.

32. Ciechanowski to Skrzyński, March 1, 1926, AAN-AL n. 84.

33. In AAN-AL, Ciechanowski to Skrzyński, March 1, 1926, n. 84, and March 8, 1926, n. 641.

34. Costigliola, "Stabilization," p. 351.

35. Stetson to Kellogg, June 15, 1926, with the appended comments of Arthur Young, July 14, 1926, SDNA 860c.51A/4. In a minute to Max Muller to Chamberlain, June 9, 1926, Laurence Collier of the Foreign Office observed, "Prof. Kemmerer is not thought much of in [British] financial circles" (PRO N2741/41/55). For the accumulated English grievances against Kemmerer, see Costigliola, "Stabilization," pp. 204–211.

36. Sthamer to Auswärtiges Amt, April 8, 1926, ADAP, ser. B, v. 2:1, pp. 289–295 and Costigliola, "Stabilization," pp. 338–339. In an exchange with Max Muller, Niemeyer expressed his hope and that of the Bank of England that the Poles would accept League of Nations tutelage and that "wilder Americans such as Dillon Reid (*sic*) . . . [will] not try to rush in on other lines" (March 29, 1926, PRO N463/41/55).

37. In ADAP, ser. B, Sthamer to Auswärtiges Amt, March 1, 1926, v. 2:1, pp. 193–197, and March 19, 1926, v. 1:1, pp. 417–421; Dirksen memorandum, March 4, 1926, v. 2:1, pp. 199–202.

38. Ciechanowski to Strong, March 7, 1926, AAN-AW n. 505; Ciechanowski to Skrzyński, March 8, 1926, AAN-AL n. 641. Also in the latter collection, Zdziechowski to

Ciechanowski, March 10, 1926. A contemporary report by an American business agent concluded that Poland required "absolutely untrammeled" foreign supervision of her finances for at least five years (J. Howard Leman to Paine, Webber and Co., May 19, 1926, J. Howard Leman Collection, HIA).

39. Wallroth to German Embassy, London, March 24, 1926, ADAP, ser. B, v. 2:1, p. 229; Niemeyer to Sir William Tyrrell, March 29, 1926, and Niemeyer to Max Muller, March 29, 1926, PRO N1463/41/55; Norman to Niemeyer, March 27, 1926, Sir Otto Niemeyer Papers, T176/23, Public Record Office, London. For this item from the Niemeyer Papers I am indebted to Dr. Thomas S. Dyman.

40. Sthamer to Auswärtiges Amt, April 8, 1926, ADAP, ser. B, v. 2:1, pp. 289–295; Henri Fischer to Norman, March 30, 1926, Niemeyer Papers T176/23. My thanks to Dr. Thomas S. Dyman for this reference from the Niemeyer Papers.

41. Max Muller to Niemeyer, April 7, 1926, PRO N1621/41/55; Stetson to Kellogg, April 23, 1926, SDNA 860c.51/566.

42. Ciechanowski to Skrzyński, March 10, 1926, AAN-AL n. 641.

43. Ciechanowski to Skrzyński, March 15, 1926, AAN-AL n. 641. Strong wanted Dillon, Read to take the lead in a Polish stabilization loan but hoped Dillon would take other banks into a syndicate so as to dilute Poland's suspicions of her American bankers (Kemmerer Diary, March 18, 1926).

44. Zdziechowski to Ciechanowski, April 7, 1926, HIA-US; Ciechanowski to Strong, April 8, 1926, AAN-AL n. 641.

45. Ciechanowski to Skrzyński, April 12, 1926. On March 26 Strong told Ciechanowski he realized that "Schacht should not take part in questions where Poland is concerned" (Ciechanowski to Skrzyński, March 29, 1926; these appear in AAN-AL n. 641). In addition, MSZ to Polish Legation, London, April 23, 1926, IHGS-AL A.12.53/8.

46. In the Strong Papers, Strong to Winston, March 3, 1926, and Strong to Norman, March 27, 1926; Ciechanowski to Strong, April 21, 1926, AAN-AL n. 641; Costigliola, "Stabilization," p. 340. On March 9 Strong hinted to Ciechanowski that he would prefer to see Poland arrive at some compromise settlement of political controversies with Germany but would not presume to dictate how this should be done (Ciechanowski to Skrzyński, March 10, 1926, AAN-AL n. 641).

47. See Strong's testimony before the House Banking and Currency Committee, April 1926, quoted in W. Randolph Burgess, ed., *Interpretations of Federal Reserve Policy in the Speeches and Writings of Benjamin Strong* (New York and London, 1930), pp. 288–289.

48. The "second fiddle" phrase was Winston's (Ciechanowski to Zaleski, October 20, 1926, AAN-AL n. 85). Strong complained to Ciechanowski of being treated by the Bank of England "with a mother's indulgence for her inexperienced child" (Ciechanowski to Skrzyński, April 12, 1926, AAN-AL n. 641).

49. Ciechanowski to Skrzyński, March 1, 1926, AAN-AL n. 84.

50. In AAN-AL n. 84, Ciechanowski to Skrzyński, February 4, 1926, and April 28, 1926; Winston to Strong, February 12, 1926, Strong Papers. One of the interested Treasury functionaries was Assistant Secretary Charles Dewey, who within two years would assume the post of American financial adviser to the Polish government.

51. Neither American nor Polish officials regarded Stetson highly. Strong slighted his abilities in a memorandum of September 16, 1926, FRB C261.1. A few years later Castle told President Hoover that Stetson was "not liked by the Poles and has not done a good job, in spite of the fact that he believes he has. . . . He is of very little value to the [Foreign] Service" (January 21, 1929, HHPP). Piłsudski dismissed him as a man "of very low intelligence" (Kazimierz Świtalski memorandum of conversation with Piłsudski and Ignacy Mościcki, April 21, 1929, AAN-KŚ n. 70).

52. In SDNA, Stetson's dispatches to Kellogg, December 7, 1925, 860c.51/543, May 10, 1926, 860c.51/567, and February 22, 1926, 860c.51/556; also Stetson to Castle, June 8, 1926, Castle Papers.

53. Ciechanowski to Skrzyński, April 19, 1926, AAN-AL n. 641. Two years later Ciechanowski encapsulated his views with the statement "in lending huge sums to Europe,

America cannot maintain *ad infinitum* a stance of complete political *désintéressement* in European questions. Of course, she will not abandon this principle quickly or all at once. This process will be one of slow evolution" (Ciechanowski to Zaleski, May 24, 1928, PIA-AL).

54. The somewhat clumsy phrase, in English original, appeared in an indignant letter from Stanisław Karpiński, president of the Bank Polski, to Norman, June 28, 1926, AAN-AW n. 482. See also Roman Dyboski, "American and Polish Democracy," *Poland*, February 1926, pp. 69–70ff., and Henryk Tennenbaum, "Czynniki gospodarcze w polityce światowej," *Przegląd Polityczny* 4 (1926), p. 203.

55. In ADAP, ser. B, v. 2:1, Dirksen memorandum, April 17, 1926, pp. 359–361, and Stresemann to German Embassy, London, April 19, 1926, pp. 363–376. Already in January the British minister to Warsaw reported that Germany had missed her chance to enforce political demands against the Poles owing to the improving Polish trade balance (Max Muller to Chamberlain, January 25, 1926, DBFP, ser. 1A, v. 1, p. 411).

56. Frederick P. Hibbard to Kellogg, May 12, 1926, SDNA 860c.00/345. For the press, see the articles by Lincoln Eyre in the *New York Times* for May 4–5, 1926, in which he asserts, among other matters, that rumors of an impending coup d'état by Piłsudski are "bosh." For the activities of Kemmerer, the text of his speech to the Council on Foreign Relations, March 12, 1926, AAN-AW n. 517, and the *New York Times*, March 18, 1926.

57. In AAN-AW n. 575, Olszowski to Western Department, MSZ, November 11, 1925, and MSZ to Ciechanowski, February 8, 1926; in AAN-AB n. 1030, Olszowski to American Department, MSZ, November 17, 1925, and Zdziechowski and Stanisław Osiecki to Harriman and Co., February 24, 1926; *Sprawozdanie*, February 25, 1926, pp. 15–18 and April 28, 1926, pp. 70–95; Lewis, p. 255; William Yandell Elliott, ed., *International Control in the Non-Ferrous Metals* (New York, 1937), pp. 707–708.

58. The painstaking course of these talks may be traced in numerous documents, spanning the period March 15–May 7, 1926, in AAN-AL n. 641 and AAN-AW nos. 482, 483, and 488.

59. The standard works on the May revolt are Joseph Rothschild, *Piłsudski's Coup d'État* (New York, 1966), and Andrzej Garlicki, *Przewrót majowy* (Warsaw, 1978). Rumors of a Piłsudskist rebellion had circulated for months and probably scared off potential American investors: Ciechanowski to Skrzyński, January 9, 1926, AAN-AL n. 84, *New York Evening Post*, April 20, 1926, and *Sprawozdanie*, April 28, 1926, p. 54.

60. Ciechanowski to Zaleski, May 20, 1926, AAN-AL n. 84. Also Kemmerer to A. W. DuBois, May 10, 1926, Kemmerer Papers; Wańkowicz economic report, June 29, 1926, AAN-AW n. 153.

61. In IHGS-AL A.12.53/8, Zdziechowski to Skirmunt, May 10, 1926, and Skirmunt to Zdziechowski, May 12, 1926.

62. In AAN-AL n. 641, A. Poklewski-Koziełł to Zdziechowski, April 29, 1926, and Skirmunt to MSZ, May 6, 1926. To Strong, the news of the coup came as "something of a shock . . . and the first effect . . . has been to greatly unsettle the minds of those who were sincerely desirous of assisting Poland, but who now may feel that the hazards are too great" (Strong to Stetson, June 5, 1926, FRB C261.1).

63. Strong to Harrison, May 15, 1926, George L. Harrison Papers, Butler Library, Columbia University; Skirmunt to Zaleski, May 19, 1926, AAN-AL n. 641. Boyle, p. 197, bases his account on the entry in Norman's diary. Strong later attributed his concessions to Norman to the coup, "which made everything most uncertain" and cast the Kemmerer mission into limbo (Strong to Ciechanowski, August 3, 1926, AAN-AL n. 85).

64. August Zaleski, *Przemowy i deklaracje* (Warsaw, 1929), p. 9. When asked by an American journalist about the future of relations between the two countries, Piłsudski enigmatically responded "only [with] a shake of [his] head" (*New York Times*, May 26, 1926).

65. Adam Krzyżanowski, *Dzieje Polski* (Paris, 1973), pp. 116–117. Directly upon the ceasefire in Warsaw, a Piłsudskist aide delivered to the Bank Polski the Marshal's "orders that the stability of the złoty be maintained" (Młynarski, *Wspomnienia*, p. 281).

66. *Głos Prawdy*, May 23, 1926; *New York Times*, May 25, 1926; Stetson to Kellogg, July 5, 1926, SDNA 860c.6355/5.

67. Stanley Hawks to Kellogg, September 28, 1926, SDNA 701.60c11/132.

68. Ciechanowski to Zaleski, June 4, 1926, AAN-AL n. 84. Piłsudski in fact offered the post to Skrzyński in hopes of pleasing world opinion, despite his personal and political contempt for the figure he called "the little bitch of Locarno"; Skrzyński refused to serve with "a man who has fraternal blood on his hands" (Piotr S. Wandycz, *August Zaleski: Minister Spraw Zagranicznych RP 1926-1932 w świetle wspomnień i dokumentów* [Paris, 1980], pp. 26–27). For the press, *New York Times*, May 18 and May 22, 1926; *New York Herald-Tribune*, May 23, 1926; *Washington Post*, May 17 and May 19, 1926; *Chicago Tribune*, May 17, 1926; *Pittsburgh Chronicle-Telegram*, May 15 and May 24, 1926.

69. Harrison memorandum, May 25, 1926, Harrison Papers; Harrison to Strong, May 18, 1926, Strong Papers; Stetson to Kellogg, June 15, 1926, SDNA 860c.51A/4; *New York Times*, May 25, 1926; Ciechanowski to Zaleski, May 20, 1926, AAN-AL n. 84.

70. In SDNA, Stetson to Kellogg, May 24, 1926, 860c.00/355, and July 5, 1926, 860c.6355/5; Wańkowicz economic report, June 29, 1926, AAN-AW n. 153; *New York Times*, May 25, June 10, and August 6, 1926. The agreement between the Polish government and Harriman and Co. of July 3, 1926, is reproduced in Landau and Tomaszewski, *Kapitały*, pp. 300–305.

71. Zbigniew Landau, *Plan stabilizacyjny 1927-1930: geneza, założenia, wyniki* (Warsaw, 1963), p. 43; Ciechanowski to Kemmerer, May 31, 1926, AAN-AW n. 517; in AAN-AL n. 84, Ciechanowski to Zaleski, June 3, 1926, and June 4, 1926; Stetson to Kemmerer, June 4, 1926, Kemmerer Papers.

72. Strong to Harrison, June 6, 1926, Strong Papers; Strong to Stetson, June 5, 1926, FRB C261.1.

73. Stetson to Strong, May 28, 1926, FRB C261.1. Also Stetson to Kemmerer, June 4, 1926, Kemmerer Papers.

74. Wańkowicz economic report, June 29, 1926, AAN-AW n. 153.

75. In ADAP, ser. B, v. 2:1, Wallroth to German Embassy, London, May 1, 1926, pp. 436–437, Dirksen memorandum of conversation with Schacht, May 17, 1926, pp. 466–467, Sthamer to Auswärtiges Amt, May 21, 1926, pp. 473–474, and Schacht memorandum of conversation with Norman, May 28, 1926, pp. 489–492.

76. Harrison to Strong, June 18, 1926, Strong Papers; in AAN-AL, Ciechanowski to Zaleski, June 7 and June 23, 1926, n. 641, and Ciechanowski to Strong, July 14, 1926, n. 85.

77. Strong to Ciechanowski, August 3, 1926, AAN-AL n. 85; Strong to Harrison, June 29, 1926, FRB C261.1; Strong to Harrison, August 3, 1926, Strong Papers.

78. In AAN-AW, Wańkowicz economic report, June 29, 1926, n. 153, and Wańkowicz to Klarner, September 18, 1926, n. 470; Strong to Ciechanowski, August 3, 1926, AAN-AL n. 85. A Dillon representative told Stresemann his bank too was waiting on the Kemmerer report before proceeding with Polish business (Stresemann to Schubert, July 12, 1926, ADAP, ser. B, v. 1:1, pp. 643–645).

79. Ciechanowski to Zaleski, August 25, 1926, AAN-AL n. 85.

80. Młynarski, *Wspomnienia*, p. 284; *Sprawozdanie*, June 25, 1926, p. 57. See as well *Sprawozdanie*, April 28, 1926, p. 17, and *Gazeta Warszawska Poranna*, June 8, 1926.

81. *Sprawozdanie*, June 25, 1926, pp. 59–64.

82. Wańkowicz's undated account of his activities of June 22, 1926, AAN-AW n. 517. Also Kemmerer Diary, July 3, 1926, and Wallroth to German Embassy, London, July 7, 1926, ADAP, ser. B, v. 2:2, pp. 95–96.

83. Romer to Ciechanowski, September 27, 1926, AAN-AW n. 517.

84. *New York Times*, August 8, August 11, August 15, August 17, August 21, September 2, and September 18, 1926. In SDNA, Stetson to Kellogg, July 20, 1926, 860c.00/371, and Arthur Young memorandum of conversation with Kemmerer, October 4, 1926, 860c.51A/7.

85. Zbigniew Landau has claimed on various occasions that Kemmerer's goal was to render Poland easy prey for the depredatory designs of German and other foreign interests.

In *Plan*, p. 129, he calls the American commission's report "an expression of Kemmerer's conscious desire to subordinate the Polish economy to the interests of Germany." In another place he asserts that "both the [Kemmerer] mission and its recommendations had as their goal the opening of the door to German economic interests for the domination of Poland, which appealed to official circles in England and the United States" (*Polskie*, p. 198). These baseless charges are derived largely from Kemmerer's connection with Dillon, Read, which Landau suspects of having collaborated with Germany to the detriment of Poland. While one might contend—as does Landau—that the practical effect of the Kemmerer recommendations would have been to make Poland an agrarian junior partner of German industry, there is no question that Kemmerer's intention was to aid Poland according to his conservative lights. He was anything but hostile to Poland or disposed toward Germany. Młynarski confirms this in *Wspomnienia*, pp. 283–286. Part of Młynarski's observations on the subjects were excised from the published version of his memoir. Examination of the typescript "Za kulisami wielkich wydarzeń: garść wspomnień osobistych," Biblioteka Ossolineum, Wrocław, reveals the following on p. 372: "Kemmerer was not an exponent of pro-German circles. He showed this not only by resisting Schacht's pressures but by . . . relating to us what Schacht had told him [concerning his aims to repossess the Polish Corridor]. In reality, then, Kemmerer was rather anti-German and represented those American circles who wished to free themselves from the patronage of Norman . . . and Schacht." This reading accords fully with all available documentary evidence of Kemmerer's actions and statements, including those of later years when from time to time he would alert Polish officials to the appearance of unfriendly "propaganda" in the American press or defend Warsaw at public gatherings: in AAN-AW, Kemmerer to Ciechanowski, May 26, 1927, n. 515, Kemmerer to Wańkowicz, March 9, 1928, n. 515, Ciechanowski to Kemmerer, November 19, 1928, n. 1187. The Princeton professor championed the contested Polish boundaries with special vehemence: Kemmerer to Francies W. Hirst, March 22, 1926, Kemmerer Papers, Ciechanowski to Zaleski, October 1, 1926, AAN-AL n. 85, and Wojciech Dzieduszycki to Mieczysław Marchlewski, December 12, 1930, Konsulat Generalny RP w Nowym Jorku, n. 507, AAN.

86. Kemmerer, *Reports*, pp. 1–48, 245–246; Młynarski, *Wspomnienia*, p. 285; Arthur Young memorandum of conversation with Kemmerer, October 4, 1926, SDNA 860c. 51A/7.

87. Arthur Young memorandum of conversation with Kemmerer, October 4, 1926, SDNA 860c.51A/7. Also Kemmerer, *Reports*, pp. 533–542.

88. Młynarski memorandum "The Polish Currency and the Problem of Free Trade," November 1926, AAN-AW n. 694. Also Arthur Young memorandum of conversation with Kemmerer, October 4, 1926, SDNA 860c.51A/7.

89. *New York Times*, September 18, 1926; text of Kemmerer's address before the American-Polish Chamber of Commerce and Industry, October 5, 1926, Kemmerer Papers.

90. Ciechanowski to Zaleski, October 8, 1926, AAN-AL n. 85; Kemmerer Diary, October 6, 1926.

91. Dufour-Feronce to Auswärtiges Amt, September 29, 1926, ADAP, ser. B, v. 2:2, pp. 283–284. Also Dufour-Feronce to Auswärtiges Amt, August 18, 1926, ADAP, ser. B, v. 1:1, pp. 91–92; Collier minute of September 28, 1926, PRO N4329/41/55; Dufour-Feronce to Auswärtiges Amt, November 24, 1926, GFMR K161 K020859.

92. Stanisław Łoś to Zaleski, September 21, 1926, AAN-AL n. 617.

93. Strong memorandum, September 16, 1926, FRB C261.1.

94. Daily press summary of American Consulate, Warsaw, August 17, 1926, Kemmerer Papers; *Sprawozdanie*, September 24, 1926, p. 13; *Echo Warszawskie*, August 19, 1926. In his memorandum "Report on Journey to London and Paris," Młynarski wrote, "up to now the post-May government has made no decision to seek a large stabilization loan" (September 29, 1926, AAN-AL n. 641).

95. Młynarski memorandum "The Polish Currency and the Problem of Free Trade," November 1926, AAN-AW n. 694.

CHAPTER V

1. Ciechanowski to Zaleski, September 17, 1926, AAN-AL n. 85; Ciechanowski to Zaleski, October 29, 1926, AAN-AW n. 448.
2. Młynarski memorandum "Report on Journey to London and Paris," September 29, 1926, AAN-AL n. 641 (emphases Młynarski's). Also Strong memorandum, September 16, 1926, FRB C261.1.
3. *New York Times*, October 5, 1926; Ciechanowski to Czechowicz, October 7, 1926, HIA-US.
4. Stetson to Kemmerer, October 15, 1926, Kemmerer Papers; Czechowicz to Zaleski, November 12, 1926, AAN-AW n. 516; *New York Times*, October 7 and November 23, 1926; Poland, Ministerstwo Skarbu, *A Budget Speech by Gabriel Czechowicz, Polish Minister of Finance* (Warsaw, 1928), p. 21.
5. Ciechanowski to Zaleski, October 20, 1926, AAN-AL n. 85.
6. Harrison memorandum, November 5, 1926, FRB C261.1. Also Ciechanowski to Zaleski, November 6, 1926, AAN-AL n. 85.
7. Ciechanowski to Zaleski, November 6, 1926, AAN-AL n. 85; in AAN-AW n. 448, Gruszka to Ciechanowski, October 17, 1926, Ciechanowski to Zaleski, October 29, 1926, and Ciechanowski to Gruszka, November 2, 1926.
8. In AAN-AW n. 484, Ciechanowski to Zaleski, July 8, 1926, and memorandum of the Polish Legation, Washington, to Dillon, Read, October 1, 1926; in AAN-AL n. 85, Ciechanowski to Zaleski, October 8, 1926, and November 6, 1926; Józef Dangel to Polish Legation, Washington, August 26, 1926, in Landau and Tomaszewski, *Kapitały*, pp. 241–242.
9. Maltzan to Auswärtiges Amt, November 2, 1926, GFMR K161 K020506; Gostomski, pp. 12–13; H. Dorsey Newson to Castle, November 17, 1926, Castle Papers.
10. Castle to Newson, December 13 and December 23, 1926, Castle Papers. In a similar vein, Leman to Paine, Webber and Co., May 19, 1926, Leman Collection. Moody's 1926 ratings of Polish bonds all fell in the less desirable B category. Of the countries of Eastern and Central Europe, only Romania ranked lower in Moody's estimation.
11. Młynarski memorandum "The Polish Currency and the Problem of Free Trade," November 1926, AAN-AW n. 694; text of note given Stetson, December 15, 1926, and Jackowski to Ciechanowski, December 20, 1926, AAN-MSZ n. 4614.
12. Stetson to Robert F. Kelley, December 7, 1926, SDNA 860c.51/639. Stetson told Kellogg that "those [Polish] groups who oppose Piłsudski are not good patriots" (November 23, 1926, SDNA 860c.00/392). For the satisfaction of American business circles with Piłsudski, Drohojowski, p. 82, and Ulen and Co. to Jeremiah W. Jenks, July 30, 1926, AAN-AW n. 595.
13. *Foreign Securities Investor*, January 5, 1927, p. 18. On a more popular level, Isaac F. Marcosson, "America in Poland," *Saturday Evening Post*, December 11, 1926, predicted the "entry of American enterprise into Poland on a big and what will undoubtedly be an increasing scale" (p. 137).
14. A Foreign Ministry official told Dillon's representative in Berlin that "it would be regarded with great disfavor in German quarters if Dillon should at present offer Poland a loan. . . . In that event, the German government could scarcely decide to permit Dillon, Read to participate in the issue of the German loan" (Zechlin [?] memorandum, November 18, 1926, GFMR K161 K020511-12).
15. Ciechanowski to Zaleski, December 22, 1926, AAN-AL n. 85. In the same collection, Ciechanowski to Zaleski, December 9 and December 10, 1926. Also Harrison memorandum, February 2, 1927, FRB C261.1.
16. Private letter sent to Ciechanowski from an unidentified friend, December 15, 1926, AAN-MSZ n. 5004. Also Młynarski, *Wspomnienia*, p. 286; Młynarski memorandum "Report on Journey to London and Paris," September 29, 1926, AAN-AL n. 641; Ciechanowski to Zaleski, December 22, 1926, AAN-AL n. 85.
17. Wańkowicz to Czechowicz, December 22, 1926, AAN-AW n. 470; Ciechanowski to

Zaleski, December 22, 1926, AAN-AL n. 85; Ciechanowski to Zaleski, December 30, 1926, HIA-US; Harrison memorandum, February 2, 1927, FRB C261.1; Newson to Kellogg, January 28, 1927, SDNA 860c.51/604. The record of Sztolcman's dealings with Dillon appears in Gruszka to Ciechanowski, December [23?], 1926, AAN-AW n. 447, and in the following in AAN-AW n. 448: Sztolcman to Brownboveri, December 27, 1926, January 15 and January 17, 1927, and Brownboveri to Sztolcman, January 17, 1927.

18. Młynarski, *Wspomnienia*, pp. 286–287; Strong to Harrison, June 29, 1926, FRB C261.1; Harrison memorandum, February 2, 1927, Harrison Papers; Monnet, p. 122.

19. Czechowicz to Monnet, December 22, 1926, Ministerstwo Skarbu, n. 4102, AAN; Młynarski, *Wspomnienia*, pp. 288–289; Monnet to Zaleski, January 18, 1927, AAN-AL n. 642; Newson to Kellogg, January 28, 1927, SDNA 860c.51/604.

20. Patrick Roberts to Charles Michael Palairet, January 12, 1927, PRO N214/23/55.

21. Czechowicz to Ciechanowski, January 20, 1927, HIA-US; Zaleski to Polish Legation, London, January 26, 1927, IHGS-AL A.12.53/9; Max Muller to Chamberlain, February 9, 1927, PRO N627/23/55. See also Krzyżanowski's typescript memoir "Kartki z kalendarza Adama Krzyżanowskiego 1873–1963," Joseph Piłsudski Institute of America, New York, which submits that "Ciechanowski . . . did not enjoy the confidence of the Marshal" (p. 46).

22. Krzyżanowski, "Kartki," p. 47. The decree of *plein pouvoir* given Młynarski and Krzyżanowski, signed by Piłsudski and Czechowicz, January 27, 1927, is in HIA-US.

23. Moreau, pp. 192, 410, 504.

24. "I was not prepared to allow [Norman] to couple the stabilization of the zloty with political conditions touching on the German-Polish frontier. . . . That is why I undertook, with the agreement of Moreau and Poincaré, and thanks to my friendly relations with Strong, to persuade the Federal Reserve Bank to counterbalance the English influence" (Monnet, p. 123).

25. Moreau, pp. 213–214, 219. Also Młynarski, *Wspomnienia*, pp. 291–292.

26. *Sprawozdanie*, January 25, 1927, pp. 28, 34–35, and February 11, 1927, pp. 55–56. Krzyżanowski wrote at the time that "the Government never intended and does not intend to adopt all of Kemmerer's recommendations" (*Dwa programy*, p. 12). See also *Foreign Securities Investor*, March 2, 1927, p. 8. From the first Kemmerer had acknowledged publicly that "it might be impossible for Poland to accept [the recommendations] all at once" (*New York Times*, August 1, 1926).

27. Stetson to Kellogg, March 1, 1927, SDNA 860c.51/616; in AAN-AW, F. Berwin to Stetson, February 4, 1927, n. 521, and Wańkowicz to Ciechanowski, February 12, 1927, n. 492; in FRB C261.1, Harrison memorandum, February 2, 1927, and Strong to Owen Young, March 3, 1927.

28. Strong to Harrison, February 20, 1927, FRB C261.1; Stetson to Kellogg, March 1, 1927, SDNA 860c.51/616. Strong regretted the rupture between Dillon and the Poles, telling Owen Young that "there has been fault on both sides: as to Poland, due partly to inexperience and the distractions of their revolution [i.e., the Piłsudski coup] and these many missions and inquiries [to other bankers]; and as to Dillon, I fear the fault has been partly a lack of the right kind of leadership . . . , possibly some neglect because of his own preoccupation with other matters" (March 3, 1927, FRB C261.1).

29. Strong to Norman, February 15 and February 25, 1927, Strong Papers. For Norman, Wallroth's memorandum of conversation with Schacht, March 7, 1927, GFMR 5462/E371134 and Moreau, p. 255. For German reaction, Wallroth to German Embassy, Washington, February (?), 1927, GFMR 5462/E371127-28; Newson to Kellogg, February 10, 1927, SDNA 660c.6231/24; Ciechanowski to MSZ, February 2, 1927, AAN-MSZ n. 48.

30. In FRB, Młynarski memorandum of February 17, 1927, and memoranda of meetings of members of Kemmerer commission with representatives of Poland, February 18 and February 22, 1927.

31. Młynarski, *Wspomnienia*, pp. 292–297; Stanisław Łepkowski to MSZ, February 25, 1927, AAN-MSZ n. 43; Federal Reserve Bank "History" of Polish stabilization loan [1927],

FRB C261.1A. Monnet codified his arguments in the memorandum "Preliminary Observations on the Financial Situation in Poland" [February 1927], FRB.

32. Młynarski, *Wspomnienia*, pp. 298–299. For the weakness of Polish credit, Orłowski to Łepkowski, February 18, 1927, AAN-AW n. 470, and *Journal of Commerce*, March 3, 1927. Czechowicz told the commercial secretary of the British legation in Warsaw that "he could not be surprised that neither of these markets [New York and London] had much confidence in Poland" (Max Muller to Chamberlain, February 9, 1927, PRO N627/23/55).

33. Młynarski, *Wspomnienia*, pp. 299–300; Ciechanowski to Zaleski, March 14, 1927, AAN-AL n. 642; "Four Gold Zlotys" to Strong, March 5, 1927, AAN-AW n. 521.

34. Młynarski, *Wspomnienia*, pp. 300–301, 303; Bankers Trust, Chase Securities Corp. and Blair and Co. to Młynarski and Krzyżanowski, March 18, 1927, AAN-AW n. 495.

35. Charles S. Hamlin Diary, March 11 and March 16, 1927, Charles S. Hamlin Papers, LC. Also Strong to Harrison, March 6, 1927, FRB C261.1. Cotton was the leading American export to Poland. In 1927 that commodity accounted for 61 percent of the total Polish import from the United States of $41.8 million.

36. Wańkowicz economic report, March 31, 1928, AAN-AW n. 154. On May 3 Dwight Morrow, a Morgan partner with ties to Coolidge, told Moreau that Harrison's Polish initiative enjoyed the backing of the president and that "a defeat would be keenly resented by the White House" (Moreau, p. 299). In his memoir *Defeat in Victory* (Garden City, N. Y., 1947), Ciechanowski credits Coolidge with helping behind the scenes to secure the loan for Poland (p. 8). For the State Department, Ciechanowski to Zaleski, March 14, 1927, AAN-AL n. 642, and Strong to Ciechanowski, March 21, 1927, AAN-AW n. 492. Ogden Mills, undersecretary of the treasury, told Ciechanowski that the Polish project was "currently perhaps the most important instance of American co-operation with Europe" (Ciechanowski to Zaleski, April 12, 1927, HIA-US).

37. On March 9, 1927, Strong wrote Harrison that "our selfish motive is of course our concern for the maintenance of an important outlet for our raw cotton and some other things we ship to Poland, but more especially to promote general stability in Europe" (FRB C261.1). S. Parker Gilbert told Norman on April 5, 1927, that "it is a matter of first-rate importance for all of us to have the area of stabilization extend as far to the East as possible" (FRB C261.1). Costigliola overstates the explicitly anti-Soviet purposes of the Americans regarding Polish stabilization ("Stabilization," p. 333).

38. Ciechanowski to Zaleski, March 17, 1927, AAN-MSZ n. 5004. See likewise Wańkowicz to Ciechanowski, March 2, 1927, AAN-AW n. 492, and Harrison to Strong, March 18, 1927, FRB C261.1. The Reserve Bank recognized that it was dealing as much with the Polish government itself as with the Bank Polski (Strong to Harrison, February 20, 1927, FRB C261.1). During their deliberations the bankers considered overtly political issues, such as the controversy over the Polish boundaries, in weighing the risks of the undertaking. See Ciechanowski's memorandum "On the Political Aspect of the Cooperation of Foreign Capital in Poland," submitted both to Strong and the State Department, March 1, 1927, FRB C261.1A and SDNA 811.503160c/2; and F.N.B. Close's memorandum "The Frontier Situation in Poland," March 17, 1927, FRB C261.1A.

39. Młynarski, *Wspomnienia*, pp. 301–305.

40. Świtalski memorandum of conversation with Piłsudski, early March 1933, AAN-KŚ n. 71. Also SDNA, Stetson to Kellogg, April 2, 1927, F. W. 860c.51/618, and April 12, 1927, 860c.51/625; *Czas*, April 8, 1927; Rataj, p. 472; Harrison to Strong and Case, April 11, 1927, FRB C261.1A; Jules Laroche, *La Pologne de Pilsudski: souvenirs d'une ambassade, 1926–1935* (Paris, 1953), pp. 28–29.

41. Krzyżanowski, "Kartki," pp. 54–55. Part of Krzyżanowski's account is reproduced in Wacław Jędrzejewicz, *Kronika życia Józefa Piłsudskiego*, 2 vols. (London, 1977), v. 2, p. 270.

42. Rataj, p. 473. Also *New York Times*, April 8 and 9, 1927; Moreau, p. 278; Hamlin Diary, April 25, 1927.

43. Moreau, pp. 267–269, 273.

44. Dirksen memorandum of conversation with Schacht, March 30, 1927, GFMR 5462/ E371141-42. Also Schubert memorandum, February 25, 1927, ADAP, ser. B, v. 4, pp. 413–414; Wallroth memorandum of conversation with Schacht, March 7, 1927, GFMR 5462/ E371134; Clay, p. 259.

45. Strong to Norman, March 25, 1927, Strong Papers. In FRB, Strong to Harrison, March 6 and March 9, 1927, C261.1, and Case to Harrison, April 8, 1927, C261.1A.

46. Harrison to Case and Strong, March 29, 1927, Harrison Papers; Hamlin Diary, April 25, 1927. Also Moreau, pp. 269–271; Stetson to Kellogg, April 12, 1927, SDNA 860c.51/625; in the Harrison Papers, Harrison memorandum of meeting with Schacht, April 1, 1927, and Harrison to Strong and Case, April 5, 1927.

47. Harrison to Strong and Case, April 5, 1927, Harrison Papers and Moreau, p. 273. In addition, Schacht to Stresemann, April 6, 1927, ADAP, ser. B, v. 5, pp. 129–131, and Moreau, p. 276.

48. Moreau, pp. 276, 278, 280; in FRB C261.1, Gilbert to Norman, April 5, 1927, and transcript of telephone conversation between Strong and Case, April 7, 1927; Hamlin Diary, April 25, 1927; New York Times, April 2, 1927.

49. Clay, p. 260; Niemeyer to Palairet, May 2, 1927, PRO N1981/23/55. Writing to Strong on April 17, 1927, Norman told "Dear old Ben" that "Poland is a most difficult problem from this end" (Strong Papers).

50. In the John Foster Dulles Oral History Collections, Mudd Library, Princeton University, see the George C. Sharp interview, pp. 6–16, and the Allen Dulles interview, pp. 43–44. Also Monnet, p. 124.

51. Czechowicz to Łepkowski, April 12, 1927, IHGS-AL A.12.53/9, and Stetson to Kellogg, April 19, 1927, SDNA 860c.51/626.

52. Krzyżanowski, "Kartki," p. 46, and Max Muller to Chamberlain, May 4, 1927, PRO N2094/23/55.

53. Hamlin Diary, April 25, 1927; Harrison to Strong and Case, April 11, 1927, FRB C261.1A; in SDNA, Stetson to Kellogg, April 19, 1927, 860c.51/626, and May 10, 1927, 860c.51/632.

54. Stetson to Kellogg, April 12, 1927, SDNA 860c.51/625; BPPP, nos. 174–175; Głos Prawdy, May 7, 1927.

55. Kurjer Warszawski, March 11, 1927. Also Krzyżanowski, Dwa programy, pp. 7, 19, 38.

56. Zygmunt Karpiński, Bank Polski 1924-1939: przyczynek do historii gospodarczej okresu międzywojennego (Warsaw, 1958), pp. 50–51; New York Times, May 2, 1927. The Socialists led the rhetorical attack on Kemmerer. In April the Socialist deputy Diamand said of him, "I marvel at the courage of the man, that he is not ashamed to speak so copiously and authoritatively to the world on subjects of which he is ignorant. . . . If he had said something worthwhile, no sacrifice would be too great, but he . . . says only: Americanize yourselves" (cited in Karol Ostrowski, Polityka finansowa Polski przedwrześniowej [Warsaw, 1958], pp. 172–173). Kemmerer expressed to Ciechanowski his satisfaction with Poland's adoption of his recommendations, May 2, 1927, AAN-AW n. 515. Others were less impressed with Polish progress toward reform. On May 31, 1927, Stetson wrote Kemmerer "until the loan negotiations with the Bankers Trust group took definite shape your suggestions were quietly sleeping in the archives" (Kemmerer Papers).

57. Stetson to Kellogg, May 10, 1927, SDNA 860c.51/632; New York Times, April 30 and May 6, 1927; Wall Street Journal, May 21, 1927. Młynarski complained to the commercial secretary of the British legation in Warsaw that the bankers conceived of the American representative more as a "controller" than an "observer" (Max Muller to Chamberlain, May 4, 1927, PRO N2094/23/55).

58. Ciechanowski to MSZ, May 1, 1927, AAN-MSZ n. 5004. In the same collection, Ciechanowski to MSZ, April 28 and May 7, 1927. Mellon favored the international advisory board, Harrison memorandum of meeting with Mellon, May 1927, Harrison Papers. Parker Gilbert believed that even the bankers' control provisions were too weak (Morrow to Russell C. Leffingwell, May 5, 1927, FRB C261.1A, and Moreau, p. 298).

59. Norman to Strong, May 7, 1927, Strong Papers. Norman seems to have facilitated a solution to the issue of the international panel of experts (Harrison to Schacht, June 9, 1927, FRB C261.1). Also Moreau, pp. 298–301. The principal American discussants were Gilbert and Morrow.

60. Młynarski and Leon Barański to MSZ, May 16, 1927, AAN-MSZ n. 5004; Ciechanowski to Harrison, May 18, 1927, AAN-AW n. 521.

61. Ciechanowski to Harrison, May 17, 1927, FRB C261.1A.

62. Moreau, p. 304. In FRB C261.1A, Federal Reserve Bank of New York to Moreau, May 9, 1927, and Strong to Moreau, May 19, 1927. On May 18 Moreau told Młynarski that "it is impossible to substitute me for the Federal Reserve Bank" (Moreau, p. 315). "The Bank [of France] is of course most anxious not to do anything which might be construed as a desire to take away the leadership of the Federal Reserve and feels that . . . the leadership should be such as to give no grounds of suspicion that the well-known political friendship of France for Poland could in any way have affected their (*sic*) judgment on the plan" (Close and Monnet to Federal Reserve Bank of New York, May 18, 1927, FRB C261.1A).

63. Ciechanowski to MSZ, May 21, 1927, AAN-MSZ n. 5004.

64. Strong to Dillon, May 26, 1927, FRB C261.1; Stetson to Kellogg, May 10, 1927, SDNA 860c.51/632; Wańkowicz economic report, June 19, 1927, AAN-AW n. 153. Stetson told Kemmerer on May 31, 1927, that the merger could not work because Blair and Dillon, Read "are after each other with a sharp knife" (Kemmerer Papers). Kemmerer's reply of July 7 also showed disdain for Blair, a firm he considered inclined toward unscrupulous methods of business competition (Kemmerer Papers).

65. Hamlin Diary, June 6, 1927; Strong to Moreau, June 7, 1927, and Harrison to W. P. G. Harding, June 22, 1927, FRB C261.1.

66. Stresemann to Schacht, May (?), 1927, GFMR K161 K020879-82; in ADAP, ser. B, v. 5, footnote #4 to Stresemann to (?) von Knebel Doeberitz, May 7, 1927, pp. 300–301, Wallroth to Stresemann, May 19, 1927, p. 378, and Dirksen to Wallroth and Zechlin, May 24, 1927, pp. 400–402.

67. In FRB C261.1A, Norman to Strong, June 8, 1927, Strong to Moreau, June 11, 1927, and B. A. Tompkins to Close, June 14, 1927; Stetson to Kellogg, June 6, 1927, SDNA 860c.51/636. Moreau gloated over the unhappiness of Norman and Schacht, noting that "the success of the Polish plan is certainly very disagreeable to them" (Moreau, p. 351).

68. Młynarski, *Wspomnienia*, pp. 307–308; Stetson to Kellogg, June 6, 1927, SDNA 860c.51/636. John Foster Dulles recalled that during the Warsaw phase of the talks Piłsudski was "the main negotiator on the Polish side . . . whose decision had to be had before anything could be done" (Sharp interview, Dulles Oral History, p. 11).

69. Młynarski, *Wspomnienia*, p. 308. Also Close and Monnet to Federal Reserve Bank of New York, May 21, 1927, FRB C261.1A.

70. Młynarski, *Wspomnienia*, pp. 309–310. Also Tompkins to Close, May 19, 1927, and Close and Monnet to Federal Reserve Bank of New York, June 14, 1927, FRB C261.1A.

71. In FRB, Tompkins to Monnet, June 16, 1927, C261.1A, and Harrison to Harding, June 22, 1927, C261.1; Stetson to Kellogg, June 13, 1927, SDNA 701.6160c/18; Wańkowicz economic report, June 19, 1927, AAN-AW n. 153.

72. In AAN-AW n. 521, Polska Agencja Telegraficzna to Polish Legation, Washington, July 6, 1927, and Tompkins to Wańkowicz, July 9, 1927; Młynarski, *Wspomnienia*, pp. 310–311. The cabinet took its formal decision on July 11 (AAN-PPRM n. 38).

73. *Moody's Investment Letters*, September 8, 1927; Czechowicz to Polish Legation, Washington, July 30, 1927, AAN-AW n. 639. A journalist by trade, Ivy Lee became the foremost practitioner of public relations of his day and lent his services widely. Warsaw retained him as permanent publicity agent for Poland at an annual fee of $20,000. Ironically, the improvement of Polish prospects in America during the summer of 1927 owed little to Lee, who had yet to begin his campaign in earnest. The Poles kept Lee on their payroll until 1929, when they dismissed him for lack of results.

74. In the Harrison Papers, Strong to Schacht, September 19, 1927, and Schacht to

Strong, September 20, 1927; Wallroth to German Embassy, London, September 23, 1927, ADAP, ser. B, v. 6, p. 495; *Times* (London), September 21, 1927.

75. Młynarski, *Wspomnienia,* pp. 311–313; Monnet, p. 124. Also Sharp interview, Dulles Oral History, p. 11. Młynarski reports that "the prospect of delivering such an ultimatum pleased [Piłsudski] greatly" (*Wspomnienia,* p. 313).

76. Stetson to Kellogg, October 20, 1927, SDNA 860c.51 P 751/13. In addition, in IHGS-AL A.12.53/9, Roman Knoll to Polish Legation, London, September 29, 1927, and Jackowski to Polish Legation, London, September 30, 1927; Krzyżanowski, "Kartki," p. 56; Fischer to Bankers Trust, September 29, 1927, FRB C261.1A; Młynarski, *Wspomnienia,* p. 311; *New York Times,* September 30 and October 1, 1927.

77. Harrison to Strong, September 29, 1927, FRB C261.1; Stetson to Kellogg, October 20, 1927, SDNA 860c.51 P 751/12. The American minister went on to note that "on several occasions [the bankers] have mentioned to me the lack of [financial] knowledge of many of the Poles, especially those in a position to determine the policy of the Government." Also Strong to Moreau, September 30, 1927, FRB C261.1A.

78. Fischer and Monnet to Bankers Trust, October 7, 1927, FRB C261.1A; Stetson to Kellogg, October 4, 1927, SDNA 860c.51 P 751/1.

79. In SDNA, Stetson to Kellogg, October 7, 1927, 860c.51 P 751/3, and October 20, 1927, 860c.51 P 751/12; *New York Times,* October 8, 1927.

80. Młynarski, *Wspomnienia,* p. 312. In his account of the loan negotiations, Młynarski routinely claims credit for devising the various compromises that permitted the parties to surmount each obstacle in turn. In this instance, at least, his statement receives independent verification (Stetson to Kellogg, October 20, 1927, SDNA 860c.51 P 751/12).

81. In FRB C261.1A, Monnet and Fischer to Bankers Trust, October 9, 1927, and Bankers Trust, Chase Securities Corp., Blair and Co. and Guaranty Trust Co. to Monnet and Fischer, October 10, 1927; Stetson and Kellogg, October 10, 1927, SDNA 860c.51 P 751/4; summary of meeting of Council of Ministers, October 11, 1927, AAN-PPRM n. 39.

82. Młynarski, *Wspomnienia,* p. 314. The text of Piłsudski's note is in FRB C261.1. On October 17 Piłsudski told Stetson he too "should not read the papers" (Stetson memorandum of conversation with Piłsudski, October 20, 1927, SDNA 760c.60 M/178).

83. The relevant documentation is reprinted in John Foster Dulles, *Poland: Plan of Financial Stabilization, 1927* (New York, 1928), pp. 39–78.

84. Polska Agencja Telegraficzna to Polish Legation, Washington, October 14, 1927, AAN-AW n. 492; *New York Sun,* October 24, 1927. According to the *New York Times* of October 18, 1927, Owen Young, a director of the New York Federal Reserve, remarked that "the new loan was in line with financial reconstruction of great importance to America. He said that as this country had a large surplus of agricultural products and a growing surplus of manufactured articles for which it was seeking markets, the maintenance of the gold standard in Europe and the stabilization of European currencies were important to this country."

85. Norman to Strong, October 16, 1927, Strong Papers. The emphasis is Norman's. See also Wallroth (?) circular, November 24, 1927, GFMR K161 K021381-82; Młynarski to Harrison, February 18, 1928, FRB C261.1; Schurman to Kellogg, October 24, 1927, SDNA 760c.62/70; Ciechanowski to Zaleski, March 27, 1928, HIA-US.

86. On October 13, 1927 the Piłsudskist paper *Epoka* proclaimed that "the country has obtained the loan for the reason that the world has confidence in our future as a state . . . , that it has confidence in our government, that it has confidence that the path chosen by the government for our internal reform is that which will reach the goal." Similar arguments appear in *Le Messager Polonais,* January 19, 1928 and Stanisław Kutrzeba, *Polska odrodzona 1914–1928* (Cracow, 1928), p. 310. The Polish legation in Washington miffed the State Department by hinting in press releases at the taboo subject of official American complicity in the negotiations (Arthur Young to Castle, October 26, 1927, SDNA 860c.51 P 751/8).

87. October 13, 1927. Note as well Stetson to Kellogg, November 8, 1927, SDNA 860c.00/

418. The *New York Times* of October 23, 1927 reported that "this American loan . . . is regarded [in Poland] as a turning point in the economic life of [the country] and . . . is being hailed in the press as 'Poland's golden key to prosperity.'"

88. See the comment signed Wł.[adysław] G.[rabski] in *Przemysł i Handel*, October 15, 1927, p. 1407. In addition, his *Idea Polski* (Warsaw, 1935), p. 35.

89. October 16, 1927. Also *Gazeta Warszawska*, October 18, 1927; in SDNA, Stetson to Kellogg, October 20, 1927, 860c.51 P 751/12, and October 24, 1927, 860c.51 P 751/13.

90. Chamberlain's minute to Max Muller's dispatch of October 12, 1927, PRO /12573; Zechlin to Auswärtiges Amt, October 19, 1927, GFMR K161 K021295-301.

91. Wysocki, "Dzieje," v. 1, reproduced in Landau and Tomaszewski, *Kapitały*, p. 99. Also record of meeting between Strong and Sir Arthur Salter, May 25, 1928, Harrison Papers; Łoś to MSZ, October 3, 1927, IHGS-AL A.12.53/9; Monnet, p. 123.

92. Zbigniew Landau described the terms of the loan as "humiliating" (Foreign Loans," p. 293), substantially the same verdict reached by an early Polish student of the transaction, H. Strońska, "Pożyczka stabilizacyjna 1927" (typescript, Szkoła Główna Planowania i Statystyki, Warsaw, 1934), p. 39. With its interest rate of 7 percent and issue price of 92, the Polish loan compared unfavorably with these contracts of the same year: Austria, 6.5 and 93.8; Germany, 6 and 96.4; Denmark, 4.5 and 98.2; Ireland, 5 and 97. Czechowicz said of the stabilization loan in 1928 that "we were obliged to make far-reaching sacrifices in order to dispel the atmosphere of lack of confidence and prejudice which had arisen, chiefly from our own fault" (Poland, Ministerstwo Skarbu, *Budget Speech*, p. 24).

93. Bernard Blumenstrauch, *Le nouveau régime monétaire en Pologne et son rôle dans l'économie nationale* (Nancy, 1932), p. 44; M. Frank, "Państwowe i samorządowe pożyczki amerykańskie w Polsce w latach 1924-1930" (typescript, Szkoła Główna Planowania i Statystyki, Warsaw, 1932), pp. 29-32; Hipolit Gliwic, *Międzynarodowa współzależność ekonomiczna a polska polityka gospodarcza: studjum ekonomiczne* (Warsaw, 1928), p. 272; *Czas*, October 17, 1927. Małecka observes in *Kredyty*, p. 136, that the sluggish sales of the loan suggest that the buying public considered the conditions of the contract "too good" for Warsaw. The Polish terms fell in the middle range of the major European stabilization loans: Austria 1923, 7 percent interest and 90 issue price; Hungary 1924, 7.5 and 87.6; Germany 1924, 7 and 92; Belgium 1925, 7 and 98.

94. "Piłsudski was not an economist, and he did not concern himself with economic matters. But I recall that he tended personally to the negotiations for the stabilization loan, and he was very satisfied when during the discussions with the Americans he managed to gain a certain reduction in the interest rate" (Wacław Jędrzejewicz, "Wypadki majowe w Polsce w 1926 r.," *Zeszyty Historyczne* 12 [1967], p. 228). See also Młynarski, *Wspomnienia*, p. 313.

95. John Foster Dulles, *Polish Stabilization Plan* (New York, 1927), p. 9.

96. The effect of the Polish stabilization controversy on the system of central bank cooperation is evaluated in Chandler, pp. 402-403; Meyer, pp. 5, 97-99, 138; Costigliola, "Stabilization," pp. 355, 372-373.

97. From the vantage point of 1932, Blumenstrauch wrote that "the foreign loan of 1927 is the capstone, the decisive achievement of monetary stabilization which [Poland] obtained through its own efforts; it was not the means or the foundation of stabilization. In this it differs advantageously from the other European 'stabilization' loans" (pp. 41-42). Krzyżanowski called the loan "our key to future prospects" (*Dwa programy*, pp. 39-41), and Leon Barański of the Finance Ministry echoed these sentiments in *Przemysł i Handel*, July 16, 1927, p. 981. See also Dulles, *Polish*, pp. 4-5; Gliwic, *Międzynarodowa*, pp. 270-271; Młynarski, *Wspomnienia*, pp. 291-292.

98. Leon Barański, "Pożyczka stabilizacyjna a program gospodarczo-finansowy," *Przemysł i Handel*, October 22, 1927, p. 1458. Dulles proclaimed that the stabilization plan "assures to Poland a new position in the world, which cannot but quickly and favorably reflect itself in all aspects of her international relations and internal economy" (*Polish*, p. 10). Also *Le Messager Polonais*, July 7, 1927, and Krzyżanowski, *Polityka*, p. 369.

CHAPTER VI

1. Landau, *Plan*, p. 245.

2. Wilbur J. Carr to Schurman, September 26, 1927, and Castle to Sullivan and Cromwell, October 11, 1927, FRUS 1927, v. 2, pp. 728-730.

3. Stetson to Kellogg, December 2, 1927, SDNA 860c.51/653. Also *New York Times*, October 28 and November 17, 1927.

4. Ciechanowski to Skrzyński, March 3, 1926, AAN-AL n. 84, and Gilbert to Norman, April 5, 1927, FRB C261.1.

5. Dewey to Strong, July 25, August 20 and August 25, 1927, FRB C261.1A. Dewey wanted out of the Treasury, having been thwarted in his ambition to advance to undersecretary (Charles S. Dewey, *As I Recall It* [Washington, 1957], pp. 144-145). Two years later Castle told Stimson that Dewey "was not much liked in the Treasury because he stuck his finger into everything and . . . there was no regret" at his resignation (August 14, 1929, SDNA 860c.51A/126). A cousin of Admiral George Dewey, the naval hero of Manila Bay, Dewey served as a Republican congressman from Chicago during the years 1941-1945. He died in 1980 at the age of 100.

6. In FRB, Strong to Dewey, August 24, 1927, C261.1, and Strong to Moreau, September 21, 1927, C261.1A; Młynarski, *Wspomnienia*, p. 314; Dewey, pp. 147-149; *New York Times*, September 30, 1927.

7. Ciechanowski to Dewey, November 5, 1927, and Strong to Harrison, November 11, 1927, FRB C261.1.

8. An anonymous memorandum of 1927 on the question of control procedures in the stabilization loan concluded that "an unfavorable report made by the American observer, may again bring about the embargo [on Polish credit abroad] at any time. The American observer's report constitutes such a powerful weapon, that even the formal right of veto could not possibly make this weapon more telling. The right of veto unnecessarily irritates the national pride and in practice it is tantamount to an adverse report" (FRB). That this indeed was the policy of the bankers is made plain in Dulles, *Poland*, pp. 9-10, and Dulles, *Polish*, pp. 7-8.

9. Castle to Hoover, October 28, 1927, HHCP. Also Castle to Stetson, November 11, 1927, Castle Papers.

10. In AAN-AW, Bankers Trust to Czechowicz, November 14, 1927, n. 494, and Ciechanowski to Harrison, December 2, 1927, n. 521.

11. Ciechanowski to Zaleski, January 3, 1928, PIA-AL; record of meeting of Council of Ministers, December 6, 1927, AAN-PPRM n. 40; in FRB C261.1, Ciechanowski to Harrison, December 2, 1927, and Harrison to Gilbert, December 6, 1927.

12. *Robotnik*, October 16, 1927; *Kurjer Poranny*, October 23, 1927; Młynarski, *Wspomnienia*, p. 315; Zygmunt Heryng, *Rola kapitału amerykańskiego w życiu państwowym i gospodarczym Polski* (Warsaw, 1928), p. 63.

13. "Installation de M. Dewey comme Membre du Conseil de la Banque de Pologne, Conseiller Financier du Gouvernement" [after December 15, 1927], FRB C261.1A; Dewey, pp. 163-165.

14. See the following items in the Charles Dewey Papers, Chicago Historical Society Library, Chicago, Illinois: Dewey to A. B. and L. S. Dewey, December 10, 1927 and March 7, 1928, Dewey to Owen Young, February 29, 1928, and Dewey to T. E. Donnelley, April 4, 1928. Note as well Dewey to Strong, December 5, 1927, FRB C261.1; Strong to Harrison, July 16, 1928, Harrison Papers; Dewey address to American-Polish Chamber of Commerce and Industry, New York, January 29, 1929, AAN-AW n. 519.

15. On January 29, 1929, Dewey told a gathering of American businessmen that "the [stabilization] plan contained certain items to give the so-called advisor a little authority. They might as well have left those items out. We work together like a bunch of brothers" (AAN-AW n. 519). The protocols of meetings of the council of the Bank Polski for the years 1927-1930 suggest that Dewey was an infrequent and passive participant in those delibera-

tions (Bank Polski w Warszawie, nos. 23, 35, AAN). Also Karpiński, pp. 58–59, and Stetson to Castle, November 15, 1928, Castle Papers.

16. Dewey's second report in Bank Polski, *Bulletin of the Bank of Poland, 1928*, n. 2, pp. 11, 14; "The Status of Agrarian Reform in Poland at the End of 1927," Charles Dewey Papers, LC; Dewey to Gilbert, October 5, 1928, Dewey Papers (Chicago); Paul F. Douglass, *The Economic Independence of Poland: A Study in Trade Adjustments to Political Objectives* (Cincinnati, 1934), pp. 48–49. On July 16, 1928, Strong wrote to Harrison that "Dewey's head is as full of schemes as one could wish" (Harrison Papers). Polish Socialists regularly attacked Dewey for his opposition to land reform (J. Webb Benton to Stimson, September 27, 1929, SDNA 860c.00 P.R./15).

17. On February 29, 1928, the counselor of the British legation in Warsaw, Reginald A. Leeper, reported to Chamberlain that "Mr. Dewey . . . assured me that he regarded it as one of his main tasks to build a bridge between London and Warsaw" (DBFP, ser. 1A, v. 4, p. 286). Leeper and Dewey conferred and corresponded frequently, and in a letter of June 10, 1930, the Briton mentioned "Anglo-American cooperation [in investment in Poland] which we have often discussed together" (Dewey Papers [Chicago]).

18. Strong to Harrison, July 16, 1928, Harrison Papers. See also Dirksen's note of April 17, 1928, ADAP, ser. B, v. 8, pp. 499–500, and Dewey to Gilbert, October 5, 1928, Dewey Papers (Chicago). Strong considered Dewey's interest in a political settlement between Poland and Germany "a rather dangerous subject for him to get into . . . visionary and impractical and very much outside of [his] duties." However, Józef Lipski states in his *Diplomat in Berlin, 1933–1939: Papers and Memoirs of Józef Lipski, Ambassador of Poland*, ed. Wacław Jędrzejewicz (New York, 1968), p. 70, that "in the years 1926–27, and during the following years . . . when attempts in general were made to attract foreign credits to Poland, I was often questioned in detail by American representatives in Warsaw about the development of Polish-German relations. I often discussed this subject with Mr. Charles Dewey."

19. Stetson to Castle, November 15, 1928, Castle Papers. See Dewey's comments in Poland, Ministerstwo Przemysłu i Handlu, *Przemysł i handel: rolnictwo, finanse, komunikacje 1918–1928* (Warsaw, 1928), pp. 36–39, and his second report in *Bulletin of the Bank of Poland, 1928*, n. 2, p. 23. Asked by a Polish associate in 1928 if his work would aid the country's credit in America, Dewey replied that "he thought his reports, impartial and prepared on location, would be properly appreciated in the States and in the end would win us better credit terms" (Wysocki, "Dzieje," v. 2, p. 39).

20. Strong to Harrison, July 16, 1928, Harrison Papers. In the same collection, Strong to Harrison, May 24, 1928. From the outset, Dewey stressed that he regarded himself as "a Polish official" and as the "servant" of his host country (Dewey, pp. 159–160, and Ciechanowski to Zaleski, October 19, 1927, HIA-US).

21. Ciechanowski to Zaleski, April 3, 1928, AAN-AW n. 519; *Buffalo Evening News*, January 29, 1929. For complimentary journalistic references to Polish stability, see *International Investor*, March 1928, pp. 13–14; *Time*, March 19, 1928, p. 16; *Literary Digest*, October 15, 1927, pp. 18–19 and Frank Simonds, "Poland Makes Good," *Review of Reviews*, May 1928, pp. 511–519. Late in 1928 the popular reporter John Gunther filed a series of laudatory articles on Poland for the *Chicago Daily News* and the *Buffalo Evening News*, and a *New York Times* editorial of March 12, 1928, commented favorably on the person and policies of Marshal Piłsudski.

22. Poland, Ministerstwo Skarbu, *Budget Speech*, pp. 23–29; *Sprawozdanie*, June 12, 1928, p. 43. Also the statement of Krzyżanowski to the Sejm, *Sprawozdanie*, May 29, 1928, pp. 8–12, and Stefan Starzyński in Instytut Gospodarstwa Społecznego, *Na froncie*, p. 20. Many of the parliamentary deputies complained that in accepting the American plan and adviser, the government had "sold out Poland to foreign capital" (Wysocki, "Dzieje," v. 2, pp. 55–56).

23. Stetson to Kellogg, May 24, 1928, FRUS 1931, v. 2, p. 925. Note as well *Epoka*, July 3, 1928, and Wańkowicz economic report, March 31, 1928, AAN-AW n. 154.

24. Leeper to Chamberlain, February 29, 1928, DBFP, ser. 1A, v. 4, p. 286. Likewise C. Budding to Zechlin, October 22, 1927, GFMR K161 K021280-81.

25. Moreau, p. 526. Reporting on his discussions in Warsaw, Pierre Quesnay wrote of Piłsudski: "The more one elaborates on the usefulness for Poland of foreign credit, of prosperity and material welfare, the more mistrustful he becomes and the more he fears that these secondary advantages may be acquired at the sacrifice of national spirit and at the cost of a diminished sense of national unity" ("La situation politique en Pologne," December 1927, FRB C261.1A).

26. Stetson to Castle, November 15, 1928, Castle Papers. Also Stetson to Kellogg, April 8, 1927, SDNA 860c.51/620, and March 20, 1929, SDNA 860c.51—Bankers Trust Company/2; Ciechanowski to Zaleski, January 12, 1928, PIA-AL; in Landau and Tomaszewski, *Kapitały*, Czechowicz memorandum for the Economic Committee of Ministers, December 5, 1927, pp. 96–97, and Kwiatkowski to Economic Committee of Ministers, November 9, 1927, p. 309.

27. Federal Reserve Bank of New York, *Annual Report: 1928*, pp. 15–16; Costigliola, "Stabilization," pp. 400–403; Derek H. Aldcroft, *From Versailles to Wall Street, 1919–1929* (Berkeley and Los Angeles, 1978), p. 263.

28. Strong to Owen Young, August 17, 1928, Strong Papers. "From the moment that the European powers stabilized their currencies . . . that co-operation [between the Federal Reserve Bank and the states of Europe] immediately began to slacken" (Ciechanowski, "Polityka zagraniczna," p. 108).

29. Strong to Harrison, March 2, 1928, FRB C261.1; Ciechanowski to Zaleski, August 30, 1928, PIA-AL; Woytkiewicz economic report, September 1, 1928, AAN-AW n. 156.

30. Economic report, AAN-AW n. 157. Note similar observations in AAN-AW, Woytkiewicz to Czechowicz, August 1, 1928, n. 156, and Wańkowicz economic report, June 13, 1928, n. 155.

31. Ciechanowski to Zaleski, January 12, 1928, PIA-AL; Ciechanowski to Tompkins, February 21, 1928, AAN-AW n. 495; Ciechanowski to Monnet, March 20, 1928, in Landau and Tomaszewski, *Kapitały*, p. 100.

32. Ciechanowski to Zaleski, April 26, 1928, PIA-AL. Also John Foster Dulles to Dewey, April 23, 1928, Dewey Papers (Chicago); Ciechanowski to Zaleski, May 24, 1928, PIA-AL; Wańkowicz economic report, June 13, 1928, AAN-AW n. 155; Wańkowicz to Czechowicz, June 13, 1928, AAN-AL n. 502; and in FRB C261.1, Case to Dewey, March 31, 1928, and Dewey to Strong, April 16, 1928.

33. Dewey to John Foster Dulles, September 12, 1928, Dewey Papers (Chicago). The issue of the central land bank also appears in Ciechanowski to Zaleski, May 24, 1928, PIA-AL; Woytkiewicz economic report, October 1928, AAN-AW n. 156; in SDNA, Benton to Kellogg, August 18, 1928, 860c. P.R./6 and Stetson to Kellogg, March 20, 1929, 860c.51—Bankers Trust Company/2; and in Dewey Papers (Chicago), Dewey to John Foster Dulles, April 19 and September 3, 1928.

34. Ciechanowski to Zaleski, January 12, 1928, PIA-AL. In AAN-AW, Hayward to A. Jechalski, September 29, 1927, n. 486; Wańkowicz to Ciechanowski, November 3, 1927, n. 493; Wańkowicz economic report, November 23, 1927, n. 154, and Ciechanowski to Hayward, March 29, 1928, n. 487.

35. Woytkiewicz economic report, September 1, 1928, AAN-AW n. 156. In the same dispatch he fumed that "it is funny how, according to each of our bankers, the step of consolidating our credit in America never is the step already achieved but always the one which needs to be achieved; and how he never takes into account the sacrifices undertaken for the previous step, but always insists on the necessity of shouldering the greatest hardships in order that—supposedly—the next step should be successful." Woytkiewicz bitterly complained of hearing nothing but "pompous promises, which come easily to each banker here and which he never sees as obligating him to anything" (economic report, January 1, 1929, AAN-AW n. 157). Also Woytkiewicz to Czechowicz, August 1, 1928, AAN-AW n. 156 and in PIA-AL, Ciechanowski's dispatches of March 21, April 26 and August 30, 1928.

36. Ciechanowski to Zaleski, January 12, 1928, PIA-AL; *New York Times*, March 7 and June 23, 1928; *Wall Street Journal*, February 8, 1928. On June 30, 1928, Czechowicz requested Zaleski to bring order to Polish loan negotiations in America, claiming that the want of governmental supervision "hurts the credit of Poland and gives the impression of a lack of co-ordination in our actions" (AAN-AL n. 642). The Poles always resisted the idea of tying themselves to one foreign banker and never fully accepted the argument that allegiance to a single firm paid dividends in the long run. Some of the tensions inherent in attempting to find a middle ground between "monopolization . . . by a given banker" and the plight of "the proverbial too-many-cooks" are shown in Sapieha, Instytut Gospodarstwa Społecznego, *Na froncie*, p. 152.

37. In FRB C261.1, Strong to Dewey, March 2, 1928, and Dewey to Harrison, July 20, 1928. Also *Bulletin of the Bank of Poland*, n. 3, p. 7; Dewey to Leon Fraser, March 27, 1928, Dewey Papers (Chicago); Stetson to Kellogg, June 19, 1928, SDNA 860c.51A/10.

38. Dewey to Gilbert, April 4, 1928, Dewey Papers (Chicago); in FRB C261.1, minutes of meeting in Bankers Trust's Paris office, July 16, 1928, and Harrison to Dewey, September 21, 1928; in FRB C261.1A, Strong to Dewey, September 12, 1928, and Dewey to Strong, September 14, 1928.

39. In AAN-AW, Woytkiewicz's economic reports of October 1928, n. 156, and January 1, 1929, n. 157; Woytkiewicz to Ciechanowski, October 25, 1928, n. 487, and Woytkiewicz to Dillon, Read, November 1, 1928, n. 487.

40. Stetson to Castle, November 15, 1928, Castle Papers. Also Stetson to Kellogg, October 11, 1928, SDNA 860c.00 P.R./7; *Sprawozdanie*, October 31, 1928, p. 11, November 6, 1928, p. 8, and November 13, 1928, p. 21.

41. Stetson to Castle, November 15, 1928, Castle Papers; E. Dana Durand typescript memoir, p. 238, E. Dana Durand Papers, Herbert Hoover Presidential Library, West Branch, Iowa. Taking note of the adviser's zest for entertaining, a *New York Times* summary of Dewey's three-year stint in Poland remarked that his return to America would be regretted by "the many friends [he and his family] made in Warsaw. . . . All Warsaw could be seen at the 'Deweys' " (November 20, 1930).

42. Stetson to Castle, November 15, 1928, Castle Papers. Castle felt little sympathy for the aggrieved minister, whom he considered incompetent; beside Stetson's plaint that "Mr. Dewey's name is on more people's lips than mine," he acidly minuted "I wonder why?" As a jurisdictional matter, however, the inability of the Warsaw legation to keep Dewey under control worried the State Department. On January 21, 1929, Castle wrote to Hoover that "Poland is a difficult post. . . . The fact that Dewey is the Financial Adviser makes the position of Minister even more difficult because Dewey likes to be considered as the principal representative of the United States" (HHPP). When a replacement for Stetson was sought a year later, a Department memorandum urged that the new head of mission in Warsaw be able to dispense financial advice to prevent "a continuation of the situation where the Ambassador is of less importance to Poland than Dewey now is" (J[oseph] P. C[otton] to Stimson, December 10, 1929, HHPP).

43. Dewey to Harrison, November 7, 1928, FRB C261.1. In the Dewey Papers (Chicago), Dewey to John Foster Dulles, September 26, 1928, and Dewey to Schacht, October 20, 1928. Dewey told Leeper that "his year in Poland had borne home on him with great clearness and force what the Germans were after. . . . He had no particular prejudices agianst the Germans in spite of the way they attacked him in their papers, and especially in the papers that they controlled in America . . . but he was not going to be duped by them" (Leeper to Sir Ronald Lindsay, December 6, 1928, DBFP, ser. 1A, v. 5, p. 532). Dewey's reference to German influence over the American press, a frequent if exaggerated complaint of the Poles, indicates that the adviser had imbibed deeply of Polish opinion.

44. Stetson to Kellogg, November 6, 1928, SDNA 860c.51A/13; Stetson to Castle, November 15, 1928, Castle Papers; *Le Messager Polonais*, October 13-14, 1928; *New York Times*, October 28, 1928. On one occasion, Dewey staged a public mock execution of certain "foreign products" (Dewey, pp. 175-176).

45. Wańkowicz economic report, January 29, 1929, AAN-AW n. 155; Hipolit Gliwic,

206 / Notes

"Nowy bankier świata," *Przemysł i Handel*, March 6, 1926, p. 306; Marie Casey-Wolko-winska, "The Crossroads of Europe," *Poland*, September 1929, pp. 587–592; Costigliola, *Awkward*, pp. 157–164. The Chase bank may well have entered the Polish stabilization group in hopes of eventual entry into Russia (Woytkiewicz to Czechowicz, August 1, 1928, AAN-AW n. 156). Both Harriman and Dillon, Read took an interest in Russian mining and transit opportunities (Stetson to Kelley, December 7, 1926, SDNA 860c.51/639, and Joseph Brandes, *Herbert Hoover and Economic Diplomacy: Department of Commerce Policy, 1921–1928* [Pittsburgh, 1962], p. 179).

46. Stetson to Castle, November 15, 1928, and March 20, 1929, Castle Papers; Stetson to Kellogg, November 28, 1928, SDNA 860c.51A/14; Dewey to A. B. and L. S. Dewey, November 23, 1928, Dewey Papers (Chicago); *New York Times*, November 11, November 14, and November 19, 1928; and in DBFP, ser. 1A, v. 5, Leeper to Chamberlain, November 29, 1928, p. 495 and Lt.-Col. K. J. Martin to Leeper, December 6, 1928, pp. 527–528. Dewey claimed Piłsudski's authorization to undertake the journey (Dewey, p. 165).

47. Leeper to Lindsay, December 6, 1928, DBFP, ser. 1A, v. 5, pp. 532–534. Also Dewey's memorandum of conversation with Maxim Litvinov [November 1928], Dewey Papers (Chicago); Łoś to Zaleski, January 21, 1929, AAN-AL n. 618; *New York Times*, November 18, 1928; Dewey, pp. 171–172.

48. *Boston Transcript*, February 23, 1929. In addition, Leeper to Lindsay, December 6, 1928, DBFP, ser. 1A, p. 532 and Wańkowicz economic report, February 28, 1929, AAN-AW n. 157. On his way to America Dewey had told a London-based diplomat that while the Polish economy was "healthy," the country's political situation was "not good and still a long ways from being stabilized" (Łoś to Zaleski, January 29, 1929, AAN-AL n. 618).

49. Woytkiewicz economic report, February 28, 1929, AAN-AW n. 157. Dewey admitted to Woytkiewicz that he did not relish the prospect of congregating with the bankers, confessing that he was not the "hard-boiled" type that commanded respect in financial circles.

50. In AAN-AW, Woytkiewicz to Finance Ministry, March 28, 1929, n. 157, and Woytkiewicz economic report, May 1929, n. 158.

51. Stetson to Kellogg, March 20, 1929, SDNA 860c.51—Bankers Trust Company/2; Stetson to Castle, March 20, 1929, Castle Papers.

52. Stetson to Castle, March 20, 1929, Castle Papers; Woytkiewicz economic report, May 15, 1929, AAN-AW n. 158. Also Stetson to Kellogg, March 20, 1929, SDNA 860c.51—Bankers Trust Company/2; in AAN-AW n. 157, Woytkiewicz's economic reports of February 28 and March 22, 1929. The credit slump in New York affected many countries. Of five governments, including Poland, that obtained major American loans in 1927, only Canada imported significant amounts of capital from the United States in 1929 (Lewis, p. 387).

53. Świtalski memorandum of conference with Mościcki, Matuszewski, and Roman Górecki, June 10, 1929, AAN-KŚ n. 70. For indications of Polish concern for avoiding dependence on Bankers Trust, see "Memorandum for the Minister on loan questions" [after 1927], AAN-AW n. 470, and Stetson to Kellogg, November 17, 1928, SDNA 651.60c31/37, in which the writer states that "a very good friend of mine who had recently seen Marshal Pilsudski told me that the Marshal had jokingly spoken of how cleverly his Government had circumvented the intentions of the bankers' plan. He added that Poland felt herself independent of America and in case of need could obtain whatever money was necessary from other sources." The Poles' dissatisfaction with Bankers Trust was encouraged by rival American bankers who criticized the consortium to serve their own purposes (Woytkiewicz economic reports of October 1, 1928, AAN-AW n. 156, and May 1929, AAN-AW n. 158).

54. Świtalski memorandum of meeting of Council of Ministers, May 8, 1929, AAN-KŚ n. 70. The Świtalski journals for this period record several instances of Piłsudski's expression of disenchantment with Dewey and the American loan (May 3, June 8, and September 23, 1929).

55. In AAN-KŚ n. 70, the entries for May 1, June 3, June 8, June 10, June 19, July 3, and July 4, 1929.

56. Wysocki, "Dzieje," v. 2, p. 72. English and American observers attributed Ciecha-nowski's downfall to the enmity of Piłsudski and the decreased importance of the envoy's

friendships on Wall Street (Sir Esmé Howard to Chamberlain, January 29, 1929, PRO A652/652/45; and in SDNA, Stetson to Kellogg of December 4, 1928, 701.60c11/157, December 5, 1928, 701.60c11/155, and December 31, 1928, 701.60c11/163). Drohojowski claims that Ciechanowski unwittingly provoked his own demise with a speech commemorating the tenth anniversary of the recovery of Polish independence that contained allusions offensive to Piłsudski, pp. 148–149.

57. Ciechanowski to Paderewski, December 31, 1929, Ignacy Jan Paderewski (archiwum), n. 1237, AAN; Wysocki, "Dzieje," v. 2, p. 59; Jackowski, pp. 345–346. American representatives had predicted as early as 1926 that Filipowicz would take the Washington post upon Ciechanowski's dismissal (Hawks to Kellogg, September 28, 1926, SDNA 701.60c11/132). Filipowicz found defenders as well as detractors. The British chargé in Washington complimented him tepidly as "cultivated and intelligent" (Campbell to Henderson, March 19, 1930, PRO A2394/943/45), but Chester McCall compared him to the leaders of the American Revolution in "Credit and New Business in Poland," *Polonian Review*, June 1930, pp. 4–5.

58. *Sprawozdanie*, March 22, 1929, p. 12, and March 25, 1929, p. 32. Also the *Sprawozdanie* for January 30, 1929, p. 39, and March 25, 1929, p. 39.

59. Dewey to A. B. and L. S. Dewey, August 9, 1929, Dewey Papers (Chicago). Also in the same collection, Dewey's letters to Klarner, March 27, 1929; to G. F. Swift, June 14, 1929, and to Leeper, April 24, 1929. In Landau and Tomaszewski, *Kapitały*, p. 103, Świtalski memorandum of conversation with Stetson, May 4, 1929.

60. Much of the correspondence between the MSZ and its delegates in the United States bemoaned the sad state of Polish trade with America. For a sampling in AAN-AW, W. Kozłowski to Zaleski, November 15, 1928, n. 176; Edmund Kaleński to MSZ, January 4, 1929, n. 155; economic report of Polish Consulate, New York, June 7, 1929, n. 185; Marchlewski to MSZ, November 25, 1929, n. 185, and March 6, 1930, n. 186. In the same vein, Wańkowicz's economic report of July 7, 1930, Konsulat RP w Buffalo, n. 27, AAN.

61. Contemporary estimates of the value of American investment in Poland varied widely and must be considered approximate. Compare the unpublished Brookings Institute report "Poland and American Capital," 1929, AAN-AW n. 1569, with Wellisz, p. 151, Zbigniew Landau, "Poland and America: The Economic Connection, 1918–1939," *Polish American Studies* 32 (1975), p. 45 and Ferdynand Zweig, *Poland Between the Wars: A Critical Study of Social and Economic Changes* (London, 1944), p. 122.

62. Stetson to Kellogg, November 19, 1928, SDNA 811.503160c/6. Also in SDNA, Stetson to Kellogg of March 28, 1927, 760c.00/12, and October 5, 1928, 811.503160c/5; Dewey's fourth report in *Bulletin of the Bank of Poland, 1928*, n. 4, p. 17; Woytkiewicz economic report, October 1, 1928, AAN-AW n. 156; E. O. Sowerwine to Eric Lord, November 22, 1928, Amerykańsko-Polska Izba Przemysłu i Handlu w Nowym Jorku, n. 36, AAN, and "Poland and American Capital," 1929, AAN-AW n. 1569.

63. Raban Graf Adelmann von Adelmannsfelden to Auswärtiges Amt, August 22, 1931, GFMR 8868 E619559. I am indebted to Prof. Hans W. Gatzke of Yale University for permitting me to examine the copy of this document in his possession. Also Elliott, p. 713.

64. In SDNA, Stetson to Kellogg of July 5, 1926, 860c.6355/5, November 8, 1927, 760c.6215/456, and July 22, 1929, 860c.00/470. The American manager of Giesche told Stetson that the German-Polish dispute in Silesia was pointless: "if left to business men, a practical modus vivendi would soon be found" (Stetson memorandum of conversation with G. S. Brooks, August 26, 1929, SDNA 860c.4016/273).

65. Stetson memoranda of conversations with Brooks and Grażyński, August 26, 1929, SDNA 860c.4016/273. Also Stetson to Kellogg, November 8, 1927, SDNA 760c.6215/456, and July 22, 1929, SDNA 860c.00/470. Late in 1928 Averell Harriman told a Polish diplomat that while he supported the goal of polonization of Upper Silesia, as a businessman he had little choice but to seek "qualified people" rather than focus on matters of "national background, language or political leanings" (Knoll to Zaleski, December 12, 1928, AAN-AB n. 1030).

66. Memorandum submitted to John N. Willys by Harriman and Co. [July 1930], Dewey

Papers (Chicago); Moraczewski's memorandum for the Economic Committee of Ministers, April 4, 1929, and record of a meeting of the Economic Committe of Ministers, May 31, 1929, reprinted in Czesław Madajczyk, "Spory wokół sprawy elektryfikacji Polski (1926-1930)," *Najnowsze Dzieje Polski: Materiały i Studia z Okresu 1914-1939* 5 (1962), pp. 172-174.

67. BPPP, n. 197; Stetson to Stimson, July 23, 1929, SDNA 860c.6463 Harriman and Co./3. Also Benton to Stimson, July 6, 1929, SDNA 860c.6463 Harriman and Co./2. M. Kozłowski, *Sprawa Harrimana* (Warsaw, 1929), is a useful compilation of contemporary press extracts. Ironically, even Brooks of Giesche opposed the electrification concession for fear that it would result in intensified nationalist pressure on his operations (Stetson to Stimson, August 13, 1929, SDNA 860c.6463 Harriman and Co./10).

68. The entries of April 26, 1929, and August 24, 1929, in AAN-KŚ n. 70; Woytkiewicz economic report, September 1, 1929, reprinted in Madajczyk, pp. 174-183; in SDNA, Stetson to Stimson, July 23, 1929, 860c.6463 Harriman and Co./3, and Stetson morandum, August 26, 1929, 860c.4016/273; Świtalski memorandum of conversation with Stetson, May 4, 1929, in Landau and Tomaszewski, *Kapitały*, p. 103.

69. Maj. Emer Yeager to Department of War, July 15, 1929, SDNA 860c.50 M.I.D./2; Frank A. Southard, *American Industry in Europe* (Boston, 1931), pp. 40-41. In 1928 Piłsudski reportedly opposed a suggestion from Bankers Trust for a loan to allow sale of the Polish state railway to a private corporation on the grounds that it would pose a military hazard in case of war (*New York Times*, March 24, 1928).

70. *Sprawozdanie* for December 5, 1929, pp. 60-61; December 6, 1929, pp. 30, 75-78, and February 10, 1930, pp. 33-34. Also Zbigniew Landau and Bronisława Skrzeszewska, ed., *Sprawa Gabriela Czechowicz przed Trybunałem Stanu: wybór dokumentów* (Warsaw, 1961), pp. 244-245.

71. Stetson to Castle, April 8, 1929, Castle Papers; Dewey to Leeper, June 15, 1929, Dewey Papers (Chicago).

72. *New York Times*, December 5, 1930. Dewey wrote to Leeper on November 14, 1929, of the general wish of Poles that "the Marshal would take matters firmly in his own hands and [temporarily] proceed to run the country without the Parliament" (Dewey Papers [Chicago]). Dewey's benevolent view of Piłsudski was not unique among Americans; note for instance the *New York Times* editorial of November 2, 1929, which said of the Marshal that Poland was being "chastened by a loving hand, and a hand that most Poles love."

73. Dewey to A. B. Dewey, June 19, 1929, Dewey Papers (Chicago). In the same collection see Dewey to Leeper, April 24, 1929, and in SDNA, Benton to Kellogg, February 25, 1929, 860c.51A/18; Harry Carlson to Stimson, March 5, 1929, 711.61/151; Benton to Stimson, July 1, 1929, 860c.51A/23, and July 6, 1929, 860c.51A/25.

74. In the Dewey Papers (Chicago), "Second Trip to Russia" [June-July 1929], and Dewey to A. B. and L. S. Dewey, July 13, 1929; Stanisław Patek to MSZ, July 9, 1929, reprinted in *Dokumenty i materiały do historii stosunków polsko-radzieckich*, v. 9, pp. 446-448.

75. These subjects are introduced in Dewey's seventh and eighth reports in *Bulletin of the Bank of Poland, 1929*, n. 7, pp. 9-12, and n. 8, pp. 10-14. The practical obstacles to a Baltic-to-Black Sea route running through Poland are catalogued in Douglass, pp. 13-18, which argues that the country consciously attempted to alter its more natural east-west trading patterns for political reasons stemming from its poor relations with Germany and Soviet Russia. Dewey's new contention contradicted his earlier opinions that Germany was Poland's natural commercial partner and that the deficiencies of the Romanian rail system rendered Polish communication with the Balkans awkward and unsatisfactory (Dewey to Harrison, November 7, 1928, FRB C261.1).

76. Charles S. Wilson to Stimson, June 6, 1929, SDNA 033.60c71/3; Dewey to A. B. and L. S. Dewey, June 11, 1929, Dewey Papers (Chicago); *New York Times*, June 4, 1929.

77. Castle to Stimson, August 14, 1929, SDNA 860c.51A/26. Also in SDNA, Stimson to Stetson, August 15, 1929, 860c.51A/40, and Benton to Stimson, August 31, 1929, 860c.516/224; and in HHPP, Dewey to Hoover, July 13, 1929, and Earl Mosburg to George Akerson, August 20, 1929.

78. Dewey to Leeper, November 14, 1929, Dewey Papers (Chicago).

79. *New York American*, January 30, 1930; Szczepański to Filipowicz, January 15, 1930, AAN-AW n. 520; "Dewey Invites American Capital to Study Poland," *Poland*, March 1930, pp. 133-136. When Harcourt Parrish of the Ivy Lee agency sent Wańkowicz a copy of the *New York Times* dispatch of February 1, 1930, carrying the news of the German protests, the commercial counselor jotted the comment, "I fear that D. is endangering his own reputation through his loyalty to Poland, but he is doing us a great service" (February 1, 1930, AAN-AW n. 223).

80. In AAN-AW n. 520, Wańkowicz to Podoski, February 21, 1930, and Podoski to Zaleski, February 25, 1930; Dewey to Lawrence Ritchie, November 27, 1929, HHPP.

81. In the Dewey Papers (Chicago), Dewey to Leeper, April 14, 1930, and Dewey to Owen Young, April 16, 1930; Ciechanowski to Paderewski, December 31, 1929, Ignacy Jan Paderewski (archiwum), n. 1237, AAN; John C. Wiley to Stimson, June 11, 1930, SDNA 860c.77/55; *Express Poranny*, March 1, 1930.

82. In AAN-KŚ n. 70, the entries for September 6, September 21, and September 25, 1929; *Journal of Commerce*, January 29, 1930; *New York Times*, October 21, 1929, January 23, and March 1, 1930; Philander Cable to Stimson, March 10, 1930, SDNA 860c.00 P.R./21; *Sprawozdanie*, December 5, 1929, pp. 50-51.

83. Record of meeting of Council of Ministers, May 26, 1930, and the memorandum of the minister of public works, Maksymilian Matakiewicz, presented to the same gathering, in Madajczyk, pp. 192-211; in SDNA, Willys to Stimson, June 5, 1930, 860c.6463 Harriman and Co./16, Wiley to Stimson, July 10, 1930, 860c.6463 Harriman and Co./24, and Willys to Stimson, November 8, 1930, 860c.6463/6. The internal MSZ bulletin *Polska a Zagranica* for June 30, 1930, instructed Polish diplomats to say that Warsaw balked at the American contract out of reluctance to grant a concession for so long a term as sixty years, AAN-MSZ n. 112.

84. *New York Times*, June 6, 1930; "Memorandum: Activities of the [State] Department with regard to Countries (Except Russia) under the Jurisdiction of the Division of Eastern European Affairs from March 4, 1929, to January 25, 1933," February 1, 1933, Stimson Papers. Poland eventually settled with Harriman by paying a fee of $100,000 (Jan Piłsudski to Zaleski, November 21, 1931, in Madajczyk, p. 220, and Lipski memorandum "Harriman Question" [September 14, 1932], AAN-MSZ n. 3235).

85. McCeney Werlich to Stimson, August 13, 1930, SDNA 860c.51/776; *New York Times*, October 30, 1930; Woytkiewicz to Jan Piłsudski, July 8, 1931, AAN-AW n. 264.

86. Wacław Babiński to Zaleski, July 7, 1930, Poselstwo RP w Belgradzie, n. 17, AAN. Also Dewey, pp. 191-198, and *New York Times*, June 29, 1930.

87. Dewey to A. B. and L. S. Dewey, May 13, 1930, Dewey Papers (Chicago). Also Dewey, pp. 177-180. Bravado aside, the American told journalists he had never been robbed in his notoriously crime-ridden home city (*New York Times*, May 7, 1930). The local constabulary apprehended the thieves and recovered the money with impressive speed; two years later the discovery was made that the chief of the Bucharest police had been an accomplice to the crime and then betrayed his confederates.

88. Dewey's twelfth report in *Bulletin of the Bank of Poland, 1930*, n. 12, pp. 12, 46-47. Also Dewey, p. 197.

89. Willys to Stimson, November 17, 1930, SDNA 860c.51/785.

90. *New York Times*, November 9, 1930. Also *New York Times*, December 5, 1930; T. Zbyszewski to MSZ, April 17, 1931, AAN-AW n. 520; outline of a speech delivered by Dewey in New York [December 1930], Dewey Papers (Chicago).

91. In his memoirs, Dewey claims to have carried to Warsaw in the spring of 1939 a Vatican-endorsed proposal for a compromise settlement of the German-Polish dispute, which ultimately led to renewed global warfare. According to his account, the archdiocese of Chicago obtained the blessing of the Holy See for his personal peace mission, Dewey, pp. 241-243.

92. Lipski memorandum of conversation with Willys [March 16, 1932], AAN-MSZ n. 3235. Willys began his summary of Dewey's work with the declaration that he had been "eminently successful" and then launched into a long catalogue of his deficiencies (Willys

to Stimson, November 26, 1930, SDNA 860c.51/788). Some months earlier Castle hedged a favorable verdict on Dewey with the complaint that "his purpose has always been to keep himself on the front pages of the papers. He has often been exceedingly tactless and our Legation feels that he has maintained his popularity through extravagant promises of American financial aid" (Castle to Stimson, August 14, 1929, SDNA 860c.51A/26).

93. Karpiński, pp. 58–59. A consistent note of faint praise runs through the memoirs of Polish officials who dealt extensively with the adviser. Wacław Konderski, *Z działalności banków polskich w latach 1928–1935: wspomnienia* (Warsaw, 1962), testifies that Dewey "behaved loyally and caused no trouble" (p. 25). With only partial accuracy, Młynarski contends that "Dewey spent three years [in Poland] and never offended anyone. He busied himself mainly with social life" (*Wspomnienia*, pp. 314–315). See as well Willys to Stimson, December 2, 1930, SDNA 860c.51A/37.

94. In DBFP, ser. 1A, v. 6, C. C. Farrar memorandum, January 15, 1929, p. 106, and Sir William Erskine to Chamberlain, March 6, 1929, p. 178; Karpiński, pp. 63–69; Młynarski, *Wspomnienia*, p. 315.

95. Lewis, p. 622; Aldcroft, pp. 264–265.

96. Strońska, pp. 58–63. Two of the principal architects of the stabilization plan subsequently registered the disappointment of unfulfilled hopes. In his "Kartki," p. 22, Adam Krzyżanowski listed the American loan in a table of "lost battles" of his life because it was "successful only at its beginning." Much the same view prevails in his more contemporary *Polityka*, pp. 637–638. With stubborn pride of paternity, Młynarski contends that the loan was a success undone only by the accident of the world economic crisis and that it did not warrant its later disrepute (*Wspomnienia*, p. 315).

CHAPTER VII

1. Ciechanowski to Zaleski, August 17, 1928, PIA-AL. In the same collection, Ciechanowski to Zaleski, May 24, 1928, and in AAN-MSZ n. 4614, text of note given Stetson, December 15, 1926, and Jackowski to Ciechanowski, December 20, 1926.

2. Kellogg to Robbins, June 5, 1928, SDNA 760c.6215/414.

3. For Stetson, note of conversation between Stetson and Lipski, October 28, 1926, AAN-MSZ n. 4614, and in SDNA, Stetson to Kellogg of August 13, 1926, 760c.62/46, and November 29, 1927, 760c.62/72; for Houghton and Schurman, Helmut Lippelt, " 'Politische Sanierung': Zur deutschen Politik gegenüber Polen 1925/26," *Vierteljahrshefte für Zeitgeschichte* 19 (1971), p. 365, and Margarete Gärtner, *Botschafterin des guten Willens: aussenpolitische Arbeit 1914–1950* (Bonn, 1955), p. 126.

4. Lipski record of conversation with Schurman, April 2, 1927, AAN-MSZ n. 4996, emphases Lipski's. See the summary of correspondence between Schurman and Kellogg in Robert Gottwald, *Die deutsch-amerikanischen Beziehungen in der Ära Stresemann* (Berlin, 1965), pp. 110, 164 note 34. Also Kellogg to Schurman, March 16, 1927, SDNA 760c.62/58.

5. In AAN-MSZ n. 4941, Szczepański to MSZ, October 31, 1927, and Ciechanowski to Zaleski, December 8, 1927.

6. Newson to Kellogg, January 31, 1927, SDNA 760c.62/55. Also Castle memorandum of conversation with Ciechanowski, January 13, 1927, SDNA 760c.62/51, and Wróblewski to Skrzyński, April 30, 1925, AAN-AL n. 83.

7. Wandycz, *Zaleski*, p. 51. Also Stetson to Kellogg, May 1, 1928, SDNA 860c.00 P.R./3; BPPP, n. 185; Ciechanowski to Zaleski, May 9, 1928, PIA-AL; Erskine to Chamberlain, May 26, 1928, DBFP, ser. 1A, v. 5, pp. 665–666.

8. Alfred Wysocki, *Tajemnice dyplomatycznego sejfu* (Warsaw, 1974), p. 66; Stetson to Kellogg, May 31, 1928, SDNA 711.60c12 Antiwar/12; Stetson to Kellogg, May 14, 1928, FRUS 1928, v. 1, pp. 63–64; Erskine to Chamberlain, May 22, 1928, DBFP, ser. 1A, v. 5, pp. 655–656; Zaleski to Ciechanowski, May 14, 1928, PIA-AL.

9. In FRUS 1928, v. 1, Houghton to Kellogg, May 7, 1928, p. 54, Stetson to Kellogg, May 14, 1928, pp. 63–64, Kellogg to Stetson, May 15, 1928, pp. 64–65, and Stetson to Kellogg, May 17, 1928, pp. 65–66; Wysocki, *Tajemnice*, p. 64; Wandycz, *Zaleski*, pp. 51–52.

10. Wysocki, *Tajemnice*, p. 65.

11. In SDNA 711.60c12 Antiwar, Stetson to Kellogg, May 30, 1928, /12, and Kellogg memorandum of conversation with Ciechanowski, June 7, 1928, /8; in PIA-AL, Zaleski to Ciechanowski, May 14, 1928, Olszowski to Zaleski, May 18, 1928, and Ciechanowski to Zaleski, June 6, 1928; Erskine to Chamberlain, May 22, 1928, DBFP, ser. 1A, v. 5, pp. 665-666; Stetson to Kellogg, June 11, 1928, FRUS 1928, v. 1, pp. 83-84; Wandycz, *Zaleski*, p. 53.

12. "Memorandum in the matter of the Kellogg proposal" [July 1928], AAN-LN n. 137. Also memorandum of conversation between Kellogg and Ciechanowski, June 23, 1928, SDNA 711.60c12 Antiwar/17; Wysocki to Skirmunt, July 6, 1928, PIA-AL; Wysocki to Stetson, July 8 [17?], 1928, FRUS 1928, v. 1, p. 119.

13. Wandycz, *Zaleski*, p. 53. In a cynical vein, Zaleski commented in his memoirs that he could not determine if Kellogg "really believed in the worth of his pact, or if he was perhaps one of those excellent actors who so enter into their role that they truly experience the given scene."

14. Stetson to Kellogg, September 1, 1928, SDNA 711.60c12 Antiwar/44; BPPP, n. 188; *New York Times*, August 26, 1928; Wysocki, *Tajemnice*, pp. 64-66.

15. Laroche, p. 64. Also Wandycz, *Zaleski*, pp. 53-54, and BPPP, n. 198.

16. Ciechanowski to Zaleski, August 17, 1928, PIA-AL. Note as well Wandycz, *Zaleski*, p. 88, and BPPP, n. 188.

17. In 1929 Hoover wrote to Stetson that "the Poles of the United States very generally supported me during the recent election" (George J. Lerski, ed., *Herbert Hoover and Poland: Documentary History of a Friendship* [Stanford, 1977], p. 35). In fact, the conventional wisdom is open to doubt: Smith outpolled Hoover among the Polonia of Chicago and Buffalo (Kantowicz, pp. 129-130, and Stefan Rosicki to Polish Legation, Washington, November 8, 1928, AAN-AW n. 977). Campaigning for the Republicans in Chicago, Charles Dewey found that Polish-Americans recalled that Hoover had aided Poland in the service of the Democrat Wilson (Dewey, p. 221). Polish publications in the United States divided more or less evenly in their preferences for the presidency (*New York Times*, October 28, 1928).

18. Benton to Kellogg, December 7, 1928, SDNA 860c.00 P.R./9; Ciechanowski to Zaleski, October 3, 1928, PIA-AL; Ciechanowski to Zaleski, February 14, 1929, AAN-AB n. 218; *Le Messager Polonais*, November 9, 1928; *New York Times*, November 8, 1928.

19. Castle to Akerson, September 6, 1929, HHPP. See as well Stetson to Stimson, HHPP; Castle memorandum of conversation with Stimson and Filipowicz, Stimson Papers; Rauscher to Auswärtiges Amt, December 27, 1929, GFMR L555 L156181. Prof. Hans W. Gatzke has kindly allowed me to examine the copy of the German document in his possession. A State Department memorandum of February 1, 1933, included in the Stimson Papers, described the elevation of the Warsaw legation as part of a policy to strengthen American representation in Eastern Europe during the Hoover administration. Even so, by 1933 Warsaw housed the only American embassy in the region.

20. In HHPP, Castle to Hoover, January 21, 1929 and Cotton to Stimson, December 10, 1929; Świtalski memorandum of conversation with Piłsudski and Mościcki, April 21, 1929, AAN-KŚ n. 70; Erskine to Henderson, October 23, 1929, DBFP, ser. 1A, v. 7, p. 66. The annual report of the British legation in Warsaw for 1926 referred to Stetson as a "busybody, whose conception of serving the interests of his country . . . is to intrigue against those of others." I am indebted to Prof. Piotr S. Wandycz, who has permitted me to examine his notes from this document. With malicious amusement, the Polish minister in Washington passed the word that Stetson had learned of his "resignation" from the newspapers (Filipowicz to Zaleski, December 16, 1929, HIA-US).

21. *Chicago Tribune*, May 8, 1930; Hoover to Simeon Fess, May 28, 1931, HHPP. See also Erskine to Sir John Simon, January 6, 1932, PRO N143/142/55; Wysocki, "Dzieje," v. 2, p. 162; Stimson Diary, November 25, 1931.

22. *Literary Digest*, June 19, 1926, pp. 11-12; Drohojowski, p. 90.

23. Olszewski, v. 4, pp. 142-143; Haiman, pp. 340, 382; Łepkowski to MSZ, July 14, 1930, AAN-MSZ n. 10881; Łepkowski to Anglo-American department, MSZ, November 12, 1930, AAN-AW n. 1053.

24. In SDNA, Stetson to Kellogg, December 4, 1928, 701.60c11/157; Stetson to Kellogg, December 31, 1928, 701.60c11/163; Stetson to Stimson, March 4, 1929, 701.60c11/170. In AAN-AW, Filipowicz to Polish Consulate, Chicago, April 26, 1929, n. 1053; Filipowicz to W. B. Błażewicz, June 5, 1931, n. 1054.

25. Olszewski, v. 4, p. 143; Haiman, pp. 407–408.

26. In AAN-AW, Zdzisław Chełmicki to Polish Legation, Washington, May 16, 1927, n. 957, and Eugeniusz Jordan-Rozwadowski to MSZ, May 15, 1929, n. 958; in AAN-MSZ, Sokołowski to MSZ, July 8, 1931, n. 10886; Drohojowski, p. 90.

27. FRUS 1931, v. 2, pp. 924–956. Note likewise the State Department memorandum of February 1, 1933, in the Stimson Papers. The United States concluded similar agreements with Estonia and Latvia during the Hoover presidency.

28. Schacht to Stresemann, February 16, 1929, ADAP, ser. B, v. 11, pp. 161–166. The text of the Schacht memorandum is reprinted in the same volume, pp. 408–412. Also see Link, pp. 459–460, and Jon Jacobson, *Locarno Diplomacy: Germany and the West, 1925–1929* (Princeton, 1972), p. 257.

29. Filipowicz to Zaleski, April 23, 1929, AAN-AL n. 840. Also *New York Times*, April 19, 1929. In ADAP, ser. B, v. 11, Friedrich von Prittwitz und Gaffron to Auswärtiges Amt, April 20, 1929, p. 424; Prittwitz to Auswärtiges Amt, April 24, 1929, pp. 443–445; Prittwitz to Walter de Haas, April 29, 1929, pp. 457–460.

30. Eric Cable to Chamberlain, March 4, 1929, DBFP, ser. 1A, v. 6, p. 175. Two years later an American diplomat in Warsaw reported that "the Polish thesis with regard to the United States [is that] . . . because of its vast financial commitment in the Reich, American concern is centered in the welfare of Germany" (Wiley to Stimson, December 2, 1931, FRUS 1931, v. 1, p. 604). A similar estimate appears in Willys to Stimson, November 4, 1931, SDNA 033.5111 Pierre Laval/239.

31. Świtalski records of conversations with Piłsudski and Mościcki, April 21, 1929 and with Piłsudski, Mościcki and Matuszewski, May 8, 1929, AAN-KŚ n. 70. An approximation of this statement appears in Filipowicz to Zaleski, November 19, 1929, PIA-AL. Representations of this nature may have been made at the American legation; a Stetson memorandum of August 26, 1929, declares that "the Poles intend to defend their territories against all comers, against the world, if necessary, and to go down fighting if they must—but fight they will" (SDNA 860c.4016/273).

32. Łepkowski to Zaleski, September 12, 1929, AAN-AL n. 31; Łepkowski to Zaleski, October 30, 1930, AAN-AB n. 218.

33. Marchlewski to Zaleski, November 24, 1930, Konsulat Generalny RP w Nowym Jorku, n. 2, AAN; Roberts Everett to Łepkowski, January 9, 1931, AAN-AW n. 1125. For German propaganda efforts in the United States, see Gärtner; Sobczak; and Zygmunt J. Gasiorowski, "German Revisionist Propaganda in 1925–1929: A Document," *Journal of Central European Affairs* 19 (1960), pp. 414–415.

34. Łepkowski to Zaleski, November 26, 1930, AAN-AB n. 218; Filipowicz to MSZ, December 14, 1931, AAN-AW n. 2619. For examples of opinion within the moderate left, Mauritz Hallgren, "The Polish Terror in Galicia," *Nation*, November 5, 1930, pp. 508–509; Negley Farson, " 'Pacification' of the Ukraine," *Nation*, January 7, 1931, pp. 14–15; Michael Farbman, "Poland: An Empire on the Make," *New Republic*, January 13, 1932, pp. 237–239; Boris Smolar, "What Polish Jews are Facing," *Nation*, January 27, 1932, pp. 99–100.

35. The quotation is taken from Frank Simonds in the *Buffalo Evening News*, February 14, 1931; the headlines, respectively, from the *New York Times*, November 16, 1930, and an article by Mauritz Hallgren in the *Nation*, January 21, 1931, pp. 82–84. Writing in *Commonweal*, February 4, 1931, p. 371, T. Hoinko complained that "the past few months have seen presented to American readers a rather large crop of articles concerning [the] . . . Polish Corridor. . . . The authors of these articles . . . almost without exception [argued] for the return of the Corridor to Germany." Publishing giant William Randolph Hearst castigated the Corridor and the Versailles treaty in front-page editorials (*Chicago Herald and Examiner*, August 29, 1930). Other examples of editorial advocacy of revision of

the Polish boundaries appear in the *Detroit Free Press*, August 21, 1930, and *New York Times*, September 2, 1930.

36. C. Warwick Perkins to Stimson, April 11, 1931, and Stimson's reply, April 15, 1931, FRUS 1931, v. 1, pp. 595–596; Franciszek Sokal to Zaleski, October 23, 1930, AAN-LN n. 22. In the spring of 1931 the head of the East European desk of the State Department delivered a lecture at Princeton in which he contended that the Corridor inevitably would revert to Germany (Robert F. Kelley, "The Polish Corridor and Danzig," John C. Wiley Papers, Franklin D. Roosevelt Presidential Library, Hyde Park, New York).

37. Stimson Diary, March 30, 1931; Josef Korbel, *Poland Between East and West: Soviet and German Diplomacy Toward Poland, 1919–1933* (Princeton, 1965), p. 264.

38. Elting E. Morison, *Turmoil and Tradition: A Study of the Life and Times of Henry L. Stimson* (Boston, 1960), pp. 404–405; Henry L. Stimson and McGeorge Bundy, *On Active Service in Peace and War* (New York, 1948), pp. 266–268. Also Stimson's memoranda of conversations with Lindsay, January 6, March 19 and May 28, 1931; Paul Claudel, January 19 and May 28, 1931; and Prittwitz, May 28, 1931, all in the Stimson Papers.

39. Stimson memorandum of conversation with Claudel, June 18, 1931, Stimson Papers; Stimson and Bundy, p. 270; Hoover to Stimson, November 9, 1943, Herbert Hoover Post-Presidential Papers, Herbert Hoover Presidential Library, West Branch, Iowa.

40. In IHGS-AL A.12.53/11, Jackowski to Polish Embassy, London, June 11, 1931, and Beck to Polish Embassy, London, June 26, 1931; in SDNA, Willys to Stimson, June 24, 1931, 462.00 R 296/4297, and Wiley to Stimson, July 21, 1931, 462.00 R 296/4860; Edward Raczyński note of conversation with Filipowicz, July 6, 1931, AAN-MSZ n. 1692; Sokołowski to Zaleski, July 27, 1931, AAN-AB n. 219. The Polish minister in Budapest opined that Britain and the United States were concerned above all with "the fate of Anglo-Saxon capital invested in Germany and an unconcealed distaste for France, which 'frustrates' the salvation of Germany from 'chaos' (that is to say: [the salvation] of Anglo-Saxon capitalists from the results of German bankruptcy)" (Łepkowski to Zaleski, July 24, 1931, AAN-MSZ n. 1619).

41. Castle memorandum of conversation with Sokołowski, July 28, 1931, SDNA 860c.51/821; Stimson memorandum of conversation with Henderson, July 15, 1931, Stimson Papers; Castle memorandum of conversation with Claudel, July 30, 1931, HHPP; Heinrich Brüning, *Memoiren 1918–1934* (Stuttgart, 1970), p. 329; Christian Höltje, *Die Weimarer Republik und das Ostlocarno Problem, 1919–1934: Revision oder Garantie der deutschen Ostgrenze von 1919* (Würzburg, 1958), pp. 214–215; Geoffrey Warner, *Pierre Laval and the Eclipse of France, 1931–1945* (New York, 1968), pp. 24–27.

42. Stimson to Hoover and Castle, July 24, 1931, FRUS 1931, v. 1, p. 549; Stimson memorandum of conversation with Claudel, June 4, 1931, Stimson Papers. For confirmation of the effect exerted by Laval's statement on Stimson's subsequent actions, see Polish Embassy, Washington, to Zaleski, June 1, 1932, AAN-AB n. 817.

43. Stimson memorandum of conversation with William E. Borah, October 6, 1931, Stimson Papers; Brüning, p. 413; Stimson Diary, July 18, 1931.

44. E. Alexander Powell, *Thunder Over Europe* (New York, 1931), p. 73. See also p. 138: "The discouraging feature of the whole sorry business is the indifference of the world to the impending peril [of the boundary question] and the weakness of the European statesmen. Courageous statesmanship, plus the pressure of world opinion, could force Poland and Germany to come to terms." Powell was an American travel journalist whose earlier book *Embattled Borders: Eastern Europe from the Balkans to the Baltic* had infuriated Polish officials as likely "paid German propaganda" (Ciechanowski to unknown recipient, September 12, 1928, AAN-AW n. 1215). The Polish embassy in Washington cited *Embattled Borders* as reason for its refusal to aid Powell's researches in Poland for *Thunder Over Europe* (Filipowicz to Ives Washburn, July 1, 1930, AAN-AW n. 1215).

45. Stimson Diary, August 6, 1931. Stimson brought the book to the attention of the East European section of the State Department, asking for an appraisal of Powell's comments on the Corridor (Kelley to Wiley, December 22, 1931, Wiley Papers).

46. Stimson memorandum of conversation with MacDonald, August 7, 1931, FRUS 1931, v. 1, pp. 514-517.

47. Stimson Diary, September 10, 1931; Stimson memorandum of conversation with Henry, September 10, 1931, FRUS 1931, v. 1, pp. 523-525. In his diary entry for the preceding day, Stimson made mention of "the provisions [of the treaties] which Germany is protesting against with respect to France, which is the Polish Corridor and other oppressive provisions." Note his identification of France, not Poland, as Germany's antagonist in the Corridor dispute.

48. Sokołowski to Zaleski, September 22, 1931, AAN-AB n. 219; Stimson memorandum of conversation with Sokołowski, September 17, 1931, Stimson Papers.

49. Stimson Diary, September 30, 1931. On September 25 Stimson had written to Mac-Donald that "I do not think permanent economic rehabilitation in Europe is possible until some of the basic political questions, which you and I discussed at Sciberscross, are settled—primarily the ones between France and Germany. The settlement of those problems virtually controls effective disarmament" (Stimson Papers).

50. Moffat Diary, September 30, 1931; Stimson Diary, October 1-2, 1931; Moffat memorandum of meeting with Stimson, Castle, Morrow, Boal, Allen T. Klots, and Herbert Feis, October 2, 1931, SDNA 033.5111 Pierre Laval/257. Melvyn P. Leffler has called these sessions "the most comprehensive reexamination since 1918-19 of American policy toward Europe" (*The Elusive Quest: America's Pursuit of European Stability and French Security, 1919-1933* [Chapel Hill, 1979], p. 262). As envisaged by Stimson, the consultative pact would consist of a presidential declaration of intent to confer with France in the event of a violation of the Kellogg pact and not to hinder actions to repel an aggressor (Stimson to Hoover, September 15, 1931, HHPP). Stimson's view of the consultative pact and its relation to disarmament is described in Moffat to Phillips, April 19, 1933, in Edgar B. Nixon, ed., *Franklin D. Roosevelt and Foreign Affairs*, 3 vols. (Cambridge, Mass., 1969), v. 1, pp. 56-57.

51. Stimson Diary, October 12, 1931.

52. A conference of financiers held October 19 in New York told two of Stimson's aides they considered "readjustment of [the] Polish Corridor" the most pressing political necessity of Europe (James Rogers and Feis to Stimson, [October 20, 1931], Stimson Papers; Feis memorandum, October 20, 1931, HHPP). Shepard Morgan of Chase National Bank presented Stimson with detailed proposals of matters to discuss with Laval, including the retrocession of the Corridor to Berlin (Stimson Diary, October 6, 1931, and Morgan memorandum "Outline Project for Realizing on the Debts," September 30, 1931, HHPP). The suggestion of the international highway appears in Warburg to Stimson, October 6, 1931, and Stimson's reply, October 8, 1931, SDNA 760c.6215/546. The idea of a "technical solution" to the Corridor also appealed to Hoover and Willys (Stimson Diary, October 12, 1931, and Willys to Stimson, October 22, 1931, FRUS 1931, pp. 601-602). Franklin Roosevelt later toyed with the possibility as well (see Chapter 8).

53. Stimson Diary, October 14, 1931. In the Wiley Papers, see Kelley's memoranda for Stimson: "Some Comments on Colonel Powell's Treatment of the Corridor Question," October 16, 1931; "Concessions Which Poland Might Be Willing to Make in Order to Bring About an 'Eastern Locarno,'" October 17, 1931, and "Considerations Underlying Polish Desire for a 'Political Moratorium,'" October 17, 1931.

54. Stimson Diary, October 9, 1931. Note the undated paper entitled "Agenda for Laval Conversations," including the entry "Territorial questions arising from Treaty of Versailles. Polish boundaries, chiefly the Danzig corridor; to a lesser degree, Upper Silesia" (Stimson Papers).

55. Castle memorandum of conversation with Claudel, October 12, 1931, SDNA 033.5111 Pierre Laval/95; Warner, pp. 43-44.

56. Moffat memorandum, October 5, 1931, SDNA 033.5111 Pierre Laval/98; Moffat Diary, October 17-18, 1931; Wilson memorandum, October 19, 1931, HHPP; J. Klahr Huddle to Stimson, July 1, 1931, SDNA 760c.6215/537-38. For a differing view, Wiley to Kelley, October 14, 1931, Wiley Papers.

57. Stimson Diary, October 2, 1931; Moffat Diary, October 5, 1931.

58. In the days preceding the Laval visit a close associate of Stimson "was asked, in private, 'whether the Secretary thought the United States Government could settle these various European questions.' The man replied that the Secretary did not think the government could do it but 'thought he could personally' " (Richard N. Current, *Secretary Stimson: A Study in Statecraft* [New Brunswick, N.J., 1954], p. 64).

59. Willys to Stimson, October 2, 1931, SDNA 701.60c11/222; Sokołowski to Zaleski, October 7, 1931, AAN-AL n. 934; Zaleski to Polish Embassy, London, October 14, 1931, IHGS-AL A.12.53/12; Willys to Stimson, October 20, 1931, FRUS 1931, v. 1, pp. 597-599.

60. Willys to Kelley, October 7, 1931, SDNA 760c.6215/554.

61. Stimson memorandum of conversation with Sokołowski, October 15, 1931, Stimson Papers; in FRUS 1931, v. 1, Willys to Stimson of October 15, 1931, p. 597, and October 20, 1931, pp. 598-599.

62. In IHGS-AL A.12.53/12, Zaleski to Polish Embassy, London, October 10, 1931, and Zaleski to Skirmunt, October 16, 1931; in AAN-MSZ n. 5075, memorandum given Dawes by Skirmunt, October 16, 1931, and Skirmunt to Zaleski, October 21, 1931; Dawes to Stimson, October 17, 1931, SDNA 033.5111 Pierre Laval/122.

63. Willys to Stimson, October 2, 1931, SDNA 701.60c11/222; Filipowicz to Polish Embassy, Washington, October 6, 1931, IHGS-AL A.12.53/12; Castle to Sokołowski, October 14, 1931, AAN-AW n. 1892.

64. Zaleski to Polish Embassy, London, October 29, 1931, IHGS-AL A.12.53/12; Castle memorandum of conversation with Filipowicz, October 22, 1931, FRUS 1931, v. 1, pp. 599-600; Castle to Frederic Sackett, October 23, 1931, Castle Papers. Zaleski later confirmed to Willys that the message was inspired directly by Piłsudski (Wiley to Kelley, November 12, 1931, Wiley Papers).

65. Castle to Stimson, October 22, 1931, SDNA 760c.6215/550. Also Kelley to Wiley, December 22, 1931, Wiley Papers. Stimson fumed that the statement was a "typical Polish production" and described Filipowicz's performance as "quite characteristic of the wretched little troublemaker that he is" (Stimson Diary, October 21, 1931).

66. Lindsay to Rufus Daniel Isaacs, Marquess of Reading, October 23, 1931, DBFP, ser. 2, v. 2, p. 303; Stimson Diary, October 17 and 20, 1931; Walter E. Edge, *A Jerseyman's Journal: Fifty Years of American Business and Politics* (Princeton, 1948), p. 206; Martin Egan memorandum of conversation with Hoover, October 21, 1931, T. W. Lamont Papers, Baker Library, Harvard University.

67. October 23, 1931. See as well *Times* (London), October 23, 1931, and *Washington Post*, October 27, 1931.

68. This account of the meeting is drawn from Stimson's memorandum of conversation with Hoover and Laval, October 23, 1931, Stimson Papers. Similar versions appear in Stimson Diary, October 23, 1931, and Lindsay to Reading, October 26, 1931, DBFP, ser. 2, v. 2, p. 307. Laval later claimed that the discussants devoted forty minutes in all to the Corridor (*New York Times*, January 20, 1933). Polish accounts of the meeting, based on sketchy and partially erroneous information, appear in Filipowicz to Zaleski, October 28, 1931, AAN-AB n. 219, and Skirmunt to Zaleski, November 13, 1931, AAN-MSZ n. 5076.

Hoover later disputed the accuracy of Stimson's account of the conference of October 23. In 1943 Stimson sent the former president a facsimile of his diary entries of the period accompanied by a request for permission to publish them. Hoover refused, and the copy of the journal—now on deposit in the Hoover Post-Presidential Papers—bears the notation in Hoover's hand "Stimson's Diary of Laval visit *very imperfect*" (emphases Hoover's). However, the likelihood is that Hoover was mistaken. Other contemporary evidence tends to support Stimson's version of the events. Hoover resented political attacks on him by the Roosevelt administration—which Stimson served as secretary of war—and in all probability his memory was clouded by the passage of time and a visceral suspicion that the extracts, if published, "could be used by the malicious to make me out a friend and supporter of Laval," then in bad odor as a collaborationist with the German occupiers of France (Hoover to Stimson, November 9, 1943, Hoover Post-Presidential Papers).

69. *New York Times*, October 24, 1931.

70. Stimson Diary, October 24, 1931; Claudius O. Johnson, *Borah of Idaho* (New York, 1936), pp. 446–447. Also Moffat Diary, October 23, 1931. For a sampling of editorial comment, *New York Times*, October 25, 1931, *Washington Post*, October 24, 1931, *Times* (London), October 26, 1931, *Le Temps*, October 26, 1931. Not surprisingly, the Borah proclamations caused a particular stir in the Polish press (Willys to Stimson, October 27, 1931, SDNA 760c.6215/560-61 and BPPP, n. 218).

71. No evidence supports the conclusion that Borah's interview was inspired. Both Stimson and the White House greeted the development with surprise (Stimson Diary, October 24, 1931, and T[heodore] G. J[oslin] memorandum for Hoover, October 23, 1931, HHPP). Furthermore, Borah had not been privy to Stimson's preparations for the Laval visit, and the senator's comments conflicted at many points with official policy regarding war debts and reparations. For the Hoover-Borah meeting, Johnson, pp. 445–446. An updated note in Hoover's hand begins cryptically: "Conversation Borah—Oct 22d; Laval; French domination—Saving Germany—Contribution to Civilization" (HHPP).

72. State Department record of Stimson's press conference of October 24, 1931, SDNA 033.5111 Pierre Laval/189. Also Stimson Diary, October 24, 1931; Johnson, pp. 448–449; White House press release, October 25, 1931, FRUS 1931, v. 1, p. 603.

73. Stimson Diary, October 25, 1931.

74. *Baltimore Sun*, October 27, 1931. Also *New York Times* and *Washington Post* of the same day. The *New York Herald-Tribune* called the Borah-Filipowicz encounter "one of the most sensational controversies [the Washington diplomatic corps] has experienced in many years" (October 27, 1931). The parties to the dispute traded barbs in the newspapers for several days. Filipowicz released a statement to the press explaining that his purpose at the gala had been to "congratulate the Senator on his great courage in admitting an inadequate knowledge of conditions prevailing in Central Europe in the same statement in which he advocated the revision of certain Central European frontiers" (October 26, 1931, AAN-AW n. 241). Borah responded that "the Polish Ambassador's memory seems to be somewhat at fault" (*Washington Herald*, October 27, 1931).

75. Castle memorandum of conversation with Grandi, November 16, 1931, FRUS 1931, v. 1, pp. 646–647; Sir Ronald Graham to Simon, December 9, 1931, DBFP, ser. 2, v. 2, p. 364.

76. Note for example the text of a skit based on the interview performed at the annual dinner of the Gridiron Club, included in Filipowicz to Zaleski, January 19, 1932, AAN-AB n. 817, and the comic verse "Borah and Laval Just Fail to Pal" by Arthur "Bugs" Baer, *New York American*, October 27, 1931.

77. In GFMR, Prittwitz to Auswärtiges Amt of October 25, 1931, K1220 K313794, and October 31, 1931, K1220 K313910-11; Höltje, pp. 215–216.

78. Zaleski to Polish Embassy, London, October 29, 1931, IHGS-AL A.12.53/12. The British chargé in Warsaw confirmed that the MSZ was "not seriously perturbed at Senator Borah's remarks" (Philip Broadmead to Reading, October 28, 1931, PRO C8094/172/62). Also see Francis White memorandum of conversation with Filipowicz, November 19, 1931, Stimson Papers; memorandum "Poland's Access to the Sea," given Willys by the MSZ [November 5, 1931], AAN-AW n. 2631; BPPP, n. 218.

79. *New York Herald-Tribune*, October 27, 1931. Lippmann's position may be considered authoritative. Stimson had taken Lippmann into his confidence so that the celebrated and influential columnist might "write some articles that would be of help on the Laval situation" (Stimson Diary, September 24 and October 21, 1931). On cue, Lippmann produced a piece centered on the Stimsonian theme that "American opinion is substantially convinced that the supreme difficulty [of European politics] lies in the Polish Corridor as now established" (*New York Herald-Tribune*, October 24, 1931). Lippmann later assured readers that Borah had said "publicly, in relation to the Corridor, what the responsible statesmen were saying privately" to Laval in Lippmann and William O. Scroggs, *The United States in World Affairs, 1931* (New York, 1932), pp. 223–224. The authors had submitted drafts of the chapters covering European topics to Stimson for his verification

prior to publication (Lippmann to Stimson, November 27, 1931, Lippmann Papers). For the record, at least, Stimson later told the Polish ambassador that the Hoover administration regarded the Borah interview as no more than pure political "exhibitionism" (Filipowicz memorandum of conversation with Stimson, December 17, 1931, HIA-US).

80. Stimson to MacDonald, January 27, 1932, Stimson Papers. During his stint as secretary of war, Stimson told President Roosevelt: ". . . from my experience in the State Department when the Polish Corridor was one of the most difficult problems we had, I had come to the conclusion that the problem of a port for Poland on the Baltic would never be settled except by force and strong armed methods" (Stimson Diary, June 8, 1944).

81. In the Wiley Papers, Wiley to Kelley, November 12, 1931; Boal to Wiley, December 21, 1931; Wiley to Kelley, February 19, 1932; Wiley to Kelley, March 9, 1932; Wiley to Kelley, May 19, 1932; Kelley to Wiley, June 23, 1932.

82. Castle to Sackett, October 23, 1931, Castle Papers. The postmortem within the State Department on the subject of the Polish warning of October 22 involved much speculation as to the authenticity of Warsaw's willingness to inflict a preventive war on Germany (Wiley to Stimson, December 2, 1931, FRUS 1931, v. 1, pp. 603–604; Wiley to Kelley, December 14, 1931, Wiley Papers; Joseph Flack to Stimson, April 6, 1932, SDNA 760c.62/ 171; Höltje, p. 197).

83. Wiley to Boal, January 18, 1932, Wiley Papers.

84. Lipski memorandum of conversation with Willys [March 16, 1932], AAN-MSZ n. 3235; Stimson memorandum of conversation with Filipowicz, December 17, 1931, Stimson Papers; memorandum of conversation among Willys, Filipowicz, and Sokołowski, November 24, 1931, HIA-US.

85. Filipowicz to Zaleski, January 19, 1932, AAN-AB n. 817.

CHAPTER VIII

1. Flack to Stimson, September 26, 1931, SDNA 860c.51/831. See similar statements in Stimson's memoranda of conversations with Filipowicz, May 21, 1931, Stimson Papers, and January 14, 1932, SDNA 860c.51/839.

2. Rudolf Nötel, "International Capital Movements and Finance in Eastern Europe 1919-1949," *Vierteljahrschrift für Sozial- und Wirtschaftsgeschichte* 61 (1974), p. 66; B. R. Mitchell, *European Historical Statistics, 1750-1975* (New York, 1981), pp. 176, 179, 377; Zbigniew Landau and Jerzy Tomaszewski, *Zarys historii gospodarczej Polski 1918-1939* (Warsaw, 1971), pp. 178-241.

3. The *New York Times* of January 25, 1931, reported that "the influx of low rate foreign credits [into Poland] would instantly materially relieve the situation, aiding both the revival of agriculture and industry." Also United States, Department of Commerce, *Commerce Yearbook, 1932*, v. 2, p. 200.

4. Iván T. Berend and György Ránki, *Economic Development in East-Central Europe in the 19th and 20th Centuries* (New York and London, 1974), p. 256; Aldcroft, pp. 264-265; Bandera, pp. 45-46.

5. Mitchell, p. 570; Royal Institute of International Affairs, *The Problem of International Investment* (London, 1937), p. 246; Teresa Małecka, "Udział kapitału amerykańskiego w kapitałach akcyjnych przemysłu polskiego w latach 1918-1939," *Materiały do sominariów z najnowszej historii gospodarczej Polski*, ed. Janusz Kaliński and Zbigniew Landau (Warsaw, 1974), p. 48. On May 7, 1935, the American ambassador in Warsaw reported that "the American investment in Polish industry has proved an unsuccessful venture" (John Cudahy to Cordell Hull, SDNA 860c.50/124).

6. "But of course the ultimate fate of the foreign capital now placed in Poland as well as the advisability of any future investment there depends after all on the political stability of that part of the world . . . the country could hardly be recommended as a safe field for foreign investment" (Charles Yost, "Foreign Investment in Poland," December 1, 1932,

SDNA 860c.51/891). Concurring judgments appear in Frank, pp. 11–12, and Woytkiewicz to Jan Piłsudski, July 8, 1931, AAN-AW n. 264.

7. Woytkiewicz to Jan Piłsudski, July 8, 1931, AAN-AW n. 264. Harrison's contention that Poland suffered less than other debtors owing to the small size of her foreign obligation is supported in Smith, p. 145.

8. Krzyżanowski, *Dzieje*, p. 118; Bandera, p. 29; Berend and Ránki, p. 261. In his *Poland and Her Economic Development* (London, 1935), Roman Górecki boasted that Poland remained among the "select and small company of states which remained faithful to the gold standard" (p. 48).

9. *New York Times*, November 8, 1931; Wandycz, *Zaleski*, p. 100.

10. Memorandum of U.S. Embassy, Warsaw, May 14, 1932, AAN-MSZ n. 3235. In FRUS 1932, v. 1, Castle to Willys, April 23, 1932, p. 630, and Flack to Stimson, April 26, 1932, pp. 630–631.

11. In SDNA, Willys to Stimson, May 23, 1932, 860c.51/872, and Sheldon Crosby to Stimson, July 20, 1932, 860c.51/878; Flack to Stimson, April 26, 1932, FRUS 1932, v. 1, pp. 630–631; *Ilustrowany Kurjer Codzienny*, July 13, 1932.

12. In FRUS 1932, v. 1, Sokołowski to Stimson, September 14, 1932, p. 799, and Harvey Bundy to Sokołowski, September 26, 1932, pp. 799–800.

13. Wandycz, *Zaleski*, pp. 106–107.

14. FRUS 1932, v. 1, pp. 861–864. Also Filipowicz memorandum of conversation with Stimson, June 9, 1932, HIA-US.

15. Stimson Diary, November 9, 1932. Note as well Crosby to Stimson, September 12, 1932, SDNA 860c.20111/2. With wisdom of hindsight, MacArthur asserted in his *Reminiscences* (New York, 1964) that Piłsudski seemed "at his wits' end trying to figure a way to avoid certain disaster, caught up geographically as he was between Germany and Russia" (p. 99). Upon MacArthur's death, a retired Polish colonel recalled that the visiting general had addressed a group of junior officers and told them, "I believe your children are born with arms in their hands. I trust you will find enough weapons to arm all your babes" (*Nowy Świat*, April 7, 1964).

16. Lipski memorandum of conversation with Willys [March 16, 1932], AAN-MSZ n. 3235; Erskine to Simon, January 6, 1932, PRO N143/142/55. Hoover directed Stimson and Castle to expedite the Belin appointment, explaining that "it means a good deal to [me] politically" and stressing the nominee's ties to the du Ponts (Stimson Diary, October 25, 1932).

17. Belin's tenure was brief. Shortly after assuming the presidency in March 1933, Roosevelt recalled him and offered the post to the mayor of Boston, James Michael Curley. The Democratic boss of Massachusetts had hoped for Rome as a reward for his contributions to the Roosevelt victory, and upon receiving Poland instead he hastily excused himself. In his autobiography *I'd Do It Again: A Record of All My Uproarious Years* (Englewood Cliffs, N.J., 1957), Curley admitted that he "did not relish the prospect of burying myself in a remote land for four years" and suggested to Roosevelt that the job was more suitable for "a Republican enemy" (pp. 251–252). By one account, Curley told Roosevelt "if Poland is such a goddam interesting place, why don't you resign the presidency and take it yourself" (Alfred Steinberg, *The Bosses* [New York, 1972], p. 172). The nomination of the roguish mayor of Boston gave rise to quips that Roosevelt "must be anti-Polish" and that Ambassador Curley would no doubt "pave the Polish corridor" (Reinhard H. Luthin, *American Demagogues: Twentieth Century* [Boston, 1954], p. 33 and Curley, p. 252). The Warsaw appointment eventually went to John Cudahy, scion of a Milwaukee meat packing family.

18. Podoski address to Polish Society of Foreign Service Officers, November 4, 1932, AAN-AW n. 50; J. Mościcki to Beck, February 20, 1933, HIA-US; Tytus Filipowicz, *Ameryka i Europa* (n.p., [1932]), p. 16; Richard A. Wojtak, "Roosevelt's Early Foreign Policy Reflected in Polish Diplomatic Dispatches from Washington (1932–1933)," *Polish Review* 21 (1976), p. 217.

19. In AAN-AW n. 69, Zbyszewski to Polish Embassy, Washington, October 22 and October 31, 1932, and Sokołowski to Zbyszewski, October 26, 1932.

20. Stimson memorandum of conversation with Filipowicz, November 10, 1932, Stimson Papers. Also *New York Times*, November 16, 1932.

21. Polish Embassy, Washington, to State Department, November 22, 1932, FRUS 1932, v. 1, p. 800; Stimson memorandum of conversation with Filipowicz, November 22, 1932, Stimson Papers. In HIA-US, the December 20, 1932, report of A. Sapieha, financial adviser to the Polish embassy, is a useful summary of the events culminating in the Polish default of December 15.

22. Castle to Filipowicz, November 26, 1932, FRUS 1932, v. 1, pp. 800–801; Castle memorandum of conversation with Sokołowski, November 26, 1932, SDNA 800.51 W 89 Poland/86.

23. Polish Embassy, Washington, to State Department, December 8, 1932, FRUS 1932, v. 1, pp. 801–806.

24. Stimson memorandum of conversation with Filipowicz, December 9, 1932, Stimson Papers.

25. BPPP, n. 228; Crosby to Stimson, November 30, 1932, SDNA 800.51 W 89 Poland/91.

26. Huddle to Crosby, March 31, 1933, SDNA 860c.51/909; *Gazeta Polska*, December 5, 1932; *New York Times*, November 26, December 6, and December 10, 1932.

27. Stimson Diary, December 14, 1932.

28. Stimson memorandum of conversation with Filipowicz, December 15, 1932, Stimson Papers; Stimson to Filipowicz, December 15, 1932, FRUS 1932, v. 1, pp. 806–807.

29. *Pittsburgh Sun-Telegraph*, December 22, 1932.

30. BPPP, n. 228; *Sprawozdanie*, December 16, 1932, p. 40; *New York Times*, December 16, 1932.

31. In SDNA, Belin's reports to Stimson, December 14, 1932, 860c.5151/63, and December 28, 1932, 800.51 W 89 Poland/101.

32. *Sprawozdanie*, December 16, 1932, p. 38.

33. Felicjan Sławoj-Składkowski, *Strzępy meldunków* (Warsaw, 1938), p. 386.

34. *New York Times*, December 21, 1932.

35. Stimson Diary, December 22, 1932; Stimson memorandum of conversation with Filipowicz, December 22, 1932, Stimson Papers. Also Filipowicz to Beck, December 22, 1932, HIA-US.

36. American diplomats claimed that Filipowicz had lost the confidence of Piłsudski and that he was removed to provide an undemanding sinecure for Patek, whose labors in Moscow had taken a toll of his health (Belin to Stimson, January 9, 1933, SDNA 701.60c11/251, and Charles E. Sherrill to Stimson, March 2, 1933, SDNA 701.60c11/257). On the other hand, the departing ambassador received commendations from U.S. sources. The *New York Times* honored him with a valedictory editorial on January 6, 1933, and the Polish consul in Pittsburgh related the opinion of his American journalistic acquaintances that official circles in Washington—including even Stimson, who had disparaged the envoy in no uncertain terms in 1931—regarded Filipowicz as a "very skillful diplomat and a man of great tact" (Jan Lech Byszewski to Polish Embassy, Washington, June 17, 1932, AAN-AW n. 1211). Considering the destination of the report, however, one hardly can imagine that Byszewski might have written anything else.

37. In SDNA, Castle memorandum of conversation with Patek, December 29, 1932, 701.60c11/243; Belin to Stimson, January 7, 1933, 701.60c11/244; Belin to Stimson, January 9, 1933, 701.60c11/251; Castle to U.S. Embassy, Warsaw, January 24, 1933, 701.60c11/250, and Kelley to Hull, March 17, 1933, 701.60c11/256. In the Wilson Papers, Belin to Wilson, January 30, 1933.

38. Stimson memorandum of conversation with Sokołowski, March 2, 1933, Stimson Papers.

39. In SDNA, Belin to Stimson, January 11, 1933, 800.51 W 89 Poland/103; Huddle to Crosby, March 31, 1933, 860c.51/909.

40. For examples of the genre, see Roman Dyboski, *Stany Zjednoczone Ameryki Północnej: wrażenia i refleksje* (Lwów and Warsaw, 1930); Roman Dyboski, *Amerykanizm* (Warsaw, 1932); Wacław Gąsiorowski, *Nowa kolchida* (Warsaw, 1932); Wacław Sieroszewski,

Wrażenia z Ameryki (Warsaw, 1930) and Aleksander Szczepański, "Amerykanizm," *Przegląd Współczesny*, March 1933, pp. 396-432. A common locution, the reference to America as the "new Rome" appears, among other places, in Sieroszewski, p. 328.

41. Roman Dmowski, *Przewrót* (Częstochowa, 1938), pp. 89, 95-96, 377-388. Likewise see the declarations of Wojciech Korfanty and Stanisław Kozicki in the records of proceedings of the Foreign Affairs Commission of the Sejm [1932], Biuro Sejmu RP, n. 66, AAN.

42. Świtalski memorandum of conversation with Piłsudski, early March 1933, AAN-KŚ n. 71.

43. According to the account of the *New York Sun* of March 17, 1933, Patek's first American news conference consisted of the following exchange:

Patek: "And now I presume you wish to know about me? I was the first Minister ever sent from my country to Japan. After that I served six years at Moscow."

Question: "And is the difficulty over the Polish corridor being settled?"

P: "While in Moscow, I signed the conciliation papers and the non-aggression pact. I also—"

Q: "But isn't it true, Mr. Ambassador, that the Polish corridor is considered the focal point of Central Europe right now?"

P: "I was appointed Ambassador to the United States during the term of President Hoover—"

Q: "And now about the Polish corridor?"

P: "So I am going right to Washington to greet the new President. . . ."

Q: "But, please, Mr. Ambassador, give us a few words about the controversy over the Polish corridor."

P: "And now, I wish to thank you all very much. The interview is at an end."

44. Kelley to Hull, March 17, 1933, SDNA 701.60c11/256.

45. The correspondence relating to the defaults of June and December 1933 appears in FRUS 1933, v. 1, pp. 905-909.

46. Phillips memorandum of conversation between Roosevelt and Herriot, April 26, 1933, FRUS 1933, v. 1, p. 111, and Hull memorandum of conversation with Patek, April 10, 1933, Cordell Hull Papers, LC. See also Hans Luther to Konstantin von Neurath, May 23, 1933, Germany, Auswärtiges Amt, *Documents on German Foreign Policy 1918-1945*, ser. I, v. 1, pp. 479-480; and in France, Ministère des Affaires Étrangères, *Documents diplomatiques français 1932-1939*, ser. I, v. 3, André de Laboulaye to Joseph Paul-Boncour, April 19, 1933, p. 246, and Herriot to Paul-Boncour, April 26, 1933, p. 327.

47. Cudahy to House, February 7, 1934, House Papers. In an exchange included in the John Cudahy Papers, Milwaukee County Historical Society, Milwaukee, Wisc., Ambassador to Berlin William E. Dodd wrote to Cudahy on March 10, 1934, that "the one trouble I was warned against when I left Washington was the Corridor. Now, we have no Corridor difficulty." In his reply of March 13, Cudahy concurred: "I am . . . not very optimistic about the European situation—but I think we here in Poland shall be removed from the scene of excitement."

48. *New York Times*, November 14, 1934.

49. Lewis, pp. 401-402; "Memorandum: Financial Questions" [1937?], HIA-US.

50. *New York Times*, May 20 and May 23, 1975; *Chicago Sun-Times*, June 1, 1975; *Wall Street Journal*, July 29, 1980; Foreign Bondholders Protective Council, *Report for the Period January 1, 1971 Through December 31, 1975*. I am indebted to Mr. Charles S. K. Scudder, a lawyer for the Council, for information supplied during an interview in New York City, October 24, 1980. The Polish action was hardly unique; to a large extent Warsaw was following the example of numerous other East European and Latin American states which during the 1940s and 1950s resettled their defaulted interwar loans.

51. Woytkiewicz to MSZ, ca. May–June 1929, in Madajczyk, p. 176.

52. Woytkiewicz economic report, May 1929, AAN-AW n. 158, emphases Woytkiewicz's.

53. Dwight W. Morrow, "Who Buys Foreign Bonds?" *Foreign Affairs* 5 (1927), pp. 225-226.

54. Nötel, p. 66.

55. In 1922, Alanson Houghton advanced a plan for European peace embracing agreement among the quartet of London, Paris, Berlin, and Rome, explaining that "I have limited my suggestion to four nations only. They are the important nations. The others can be dealt with when we see fit" (Houghton to Hughes, October 23, 1922, FRUS 1922, v. 2, p. 174). Several years later Frank Simonds told a British diplomat that "there was the same tendency in England as in America to treat with scant respect or interest anything that lay east of Germany" (Leeper to Chamberlain, February 29, 1928, DBFP, ser. 1A, v. 4, p. 285).

56. In the *Buffalo Evening News* of November 7, 1931, Frank Simonds wrote of the "clear misapprehension . . . , one shared widely in this country, namely that in some way France could prevail upon Poland to return the corridor to Germany peacefully." In his article "In Europe's New Tenseness the 'Corridor' Looms Large," *New York Times*, March 19, 1933, Shepard Arthur Stone stated that the qeustions of Danzig and Pomerania "are really German-French controversies." At the time of Locarno, Houghton reported to Kellogg that "[the German] eastern frontier is primarily a question between Germany and France [that] must be worked out between them" (Coolidge Papers).

57. Marchlewski to Beck, January 9, 1933, AAN-AW n. 892.

58. Sokołowski to Zaleski, October 7, 1931, AAN-AL n. 934. Three weeks later Filipowicz told Zaleski that the standard American position on the Corridor was that "we don't know the facts of the matter, but we do know that it stands as a barrier to disarmament and the stabilization of peace in Europe, and for that reason we think the problem should be settled in some manner" (October 28, 1931, AAN-AL n. 934).

59. Lippmann to Gibson, April 16, 1919, Lippmann Papers.

Bibliography

The following selective essay does not claim to be a comprehensive guide to the vast literature on interwar diplomacy or even Polish and American foreign policies. As a rule, the entries included bear directly on the subject of this study or on related issues raised in the text. Nor does this list exhaust the sources consulted; many items omitted here are cited in the notes where appropriate.

I. *Archival Holdings*

The best sources for examination of relations between Poland and the United States in the interwar era consist of unpublished primary material housed principally in archives and libraries in the two countries under consideration. The greatest concentration of relevant documents resides at the Archiwum Akt Nowych in Warsaw, the branch of the Polish state archives devoted to the modern history of Poland. The most valuable of its collections for our purposes are those of the Ministerstwo Spraw Zagranicznych and its embassy and consulates in the United States. Much of interest may also be found in the files of the other major diplomatic missions, particularly the embassies of London and Berlin, and in the records of meetings of the Council of Ministers.

In addition to these official files, the Archiwum Akt Nowych holds several private collections of basic importance to the topic. The papers of Stanisław Kauzik cast light on the financial diplomacy of the Grabski government, and the journals of Kazimierz Świtalski do the same for the Piłsudski regime. Selections from the voluminous papers of Ignacy Jan Paderewski have been published, but in the process of winnowing a few intriguing items have fallen through the editorial sieve.

The researcher will profit as well from excavation in other Polish locations. The chief attraction of the Biblioteka Narodowa (Warsaw) is the diary of Maciej Rataj, also available in published form. The Biblioteka Ossolineum (Wrocław) holds the manuscript recollections of Feliks Młynarski and Alfred Wysocki. Both of these invaluable sources have been published in abridged versions, but the omissions make perusal of the originals well worthwhile. Composed in the infirmity of age, the memoirs of Konstanty Skirmunt are not wholly reliable but contain some useful observations on the American policy of Skrzyński; copies exist at the library of the Katolicki Uniwersytet Lubelski (Lublin) and the Biblioteka Jagiellońska, Uniwersytet Jagielloński (Cracow).

Most of the remaining stores of pertinent unpublished European documents are to be found in the United States or England, exiled in many cases by the dislocations of war and postwar political emigration. Held in custody of the National Archives, the microfilmed records of the German Foreign Ministry

(R.G. 242) are a mine of information. The Joseph Piłsudski Institute of America in New York possesses the Archiwum Adiutantury Generalnej Naczelnego Dowództwa—the so-called "Belvedere Archive"—which illuminates Polish foreign policies for the years 1918-1922. This as well as other assets of the Institute, including its files from the Polish embassy in London, have become available in microform at Sterling Library, Yale University. The Piłsudski Institute also holds a profitable manuscript memoir of Adam Krzyżanowski. Among the collections of the Instytut Historyczny im. Generała Sikorskiego, London, is a notable set of transcripts of the cable traffic between the MSZ and the Polish embassy in the British capital. In the same city, the Public Record Office maintains the papers of the Foreign Office, which are of abundant interest.

The chief stocks of American documents reside in Washington, D.C., and New York. The National Archives possesses the decimal file of the State Department (R.G. 59), the foremost source for official policy toward Poland. Several entries at the Library of Congress merit attention, including the papers of Bainbridge Colby and Charles Evans Hughes. In addition, the manuscript diaries of Charles S. Hamlin contain a few meaty references to the question of Polish stabilization in 1927. The best resource for study of American financial dealings with Poland is the archive of the Federal Reserve Bank of New York, which preserves the papers of Benjamin Strong and the records of the Bank's activities in Polish matters. These rich collections may be supplemented by scrutiny of the George L. Harrison papers at Butler Library, Columbia University.

The archives of the Hoover Institution on War, Revolution and Peace at Stanford University include an abundance of important relevant sources, chiefly the files of the Polish embassy in Washington—part of the massive "Ciechanowski Deposit"—and the papers of Hugh Gibson. References to Poland appear frequently in the center's enormous Herbert Hoover collections as well as in various smaller items, such as the intriguing reports of the businessman J. Howard Leman and the papers of Henry B. Smith.

The student also will wish to inspect the libraries established in commemoration of two American presidents of the era. At the Franklin D. Roosevelt Library in Hyde Park, N.Y., the John C. Wiley papers are revealing of American-Polish relations for the years 1930-1932. The Herbert Hoover Library at West Branch, Iowa, holds a wealth of rewarding material. Aside from the estimable collections relating to the career of his namesake, the Hoover Library shelters the papers of William R. Castle and a manuscript memoir of E. Dana Durand. As for the other interwar American presidents, the papers of Calvin Coolidge (Library of Congress) are of merely occasional interest and those of Warren G. Harding (Ohio Historical Society, Columbus) hold no utility for the subject at hand.

Small Charles Dewey collections rest at the Library of Congress and the Hoover Institution, but the bulk of his correspondence is at the library of the Chicago Historical Society, and this is the best source for his Polish service. Mudd Library of Princeton University has the papers of Edwin W. Kemmerer, the other principal American financial adviser to Warsaw. The same center also keeps transcripts of interviews conducted for the John Foster Dulles Oral History Collections, and the conversations with George C. Sharp and Allen Dulles touch on the negotations for the Polish stabilization loan.

Sterling Library of Yale University holds a plenitude of American diplomatic documents relating to the Paris Peace Conference and the immediate postwar period. Included in this category are the papers of Edward M. House, Frank Polk,

Arthur Bliss Lane, and the Inquiry. For the later years, the papers and diary of Henry L. Stimson are essential for the Hoover foreign policy. Walter Lippmann's circle of correspondents was broad, and his papers are well worth a glance. At Harvard University, Houghton Library maintains the useful diaries and papers of Jay Pierrepont Moffat, while the John Cudahy papers at the Milwaukee County Historical Society, Milwaukee Wisc., are of value for the 1930s.

II. *Published Documents*

Of the various official sets of published foreign ministry papers, three are of particular importance for the topic. The German *Akten zur deutschen auswärtigen Politik 1918-1945* shed much light on financial diplomacy concerning Poland. The American *Foreign Relations of the United States* and the English *Documents on British Foreign Policy, 1919-1939* are also of general value. A few relevant items appear in the *Documents diplomatiques français 1932-1939* and the *Documents on German Foreign Policy 1918-1945*, but these have mostly to do with a later period than mine.

Among other works of this type, *Kapitały obce w Polsce, 1918-1939: materiały i dokumenty* (Warsaw, 1964), edited by Zbigniew Landau and Jerzy Tomaszewski, is an excellent compendium of documents on the Polish experience with foreign capital. In the same vein, Czesław Madajczyk, "Spory wokół sprawy elektryfikacji Polski (1926-1930)," *Najnowsze Dzieje Polski: Materiały i Studia z Okresu 1914-1939* 5 (1962), pp. 153-220, deals with the Harriman electrification project. The second and third volumes of Polska Akademia Nauk, Instytut Historii, *Archiwum polityczne Ignacego Paderewskiego*, 4 vols. (Wrocław, 1973-1974) are enlightening, and John Foster Dulles, *Poland: Plan of Financial Stabilization, 1927* (New York, 1928), reproduces many of the agreements and public proclamations associated with its subject. Portions of George J. Lerski, ed., *Herbert Hoover and Poland: Documentary History of a Friendship* (Stanford, 1977), also relate to matters at hand.

III. *Official and Central Bank Publications and Statistical Handbooks*

The primary attraction of the Bank Polski's *Bulletin of the Bank of Poland* are the appended advisory reports of Charles Dewey, appearing between 1927 and 1930. The *Annual Report* and *Monthly Review of Credit and Business Conditions* of the Federal Reserve Bank of New York aid in analysis of the behavior of American overseas investment. Commentary on the United States abounds in the parliamentary debates transcribed in Poland, Sejm, *Sprawozdanie stenograficzne z posiedzenia Sejmu Rzeczypospolitej*. Polish matters rarely disturbed the thoughts of U.S. legislators, however, so the *Congressional Record* is of minimal utility.

The best American statistical guides for the period are the Department of Commerce annuals *Commerce Yearbook* and *Statistical Abstract of the United States*. For their Polish counterparts see the various serial publications of the official Główny Urząd Statystyczny, mainly the *Rocznik statystyczny*, *Rocznik statystyki* and *Rocznik handlu zagranicznego Rzeczypospolitej polskiej i wolnego miasta gdańska*. Much of this material appears in conveniently digested form in United States, Bureau of the Census, *Historical Statistics of the United States*,

Colonial Times to 1970, 2 vols. (Washington, 1975) and B. R. Mitchell, *European Historical Statistics, 1750–1975* (New York, 1981).

IV. Press

As much owing to its excellent index as its quality, the *New York Times* is the most useful American newspaper of the time. The *Wall Street Journal* and the *New York Herald-Tribune* and its predecessors also have been extensively consulted. *Le Messager Polonais* served as the quasi-official voice of the Polish government from 1925 to 1929, when its authoritative position was assumed by the Piłsudskist *Gazeta Polska*. The serious Cracow journal *Czas* devoted considerable space to discussion of Poland's financial relations with the outside world. Among other papers, *Le Temps* (Paris) and the *Times* of London are the most beneficial. The French Ministère des Affaires Étrangères produced handy summaries of the foreign press at regular intervals; of these, the most informative for present purposes is the *Bulletin périodique de la presse polonaise*.

Aside from the dailies, numerous contemporary periodicals of politics or finance have proved rewarding. Polish examples of the genre are *Przegląd Polityczny*, *Przegląd Współczesny* and *Przemysł i Handel*. Then as now, the quarterly *Foreign Affairs* ranked as the leading publication of its type in the United States. As the organ of the American-Polish Chamber of Commerce and Industry, *Poland* is of special interest, and *Foreign Securities Investor* is of aid in monitoring the moods of the foreign bond market. Of the more popular American magazines, perhaps the *New Republic* paid most attention to Poland.

V. Published Diaries and Memoirs

Within this grouping three Polish entries stand head and shoulders above the rest. The *Wspomnienia* (Warsaw, 1971) of Feliks Młynarski is an unmatched firsthand account of Polish financial diplomacy for the years 1925–1927, but the reader must exercise constant vigilance in separating fact from the author's attempts to congratulate himself. Władysław Grabski's *Dwa lata pracy u podstaw państwowości naszej* (Warsaw, 1927) is similarly indispensable and self-serving. The published version of the diary of Maciej Rataj, *Pamiętniki 1918–1927* (Warsaw, 1965), records the salty observations of a prominent parliamentarian.

Other Polish memoirs are of secondary importance. Alfred Wysocki, *Tajemnice dyplomatycznego sejfu* (Warsaw, 1974), an abridgement of the original manuscript, has deleted all but a few—and not necessarily the best—of the references to American subjects. The diplomatic reminiscences of Tadeusz G. Jackowski, *W walce o polskość* (Cracow, 1972), and Jan Drohojowski, *Jana Drohojowskiego wspomnienia dyplomatyczne* (Cracow, 1970), are occasionally interesting, as are Zygmunt Karpiński, *Bank Polski 1924–1939: przyczynek do historii gospodarczej okresu międzywojennego* (Warsaw, 1958), and Wacław Konderski, *Z działalności banków polskich w latach 1928–1935: wspomnienia* (Warsaw, 1962), for banking matters. Jan Ciechanowski, *Defeat in Victory* (Garden City, N.Y., 1947), concentrates on the Second World War and devotes only a few paragraphs to the author's interwar ministry in Washington.

Fewer American memoirs warrant attention for U.S. dealings with Poland. Of these, the most useful is the chatty Charles S. Dewey, *As I Recall It* (Washington, 1957). Herbert Hoover, *Years of Adventure, 1874–1920* (New York, 1951), affords a bland recollection of the ARA. Nancy Harvison Hooker has edited *The Moffat Papers: Selections from the Diplomatic Journals of Jay Pierrepont Moffat, 1919–1943* (Cambridge, Mass., 1956), extracts from the diaries of a well-connected State Department hand whose career began with a stint in Warsaw. Henry L. Stimson and McGeorge Bundy, *On Active Service in Peace and War* (New York, 1948), must be read but is no substitute for the Stimson collections at Yale.

The outstanding French contribution is Émile Moreau, *Souvenirs d'un gouverneur de la Banque de France, histoire de la stabilisation du franc, 1926–28* (Paris, 1954), one of the better sources for the origins of the Polish stabilization loan. The same subject receives pungent if unfortunately skimpy mention in Jean Monnet, *Mémoires* (Paris, 1976), and the reader will find scattered nuggets in Jules Laroche, *La Pologne de Pilsudski: souvenirs d'une ambassade, 1926–1935* (Paris, 1953). Preoccupied with other concerns, German memorialists add little to our knowledge of the matters at hand. Heinrich Brüning, *Memoiren 1918–1934* (Stuttgart, 1970), is of some help for the events of 1931, but in *My First Seventy-Six Years* (London, 1955) Hjalmar Schacht tells much less than he might.

VI. *Contemporary Works*

This category includes polemical literature and serious commentaries dating from the period. At the least, these works afford a glimpse into informed opinion of the day, while in some instances—especially where the writer is also a participant in the narrative—they may reflect the view of protagonists or even sway the course of events. The clearest example of this last type is Edwin W. Kemmerer, *Reports Submitted by the Commission of the American Financial Experts* (Warsaw, 1926), which laid the basis for the stabilization plan of 1927. Along the same lines, Kemmerer's *Praca ekonomicznego doradcy rządów*, trans. S. Ropp (Poznań, 1927), illustrates the author's approach to his advisory chores.

On the general subject of American economic activity overseas, Cleona Lewis, *America's Stake in International Investments* (Washington, 1938), is a virtual encyclopedia of facts and statistics. Benjamin H. Williams, *Economic Foreign Policy of the United States* (New York, 1929), and John T. Madden and Marcus Nadler, *Foreign Securities* (New York, 1929), are worthy of note. See as well two articles in *Foreign Affairs*: Herbert Feis, "The Export of American Capital," 3 (1925), pp. 668–686, and Dwight W. Morrow, "Who Buys Foreign Bonds?" 5 (1927), pp. 219–232. The governor of the Federal Reserve Bank of New York presents his opinions on these and other matters in W. Randolph Burgess, ed., *Interpretations of Federal Reserve Policy in the Speeches and Writings of Benjamin Strong* (New York and London, 1930).

The state of Poland's economy and finances received considerable attention in print during these years. American reflections on the chaos of the postwar period appear in the articles of E. Dana Durand, "Finance and Currency Situation in Poland," *Annals of the American Academy of Political and Social Science* 102 (1922), pp. 32–39, and "Currency Inflation in Eastern Europe," *American Economic Review* 13 (1923), pp. 593–608. Feliks Młynarski analyzed a later bout of inflation in *The International Significance of the Depreciation of the Zloty in 1925* (Warsaw, 1926). Instytut Gospodarstwa Społecznego, *Na froncie gospodarczym: w dziesiątą rocznicę odzyskania niepodległości 1918–1928* (Warsaw, 1928), mirrors the optimism of Polish officialdom after the achievement of stabilization. The consequences of the Grabski financial reforms occupy Bernard Blumenstrauch, *Le nouveau régime monétaire en Pologne et son rôle dans l'économie nationale* (Nancy, 1932), Pierre Robin, *La réforme monétaire en Pologne* (Paris, 1932), and Lawrence Smith, "The Zloty, 1924-1935," *Journal of Political Economy* 44 (1936), pp. 145-183.

Polish trade patterns are discussed in Paul F. Douglass, *The Economic Independence of Poland: A Study in Trade Adjustments and Political Objectives* (Cincinnati, 1934), and the nature and extent of outside investment in the country is the theme of Leopold Wellisz, *Foreign Capital in Poland* (London, 1938). Hipolit Gliwic examines the place of Poland in the world economy in *Międzynarodowa współzależność ekonomiczna a polska polityka gospodarcza: studjum ekonomiczne* (Warsaw, 1928). Polish foreign borrowing is the focus of two works by Józef Zajda, *Długi państwowe Polski* (Warsaw, 1927), and *Zagraniczne pożyczki państwowe* (Warsaw, 1927).

The United States held a particular fascination for Poles. For examples of Polish popular or literary approaches to American society and civilization, see Roman Dyboski, *Stany Zjednoczone Ameryki Północnej: wrażenia i refleksje* (Lwów and Warsaw, 1930), Roman Dyboski, *Amerykanizm* (Warsaw, 1932), Wacław Gąsiorowski, *Nowa kolchida* (Warsaw, 1932), and Wacław Sieroszewski, *Wrażenia z Ameryki* (Warsaw, 1930). Jerzy Krahl described U.S. foreign policy in "Polityka zagraniczna Stanów Zjednoczonych," *Przegląd Polityczny* 4 (1926), pp. 17-27, and four years later Jan Ciechanowski presented an identically-titled piece in *Przegląd Polityczny* 13 (1930), pp. 93-112. Ciechanowski's successor as chief of mission in Washington, Tytus Filipowicz, expresses regret for lost opportunities of bilateral cooperation in his *Ameryka i Europa* (n.p., [1932]).

Fewer U.S. writers of those days showed a reciprocal interest in the Polish republic, although H. H. Fisher, *America and the New Poland* (New York, 1928), is a notable exception. Hugh Gibson and Samuel M. Vauclain, *Poland, Her Problems and Her Future* (New York, 1920), advocates American aid to the infant Polish state, and some of the efforts of the ARA to this end are outlined in A. B. Barber, *Report of European Technical Advisers Mission to Poland, 1919-1922* (New York, 1923). Many of the observations in Elmer Davis, "Character of American Influence on Eastern Europe in the Near Future," *Annals of the American Academy of Political and Social Science* 102 (1922), pp. 121-126, pertain to Poland.

Several entries deal with differing aspects of financial relations between Poland and the United States. Stanisław Arct, *Projekt odbudowy Polski przy pomocy amerykańskiej* (Warsaw, 1920), is an early argument for rebuilding and modernizing the Polish state largely with U.S. assistance. American dollars tended instead to flow toward Germany, and Wacław Fabierkiewicz, *O konsekwensjach Planu Dawesa* (Warsaw, 1925), typifies the unease of the Poles at this development. Polish prospects in American capital markets occupy A. Gostomski, *Pozycja polska na amerykańskim rynku kapitału* (Warsaw, 1926), and Zygmunt Heryng, *Rola kapitału amerykańskiego w życiu państwowym i gospodarczym Polski* (Warsaw, 1928).

In his *Dwa programy finansowe* (Cracow, 1927), and *Polityka i gospodarstwo: pisma pomniejsze oraz przemówienia, 1920-1931* (Cracow, 1931), Adam Krzyżanowski argues for acceptance of the stabilization loan and plan of 1927, and John Foster Dulles appraises the same program from the lender's point of view in *Polish Stabilization Plan* (New York, 1927). The library of the Szkoła Główna Planowania i Statystyki, Warsaw, holds typescripts of two early unpublished studies of the effects of American loans to Poland, M. Frank, "Państwowe i samorządowe pożyczki amerykańskie w Polsce w latach 1924-1930" (1932), and H. Strońska, "Pożyczka stabilizacyjna 1927" (1934). M. Kozłowski, *Sprawa Harrimana* (Warsaw, 1929), is a useful volume of extracts from the Polish press on the embattled American electrification venture.

A scattering of titles are important for particular episodes in the course of relations between the two countries. The major addresses delivered by Aleksander Skrzyński during his American tour are reprinted in *American and Polish Democracy* (Washington, 1925), *American Policy Towards Europe as Viewed by a European* (Washington, 1925), and *Poland's Problems and Progress* (Washington, 1925). Neither better nor worse than countless other popular treatments of European affairs dating from the period, E. Alexander Powell's *Thunder Over Europe* (New York, 1931) merits special mention for its impact on the thinking of Henry L. Stimson. Owing to Stimson's collaboration in its preparation, Walter Lippmann and William O. Scroggs, *The United States in World Affairs, 1931* (New York, 1932), is a noteworthy exposition of American attitudes toward the issue of the Pomeranian frontier.

VII. *Secondary Works*

The catalogue of studies bearing on the subject of American-Polish relations after the First World War is growing steadily. For a cogent introduction to the characteristics and goals of U.S. diplomacy in Europe, see Melvyn P. Leffler, "American Policy Making and European Stability, 1921-1933," *Pacific Historical Review* 46 (1977), pp. 207-208. The same author has expanded his arguments and organized them about the theme of Franco-American relations in *The Elusive Quest: America's Pursuit of European Stability and French Security, 1919-1933* (Chapel Hill, N.C., 1979). An admirably broad survey, useful primarily for the U.S. perspective, is Frank Costigliola, *Awkward Dominion: American Political, Economic, and Cultural Relations with Europe, 1919-1933* (Ithaca and London, 1984). American financial influence on Europe is portrayed in Costigliola's "The Politics of Financial Stabilization: American Reconstruction Policy in Europe, 1924-30" (Ph.D. dissertation, Cornell University, 1973), and Stephen A. Schuker, *The End of French Predominance in Europe: The Financial Crisis of 1924 and the Adoption of the Dawes Plan* (Chapel Hill, 1976). Two examinations of the State Department of those days, Robert D. Schulzinger, *The Making of the Diplomatic Mind: The Training, Outlook, and Style of United States Foreign Service Officers, 1908-1931* (Middletown, Conn., 1975), and Martin Weil, *A Pretty Good Club: The Founding Fathers of the U.S. Foreign Service* (New York, 1978), contain observations on several figures who served in Poland.

Roman Dębicki, *Foreign Policy of Poland, 1919-39: From the Rebirth of the Polish Republic to World War II* (New York, 1962), is the only survey in English of Polish interwar diplomacy. Piotr S. Wandycz, *France and Her Eastern Allies, 1919-1925: French-Czechoslovak-Polish Relations from the Paris Peace Conference to Locarno* (Minneapolis, 1962), and *August Zaleski: Minister Spraw Zagranicznych RP 1926-1932 w świetle wspomnień i dokumentów* (Paris, 1980), as well as Anna M. Cienciała and Tytus Komarnicki, *From Versailles to Locarno: Keys to Polish Foreign Policy, 1919-1925* (Lawrence, Ks., 1984), are essential for the period preceding the ministry of Józef Beck. As yet there exists no adequate biography of Józef Piłsudski, the dominant Polish personality of the age; in its absence, Wacław Jędrzejewicz, *Kronika życia Józefa Piłsudskiego 1867-1935*,

2 vols. (London, 1977), a reconstruction of the Marshal's life composed of extracts from other sources, is a serviceable substitute.

The economic history of the Second Republic forms a necessary background for many of the events depicted here. Zbigniew Landau and Jerzy Tomaszewski, *Zarys historii gospodarczej Polski 1918-1939* (Warsaw, 1971), and *Druga Rzeczpospolita: gospodarka, społeczeństwo, miejsce w świecie* (Warsaw, 1977), sketch the main outlines of the problem; Jack Taylor, *The Economic Development of Poland, 1919-1950* (Ithaca, 1952), and Ferdynand Zweig, *Poland Between the Wars: A Critical Study of Social and Economic Changes* (London, 1944), do the same in English. The currency and financial reforms of Władysław Grabski receive capable monographic treatment in Jerzy Tomaszewski, *Stabilizacja waluty w Polsce: z badań nad polityką gospodarczą rządu polskiego przed przewrotem majowym* (Warsaw, 1961).

V. N. Bandera, *Foreign Capital as an Instrument of National Economic Policy: A Study Based on the Experience of East European Countries between the World Wars* (The Hague, 1964), Rudolf Nötel, "International Capital Movements and Finance in Eastern Europe 1919-1949," *Vierteljahrschrift für Sozial- und Wirtschaftsgeschichte* 61 (1974), pp. 65-112, and Iván T. Berend and György Ránki, *Economic Development in East-Central Europe in the 19th and 20th Centuries* (New York and London, 1974), assess the place of Eastern Europe in the interwar financial system. For general aspects of the impact of foreign capital on Poland, see Zbigniew Landau, "Wpływ kapitałów obcych na gospodarkę polską 1918-1939 (Uwagi ogólne)," *Finanse* 15 (1965), pp. 37-47, and the disconcertingly polemical *Anonimowi władcy: z dziejów kapitału obcego w Polsce, 1918-1939* (Warsaw, 1968) by Landau and Jerzy Tomaszewski. Two more titles by Landau, *Polskie zagraniczne pożyczki państwowe 1918-1926* (Warsaw, 1961), and "The Foreign Loans of the Polish State in Years 1918-1939," *Studia Historiae Oeconomicae* 9 (1974), pp. 281-297, analyze the Polish experience as a borrower abroad.

The best introduction to American foreign policy as it affected Eastern Europe is Piotr S. Wandycz's essay *Stany Zjednoczone a europa środkowo-wschodnia w okresie międzywojennym 1921-1939* (Paris, 1976); unfortunately, it finds no satisfactory counterpart in English. Zsuzsa L. Nagy, *The United States and the Danubian Basin 1919-1939* (Budapest, 1975), is thin, and Marian Wojciechowski, "The United States and Central Europe Between the Two World Wars (1918-1939/41)," *Polish Western Affairs* 16 (1975), pp. 65-73, amounts to a simplistic and misleading attack on Washington as a handmaiden of German expansionism.

Few have attempted to trace the course of U.S.-Polish relations of the interwar years, and still there is no full-length study of the subject. The relevant sections of Piotr S. Wandycz, *The United States and Poland* (Cambridge, Mass., 1980), are superior to those in Samuel L. Sharp, *Poland, White Eagle on a Red Field* (Cambridge, Mass., 1953). Longin Pastusiak devotes a superficial chapter to the topic in *Pół wieku dyplomacji amerykańskiej 1898-1945* (Warsaw, 1974), and some of the collected articles in Marian M. Drozdowski, *Z dziejów stosunków polsko-amerykańskich 1776-1944* (Warsaw, 1982), are pertinent if derivative. For the period extending through the Coolidge presidency, Frank Costigliola, "American Foreign Policy in the 'Nut Cracker': The United States and Poland in the 1920s," *Pacific Historical Review* 48 (1979), pp. 85-105, is informative, if lacking in reference to Polish sources. Costigliola has contributed a chapter on John Stetson's service as minister to Poland in Kenneth Paul Jones, ed., *U.S. Diplomats in Europe, 1919-1941* (Santa Barbara, Calif., 1981).

The financial side of the association between the two countries is encapsulated in Zbigniew Landau, "Poland and America: The Economic Connection, 1918-1939," *Polish American Studies* 32 (1975), pp. 38-50. Teresa Małecka has written an impressive monograph on American lending to Poland, *Kredyty i pożyczki Stanów Zjednoczonych Ameryki dla rządu polskiego w latach 1918-1939* (Warsaw, 1982), a reprint of her doctoral dissertation at Warsaw's Szkoła Główna Planowania i Statystyki. Małecka has dealt with the related matters of debt service and direct American investment in Polish joint stock companies in her articles "Spłata amerykańskich pożyczek i kredytów przez Rząd Polski (1919-1939)," in *Materiały do seminariów z najnowszej historii gospodarczej Polski*, v. 4, eds. Zbigniew Landau and Janusz Kaliński (Warsaw, 1978), pp. 33-54, and "Udział kapitału amerykańskiego w kapitałach akcyjnych przemysłu polskiego w latach 1918-1939," in *Materiały do seminariów z najnowszej historii gospodarczej Polski*, eds. Zbigniew Landau and Janusz Kaliński (Warsaw, 1974), pp. 34-54. The Polish foreign debt crisis of recent years prompted the appearance of "Poland's Relations with its International Bankers in the 1920s," *International Currency Review* 14 (1982), pp. 29-36, drawn from previously published works.

A relative abundance of material is available concerning Poland and the United States immediately following the First World War, notably Zbigniew Landau, "O kilku spornych zagadnieniach stosunków polsko-amerykańskich w latach 1918-1920," *Kwartalnik Historyczny* 65 (1958), pp. 1093-1108, and Lubomir Zyblikiewicz, "Stany Zjednoczone a Polska w latach 1920-1921," in *Ameryka Północna*, ed. Marian M. Drozdowski (Warsaw, 1975), pp. 220-258. Kay Lundgreen-Nielsen, *The Polish Problem at the Paris Peace Conference: A Study of the Policies of the Great Powers and the Poles, 1918-1919* (Odense, 1979), covers American diplomacy at Versailles. For U.S. loans and relief assistance, consult Zbigniew Landau, "Pierwsza polska pożyczka emisyjna w Stanach Zjednoczonych," *Zeszyty Naukowe Szkoły Głównej Planowania i Statystyki* 15 (1959), pp. 59-76, and Teresa Małecka, "Pomoc rządowa Stanów Zjednoczonych Ameryki dla państwa polskiego po I wojnie światowej," *Przegląd Historyczny* 70 (1979), pp. 73-88. The activities of the American legation in Warsaw are portrayed in Zygmunt J. Gasiorowski, "Joseph Pilsudski in the Light of American Reports, 1919-1922," *Slavonic and East European Review* 49 (1971), pp. 425-436, and the relevant pages of Ronald E. Swerczek, "The Diplomatic Career of Hugh Gibson, 1908-1939" (Ph.D. dissertation, University of Iowa, 1972).

Zbigniew Landau has established a virtual monopoly over American-Polish financial relations of the years 1924-1926. Loans of this period are considered in his articles "Pożyczki ulenowskie," *Najnowsze Dzieje Polski: Materiały i Studia z Okresu 1914-1939* 1 (1958), pp. 123-160, "Pożyczka dillonowska. Przyczynek do działalności kapitałów amerykańskich w Polsce," *Kwartalnik Historyczny* 64 (1957), pp. 79-85, and "Bank Dillon, Read and Co. a Polska," *Sprawy Międzynarodowe* 12 (1960), pp. 53-75; the advisory tours of Edwin Kemmerer are the subject of "Misja Kemmerera," *Przegląd Historyczny* 48 (1957), pp. 270-284. Wiesław Balcerak, *Polityka zagraniczna Polski w dobie Locarna* (Wrocław, 1967), contains information on the American policies of Aleksander Skrzyński. The role of the Harriman properties in the economic system of Polish Silesia receives passing mention in Józef Popkiewicz and Franciszek Ryszka, *Przemysł ciężki Górnego Śląska w gospodarce Polski międzywojennej (1922-1939): studium historyczno-gospodarcze* (Opole, 1959).

The fullest account of the genesis and execution of the Polish stabilization plan is Zbigniew Landau, *Plan stabilizacyjny 1927-1930: geneza, założenie, wyniki*

(Warsaw, 1963), which completes the story begun in his *Pierwszy etap rokowań o pożyczkę stabilizacyjną* (Warsaw, 1962). In English, the stabilization loan occupies a chapter in Richard Hemmig Meyer, *Bankers' Diplomacy: Monetary Stabilization in the Twenties* (New York and London, 1970), and several pages in Lester V. Chandler, *Benjamin Strong, Central Banker* (Washington, 1958). The governor of the Bank of England played a substantial part in the business, and his principal biographies—Andrew Boyle, *Montagu Norman: A Biography* (New York, 1967), and Sir Henry Clay, *Lord Norman* (London and New York, 1957)—are useful.

The bibliography of scholarship on American-Polish ties of the Hoover period is much shorter than the list for the Coolidge years. Teresa Małecka, "Stosunek kapitału amerykańskiego do Polski na przykładzie rokowań o Centralny Bank Ziemski (1928-1929)," in *Materiały do seminariów z najnowszej historii gospodarczej Polski*, v. 2, eds. Zbigniew Landau and Janusz Kaliński (Warsaw, 1975), pp. 43-66, is the sole entry for the financial side. On political matters, Robert H. Ferrell, *American Diplomacy in the Great Depression: Hoover-Stimson Foreign Policy, 1929-1933* (New Haven, 1957), includes relevant passages, while Elting E. Morison, *Turmoil and Tradition: A Study of the Life and Times of Henry L. Stimson* (Boston, 1960), is the standard life of the subject. Neal Pease, "The United States and the Polish Boundaries, 1931: An American Attempt to Revise the Polish Corridor," *Polish Review* 27 (1982), pp. 122-137, focuses on Stimson's effort to refashion the Pomeranian frontier. The transition to the Democratic era receives notice in Richard A. Wojtak, "Roosevelt's Early Foreign Policy Reflected in Polish Diplomatic Dispatches from Washington (1932-1933)," *Polish Review* 21 (1976), pp. 217-224.

A number of works devoted to supplementary issues deserve mention. More often than not, Germany figured as a factor in relations between the Poles and Americans, and this three-cornered relationship may be traced in Robert Gottwald, *Die deutsch-amerikanischen Beziehungen in der Ära Stresemann* (Berlin, 1965); Christian Höltje, *Die Weimarer Republik und das Ostlocarno Problem, 1919-1934: Revision oder Garantie der deutschen Ostgrenze von 1919* (Würzburg, 1958); Werner Link, *Die amerikanische Stabilisierungspolitik in Deutschland 1921-1932* (Düsseldorf, 1970); Helmut Lippelt, " 'Politische Sanierung': Zur deutschen Politik gegenüber Polen 1925-26," *Vierteljahrshefte für Zeitgeschichte* 19 (1971), pp. 323-373, and Barbara Ratyńska, "Niemcy wobec stabilizacji waluty polskiej w latach 1925-1926," *Sprawy Międzynarodowe* 12 (1960), pp. 70-83. In English, note Zygmunt J. Gasiorowski, "Stresemann and Poland After Locarno," *Journal of Central European Affairs* 18 (1958), pp. 282-317, and Hans W. Gatzke, *Germany and the United States: A "Special Relationship?"* (Cambridge, Mass., 1980). Mieczysław Haiman, *Zjednoczenie Polskie Rzymsko-Katolickie w Ameryce 1873-1948* (Chicago, 1948), Adam Olszewski, *Historia Związku Narodowego Polskiego*, 6 vols. (Chicago, 1957-1968), and Donald E. Pienkos, *PNA: A Centennial History of the Polish National Alliance of the United States of North America* (Boulder, Colo., 1984), are the leading histories of political currents within the American Polonia.

Index